# BORN TO CHOOSE

*Born to Choose* is John H. Falk's compelling account of why and how we make the endless set of choices we do, every second of every day of our lives. Synthesizing research from across the biological and social sciences, Falk argues that human choice-making is an evolutionarily ancient and complex process. He suggests that all our choices are influenced by very basic and early evolving needs, and that ultimately each choice is designed to support survival in the guise of perceived well-being. This engaging book breaks new intellectual ground and enhances our understanding not just of human choice-making but human behavior overall.

**John H. Falk** is Executive Director of the Institute for Learning Innovation and Professor Emeritus of Free-Choice STEM Learning at Oregon State University, USA. He holds a joint doctorate in ecology and science education, and has published widely on a range of topics.

# BORN TO CHOOSE

## Evolution, Self, and Well-Being

*John H. Falk*

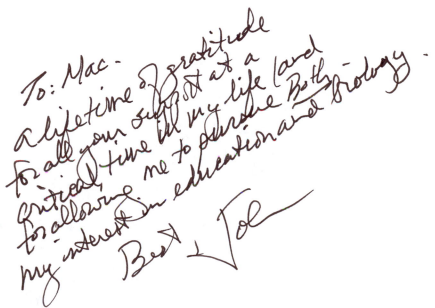

To: Mac –
a lifetime of gratitude
for all your support at a
critical time in my life and
for allowing me to pursue Both
my interest in education and Biology –
Best ⅃ John

**Routledge**
Taylor & Francis Group

NEW YORK AND LONDON

First published 2018
by Routledge
711 Third Avenue, New York, NY 10017

and by Routledge
2 Park Square, Milton Park, Abingdon, Oxon, OX14 4RN

*Routledge is an imprint of the Taylor & Francis Group, an informa business*

*Library of Congress Cataloging-in-Publication Data*
A catalog record for this book has been requested

ISBN: 978-1-62958-562-8 (hbk)
ISBN: 978-1-62958-563-5 (pbk)
ISBN: 978-1-31510-594-9 (ebk)


Typeset in Bembo
by Apex CoVantage, LLC

*Needs are our bow.*

*The arrows are our choices.*

*Well-being is the target at which we aim unceasingly.*

# CONTENTS

# FIGURES

# 1

# BORN TO CHOOSE

## An Introduction

People were born to choose. And choose they do, from birth to death each human being spends every second of his or her life making choices. To be alive is to make choices. Some choices are momentous and life-altering; most are tiny. Collectively, choices define the trajectory of a person's life.

Life involves choices, such as who one associates with, how one raises children or how one practices one's religion, as well as how one moves through an average day, deciding what time to get up, when to head to bed, what clothes to wear and how to entertain oneself in the evening. Little is more characteristic of what it means to be alive and human than the choices a person makes, but surprisingly, few aspects of choice-making are understood. Despite thousands of years of wondering about why people make the choices they do, no one has yet developed a completely satisfactory answer, one that suitably accommodates all human choices, choices large and small, those made by Americans, Chinese and Inuit, and those made consciously, as well as the innumerable choices a person makes unconsciously.

The purpose of this book is to address the following major questions: Why do humans make the choices they do? What mechanisms regulate human choice-making? And ultimately, does an understanding of the whys and hows of human choice-making afford a better understanding of human behavior overall?

It is not the case that there are no theories of human choice-making. There are many.[1] Most are highly domain-specific, providing reasonable insights and predictions about choice-making for certain groups of people within specific circumstances, but few if any are truly generalizable to all humans under all circumstances. In great part this is because virtually all have attempted to answer such questions based on two highly flawed assumptions.

The first is the interesting and peculiar modern, primarily Western assumption that choices, like so much else related to life processes, are isolatable events; something that can be dissected, analyzed and a-contextually studied. Most social scientists have approached choice-making as if it was a process with a definable beginning, middle and end point; a person is confronted with a problem, ponders it and then chooses. If true, then it follows that the rules of choice-making can be examined through constructed experiments designed to test specific hypotheses and resulting in generalizable conclusions. In reality, though, choice-making is not so readily manipulated. All choices are "situated," meaning they are made within specific contexts, and all are parts of never-ending loops; loops with no clearly defined beginning or end. Of course it is possible to arbitrarily define the boundaries of a choice, but that is the point. Any effort to place boundaries around a choice is always going to be arbitrary and by necessity distort the true context in which that choice is made. Every human choice is part of a much larger system of influences, each part of a continuum of choices, with all current choices dependent upon previously made experiences and choices. Every choice builds upon not only the choices made over the lifetime of that individual but upon the choices made over the lifespan of that individual's entire genetic lineage going back to beginnings of life itself. Every previous choice affects, even if only in the tiniest way, the outcomes of future choices.

The second flawed assumption is the presumption that human choice-making is a uniquely human process requiring a complex mind, largely achieved through the conscious awareness that one is initiating, executing and controlling one's actions, what social scientists refer to as agency.[2] However, choice-making is not uniquely human, nor is it always or typically driven by complex, conscious processes. In fact, nearly all human choices are simple dichotomous, concrete choices between continuing to do more of the same or doing something different, with well over 90% of the time the choice being to continue on as before. Only a small percentage of choices involve new actions, and even in these cases, surprisingly few involve conscious deliberation. Admittedly some of these "new action" choices can be quite interesting, and seemingly do involve consciousness, but it is problematic when one's generalized models of choice are based on only these few exceptions rather than the norm.

A truly comprehensive model of human choice-making needs to provide an understanding of all choices made, not just the exceptional choices. It needs to explain both simple and complex choices, and it needs to do so in a way that is consonant with all the facts, not just some. Given how fundamental choice-making is to life, a robust model must transcend a single intellectual tradition, be it psychology, philosophy, anthropology, neuroscience, physiology, immunology or evolutionary biology, and accommodate understandings deriving from all of these domains.

## Towards a Unified Model of Human Choice-Making

My major premise is that human choice-making is an evolutionarily ancient and complex process involving multiple biological as well as psychological processes. Only a small fraction of human choices involves any measure of conscious deliberation. At its core, choice is an on-going mechanism for insuring survival using feelings of well-being as a proxy. All living things, from the tiniest microbe to the most complex social primate, strive to achieve well-being through functionally similar processes of choice-making. Although some choices humans make are distinctly human, and, in some cases, even culturally specific, a surprisingly large number of human choices are not specific to any particular human group or even to humans in general. Most social science theories of choice-making ignore the thousands of survival-oriented choices people make daily, ranging from temperature control to the need to consume a sufficient number of calories, instead focusing on choices such as making a decision about one's career or investments or whom to vote for in the upcoming election.

The focus on these latter choices is understandable at one level, yet such a narrow focus on a small subset of human choices has resulted in a distorted view of the causative mechanisms underlying choice. Even more importantly, despite these "big" choices being highly salient and thus memorable, they are typically not the most important choices a person makes in any given day. Far and away the thousands of small, mostly unconscious choices a person makes over the course of each day—choices about diet, general health and social relationships—are much more likely to directly influence a person's well-being. Ultimately though, as I will describe in this book, all the choices people make—both the myriad "small" ones, as well as the few "big" choices—share a common structure and pedigree.

The model I propose posits that choice-making is only one step in a whole process. Choices are always self-referential and always focused on well-being. Choice-making is one step in a cyclical, highly integrated Well-Being System; a system with no real beginning or end. The System consists of a continual series of feedback loops in which events going on outside and within the individual trigger needs, which necessitate choices, which trigger actions, which influence perceptions of self-related needs, which in turn trigger more choices; all of which collectively generate feelings of well-being. In such a System, past choices are recalled relative to the feelings of well-being they generated, which in turn influences the making of future choices. Take for example the following discussion with my wife Lynn about cooking, where it is clear that her past positive feelings of well-being influenced her current choice-making.

> I love cooking. My mother was a good cook, and I used to love to watch her bake or prepare meals. I always wanted her to let me help, however, she controlled the kitchen. She'd choose small jobs for me to do. Like at Thanksgiving, she'd give me the job of preparing the relish trays, cutting up the carrots and stuff. . . . I used to go grocery shopping with her too, and I enjoyed watching how and what she selected to buy. Maybe that's why I like shopping for food so much myself.
>
> Something I really enjoy now is going to the local Farmer's Market. Over the years I've established strong relationships with some of the people there. I learned who grows the best tomatoes, the best lettuce. There's one person

who's always there at the end of the summer with melons. He's a connoisseur of melons. If you say I want a melon that will be ripe in three days he'll find it for you. I like to try and pick the perfect apple or tomato, choosing one that will be right for the meal I'm planning. I'll be thinking ahead to the meals I want to make the next week and try to choose just the right ingredients for that meal.[3]

Lynn's feelings of well-being around cooking build on her early childhood experiences with her mother, and her mother's attitudes around cooking no doubt derived from her early experiences with her family, and so on back generations. The processing and preparation of food for meals is one of the most basic of life's routines, a distinctively human approach to one of life's most essential needs—eating. The time-intensive choice-making involved in the selection and preparation of plants and animals for eating has been a fundamental part of the human experience for millions of years,[4] with every human culture in every corner of the globe developing their own unique solutions.[5] As the example above illustrates, cooking provides a wonderful example of the continuous, cyclical nature of Well-Being Systems; it also serves as a useful metaphor for thinking about how these systems work. For example, regardless of approach, all cooking starts with the ingredients; so too all Well-Being Systems.

## The Ingredients of Well-Being

You can't make a good meal without first having good ingredients. That's essential. When I am choosing ingredients for a dish I try to balance nutrition and aesthetics. You need to start with a good nutritional foundation but I also like to think about the look and feel I might want to have in the finished product. A simple and quick meal I like to prepare is an Italian dish called *Aglio Olio*. It is a pasta dish, literally translated it means garlic oil, but I usually make it with not only garlic and oil, but red pepper flakes, anchovies, capers, and depending upon how I feel and what I have available, I always add yellow, red or orange capsicum peppers for color. Texture is also important, so I will think about perhaps adding something like roasted pine nuts to the dish as I serve it, since that will add a little extra "crunch."[6]

The five key ingredients of all Well-Being Systems are: *Choice, Actor, Need, Sensor,* and of course *Well-Being*. Before I define each of these key ingredients, I need to provide some framing about my terminology.

I purposefully avoided "scientific," jargon-laden terms and the use of acronyms. I wanted words that might be readily recognized and understood by a wide readership spanning both the social and biological sciences. There is an obvious advantage to this approach. The goal of language is effective communication; it is always easier to communicate with a person if she does not have to constantly refer to a glossary to understand the words used. However, there also is an inherent danger in using common terms. All these words already come with a variety of meanings, particularly key terms like Choice, Need and Well-Being. Each has a long history of vernacular use. These terms also have a long history of use within the social sciences, humanities and biology; though interestingly and significantly there are no universally agreed upon definitions for any of these terms. I would implore the reader to try to set aside prior conceptualizations and understandings of these terms and think about them only in the specific ways I define here.

> **Choice**: Is the active response to Self-Related Needs and selection between options. I use the term choice to include selections that involve both conscious agency, but also those decisions processed unconsciously, including choices that other theorists have categorized as "instinct." Even "instinctual" choices arise through active selection of options and are subject to change and manipulation. Also important to appreciate is that the most frequent choices people make are the "choices" to continue doing the same thing they are currently doing. In humans, choice-making typically though not exclusively involves some kind of brain-based, neural processing.
>
> **Actor**: Is the structure; it can be a collection of nerves, muscles, a whole person or even a group of people that responds to choices. Actions typically involve physical responses, ranging from simple movements to more complex behaviors, but actions can and do happen at every organizational level, from the biochemical to the collective efforts of groups of people.
>
> **(Self-Related) Need**: Is a perception of an underlying state; a threshold-like, regulatory "construct." Perceived needs can be based on an actual physical entity such as a molecule or possession, but they can also be based on totally abstract, entirely mental constructions such as a relationship or an idea. Whether physical or mental, individual or social, Needs are always self-referential and based on previous lived experiences, always framed in relationship to the balance of a person's perceived requirements as compared with some intended internal or external reality.
>
> **Sensor**: Is the bodily structure that takes in information and is capable of perceiving the status of Self-Related Needs relative to the internal and external environment. Some sensors are externally focused, such as eyes and ears, but others are internally focused, attuned to electrical and biochemical signals coming from the gut or circulatory system.
>
> **Well-Being**: Is the holistic perception of the entire dynamic system. Well-Being is the feeling one has when there is an optimal satisfaction of Self-Related Needs, monitored by Sensors, regulated by Choice and maintained through Actions. Well-Being, in particular short-term Well-Being, has evolved as a perceptible proxy for fitness. People perceive Well-Being when they feel they are healthy, part of and appreciated by their group, physically safe and secure and intellectually and spiritually satisfied. Perceived states of Well-Being generally correlate with enhanced survival.

However, ingredients alone do not make a dish. The cook needs to combine the ingredients in just the right way; he needs a recipe.

## A Recipe for Well-Being

> One of the things that cooking does for me is provide an outlet for creativity. I've always appreciated art and music but never pursued either. Cooking is an area in which I can express my creativity. As I'm thinking about the colors, tastes and textures it's an opportunity for me to explore how these elements can be combined into a tasty and beautiful dish or meal. I usually start with a recipe in mind that forms the basic framework of what I'm cooking. But when I actually cook, I see how it is all coming together. Sometimes I realize that it isn't quite what I had in mind so I try to think creatively about what I need to add, perhaps some spice or herb, something that will insure that the whole ends up greater than the sum of the parts.[7]

Every pasta dish, cake or curry is more than just a random collection of ingredients. Each is a complex whole, a product of an orderly and purposeful assembly of elements. So too are Well-Being Systems. Every meal, every Well-Being System is a complex whole greater than the sum of its parts.

Well-Being Systems emerge from the complex interactions of the five ingredients; Choices and resulting Actions are always the result of a whole, integrated, purposeful process. People do not randomly Act, they make Choices for a purpose. That purpose is enhanced survival. Since people cannot directly perceive "survival," perceptions of Well-Being have evolved as a proxy. Over time, feelings of Well-Being have evolved to significantly correlate with fitness. But Well-Being is not a thing, it is a state and thus is always relational. Well-Being needs to be assessed relative to something else, something has to be better or different than something else. Well-Being is always determined relative to some perceived Need. Every individual is attuned to Sensing whether their Needs are being met, whether the state of a person is indeed in positive equilibrium with the world. Based on that assessment, new Choices are made. All human choice-making involves these five ingredients, these five steps; all are assembled into this singular recipe. This universal recipe for choice-making, or more accurately the universal Well-Being System, is represented in Figure 1.1.

The essence of this model is that all choices are designed to support survival, in the guise of perceived well-being. Typically a person strives to achieve a short-term sense of well-being. Typical short-term well-being goals include eating when one feels hungry, trying to get warm when feeling cold or trying to get the person one is with to pay attention and respond positively. Occasionally well-being goals are longer term, such as a person wanting to save money for college or retirement, or plotting how to get a date with someone just met. No matter the time-line of well-being, the process is always the same. Individuals are constantly attempting to optimize their state relative to the world, which is perceived as self-related needs. Based on an appraisal of whether those needs are or are not in balance, a choice is made which in turn precipitates a self-appropriate action (or inaction). The purpose of the action is to affect the relative balance of perceived need. So, for example, if a person is engaged in conversation with another person, choices are constantly being made based

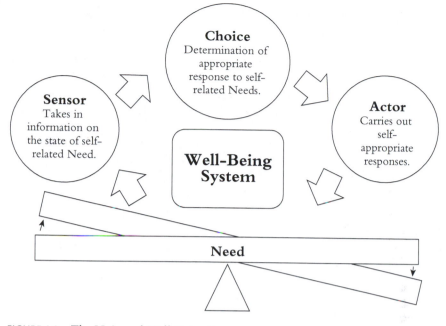

**FIGURE 1.1**    The Universal Well-Being System

on whether or not the individual perceives the person she is talking to is paying attention or not. When a person hums a tune, he is continuously listening to hear whether he is humming the correct melody and is on-or off-key and alters his actions accordingly. Over the course of a day, a person is informed by her body whether her belly is empty or full; if empty then she decides it is time to eat something. Every second the individual monitors his multitudinous self-related needs, appraises their state, makes choices and initiates well-being-appropriate actions. Most choices are easy and dichotomous—either continue on as before, or alter course and make a new choice. Each choice activates an action, and so on and on without a stop.

## The Foundations of Well-Being Systems

I grew up with primarily English, German and American types of foods—basically meat and potatoes. These days I love to eat and cook all kinds of foods. Obviously Italian, but also Indian, Thai, Japanese, Lebanese, Mexican and Peruvian, just to name a few. We live in a wonderful time for food. It is wonderful to be able to discover and celebrate all the world's rich and diverse culinary history.[8]

Up until now most of the examples I have used to discuss cooking, as well as choice, derive from current 21st century culture. Despite the evolution of thousands of highly sophisticated cuisines, and the surfeit of affluent individuals around the world who "live to eat" these many cuisines, the primary purpose of preparing and cooking food stuffs is much more fundamental. Every human on earth needs to eat in order to stay alive. At its core, the acquisition, preparation and eating of food is not an optional activity; it is a necessity of life. The same is equally true for the making of choices.

Because of how fundamental eating and choice-making are to human existence, they have been subject to intense evolution—both biological and cultural. The result has been the build-up of layer upon layer of behavioral complexity. One can observe staggering complexity and diversity in both human cooking styles and human choice-making. This complexity and diversity, almost without exception, represents important adaptations to local conditions, and each unique example is worthy of study in its own right. But surface complexities and diversity should not prevent one from equally noticing the similarities that lie at the core of each of these practices. In other words, just as sweets take many different forms throughout the world and people use a wide range of different names to describe these sweets, what's on the inside is surprisingly similar. All sweets are largely comprised of some form of calorie-rich carbohydrate, usually in the form of sugar. And not unlike the chocolates in a sampler box, sometimes the only way to know what a chocolate is really like is to actually bite into it and see how it tastes.

Human experience tells us that the inside of a chocolate candy nearly always dramatically influences its taste; some we like and some we do not. Food science tells us that the chocolate's insides only marginally alter the chocolate's nutritional or caloric value; from a biological perspective, subtle differences in taste are largely irrelevant. Every piece of chocolate contains roughly the same number of calories per unit of weight and roughly the same quantity of carbohydrates, proteins and fats. Just as it is normal for people to focus on the taste differences between two pieces of chocolate, rather than the overriding nutritional similarities, it is equally typical that people focus on the cultural differences between human choice-making, rather than the underlying biological similarities. Language only confounds this discrepancy further.

People give lots of names to their various food stuffs, often making amazingly fine-grained distinctions between even tiny differences in the ways one type of chocolate, coffee, wine, cheese, vegetable, meat or bread tastes. But at their core, when defined by their chemical constituents, all food items are just varying combinations of carbohydrates, proteins, fats and minerals, and most similar types of food contain very similar quantities of these basic chemicals. Although the specific food items in peoples' diets vary widely from culture to culture, the basic nutrients within human diets, the nutrients people require in order to survive, do not vary widely. Thus, although historically Asia had a rice-based cuisine, Europe was wheat based and the Americas maize based, peoples living in Asia, Europe or the Americas on a daily basis require roughly the same basic complement of calories, carbohydrates, proteins, fats and nutrients in order to remain healthy and reproductively successful. It is the same for the varied Well-Being Systems of humans globally. Although outwardly the Well-Being Systems of individuals from different cultures appear wildly different, internally they possess a high degree of similarity and serve similar goals.

## The Limitations of Language

> I love to try and describe the tastes of things. I often talk about "high" and "low" notes and of course sweet, spicy and salty. But no matter how hard I try, language, at least the English language, is not rich enough to capture all the subtlety of flavor.[9]

Humans are linguistically-driven creatures, and the names and descriptions they use, although informative, at best only partially capture the full richness and complexity of life. And sometimes, language can actually be a hindrance, leading to miscommunication. Take for example the names people use to describe the foods they eat. It is not uncommon for people in different countries to use the same name to describe vastly different foods. For example, a pepperoni in Italy and the U.S. is a spicy dry sausage, but the same name is used by people in many other countries to describe a capsicum sweet pepper. While andouille in the U.S. is a garlicky sausage made using primarily smoked pork shoulder, garlic, pepper, onions, wine and seasoning, in France, particularly in Brittany, a sausage by the same name is made from chopped pig's colon, chitterlings, tripe, onions, wine and seasoning. Not surprisingly, the two sausages with the same name look and taste entirely different.[10] A stuffed pastry with meat, potato and other vegetables is called a samosa in India, a salteña in Bolivia and a Cornish pasty in the U.K., yet all are functionally identical.[11] Even within the same country, the same "food" can have hundreds of different variations. For example, in the case of the U.S. Thanksgiving standard "cranberry sauce," there are literally hundreds of different cranberry sauce recipes with the resulting dishes ranging in taste from sweet to savory, salty to spicy, and everywhere in between. The only thing all the dishes have in common is the presence of cranberries.

It is the same with the Well-Being System. Individuals from differing cultures are highly likely to use very different words and metaphors to describe the same basic phenomenon, or in some cases, very similar words and metaphors to describe different phenomena. And even individuals from the same culture can frame their experiences in starkly different ways. The fact that most people seem capable of generating an explanation for why they believe they acted in the ways they did does not mean that these descriptions accurately reflect the actual underlying psychological, neurological and/or biochemical processes at play. With this in mind, there is one additional important term to define.

> **Self-Aspects** are the self-related linguistic inventions that people use to describe their needs and justify their need-related choices and actions. As the name implies, all facets of the Well-Being System—perceptions of need, choices, actions, sensations and even perceptions of well-being itself—are linguistically expressed in relation to perceptions of self.

As I will describe later in detail, these consciously-generated self-aspects are useful linguistic indicators of essential underlying processes, but they should *never* be uncritically accepted as totally faithful or complete descriptions of what is actually going on inside an individual. Much of the current misunderstanding about the nature of choice-making has resulted from the assumption that an individual's choice-related self-aspects could and should be taken literally; that these linguistic interpretations of choice actually represent a true and unaltered explanation of why and how people made the choices they did.

No matter how explained, choice-making is always at its core about enhancing well-being (i.e., survival). Although collectively humanity has evolved an almost infinite number of self-aspects as ways to describe and justify their choices, in actuality, all of these self-aspects describe a much smaller, very finite number of survival-oriented Well-Being Systems. These two insights are at the heart of this model and are reflective of my effort to synthesize understandings derived from the social and biological sciences in building it. The Well-Being Systems model recognizes and celebrates the inherent diversity and complexity of human experience and the seemingly infinite expressions of choice-making that humans exhibit, while simultaneously appreciating that beneath this diversity is a more finite, evolutionarily stable, underlying set of mechanisms that reflect humanity's shared evolutionary history.

## Fostering a Social-Biological Science Fusion

> Some of my favorite dishes are fusions. I love all kinds of Asian fusion dishes—the mixing of Thai, Chinese and Japanese cuisines. Increasingly people are even exploring the fusion of seemingly dissimilar cuisines such as Indian and Italian or South American and Thai. It seems to be the nature of the world at the moment. The boundaries between all kinds of traditionally distinct entities are dissolving.[12]

This book too represents the dissolving of traditional boundaries, in particular the boundaries between the social and biological sciences. There is no question that every human possesses a vast array of different Well-Being Systems, each of which is extraordinarily sophisticated and strongly molded by that individual's unique psychological, social and cultural experience. However, I argue that despite the amazing burst of cultural capabilities that accompanied the rise of modern humans over the past 40,000 or more years, as well as the exponential increase in individual differences amongst humans over the last several thousand years, humanity's highly sophisticated, socially and culturally influenced Well-Being Systems are still connected to, and influenced by, a wide assortment of very basic and early evolving needs. As I show throughout the book, these early evolving modalities of self-related need, some of which not only all people but all living things possess, continue to influence human choice-making and behavior in both subtle and not so subtle ways.

In arguing that biology plays a critical role in how and why people make the choices they do, I am not trying to replay the appropriately disparaged debate about which is more important, nature or nurture. I take the position that all human functions, from the biochemistry of a person's synapses, to complex behaviors like writing poetry, involve some combination of genetic and environmental influence; nothing is solely nature or nurture.

It is now widely accepted within biology that genes are always expressed within an environmental context; hence the influences of one's DNA[13] are not deterministic but emergent.[14] Equally true, but not as widely acknowledged, is that all human behaviors have a genetic component, hence even the most culturally-influenced behaviors are constrained to some degree by a person's genes.[15] It is not an either-or situation, but always *both-and* regarding the influence of the environment and genes. As will become clear over the course of this book, a person's specific genetic code does have some influence on how a person perceives needs and makes choices, but even the most biological of these needs and choices are subject to environmental influences. The result is that Well-Being Systems are always highly variable from person to person, and even within a single individual vary from situation to situation,[16] and over the lifespan.[17] Research demonstrates that even seemingly instinctual choices such as an aversion to snakes or fear of heights are modifiable through training and effort.

The disciplines of biology and the social sciences have developed in intellectual siloes, such that most biologists know little about current thinking within the social sciences, and few social scientists know much about current thinking within biology, even human biology. That said, there are historical reasons why many biologists still resist fully embracing the idea that living systems are fundamentally open-ended and often unpredictable, including genetic systems. Biological traditions derive from positivist and mechanistic epistemologies, where cause and effect are assumed to be both predictable and quantifiable. If one only studies organisms where individual differences are difficult to perceive, it is easy to see how one can believe that within the limits of measurement error, organismic behavior can be accurately predicted using a simple cause and effect equation. Likewise, there are a number of reasons why many social scientists continue to operationally reject the idea that human evolutionary history plays any significant role in human behavior. If one assumes that genes operate like a computer program, where an individual's genetic code specifically and unvaryingly dictates behavioral outcomes, it is understandable why many social scientists question the importance of such a system given how observably responsive and endlessly variable humans are.[18] If these are the battle lines in the debate then I understand why nature and nurture should continue to be hotly debated, but these are false battle lines. Humans are indeed too variable, complex, responsive and adaptable to have derived from a fixed genetic blueprint. However, so too are all other forms of life. All living things, even the simplest bacterium or blue green algae, are much too variable, complex, responsive and adaptable to be the direct, pre-programmed products of their genetic code. Individual differences in both structure and function exist in all species, and not all of this variability is due to genetic diversity. A surprisingly large amount of variability derives from variations in gene expression in response to environmental conditions.[19]

The new consensus emerging is that life processes are inherently dynamic and adaptable.[20] I would argue that major drivers of this flexibility are the Well-Being Systems on which all life-processes are built; life is flexible because Well-Being Systems are inherently dynamic and adaptable. Natural selection, and hence evolution, operates at multiple levels of complexity, influenced equally by genes and context; learning and memory, biology and culture can and do act as powerful vehicles for long-term evolutionary change.[21] Although these ideas are now accepted by mainstream genomic scientists, widespread appreciation of this seismic shift has been slow to creep into the awareness of some biologists and those outside of biology, including many social scientists. Human Well-Being Systems are a prime example of this fusion of genes and environment, biology and culture. My Well-Being Systems model exemplifies such a fusion, a new kind of model in which fundamental ideas within the social and biological sciences are combined into a single, dare I say delectable, whole.

## Cookbook for Understanding Well-Being Systems

In the spirit of the food metaphor of this initial chapter, *Born to Choose* is a book serving up an understanding of human Well-Being Systems in three courses. The reader can choose to consume the courses in any order, including dessert first, but there is a logic to the current presentation of ideas (courses). The first and main course develops, over the next five chapters, the key ideas that underlie the Well-Being Systems model.

In these initial chapters I use specific examples to illustrate how Well-Being Systems operate. A key goal of Chapter 2 is further elucidating how well-being acts as the driver of these systems. Chapter 3 specifically focuses on needs and how humans use their self-perceptive capacities to activate and assess their Well-Being Systems. Chapter 4 focuses on the biological basis of Well-Beings Systems. Although not all human Well-Being Systems are localized within the mind, many are. So Chapter 5 specifically focuses on the neural basis of choice-making. The sixth and final chapter of this first course/section reiterates these key ideas and offers some insights as well as cautionary notes about how to make sense of observable examples of Well-Being Systems. To provide context and "flavor"[22] in this first section, I use excerpts from a single case study, an interview with a Mexican American woman who describes the many harrowing experiences and difficult choices made during her undocumented emigration to the U.S.

The second course on offer can be thought of as an *à la carte* meal in itself. Over seven chapters I highlight the evolutionary origins of Well-Being Systems and key aspects of how they function. I tell the story through the lens of the seven distinct need-related modalities that form the fulcrum of all human Well-Being Systems. Unlike the first course which has a consistent flavor principle, I have grouped the chapters in this section into three distinct flavor groupings—examples from war for the first three "bodily" needs-related modalities of Well-Being, examples from commerce for the two "relational" needs-related modalities of Well-Being and examples related to "genius" for the final two "reflective" needs-related Well-Being modalities. Although the dominant "taste" of this course is decidedly biological, each chapter is amply seasoned with examples from the social sciences.

The third and final course of the book can be thought of as dessert. There are three chapters in this applications-oriented section. The first two utilize a single, leisure-oriented case study to describe how the Well-Being Systems model can be practically applied to understanding how individuals respond to needs and make choices. The third and final chapter discusses ways the model can be extended to answer questions about Well-Being Systems operating below as well as beyond the level of a single individual. Collectively, these three chapters strive to answer the key questions posed at the beginning of this chapter: Why do humans make the choices they do? What mechanisms regulate human choice-making? And ultimately, does an understanding of the whys and hows of human choice-making afford a better understanding of human behavior overall? In the final chapter I also touch on some of the potential opportunities and challenges that remain, both with regards to developing further understanding about how Well-Being Systems actually work, as well as potentially with the Well-Being Systems model itself.

Clearly this is an ambitious book, but one I hope will usefully break new intellectual ground. At a minimum, my Well-Being Systems model should result in a much clearer understanding of why and how humans make choices. Ideally it will also help social scientists and biologists make connections between what were historically viewed as disconnected life processes. I know it is a hearty intellectual meal. Hopefully the time invested in consuming it will prove worthwhile and readers will find it sufficiently nourishing and pleasurable to warrant coming back for seconds.

## Notes

1.  e.g., Nozick, R. (1990). *A normative model of individual choice*. New York: Garland Press.
    Fernández-Huerga, E. (2008). The economic behavior of human beings: The institutional/Post-Keynesian model. *Journal of Economic Issues*, 42(3), 709–726.
    von Neumann, J. & Morgenstern, O. (1972). *Theory of games and economic behavior*. Princeton: Princeton University Press.
    Kahneman, D. & Tversky, A. (1972). Subjective probability: A judgment of representativeness. *Cognitive Psychology*, 3, 430–454.
    Bell, D.E. (1982). Regret in decision making under uncertainty. *Opinions Research*, 30(5), 961–981.
    Simon, H.A. (1956). Rational choice and the structure of the environment. *Psychological Review*, 63, 129–138.
    Fishbein, M. & Ajzen, I. (1975). *Belief, attitude, intention, and behavior: An introduction to theory and research*. Reading, MA: Addison-Wesley.
    Shiffrin, R. & Schneider, W. (1977). Controlled and automatic human information processing: II: Perceptual learning, automatic attending, and a general theory. *Psychological Review*, 84(2), 127–190.
    Deci, E.L. & Ryan, R.M. (2000). The 'what' and 'why' of goal pursuits: Human needs and the self-determination of behavior. *Psychological Inquiry*, 11, 227–268.
2.  e.g., Jeannerod, M. (2003). The mechanism of self-recognition in human. *Behavioral Brain Research*, 142, 1–15.

3. Unpublished interview with Lynn Dierking, conducted November 12, 2016.
4. Lieberman, D.E. (2013). *The story of the human body*. New York: Pantheon.
5. Mintz, S.W. & du Bois, C.M. (2002). The anthropology of food and eating. *Annual Review of Anthropology*, 31, 99–119.
6. Unpublished interview with Lynn Dierking, conducted November 12, 2016.
7. Unpublished interview with Lynn Dierking, conducted November 12, 2016.
8. Unpublished interview with Lynn Dierking, conducted November 12, 2016.
9. Unpublished interview with Lynn Dierking, conducted November 12, 2016.
10. BobB. (2010). Same name, two different things. *Chowhound*. Retrieved November 13, 2016. www.chowhound.com/post/725469
11. Tobin, C. (2012). What are some examples of the same dish being prepared or served differently across different countries and/or cultures? *Quora*. Retrieved November 13, 2016. www.quora.com/What-are-some-examples-of-the-same-dish-being-prepared-or-served-differently-across-different-countries-and-or-cultures
12. Unpublished interview with Lynn Dierking, conducted November 12, 2016.
13. DNA is an acronym for the complex molecule deoxyribonucleic acid. DNA molecules create the biochemical foundation on which all human genetic inheritance is built.
14. Gilbert, S.F. (2001). Ecological developmental biology: Developmental biology meets the real world. *Developmental Biology*, 233, 1–12.
    Hodgins-Davis, A., Adomas, A.B., Warringer, J. & Townsend, J.P. (2012). Abundant gene-by-environment interactions in gene expression reaction norms to copper within Saccharomyces cerevisiae. *Genome Biology and Evolution*, 4(11), 1061–1079.
    West-Eberhard, M.J. (2004). *Developmental plasticity and evolution*. New York: Oxford University Press.
15. e.g., Goldman, D. (2012). *Our genes our choices: How genotype and gene actions affect behavior*. Amsterdam: Elsevier.
    Breed, M. & Sanchez, L. (2012). Both environment and genetic makeup influence behavior. *Nature Education Knowledge*, 3(10), 68.
    Meany, M.J. (2010). Epigenetics and the biological definition of gene environment interactions. *Child Development*, 81(1), 41–79.
16. cf., Jablonka, E. & Lamb, M. (2014). *Evolution in four dimensions: Genetic, epigenetic, behavioral and symbolic variation in the history of life*. Cambridge: MIT Press.
17. Torday, J.S. & Miller, W.B., Jr. (2016). Phenotype as agent for epigenetic inheritance. *Biology*, 5, 30–36.
18. For example Tedeschi and Felson (1994) stated: "Although lower organisms may inherit instinctual behavior, humans do not. Furthermore, the development of language and culture by humans has transformed, redirected and obscured whatever biological tendencies that may be coded in genes . . . Biological capacities do not provide an adequate explanation for complex human actions." (Tedeschi, J.T. & Felson, R.B. (1994). *Violence, aggression & coercive actions*. Washington, DC: American Psychological Association, p. 36.).
19. Jablonka, E. & Lamb, M. (2014). *Evolution in four dimensions: Genetic, epigenetic, behavioral and symbolic variation in the history of life*. Cambridge: MIT Press.
20. Jablonka, E. & Lamb, M. (2014). *Evolution in four dimensions: Genetic, epigenetic, behavioral and symbolic variation in the history of life*. Cambridge: MIT Press.
21. Jablonka, E. & Lamb, M. (2014). *Evolution in four dimensions: Genetic, epigenetic, behavioral and symbolic variation in the history of life*. Cambridge: MIT Press, p. 1.
22. A useful additional insight into the ultimate nature of how a selection of dishes might taste comes from knowing a little something about what cooking expert Elisabeth Rozin refers to as the "flavor principle"—the distinctive appearance, aroma, texture and tastes that give different ethnic cuisines their distinctive qualities (Rozin, E. (1973). *The flavor-principle cookbook*. New York: Penguin.). For example, Rozin suggests that Indian cuisines are known for their distinctive combinations of gingerroot, garlic, cumin, coriander, cardamom, turmeric, fenugreek, cloves, cinnamon, mustard seed and fresh coriander leaf—a

mélange often generically called "curry" (pp. 44–45), while the cuisine of Korea typically includes a combination of soy sauce, garlic, brown sugar and sesame (p. 26). The flavor principle can be thought of as the "theme" of the food, the distinctive social and cultural traditions and practices that will influence not only what ingredients are selected but also how the food is actually prepared. Flavor principles do not of course apply only to food, they equally apply to languages, beliefs and of course, choices, actions and perceptions of well-being. So knowing something about the theme that underlies the chapters in this section provides an essential clue as to the flavor of this section.

**PART I**

# Developing the Well-Being Systems Model

# 2

# WELL-BEING AND CHOICE

This chapter explores what Well-Being Systems look like in action, specifically how the individual pieces of the system work together to support well-being. An interview with a woman named Teresa[1] provides a concrete example.

> I had thought about coming [from Mexico to the U.S.] because [my niece] Yese's grandma [Mariana] told me "There's an opportunity for us to go [to the U.S.]." She told me, "I'm going over there, and if you want we can go in my truck all the way to the border, you only have to give me 1,500 pesos[2] and we will all go. So I told my husband [via telephone], "You know? There's an opportunity, I can go." Because my husband was already here [in the U.S.], for a longer time, and I was in Mexico taking care of my own and my brother's children [Yese and her brothers], they were with me. Then I told my husband "What do you think? Mariana is leaving; do you think I can go with her?" And he said, "It would be ok." But time passed, because for me it was [hard] making the decision to come. [It] meant changing my life. It was risking my children's lives. Because for me they were my kids, all of them were my children. Taking [such] a responsibility is extremely hard, so then I got depression, when suddenly, making the decision to come, I remember I was like, "Oh, what should I do? What should I do? I can't [decide]."[3]

Teresa is an intelligent, attractive, 45-year-old woman with straight dark brown hair pulled back in a ponytail. At the time of this interview, Teresa was living in a small, weathered ranch-style house, surrounded by agricultural fields in a rural part of eastern Washington State. After setting out food for her interviewer/ guest—a generous selection of homemade tamales and beans accompanied by spicy salsa and water—Teresa began to tell the story of her undocumented emigration to the U.S. Occurring roughly ten years earlier, the trip she described was a harrowing, many-week journey of more than 7,000 kilometers (4,400 miles), from a rural part of central Mexico, to the Mexican border with the U.S., through the Sonoran Desert into the U.S with various stops in Arizona and California, up the entire West Coast of the U.S. and then finally back inland again to her current location.

Teresa suggests that she chose to make this dangerous journey to insure a better life for herself and her children by reuniting with her husband, brother and sister-in-law, all of whom were already living in the U.S. What did her choice-making process look like? As discussed in the previous chapter, all human choices can be represented by a set of complex, multi-step feedback loops, what I refer to as a Well-Being System. Teresa's experiences and choices, including her momentous choice to emigrate to the U.S. and continuing through the many other decisions she needed to make along the way, are illustrative of this process.

## Choice-Making Illustrated

I start the story of Teresa's Well-Being Systems related to emigration (see Figure 2.1) with a snapshot of what occurred when Teresa's niece's grandmother, Mariana, informed her that she would be emigrating to the U.S. and invited her to join her, even offering a low price for the first leg of the journey.

Although Teresa began her story at the point when Mariana invited her to join her in illegally emigrating to the U.S., it is reasonable to assume that this issue had

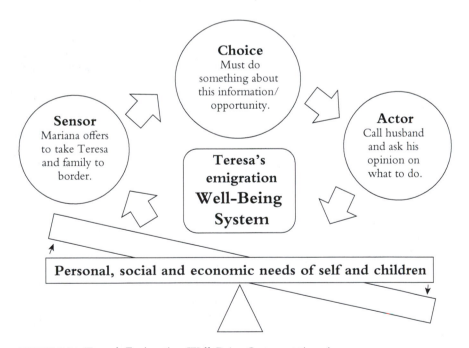

**FIGURE 2.1** Teresa's Emigration Well-Being System at time 1

been on Teresa's mind for a great deal of time; she had long perceived a need to do something about her and her children's personal, social and economic welfare. But hearing, i.e., sensing, this new information created a more pressing urgency to make a choice. She could decide to go or she could decide to stay, but instead she chose to get further input. She acted by calling her husband, trying to see if he could help her make this difficult choice.

Although Teresa's husband said he thought it was a good idea and she should come, she considered this choice relative to her current perceptions of her own happiness, security and quality of life in Mexico as well as the known risks emigration were likely to pose for her children if she undertook this difficult and dangerous journey. She chose to maintain the status quo, to stay in Mexico but also continued to ponder whether she should or should not emigrate to the U.S. (see Figure 2.2).

This action resulted in Teresa still faced with the same need to decide which of the options—stay or go—would best satisfy her need to provide for herself and her children's personal, social and economic stability and opportunity, setting off another Well-Being System cycle (see Figure 2.3). The more she thought about it the more she became convinced that the dangers her children would face during the journey outweighed any potential benefits that might accrue once in the U.S. She decided she should remain in Mexico. She acted on this choice and did nothing further related to emigrating, but she also continued to fret about this choice, causing her to feel depressed. One can presume that the reason Teresa got

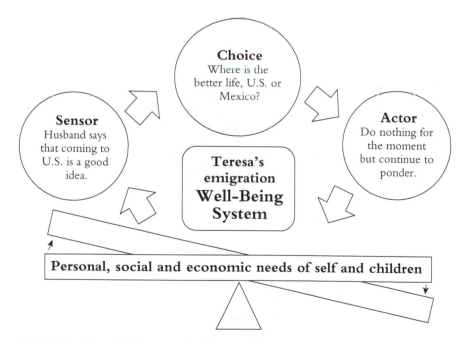

**FIGURE 2.2** Teresa's Emigration Well-Being System at time 2

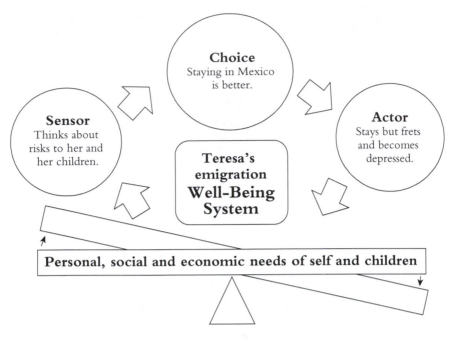

**FIGURE 2.3** Teresa's Emigration Well-Being System at time 3

depressed was because the basic need that precipitated these events remained unresolved. She knew that there would be benefits for her and her children if they were in the U.S., not the least of which would be to be reunited with loved ones. But she also knew that there were significant risks posed by the journey, particularly for her children.

Below is Teresa's narrative version of these multiple Well-Being System loops, loops that included an incessant stream of new input as she sought the counsel of a friend, talked again with her husband and continued to think and fret about the decision. And then she got some additional information.

> It was very hard to make a decision, so I talked to a friend I had, she was a Jehovah's Witness, and I told her, "You know? I'm leaving to go to Los Angeles." And she told me, "Oh my friend, that's good, at least you will be with your husband and he will help you with your kids." And I told her, "Yes." But she said, "You are going with a visa, right?" And I said, "No, I'm going through the desert." And she told me, "Oh no, don't do that, I know Jehovah is very good, I know he is good, but don't test him, don't ask him to see if he is really with you. Okay?" And that left me like, thinking, and I said, "I don't want to leave." I knew, I knew that entering the desert was risking death, because a lot of people die. So then when I arrived home, I was in deep depression. I felt a general tiredness in my body. I felt so fatigued and I felt it was a lot of a burden for me, a lot. So then I told my husband, "You know what? I'm not leaving." And then I remember that when I went

to call him, when I made that decision, I said, "No, I don't want to go, no, no. Because if I go to the desert my children will die and we will all die. And I'm responsible because I took them, and that will never be something I would do [to them]." I thought, "If I stay alive, [and they don't] . . ." I used to say, "If I die with them, that's fine. But if I stay alive and they die, I will never forgive myself for that." Right? So then I went [to call him] and tell him, "I don't want to leave."

But just when I was going [to call him again and tell him my final decision], my children were playing like, like *cholos* [gangs], one against the other. And I was going to tell my husband that I no longer wanted to come, but when I was on my way [to call him], my son, the one who is now working here [in the U.S.], he had a stick in his hand, and he was breaking bottles. And they were acting like, like fighters. They were little, they were only playing, but that stayed with me. And I said, "If they are doing this right now, if they are only practicing, what will they do [when they are older]? And that's not going to be easy for me." And I said, "Oh, that's not good." And I was thinking that if I stayed, because I had already decided to stay, and if my children did wrong, it was because [of what] I had already decided. [Then I thought], if I could bring them over here [to the U.S.], everything would be better. [So] I thought about that. But during the whole time I was praying. Since the idea of coming here came to me, every day I told the Lord, "Lord, if I go a step outside my house, don't let me go a step if that step is not directed by you. If not, close doors, close doors. May no door be open, [that is not directed by you] because [without your guidance] my children are going to die! They will die."

Teresa's Well-Being System at this moment is represented in Figure 2.4.

Based on the discussion in Chapter 1 and thus far in 2, it is possible to infer Teresa's basic choice-making process, as represented in Figure 2.4:

1. **Need**—Teresa is struggling economically and knows that her children's future prospects are diminished if she stays in Mexico. She desires to be reunited with her husband and she knows that her nieces and nephews have a right to be reunited with their parents. But tempering the urgency of this need is the fact that although not optimum, her future if she stays in Mexico is at least predictable; her children are with her and they are safe and happy and she has her house and her friends. Further complicating things is the subtle pressure her relatives and friends are exerting to have her emigrate to the U.S.

2. **Sensor**—Teresa looks out the window and sees her children playing as though they are gang-members (*cholos*) and she fears for her children's future.

3. **Choice**—Teresa again weighs the options and changes her mind; this time she decides that she needs to leave Mexico and emigrate to the U.S.

4. **Actor**—Teresa initiates actions towards emigration but she is still not entirely certain, so she prays and asks God to guide her and make sure that if this is the wrong decision he will "close doors" and not allow her to leave.

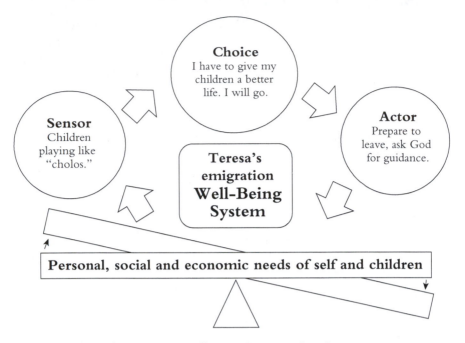

**FIGURE 2.4** Teresa's Emigration Well-Being System at time 4

5. **Need**—Teresa continues to be concerned about her own and her children's personal, social and economic security, but now she also is paying particular attention to any signs from God that might let her know whether or not she is doing the right thing.

However, between this moment and the day of departure, Teresa changed her mind again. She decided that only the oldest child, her niece Yese, would leave for the U.S. Yese would accompany her grandmother, Mariana on the journey. Teresa and her other children would stay in Mexico.

Then, the day arrived and I already had Yese's suitcase packed and ready, I was not coming [TERESA STARTS CRYING AT THIS POINT IN THE INTERVIEW]. Yese had everything ready, and she was crying. And she says, "Aunt, I don't want to go alone with my grandma, I want you to go [too]." And I said to her, "You have to go, because I can't go *hija*." And then, then Yese kept crying, and I had everything ready for her, her little suitcase. And then I said, "well, *hija*, don't go if you don't want to go. Your mom should come [here instead]." Then we talked on the phone and I said to my brother, "You know what? Yese doesn't want to go and she won't go." And he said, "Ok, if she doesn't want to come that's fine." But later the grandma arrived. [She came after] I had already spoken with my brother and told him nobody was leaving. After a while her grandma came and said [to Yese],

"Daughter, you have to leave, because your dad left with much sacrifice and he took your mom, and they still owe the [border] crossing [fee] and you can have a future there. Because if you stay here, [you have no support]." Because my brother told me, "Ok, if Yese doesn't want to come, I will send my wife, their mother, over there in a month, to take care of them because she won't stay here [in the U.S.] if they are not coming." So, when Mariana, her grandma, told her, "You have an opportunity there, *hija*, you have to go." For me those words were like, like something that gave me confidence. Because I said, "Well." I think the Lord put that on my mind, because I prayed so much and asked him what to do. "What should I do? Because I can't make the decision." So, when [Mariana] said, "You can go, you have to go." I felt as if God had told me, "Everyone is going to cross. Everyone is going, GO!"

So when I felt that, like an answer, like a confidence, suddenly [I went] from being like not knowing what to do [to knowing]. Then I said, "Let's all go." Then my children said, "Everyone?" And I said, "Yes. Everyone take a suitcase and get on the truck, let's all go."

Then I called my husband and I told him. Oh, first I called my brother and I told him, "You know what? We're all leaving," I told him, "I'm going. Do you want me to take your children with me, or should I leave them here?" And he says, "No, I don't want you to leave them there, bring them with you." And I said, "Are you sure? I'm going through the desert." And he said, "Bring them." And when he told me that, I told [the children], "Take a suitcase, put it on the truck, and let's go!"

That was, [SOBBING AGAIN], was something very difficult. To make that decision, [was] very difficult. But I suddenly felt [a great sense] of security. That I was not coming alone. In spite of everything, in spite of how I felt, I had a great faith that God was coming with us.

At the final moment, Teresa felt that God had spoken to her, and that was the "signal" she needed in order to confidently make what she had for months perceived as an impossibly difficult choice (see Figure 2.5).

## Well-Being

Teresa and all of her children climbed onto the truck and headed north toward the U.S. In that moment Teresa felt a sense of well-being. She perceived that she had achieved a suitable balance between risk and reward, and that the personal, social and economic well-being of herself and her children was being advanced. This perception of having satisfied this pressing need, of doing what was required for her own and her children's personal, social and economic well-being, made her feel confident and joyful.

Well-Being is an oft used, but historically poorly defined concept. This reality began to change several decades ago when a group of psychologists began to

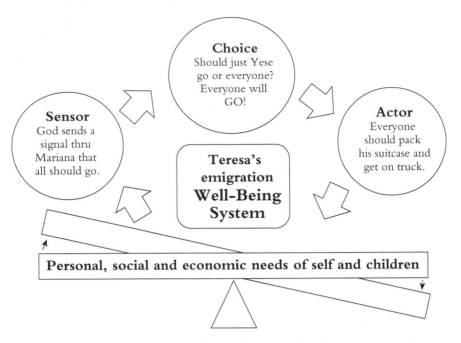

**FIGURE 2.5**  Teresa's Emigration Well-Being System at time 5

apply theoretical and experimental rigor to the understanding of what it means to cultivate and maintain well-being.[4] Often referred to as "positive psychologists," in response to the fact that psychology was, and in large measure still is concerned primarily with the study of human dysfunction and malaise, these researchers focused on better understanding and measuring what it means to be happy and life-satisfied.[5] One such model is that of behavioral economist Paul Dolan.[6] Like most well-being researchers, Dolan conceptualizes well-being as multi-dimensional, but rather than three, four, or in some cases, six or seven modalities or dimensions, Dolan believes that feelings of well-being can be adequately defined using just two dimensions—pleasure and purpose. Dolan defines pleasure as how one feels, both positively and negatively, what he generically refers to as "pleasure" and "pain." He defines purpose as an additional sense of one's accomplishment, meaning, worthwhileness or fulfillment.[7] Using this conceptualization, at the moment Teresa chose to get on the truck and head to the U.S., she was feeling extreme pleasure and also had a high level of purpose and sense of fulfillment.[8]

However, the fact that Dolan parses well-being into two broad domains, rather than multiple dimensions, is not the important distinction that separates him from most other positive psychologists. What really distinguishes Dolan's ideas from many others is his insistence that a person's perceptions of well-being are not based on some generic life evaluation, but rather on the moment-to-moment perception of current conditions.[9]

This was clearly the case with Teresa. As the moment for going arrived, she remained torn with indecision, even about whether her niece Yese should go. Then she perceived she got a signal from God and the choice of going or staying was resolved. In just a matter of minutes, she went from the depths of despair to the heights of joy, from feeling diminished well-being to feeling a highly positive sense of well-being. But this heightened sense of well-being, too, turned out to be short-lived.

[The truck we were in] was not going well. They supposedly did a repair on it and it was working. And they were driving very fast, really fast on that truck. And there was a moment in which I felt as if we were falling out because they were going really fast. And I [prayed to God] . . . "Lord, please, touch their hearts, the drivers' hearts, because they are going really fast. Make them think they shouldn't go at that speed because [it] is a danger for my children." And when I had told that to the Lord, they suddenly stopped, and went off in a part where they were going slow, where the truck could stop. So then I told the [driver], "Don't drive that fast. Why don't you slow down? You're going very fast. In addition, if the truck stopped it is because it has a problem. Please take it to a repair shop. I have money for it to be checked, because it's not normal for it to turn itself off." And he said "Let's see, we'll see in a moment," and they turned it on and it worked.

We kept moving, but I felt much better. By now we were almost reaching the place where we were going. We were already at the desert. . . . We were heading to [the Mexican border town of] Altar, where we had to arrive before entering the desert [where we would cross the border into Arizona].

Hence, well-being not only can, but does fluctuate widely over time, not only across a year, but even over the course of a day. No one can expect to constantly be happy or in a continuous state of well-being. However, Dolan believes people do not need to passively accept their state of well-being; they can monitor and to a large degree proactively manage it. According to Dolan, the ability to regulate one's well-being begins with a degree of self-knowledge, knowing what it is that provides one pleasure, what constitutes purpose and what one perceives is the right balance between pleasure and purpose.[10] Of course some situations are easier to control than others. Teresa exercised every tool she possessed in an effort to control her situation, including praying and, when offered the opportunity, providing rational alternatives to the driver. Because she perceived that her efforts to control the circumstance worked, her sense of well-being returned again.

Because well-being is always subject to fluctuation, it must be constantly monitored and attended to. Though it is theoretically possible to synoptically evaluate one's life,[11] to look back and say it was a good year for example, this type of summary assessment does not accurately capture the realities of personal well-being. Well-being is too varied and ephemeral to be accurately measured by this kind of an annual, summary assessment. Well-being is not a destination, it is a journey, more like a river than a lake. Well-being is never totally static, but always dynamic. Well-being is a judgment about experience, particularly the experiences happening in the immediate here and now.

Although people can derive a sense of well-being based on imagining a better future, this is not the norm. Based on a range of experiments, psychologists have hypothesized that humans perceive their well-being, and hence make choices differently, depending upon the timeframe involved.[12] The idea is that even though an individual reflectively knows that the person he will be in a month, his "future self," is theoretically the same person that he is today, his "present self," the present self has little concern, understanding or empathy for that future person.[13] Reinforcing this view, psychologist Hal Hershfield stated, "When making long-term decisions, [people] tend to fundamentally feel a lack of emotional connection to their future selves. . . . So even though I know on some fundamental level in a year's time, I'll still be me, in some ways I treat that future self as if he's a fundamentally different person, and as if he's not going to benefit or suffer from the consequences of my actions today."[14]

Reinforcing this idea, brain research conducted by Hershfield and his colleagues showed that individuals process conceptualizations of their present and future selves in different parts of the brain.[15] Not only do people generally experience pleasure in the moment, but pleasure is so fleeting that it generally pays for people to maximize immediate pleasure, rather than delay gratification.[16] Pleasurable memories seem to be disproportionately connected with the "present self" part of the brain. This discrepancy in where positive emotional connections occur appears to have consequences. It is hypothesized that the paucity of positive emotional connections to the future self negatively affects future choice-making.[17] People most of the time selectively opt to make choices designed to satisfy short-term rather than long-term needs. This is because, based on prior experiences, people perceive that satisfying short-term needs are much more likely to result in feelings of positive well-being.[18]

## How the Well-Being Systems Model Compares to Other Models

There are many models of choice-making, and many of them would seem to explain the hows and whys of Teresa's choice-making trials and tribulations described above just as readily as does the model I propose. In fact, some models, such as Deci and Ryan's Self-Determination Theory, might even do so more analytically and less descriptively.[19] Self-Determination Theory is predicated on the assumption that all choices are motivated by the need to fulfill the three fundamental psychological needs that Deci and Ryan assert underlie all human behavior. These are the needs of: *Autonomy, Competence* and *Relatedness*; evidence for all three can be found in Teresa's tale.

*Autonomy* is defined by Deci and Ryan as the desire to have control over the direction of one's activities and Teresa certainly was desirous of control. The main reason she felt she could not decide on whether to travel to the U.S. revolved around her perceptions of control. Teresa understood that staying in Mexico doomed her and her children to limited economic opportunity and would permanently separate her from her family, but she also perceived that staying in Mexico insured her considerable control over her life and that of her children. She had friends in Mexico, a home to live in and a reasonably predictable life. Emigrating to the U.S. held the promise of not only significantly increasing the likelihood her family achieving economic advancement, but would reunite her with her husband and her brother and his family. However, in order to get to the U.S., Teresa would risk total loss of control. Her experience in the truck shortly after leaving her home is just one example of what she feared. Although Teresa had not anticipated the truck issues, she did anticipate what would happen once they got to the border, where she would be forced to put her fate, and that of her children, in the hands of the "Coyotes"—the name Mexican migrants use to describe the men they pay to guide them into the U.S. She knew that most Coyotes were untrustworthy criminals, individuals who would put her and her children at great physical risk, risks that she would have only the most marginal ability to mitigate. This conundrum caused her great stress, even depression. Ultimately in the 11th hour, she decided to go. Throughout her ordeal, Teresa turned to God, who she believed spoke to her and told her what to do. She believed that God would listen to her prayers and intervene at critical moments, such as he had in the truck, and this provided her an additional sense of control.

*Competency*, according to Deci and Ryan, reflects the need to feel successful in one's environment. While in Mexico, Teresa felt that she was a competent mother and aunt, a capable, albeit challenged provider for her extended family. By contrast she had no confidence in her ability to keep her children safe on the journey to the U.S. Her concerns were reinforced by her experience in the truck, where she was relegated to the back of the truck; she was just another passenger. In this situation she had no more say about how fast the truck should be driving than did her children. Once the truck stopped, though, Teresa had an opportunity to intervene and offer solutions, such as helping to pay for repairs. In this way she felt she was able to be a part of the decision-making process; she was helping to manage the situation.

*Relatedness* is the third need highlighted by Deci and Ryan. In their theory, relatedness refers to the need to feel part of and accepted by one's group. This need too is apparent in Teresa's account of her decision-making process of whether to leave for the U.S. or stay in Mexico. Teresa continuously sought the counsel of others—her husband, her brother, her friend. Each of these individuals in his/her own way exerted an influence on Teresa. Each gave Teresa mixed messages; all expressed understanding of her predicament but none gave an unequivocal answer. Each person both encouraged and discouraged her from leaving Mexico. Teresa's need to do what was "right," to make a choice that did not disappoint her friends and relations, ultimately figured prominently in her choice-making dilemma. Ultimately the one "voice" that was unequivocal was the voice of her God. Far and away Teresa's most cherished association is the one she has with her religion. She clearly believed she was close to God, after all God spoke directly to her. Once she felt that she heard the voice of God telling her to go, there was no longer a choice. For a devout person like Teresa, one cannot disobey one's God. In this way, Teresa's choice was the ultimate act of acceptance, a fulfillment of her relationship with her religion and her God.

According to Deci and Ryan, when individuals engage in activities in which these three needs are fulfilled, individuals feel that their motivations are "self-determined" and they find the activity itself pleasurable. When these needs are not fulfilled, individuals feel that their motivations are not "self-determined" and that the experience is coerced and often unpleasant. From the perspective of Self-Determination Theory, Teresa's decision-making process involved this triage of considerations, each requiring Teresa to weigh the relative pros and cons of the three dimensions of need. Teresa's explanations for why this was such a difficult choice, as well as her description of why she finally decided to seize the moment, climb onto the truck and head for the U.S., all appear to conform to the basic outlines of Deci and Ryan's model. A number of researchers have applied the tenets of Self-Determination Theory to a variety of settings and situations and similarly found that the model successfully captures critical aspects of people's choice-making.[20]

Choice clearly involves a complex dance between personally and socially weighed considerations, including important factors like perceptions of self-efficacy, social norms, belief systems and social and personal consequences. Self-Determination Theory captures much of this complexity. However, the Achilles heel of this and other comparable psychological models of choice is that they place a premium on conscious deliberation, even if that conscious deliberation is skewed by some kind of psychological, social or personal bias. Psychological models like Self-Determination Theory also inadequately accommodate the biological propensity of people to focus on short-term rather than longer term well-being. Some aspects of Teresa's choice-making during her journey seem to fit Deci and Ryan's model, but other pieces less so; at times Teresa was acting more reflexively and less deliberately. In such cases, Deci and Ryan's model does not seem to adequately describe the choices Teresa made since they do not appear to be the product of conscious or even subconscious deliberation, nor do they seem to reflect a balance between a desire for *Autonomy, Competence* and *Relatedness*. In particular, I am referring to all the survival and security-related choices that Teresa was constantly forced to make.

After her long, sometimes harrowing truck ride, Teresa and her family finally arrived at the Mexican border town of Altar where they would wait until the Coyote told them it was safe to make the desert crossing into the U.S. They needed to stay in Altar several days, and all that time Teresa needed to make choices related to basic needs, finding food and a place to stay where she and her family members would not be raped, robbed or otherwise injured. In this foreign and threatening environment, even typically common-place behaviors required careful thought and choice. But even these challenging survival-oriented choices paled in comparison with the ones she needed to make once they actually began their 17-hour walk through the desert. Teresa continued to share her story:

> What happened is that we walked for many hours [but] we weren't walking during the daytime, everything was at night. [The Coyotes] know where there are places like sand [away from the cactus], and there you can sit to rest on the sand. Because in the desert there are a lot of thorns and it's really bad, full of thorns, those that stick in you [and don't come out]. But when he said, "Rest here," we knew, we had seen that there are many scorpions on the sand around there. And [there] could also be [rattle] snakes. And I was so close to a snake. . . . I was like, this far [INDICATES ABOUT A THIRD OF A METER/ONE FOOT WITH HER HANDS] from stepping on it. But I just quickly stepped to the side and walked around it. And nothing happened, thank goodness.

Psychological models like Self-Determination Theory do not consider these kinds of choices as relevant for consideration. Since it is assumed that Teresa's reaction was instinctual, rather than consciously agentic, it does not rise to the level of being considered a "choice." However, the evasive action Teresa took to side-step the snake was indeed a choice, albeit what another behavioral economist, Daniel Kahneman, would refer to as involving thinking fast rather than thinking slow.[21] This is because in this particular instance, Teresa's choice-making process bypassed the route involving conscious deliberation, instead utilizing more primordial, faster acting neural pathways that first evolved hundreds of millions of years ago. Even though no conscious choice was involved, except after the fact, it still must be considered a choice. This is because virtually all of a person's neural pathways, including the ones Teresa used to make this avoidance choice, are not unalterably hardwired. Individuals can learn to find snakes appealing rather than scary, even rattlesnakes. People can even learn to react to the presence of snakes by instantly pouncing on it rather than automatically sidestepping it. The fact that Teresa lacked that kind of training and responded in a more "instinctual" way to the signals alerting her to the presence of a snake does not mean her actions were not the result of a choice, were not part of a Well-Being System. Of course the exact neural networks in Teresa's brain involved in choosing to avoid the snake were different than the neural networks used to enact her choice(s) of whether or not to emigrate to the U.S. The same basic Well-Being Systems model I used earlier to diagram "conscious" choice-making can equally be used to represent this type of "unconscious" choice-making (see Figure 2.6).

Avoiding stepping on a rattlesnake was obviously a highly salient event for Teresa, and thus highly memorable, but over the course of her multi-month ordeal Teresa made thousands of equally important survival-oriented choices, most of which she did not find sufficiently salient to remember. Each day she was making choices of when to eat, drink, defecate and urinate. Some days those choices were easy to make, but on other days they were more challenging. Each day she was

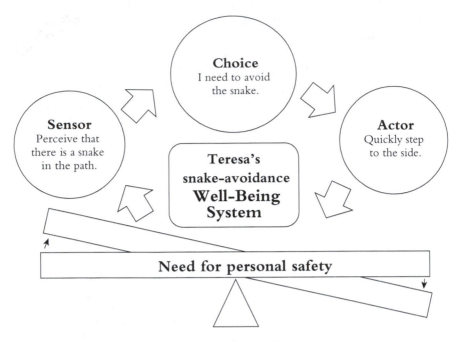

**FIGURE 2.6**   Teresa's Snake-Avoidance Well-Being System

making choices about her body temperature, trying to stay warm at night and cool during the day. Again some of those choices were made without thought, while others required considerable thought as she found herself in unfamiliar settings and circumstances. Whenever Teresa was walking she would have had to select where to place her feet. Most of the time she would not have had to consciously focus on this task, but while walking through the desert at night Teresa would have been constantly watching the ground and carefully choosing to follow a particular path so as to avoid stepping on rocks or snakes or getting stuck by a cactus. Each day Teresa's body also would be making choices for her, for example, how quickly to breathe and/or how fast her heart should beat, all to insure that the proper amounts of oxygen and nutrients were distributed throughout her body. Again, Teresa would typically not be aware of such choices. Perhaps even during the initial phase of her trek through the desert, she might have been oblivious to these bodily choices, but over time as she walked further and became increasingly fatigued she would have become increasingly aware of even these normally subconscious choices. Of course, she would not have perceived this deficiency in this way, but instead would have perceived these as needs. She would have become aware of being fatigued, or even worse, having muscle cramps, and feeling the need to stop and rest.

Clearly each of these choices were fundamental to Teresa's health and well-being. Each of these choices could be readily diagramed using the Well-Being Systems model, as I did for her snake encounter. However, as I pointed out in

Chapter 1, these survival-oriented choices are not easily reconciled using traditional social science models of choice that begin with the assumption that all choices require conscious agency, let alone rational decision-making. Even models that take into consideration the role of the subconscious and emotion can only marginally explain this entire spectrum of choice; psychological constructs like *Autonomy, Competence* and *Relatedness*, though useful in understanding some choices, are irrelevant for understanding others. A robust model of human choice-making requires understanding and explaining the full range of human choice-making, not just a selected subset.

The same issues pertain to how well-being has been conceptualized. Social science models of well-being tend to focus on only the most salient and conscious aspects of life.[22] A good job and a healthy social life are important, but so too is being physically healthy and feeling safe and secure.

## The Fulcrum of Well-Being Systems

Whether trying to decide whether or not to emigrate, insuring that she and her family did not die in a truck accident or avoiding getting bit by a snake or stuck by a cactus, all of Teresa's choices were made to maximize her and her family's well-being. The impetus for the entire journey was her concern about the long-term economic well-being and safety of her children as she watched them play like gang members. Over the course of the crossing though, more immediate, tangible concerns framed her choices, such as thirst, sleep-deprivation, exposure to the elements and the safety of her and her children. As suggested by Paul Dolan, Teresa's feelings of well-being were constantly in flux; her feelings of positive well-being highly ephemeral.

Despite beginning her journey feeling good about her choice to better her and her family's well-being, for much of the journey Teresa did not feel either happy or satisfied. Much of the time she felt a lack of control, was fearful for her life and the lives of her children and was surrounded by strangers and authority figures who showed no real regard for her or her interests. Despite her continuing faith that God would take care of her and her family, her sense of well-being was significantly tested and diminished. However, once safely reunited with her husband and family in the U.S., in a situation where she felt able to satisfy her own and her children's short and longer-term economic, social and biological needs, her perception of well-being again revived:

> I felt very discouraged [during much of the journey] but at the same time when we entered the desert, watching [the youngest boy], saying "Oh, I'm almost there with my parents." Then I said to myself, "Ok, ok." I repeated to myself, "I have to be positive, because we already are in the field, we are in the desert and I can't be like this." Even if I was, even if I couldn't really [control things], I needed to be positive for the children. It was a lot of pressure. And since I couldn't sleep, I didn't sleep. I was awake there, taking

care of them in the desert while they were sleeping. I felt weak. But, we are here [in the U.S.] [SMILES], and that is what is important. Yeah, now I feel good. . . . My life is better now and so are the lives of my children. I am happy.

Teresa based her feelings of well-being, before, during and after her journey, on a wide diversity of needs, including her perceptions of pleasure and purpose.[23] However, fundamental to appreciate is that all of Teresa's perceptions of well-being and need were self-referential.

The only way an individual like Teresa could ever judge whether or not she had achieved well-being, whether her perceived needs are/were satisfied, is to make that judgment relative to her perceptions of self. When a person perceives that their self-related needs are satisfied, when they perceive that their well-being is strong and well-supported, the individual feels good. Teresa felt good because she perceived that God was answering HER prayers. She felt positive because she perceived that HER children were safe. When a person perceives that they cannot satisfy their needs, when they perceive forces/others beyond their control are determining events, the individual feels tested and diminished. Teresa felt unhappy and scared when she perceived the truck she was riding in was going too fast to be safe for HER and HER children. She felt her life threatened when SHE almost stepped on a rattlesnake. All choices are about satisfying needs in order to achieve feelings of well-being, and all perceptions of need are framed in terms of the self (either the individual self or the collective self of family and/or community). Self-related Needs are the "fulcrum" on which the whole Well-Being System pivots and are the focus of the next chapter.

## Notes

1. Teresa is a pseudonym, as are all the other names used in her subsequent interview transcripts.
2. 1,500 pesos is roughly the equivalent of $75 (U.S.).
3. This excerpt and the remainder of the interview with Teresa included in this chapter were conducted in the summer of 2016 by my associate Nelda Reyes expressly for this book. A full transcript is available from the author upon request.
4. cf., Ryff, C.D. (1989). Happiness is everything, or is it? Explorations on the meaning of psychological well-being. *Journal of Personality and Social Psychology*, 57(6), 1069–1081.
5. e.g., Ryff, C.D. (2014). Psychological well-being revisited: Advances in the science and practice of Eudaimonia. *Psychotherapy & Psychosomatics*, 83(1), 10–28.
   Cloninger, C.R. (2004). *Feeling good: The science of well-being.* Oxford: Oxford University Press.
   Eid, M. & Larsen, R.J. (Eds.). (2008). *The science of subjective well-being.* New York: The Guildford Press.
   Diener, E. & Biswas-Diener, R. (2008). *Happiness: Unlocking the mysteries of psychological wealth.* Malden, MA: Blackwell Publishing.
6. Dolan, P. (2014). *Happiness by design: Finding pleasure and purpose in everyday life.* London: Penguin.
7. In my model, purpose is equivalent to "NEED." Typically short-term but occasionally long-term, an individual's self-related needs are perceived as the purpose, the "reason" why that person acts in the way she does.

8. Interestingly, most positive psychologists, like Aristotle before them, make a point of distinguishing between feelings of pleasure related to "simple pleasures" like a good meal or sex and the higher "meaningful pleasures" of knowledge and altruism. For example, Martin Seligman, one of the founders of positive psychology, is quoted as saying, "[Positive Psychology] takes you through the countryside of pleasure and gratification, up into the high country of strength and virtue, and finally to the peaks of lasting fulfillment: meaning and purpose" (Seligman, M. (2002). *Authentic happiness: Using the new positive psychology to realize your potential for lasting fulfillment.* New York: Free Press, p. 61).

   I would argue that each of these various dimensions are equally valid, all are variations on the same thing, feedback that one is engaged in a positive survival-oriented experience. As I will describe more fully in Chapter 4, my model outlines seven modalities of well-being-related needs. The multiple dimensions of well-being that have been defined reflect feedback from one or combinations of these seven modalities.

9. Dolan's ideas are consistent with Daniel Kahneman's assertion that well-being/happiness is always situated in the moment and relative, rather than some absolute state (cf., Kahneman, D. (2000). Experienced utility and objective happiness: A moment-based approach. In D. Kahneman and A. Tversky (Eds.). *Choices, values and frames* (pp. 673–692). New York: Cambridge University Press).

10. Dolan, P. (2014). *Happiness by design: Finding pleasure and purpose in everyday life.* London: Penguin.

11. A large number of wide-scale surveys and assessments of well-being, typically referred to in the psychological literature as "subjective well-being" have been developed. These assessments have now been administered to individuals, groups and even whole nations (e.g., Hicks, S. (2012). Measuring subjective well-being: The UK Office for National Statistics experience. In J.F. Helliwell, R. Layard & J. Sachs (Eds.), *World happiness report.* New York: Earth Institute. Retrieved December 8, 2016. http://worldhappiness. report/wp-content/uploads/sites/2/2015/04/WHR15.pdf); Diener, E. (2015). *Subjective well-being scales.* Retrieved December 8, 2016. https://internal.psychology.illinois. edu/~ediener/scales.html

12. Blouin-Hudon, E.-M. & Pchyl, T. (2015). Experiencing the temporally extended self: Initial support for the role of affective states, vivid mental imagery, and future self-continuity in the prediction of academic procrastination. *Personality and Individual Differences,* 86, 50–56.

13. Eagleman, D. (2011). *Incognito: The secret lives of the brain.* New York: Vintage.

14. Quoted in: Swanson, A. (2016). The real reasons you procrastinate—And how to stop. *Washington Post.* Retrieved April 28, 2016. www.washingtonpost.com/news/wonk/wp/2016/04/27/why-you-cant-help-read-this-article-about-procrastination-instead-of-doing-your-job/?hpid=hp_hp-more-top-stories_wonk-procrastinate-652pm%3Ahomepage%2Fstory

15. Ersner-Hershfield, H., Elliott Wimmer, G. & Knutson, B. (2009). Saving for the future self: Neural measures of future self-continuity predict temporal discounting. *Social Cognitive and Affective Neuroscience,* 4(1), 85–92.

16. Mischel, W. (2014). *The marshmallow test: Conquering self-control.* New York: Little, Brown.

17. Eagleman, D. (2011). *Incognito: The secret lives of the brain.* New York: Vintage.

18. Although perceived well-being/happiness is ultimately determined by a range of factors, including environmental conditions and active choice, genetic factors appear to play a surprisingly large role (Simandan, D. (2014). Omitted variables in the geographical treatment of well-being and happiness. *Geography Journal,* 2014, http://dx.doi. org/10.1155/2014/150491 Retrieved May 18, 2017).

19. Deci, E.L. & Ryan, R.M. (1985). *Intrinsic motivation and self-determination in human behavior.* New York: Plenum.

   Deci, E.L. & Ryan, R.M. (2000). The 'what' and 'why' of goal pursuits: Human needs and the self-determination of behavior. *Psychological Inquiry,* 11, 227–268.

   NOTE: I have opted in this book not to invest time and space in exhaustive reviews of the literature. Deci and Ryan's Self Determination theory is one of dozens of models of choice. I selected it because I believe it to be one of the better psychological models.

20. See review by Lapointe, M.-C. & Perreault, S. (2013). Motivation: Understanding leisure engagement and disengagement. *Society and Leisure*, 36(2), 136–144.
21. Kahneman, D. (2011). *Thinking, fast and slow.* New York: Farrar, Straus and Giroux.
22. e.g., Ryff, C.D. (2014). Psychological well-being revisited: Advances in the science and practice of Eudaimonia. *Psychotherapy & Psychosomatics*, 83(1), 10–28.
      Cloninger, C.R. (2004). *Feeling good: The science of well-being.* Oxford: Oxford University Press.
      Eid, M. & Larsen, R.J. (Eds.). (2008). *The science of subjective well-being.* New York: The Guildford Press.
      Diener, E. & Biswas-Diener, R. (2008). *Happiness: Unlocking the mysteries of psychological wealth.* Malden, MA: Blackwell Publishing.
      Seligman, M. (2002). *Authentic happiness: Using the new positive psychology to realize your potential for lasting fulfillment.* New York: Free Press.
      Dolan, P. (2014). *Happiness by design: Finding pleasure and purpose in everyday life.* London: Penguin.
23. Dolan, P. (2014). *Happiness by design: Finding pleasure and purpose in everyday life.* London: Penguin.

# 3

# WELL-BEING, SELF AND SELF-RELATED NEEDS

This chapter addresses two major questions: 1) How does self-perception enable the perception of need? and 2) How do perceptions of self-related need support and enable choice-making? Current social science theory provides a useful foundation for answering these questions, particularly when bolstered by findings from the neurosciences. Ultimately though, neither social science nor neuroscience theory alone provides a full and adequate explanation. Teresa's emigration story is again illustrative.

We pick up Teresa and her family's emigration story as they arrived in Altar, the Mexican border town used as a staging area for undocumented crossings into the U.S. Although faced with challenges and choices before this point, once in Altar and beyond, Teresa and her family's challenges and choices escalated in both frequency and urgency.

> We had to go [to Altar] where we were going to meet the people who were going to cross us. . . . That place is very ugly, the place where you arrive, because there are a lot of bad people. . . . There is a lot of risk, there's a lot of risk for the girls getting raped, older people getting raped. Because they do drugs, because the people [in charge there] do drugs. Staying at those houses is not safe at all. I found a hotel and all of us stayed in a [single] room. It was safer. It was an ugly place, but thank God, we could stay in a room and be there the whole time we stayed before leaving to the desert.
>
> So we didn't go out, you can't go out, except to grab food, and that was all. [We told the children], "Don't speak with anyone, don't speak with anyone. Don't open the door for anyone." Because apparently, there are other people [who try to] take you to a different person who [tries to get more money from you]. It's like a business. That's their business. Your business [when you are crossing like we did], is taking care of your money, taking

care of the people you are taking [with you]. That's why we didn't speak to other people. Only the grown-ups went out. Not the children, they had to remain there inside. One of the grown-ups always stayed with the children. Actually there's no place to be either inside or outside in that place, because it's super-hot. Picture yourself at the foot of the fireplace.

Teresa made a clear distinction between herself and her family and the other people of Altar. Her family she could trust, but the others she could not. Under the circumstances this was entirely understandable, and very human. All humans see themselves as unique selves, individually and collectively distinct from some perceived "other"—be it other people or other physical aspects of the world.[1] This idea of human uniqueness and separation has great survival value, clearly a value that has existed for as long as humans have been a unique species. The idea of human uniqueness and separation is central in one way or another to all creation myths; "we" are self, everything and everyone else is the other.[2] This tendency to distinguish self from other[3] has been a central focus of much of both Western and Eastern philosophy,[4] and more recently social science theory.[5]

At the most basic level, the ability to perceive self, to envision one's physical essence, actions and even thoughts as distinctive from one's surroundings affords humans (and other organisms) the most fundamental and important of all life-capabilities: The ability to distinguish one's current state or situation relative to the environment; to determine whether everything is currently satisfactory and in-balance or out-of-balance and thus unsatisfactory.

Without the ability to perceive and distinguish self from non-self, humans (and other organisms) would not be able to perceive needs; it would not be possible to act purposefully in the world. For example, it would not have been possible for Teresa to proactively try to maintain her family's Well-Being while staying in Altar. Teresa used her notions of self to determine not only that Altar was a potentially unsafe place but also what the nature of that danger might be. Only by determining what her needs were could she try to define the nature of the problem and arrive at a solution—act to isolate and protect her family so that they would be insulated from the dangers posed by the "bad" others of Altar (see Figure 3.1).

## Self-Perception

Thousands of years of thinking about human self-perception have resulted in some deep insights, but surprisingly little consensus. More than 2,500 years ago Aristotle said, "Knowing yourself is the beginning of all wisdom."[6] Halfway around the world at roughly the same time, Confucius was also lecturing about the relationship between self and other. Confucius though framed self-perception in a social rather than an individual context, focusing on the relationship between a child and his parents, or a citizen and his ruler. Although there is a lack of written records to substantiate the fact, I think it is a fair guess that people long before Aristotle and Confucius were also pondering the importance of knowing how

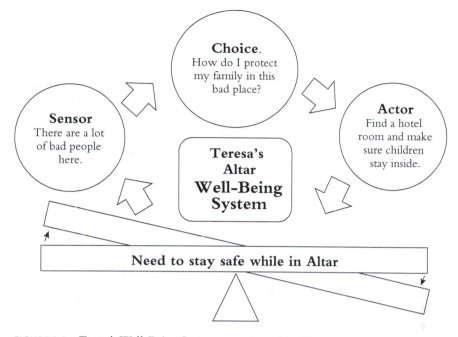

**FIGURE 3.1**   Teresa's Well-Being System upon arrival in Altar

to understand and distinguish self from other. Notions of self-perception have of course not remained constant over time. How a Greek or Chinese in the fifth or sixth century BC conceptualized self was different from how a Greek or Chinese would have done so in the thirteenth century, which in turn would have been different from how similar people do so today.[7]

Despite millennia of speculation, serious empirical investigation on the nature of self-perception is actually quite recent, in its broadest outline only a little more than a hundred years old.[8] Building on intuitive understandings of the self, early on social scientists appreciated that self-perception was "reflexive" in the social science sense of the word—not instinctual but relational. In other words a person's sense of *self* is not only based on how an individual perceives himself, but also on how that person perceives others perceive him; and the two are interconnected.[9] An individual both projects a sense of self that influences how others perceive him, as well as modifies that sense of self based on how his self is responded to by others. As early as 1890, pioneering psychologist William James talked about the self as being both the known self—"me"—and the self as knower—"I."[10] Importantly though, James also appreciated that a person's self-non-self boundary is psychologically rather than physically defined, and thus subject to considerable fluidity.

> In its widest possible sense, however, a man's Self is the sum total of all that he *can* call his, not only his body and his psychic powers, but his clothes and his house, his wife and children, his ancestors and friends, his reputation and

works, his lands and horses, and yacht and bank account. All these things give him the same emotions. If they wax and prosper, he feels triumphant; if they dwindle and die away, he feels cast down.[11]

James' definition of self, despite being more than 125 years old (and reflective of the social realities and values of his time), remains a cogent and useful way to conceptualize the nature of how humans perceive self. According to James, what determines the boundary between self and other is a person's emotional attitude toward an object or thought. The things, people or thoughts with which a person perceptibly identifies are quite literally part of self; what happens to them is experienced as something happening to one's self. The boundary of perceived self can, and typically does, extend beyond an individual's skin and body and includes a person's pets, loved ones, possessions, and even her ideas.

There was a period when James' view of self as a psychologically constructed, multifarious and changeable entity lost favor among social scientists, replaced by a view of self as more monolithic and stable. According to this conceptualization, the "self" developed during childhood and adolescence, and was strongly influenced by genetically-determined personality traits. Once established, the self exhibited great constancy.[12] However by the end of the twentieth century and into the current century, most social scientists, including me, accept the Jamesian view of self.[13] Social scientists such as James Gee, Stuart Hall, Etienne Wenger and Kath Woodward further argue that part of what makes understanding self-perception so complex is that there are multiple layers of self, for example, individual, social and societal selves.[14] To this list of multiple selves I have added the "s" selves reflective of the roles and relationships a person enacts in the moment, aspects such as "helpful neighbor," or "curious tourist," rather than the traditional, demographically-derived "S" selves of race/ethnicity, gender, nationality and religion that have historically dominated discussions of the self.[15] However, whether self-related needs are framed in terms of "s" or "S"-type perceptions of self, all derive from lived experience. Combining these perspectives, self-perception emerges as something that is malleable and continually constructed by the individual as need requires. Importantly, perceptions of self are not exclusively a conscious process, but reflective of the vast unconscious set of genetic, cultural and personal histories that define an individual.[16] Each person is continuously constructing and maintaining not one but numerous levels of self-perception which are expressed collectively or individually at different times, depending upon need and circumstance.[17] From this perspective, self-perception is best defined as an emergent, rather than permanent, property of the individual, nimble, ever-changing, always responsive, situated and reactive to the immediate realities of the perceived physical and sociocultural world. Over the course of a lifetime, each individual develops a unique, ever-developing set of selves that she uses as a device for navigating and surviving in the world. Each of these self-perceptions influences how a person perceives her needs, and thus the choices she makes; in this way directly and indirectly shaping how that person selectively presents herself to the world.[18]

These social science paradigms of self-perception provide a framework for understanding Teresa's response to Altar, as diagrammed in Figure 3.1. To begin with Teresa's perception of "self" included not just her own person, but those of her children (which included her own two children plus her brother's three children), and the other adult traveling with her, her brother's wife's mother, Mariana. She defined as "non-self" everyone else she encountered in Altar.

Based in large part on prior knowledge and experience, but reinforced by direct observations, Teresa perceived that this town was filled with "bad" people. She decided that she could not trust any of these people, and therefore needed to find a way to keep her and her family safely separated from these bad people. Acting on this need, Teresa found a room in a hotel that she deemed safe, and then instructed everyone to stay inside the room, and not to open the door to anyone. Only the adults left the room, and only when necessity demanded it. And through this process, Teresa's well-being was maintained by acting in a way that minimized contact between the people she considered self and those she perceived as the dangerous other, i.e., bad people. The threshold trigger, the self-related NEED that regulated this System, was Teresa's desire to stay safe during her forced stay in Altar. She used a simple rubric for helping her decide how to satisfy this need. She assumed no one could be trusted, thus the simplest strategy for insuring safety was to keep everyone in the family as sequestered from others as possible, for as long as possible.

For this Well-Being System to work, everyone in the family needed to understand the System; needed to have a shared understanding of the Need. Fortunately, Teresa was able to communicate at least the basic action part of the System to even her youngest children by using a few simple directives: "Don't speak with anyone and don't open the door for anyone." Although she did not say this in her narrative, one can assume she added or prefaced her directive to her children with some kind of explanation, such as, "It is not safe here." It helped in this case that the Need, the idea Altar was an unsafe place, was so concrete. Self-perceived needs are not always so tangible.

## The Illusive Nature of Self-Perceived Needs

Every microsecond the brain is flooded with signals, both electrical and chemical. Some of these signals come from sense organs like the eyes or ears as a person scans the environment or processes conversation. Some signals come from other parts of the body, for example the digestive tract communicates whether it is sated or hungry and muscles communicate when they are fatigued.[19] Still other signals originate within the brain itself, as different parts of the brain communicate with each other. All of these signals collectively result in the firing of millions of neuronal arrays, but the individual cannot act on all of these attentional demands. So each array of stimulated neurons competes with other arrays for primacy. Every human choice and action is the result of the competition between, and the sorting out of all these electrical and chemical signals, each choice and action the product of a compromise between competing needs.[20]

Favored signals are always the ones that are perceived as best/most critically fulfilling self-related needs. For example, as Teresa entered the town of Altar, her brain was screaming DANGER! DANGER! DANGER! And danger is a signal that human minds have evolved to pay attention to. Of course in Teresa's case, this was not the same kind of danger signal as a snake, but rather a more subtle signal. These messages of danger were not actually based on an immediate reality, but rather an anticipation of danger. As Teresa looked around Altar she imagined a range of possible threats that could endanger her and her family. The danger signals flooding Teresa's brain were technically an illusion; a (justifiable) mental invention.

The danger signals Teresa perceived and processed in her the brain had a basis in external reality—there were real people in Altar who potentially posed a threat. But the attributes of these men were converted by Teresa's brain into chemical and electrical signals, into secondary messages constructed by her mind. As such, they fit the definition of an illusion.

Psychologists and neuroscientists have determined that every signal humans mentally perceive and respond to falls into this "illusion" category; all signals are constructions of the mind[21] (and as I have, and will continue to emphasize, equally constructions of the body[22]). Every second, of every day, a person takes the cacophony of external and internal sensations and converts them into electrical and chemical signals, which when compared with memories of past concentrations of similar chemicals and electrical signals enables the mind to build a mental model of the present. In this way, past and present signals are constructed into a coherent self-referential story that enables the person to interpret and determine what to do next.[23] In this way, all mental signals, ALL perceptions of need, are self-related mental inventions. All are one step removed from reality; all are technically illusions.[24]

However, saying that self-perceptions are an illusion does not by any means suggest that these perceptions can or should be dismissed as unimportant or without any basis in reality. When Teresa stepped off the truck in Altar and looked around at the men hanging around the street, she mentally converted this information into chemical and electrical signals, which she evaluated based on her existing mental models of men she had seen and met before as well as what she had heard or read about this and other similar towns along the border. The resulting perception of threat that Teresa formed was an illusory construction of her mind, but it was based on what she perceived as reliable past experiences, both her own and those of others. Although her feelings of threat may have technically been an illusion, they had real consequences as these constructed perceptions were translated into concrete actions.[25]

Constructed self-related mental illusions of need form the foundation of all Well-Being Systems. People base their every interaction with the world, whether with other people, ideas or physical phenomena, on mentally constructed self-related needs. Everything a person perceives, from the most tangible aspects of the world such as perceptions of temperature, texture and color to the most intangible such as perceptions of love and hate, are translated into self-referential mental constructions and evaluated as a function of self-related need.[26] From this perspective, every human action, from the most basic act of breathing to the most elevated act of creativity, begins through a process of converting sensory information into self-referential signals.[27]

Over the course of a day, millions upon millions of incoming self-referential signals are evaluated in relation to self-related needs. This represents a huge processing challenge, but the human brain is up to it. An average brain has something on the order of 100 billion neurons, and each neuron is connected to up to 10,000 other neurons, resulting in between 100 trillion and 1,000 trillion possible connections. Collectively these connections are organized into billions of neural networks. Each of these billions of brain-based neural networks represents a single Well-Being System.[28]

Evolution, as well as each person's unique life history, has dictated that these millions of signals get routed to the "right" set of Well-Being Systems. There are Systems related to the perception of social threat[29] and others related to temperature regulation,[30] and although these and other Systems typically have some form of interconnection, they are also semi-autonomous, self-functioning modules—with social threat-related Well-Being Systems localized in one part of the brain and temperature regulation-related Well-Being Systems in yet another. The neural organization and structures that define these various Well-Being Systems derive from two main histories—the individual's personal history and human evolutionary history.

So for example, initially Teresa's social threat Well-Being Systems may not previously have had any significant connections with her temperature regulation Well-Being Systems, but once she got to Altar and experienced both social threat and overwhelming heat stress together at the same place and time, Teresa's brain formed connections between these two Systems. And as suggested by her personal narrative, even years later, thinking about Altar activated both Systems. In other words, many of the relationships that exist between a person's various Well-Being System modules are likely quite unique to that person, reflective of that person's own idiosyncratic personal life-history and experience.

In general, though, the basic structure and relationships of a person's various Well-Being Systems modules are anything but idiosyncratic. All humans, not just Teresa, possess social threat and temperature regulation Well-Being Systems. Each of these Systems are products of a long evolutionary history, a history shared by all humans. This is why every human on the planet not only has these Systems, but why across all humans these particular Well-Being Systems are always located within the same areas of the brain, why the same types of sensory signals are likely to activate every human's social threat or their temperature regulation Well-Being Systems and result in a similar suite of choices and actions. Genetic history is not destiny but it is not irrelevant.

Human evolutionary history has affected not only the structure of each individual Well-Being System but also how the entire collection of Systems process and prioritize self-related needs. Although in general each of the various Well-Being Systems within the brain work collectively to maximize the total well-being of the person, they do this primarily by attending to their own well-being; their own self-related needs. The social threat Well-Being System is chiefly concerned with meeting needs related to social threat while the temperature regulation Well-Being System focuses on needs related to temperature regulation. At any given moment, the brain is processing signals related to multiple competing needs. Although a person is capable of doing many things simultaneously, it cannot obviously do an infinite number of things at the same time. Inevitably then, there needs to be some triage, some prioritizing at the level of the whole organism as to which of these various needs are most important, which Well-Being Systems should be activated and in which order. People are only consciously aware of some fraction of these complex goings on in their mind.

## Well-Being Systems and the Adaptive Unconscious

After leaving Altar, Teresa and her family followed the Coyote across the border, through the desert. They walked for hours, traveling at night and resting during the day.

> We kept on walking at night, we were very far from the Immigration [authorities], and I remember [my son] Ernesto was crying and Ernesto said he wanted the light, he said "I want light," because we were in the darkness, walking among the weeds, there. And I told him "There's the light" [SIGNALING UP TO THE CEILING], and there was a beautiful moon. I say "Look, there's the bulb, calm, don't cry," and then I said to him "Shut up!" And then the Coyote guide says, "Let him cry, we are really far from anyone." There was no problem. But he was also crying because he had thorns in him. We pulled it out of him. But I too had lots of thorns in me, over here [POINTS TO HER ARM].

It is reasonable to assume that people make choices along a continuum of conscious awareness. At one end of the continuum are choices that are made "mindfully" through conscious reflection. Choices at the other end of the continuum are made entirely subconsciously through some kind of semi-automatic process.

An example of a choice at the conscious end of the continuum is Teresa's choice to emigrate to the U.S. These kinds of choices often require considerable deliberation, time and even the creation of (mental or physical) checklists and consultations. At the other, unconscious end of the continuum are physiological decisions such as Ernesto crying when scared and poked by thorns. In the middle are a whole range of common, often highly routinized decisions, like opening the door of the hotel room when someone knocks; presumably these decisions involve some mix of conscious and unconscious, habitual choice-making. Arguably, from a purely quantitative point of view, people almost certainly make more choices that fall on the unconscious end of the continuum than the conscious end. It would seem most philosophers and social scientists believe that conscious choices are of greatest importance since these are the ones they have almost exclusively focused on. Of course this conclusion of importance is debatable, since the decision to avoid stepping on a snake or crying out in pain when stuck by a thorn even while trying to hide from authorities are hardly trivial life-choices.

How would a person, let alone a scientist, actually determine which of the many life choices made in a day, a year or a lifetime are most important? Part of the difficulty is that there is an inherent bias in people's ability to decide which of their choices are important, since the only ones they are likely to remember, in other words have awareness of, and thus encode into their autobiographical memory, are the ones that involve some or perhaps even a great deal of conscious awareness. Even in the absence of direct evidence for this statement it seems inarguably true. To begin with, people generally do not think about, let alone "recall," the choices of which they are unaware. People only remember choices they find salient, i.e., are consciously aware of. As a consequence, it seems reasonable to conclude that people have a strong "consciousness" bias in their beliefs about what choices were important in their life, as well as what factors or circumstances were involved in making those choices. Should anyone continue to doubt this reality, based on the logical argument just made, then the evidence emerging from research in the cognitive and neurosciences should put those doubts to rest.

Research on the mind is revealing that much, if not all choice-making, and even "thought," is unconscious. According to most estimates, more than 95% of thought and choice-making occurs entirely below the level of conscious awareness.[31] And the 5% figure is said to only apply to the most cognitively aware people; most people operate at just 1% conscious awareness.[32] In addition, most of the ways people formulate thoughts about why they act in the ways they do occur nonverbally. Thus, despite the fact that people store, process and communicate what is going on in their minds to others through language, verbal language is capable of only capturing a fraction of what is actually transpiring within the mind. In particular, words are notoriously poor for communicating inner feelings, needs or even actions.[33] Although by necessity, researchers like me depend upon individuals like Teresa to verbally describe why they do what they do, such conscious, verbal self-reflections are likely to be incomplete and reflective of only a little of what actually transpired in the person's mind.

It is not that Teresa, or any other person, does not want to share her choice-making process; she simply cannot do it. As a consequence, there is growing evidence that much of what people relate to each other during normal conversations, as well as during interviews such as the one my colleague conducted with Teresa, is actually "made up" on the spot in order to satisfy both parties—the listener and the teller.[34] By saying Teresa made up her story, I am not trying to suggest she purposefully lied about the ordeal, but rather that her memory of her emigration to the U.S. was selective and incomplete. She can remember many parts of it, but not all of it, or even necessarily as much as she related. However, people's conscious minds do not like this kind of ambiguity, so according to cognitive psychologist Daniel Wegner and others, they construct a plausible reality to "cover up" what they cannot actually remember.[35]

The reality is that people do not consciously think about most of the things they do over the course of the day.[36] A person's conscious intentions are at best vague and undeveloped, or more often, entirely nonexistent. This lack of clear intentionality or even awareness, though problematic for social science researchers, is actually not a problem for "real" people most of the time, since it rarely prevents them from making thousands of choices in an effective and "appropriate" manner. Teresa was asked to describe her ordeal in detail, from beginning to end, and so she did. How much of what she communicated was actually based on her memory of events, or inferred as events that must have happened, cannot be known, even by Teresa. More importantly, how much of what Teresa reported as conscious choice-making really was?

According to Wegner, although people strongly believe that their choices and actions are made consciously, there is little substantive evidence that this is actually true. Research has long shown that the brain begins to prepare for action just over a third of a second before the person consciously decides to act. In other words, even when a person "thinks" they are consciously aware of a decision to act, it is their unconscious mind which is actually making the decision for them.[37] Conscious will, according to Wegner, is similar to perceptions of self, merely an illusion.[38] Wegner goes on to say that "the illusion of will is so compelling that it can prompt the belief that acts were intended when they could not have been. It is as though people aspire to be ideal agents who know all their actions in advance."[39] He argues that people conflate the feeling of willfulness with actual causality of experience. People do feel like they will their actions, even when they do not actually do so. Again according to Wegner, "the experience of will, then, is the way our minds portray their operations to us, not their actual operation."[40] There are actual causal agents in the mind that cause actions, i.e., Well-Being Systems, but these parts of the mind operate primarily unconsciously.[41]

The ubiquitous human perception of will, the conscious sense of making choices, is likely just a byproduct of the mind.[42] Wegner speculates that this process evolved to allow people to "preview" actions, rather than control actions. Previewing what will happen has great evolutionary benefits, even if it does not directly control actions. From an evolutionary perspective, feeling in control is almost as good as actually being in control. Interestingly, such "previewed" actions are disproportionately found amongst those actions with lengthier lead times—for example, decisions involving at least some "rational" decision-making, such as Teresa deciding whether or not to emigrate to the U.S.—rather than those involving rapid responses, such as whether to "fight" or "flee" when faced with a threat such as Teresa's decision to sidestep the rattle snake. As I will describe in more detail in a later chapter, these conscious justifications become encoded in autobiographical memory and form the recalled stories of life. In these recalled narratives, such as Teresa's tale of her journey from Mexico, across the desert, and into the U.S., everything emerges as consciously considered and willed, regardless of the actual reality of the circumstances.

Despite the fact that at any given moment there are always many things going on simultaneously in a person's body, mind and the surrounding environment, people are only capable of consciously perceiving one, or at most two or three things at a time.[43] For example, most of the time a person is oblivious to their breathing or heart beating. It is possible to focus conscious awareness on any one of these physiological processes, but when one does focus on one of these processes, one cannot simultaneously add up a list of numbers.[44] This tendency of the conscious mind to concentrate on a single track provides a useful focus and singular frame of reference for people, and both of these qualities have great survival benefits, but they also tend to create significant problems for understanding the nature of Well-Being Systems. As a consequence of consciousness' concentration on a single track, people are functionally deaf to the cacophony of competing signals and myriad Well-Being Systems simultaneously operating within their minds and bodies. Consciousness serves to filter all this "noise" into a single, perceptually homogenized whole. As a result, when people like Teresa share their experiences, these narratives tend to be described very linearly, with one series of choices/actions following another—I did this, then I did that, then this happened. Since a person's conscious mind does not actually know with certainty all the various things that were happening concurrently, nor even why it selected certain things to be conscious of, and not others, recalled narratives emphasize those things which plausibly should have happened, presented in a seemingly reasonable and logical progression. For example, Teresa's narrative includes huge gaps in time and detail. If probed, she undoubtedly could fill in some of the holes. But she could never credibly fill in all of the missing details about all of the perceived needs and choices she made during that time period, even if she had a photographic memory.

The truth is that the vast majority of what transpired in Teresa's life over the several months in question occurred outside of her conscious awareness. Despite Teresa's selective memory, her narrative describes her response to a wide array of needs—physiological ones, socially-oriented ones and more intellectual ones, including especially Systems revolving around her religious beliefs—collectively dozens upon dozens of needs, each associated with a different Well-Being System. However, despite all the variety and individuality of Teresa's various needs, it is possible to sort them into seven basic categories. These seven broad categories of need can be applied to not only all of the various choices and actions exhibited by Teresa, but to all humans.

## Notes

1. cf., The Human Condition, https://en.wikipedia.org/wiki/Human_condition retrieved June 26, 2013.
2. Leeming, D.A. (2010). *Creation myths of the world* (2nd ed.). Santa Barbara, CA: ABC-CLIO.
   Long, C.H. (1963). *Alpha: The myths of creation.* New York: George Braziller.

3. The terms self and identity are typically used interchangeably in the literature, even when sometimes it is not always clear that they are referring to the same thing. I distinguish between the two terms. I use the term self inclusively to refer to all examples of an organism distinguishing between itself and the world, ranging from distinctions at the molecular level all the way to complex associations of people and communities. By contrast I restrict the use of the term identity to a very specific subset of self-related perceptions, those that are primarily consciously-driven and reflective of more complex inter-human relationships and situations.

4. As discussed earlier, there is debate about the difference between Western and Eastern traditions. Some have argued that the Western conception of self unduly emphasizes the individualistic nature of the person with a focus on the person's uniqueness, sense of direction, purpose and volition. In this world view, the individual is at the center of the perception of self and other and the two are sharply demarcated with the self "belonging" to the individual and to no other person (Sampson, E.E. (1988). The debate on individualism. *American Psychologist*, 43, 15–22). According to comparative psychologist David Ho, these ideas are deeply rooted in the Western concept of individualism. He points out that the English word "individual" is derived from the Latin *individuus*, which means not divisible. Thus, even the language Westerners use to talk about self-perception reflects how deeply entrenched is the Western belief in the self as a distinct, holistic entity (Ho, D.Y.F. (1995). Selfhood and identity in Confucianism, Taoism, Buddhism, and Hinduism: Contrasts with the West. *Journal for the Theory of Social Behaviour*, 25(2), 115–139). Although some Eastern religious traditions, for example Buddhism, take great pains to distinguish between the self of the material world and the self of the spiritual world, in general, Ho argues that at a minimum many Eastern cultures have a very different, more inclusive and relational interpretation of the boundaries of the individual. Psychologists Hazel Markus and Shinobu Kitayama argue that individuals in many Asian cultures perceive the self in relation to others as interdependent, not independent as in the West (Markus, H.R. & Kitayama, S. (1991). Culture and the self: Implications for cognition, emotion, and motivation. *Psychological Review*, 98, 224–253). In East Asia, the dominant ethical system underlying this interdependent construal of self is Confucianism (Ho, D.Y.F. (1995). Selfhood and identity in Confucianism, Taoism, Buddhism, and Hinduism: Contrasts with the West. *Journal for the Theory of Social Behaviour*, 25(2), 115–139). From a Confucian worldview, the boundaries between the individual and the group are not as sharply demarcated and separate. According to Ho, this traditional Eastern view of self as more socially-personal and inter-relative is actually quite similar to more recent Western post-modernists views of self-perception, for example the views of American psychologist Frank Johnson (Johnson, F. (1985). The Western concept of self. In A.J. Marsella, G. DeVos & F.L.K. Hsu (Eds.), *Culture and Self: Asian and Western perspectives* (pp. 91–138). New York: Tavistock.), who defines the self as an intersubjective unit.

5. Leary, M.R. & Tangney, J.P. (2003). The self as an organizing construct in the behavioral and social sciences. In M.R. Leary & J.P. Tangney (Eds.), *Handbook of self and identity* (pp. 3–14). New York: Guilford Press.

6. Aristotle, *Metaphysics,* Book I, chapter II. http://classics.mit.edu/Aristotle/metaphysics.1.i.html Retrieved January 17, 2016.

7. Taylor, C. (1989). *Sources of the self: The making of the modern identity.* Cambridge, MA: Harvard University Press.

8. www.encyclopedia.com/topic/social_science.aspx# Retrieved January 17, 2016.

9. James, W. (1890). *The principles of psychology.* New York: Henry Holt and Company. Goffman, E. (1959). *The presentation of self in everyday life.* New York: Doubleday.

10. James, W. (1890). *The principles of psychology.* New York: Henry Holt and Company.

11. James, W. (1890). *The principles of psychology.* New York: Henry Holt and Company.

12. This idea was arguably most strongly proposed by Erik Erikson who is typically credited with bringing the concept of identity to the fore in discussions of self. cf., Fearon, J.D. (1999). *What is identity (as we now use the term)?* Unpublished Manuscript. Retrieved July 10, 2013. www.stanford.edu/~jfearon/papers/iden1v2.pdf

13. e.g., Bronfenbrenner, U. (1979). *The ecology of human development.* Cambridge, MA: Harvard University Press.

    Holland, D., Lachicotte, W., Jr., Skinner, D. & Cain, C. (1998). *Identity and agency in cultural worlds.* Cambridge: Harvard University Press.

    Simon, B. (2004). *Identity in modern society: A social psychological perspective.* Oxford, UK: Blackwell.

    Taylor, C. (1989). *Sources of the self: The making of the modern identity.* Cambridge, MA: Harvard University Press.

    See also review by Falk, J.H. (2009). *Identity and the museum visitor experience.* Walnut Creek, CA: Left Coast Press.

14. Gee, J.P. (2001). Identity as an analytic lens for research in education. *Review of Research in Education*, 25, 99–125.

    Wenger, E. (1998). *Communities of practice: Learning, meaning, and identity.* Cambridge: Cambridge University Press.

    Hall, S. (1992). The question of cultural identity. In S. Hall & T. McGrew (Eds.), *Modernity and its futures* (pp. 273–326). Cambridge: Polity Press.

    Woodward, K. (2002). *Understanding identity.* London: Arnold.

15. Falk, J.H. (2009). *Identity and the museum visitor experience.* Walnut Creek, CA: Left Coast Press.

16. Dweck, C. (2000). *Self-Theories: Their role in motivation, personality and development.* New York: Psychology Press.

    Also, Jerome Bruner and Bernie Kalmar (1998) and Neisser (1988).

17. Cooper, C.R. (1999). Multiple selves, multiple worlds: Cultural perspectives on individuality and connectedness in adolescence development. In A. Masten (Ed.), *Minnesota symposium on child psychology: Cultural processes in development* (pp. 25–57). Mahwah, NJ: Lawrence Erlbaum Associates.

    McAdams, D.P. (1990). *The person: An introduction to personality psychology.* Orlando, FL: Harcourt Brace Jovanovich.

18. Goffman, E. (1959). *The presentation of self in everyday life.* New York: Anchor Books.

19. And as will be discussed in more detail later, many of these internal messages derive from the denizens of the vast microbiome we harbor within us (cf., Miller, W.B. Jr. (2013). *The microcosm within.* Boca Raton, FL: Universal-Publishers).

20. Eagleman, D. (2015). *The brain: The story of you.* New York: Pantheon.

21. Calvin, W.H. (1997). *How brains think.* New York: Basic Books.

22. Clark, A. (1997). *Being there: Putting brain, body and world together again.* Cambridge: MIT Press.

23. Hood, B. (2012). *The self illusion.* Oxford: Oxford University Press.

24. Hood, B. (2012). *The self illusion.* Oxford: Oxford University Press.

25. Damasio, A.R. (1999). *The feeling of what happens: Body and emotion in the making of consciousness.* New York: Harcourt Brace & Company, p. 134.

26. Hood, B. (2012). *The self illusion.* Oxford: Oxford University Press.

27. Eagleman, D. (2015). *The brain: The story of you.* New York: Pantheon.

28. Although all neural networks are part of Well-Being Systems, the two are not synonymous. Some of the billions of Well-Being Systems reside exclusively within the brain, existing as nothing more than neural networks, but billions more extend beyond the brain, including in addition to neural networks other bodily constituents such as the villi of the gut or the fibers of skeletal muscles. Importantly, billions of other Well-Being Systems exist totally outside of the brain and contain no neurons or other nervous tissue.

29. cf., Green, M.J. & Phillips, M.L. (2004). Social threat perception and the evolution of paranoia. *Neuroscience and Biobehavioral Reviews*, 28, 333–342.

30. cf., Gordon, C. & Heath, J. (1986). Integration and central processing in temperature regulation. *Annual Review of Physiology*, 48, 595–612.

31. Wegner, D.M. (2002). *The illusion of conscious will.* Cambridge, MA: MIT Press.

    Edelman, G. & Tononi, G. (2000). Reentry and the dynamic core. In T. Metzinger (Ed.), *Neural correlates of consciousness: Empirical and conceptual questions* (pp. 121–138). Cambridge, MA: MIT Press.

Freeman, W. (2000). *How brains make up their mind.* New York: Columbia University Press.

32. Wegner, D.M. (2002). *The illusion of conscious will.* Cambridge, MA: MIT Press.
    Edelman, G. & Tononi, G. (2000). Reentry and the dynamic core. In T. Metzinger (Ed.), *Neural correlates of consciousness: Empirical and conceptual questions* (pp. 121–138). Cambridge, MA: MIT Press.
    Freeman, W. (2000). *How brains make up their mind.* New York: Columbia University Press.

33. Cf., Galaburda, A.M. & Kosslyn, S.M. (2002). *Languages of the brain.* Cambridge, MA: Harvard University Press.
    Pinker, S. (1994). *The language instinct.* New York: Harper Collins.
    Lieberman, P. (2000). *Human language and our reptilian brain: The subcortical bases of speech, syntax and thought.* Cambridge, MA: Harvard University Press.

34. Hastie, R. & Park, B. (1986). The relationship between memory and judgment depends on whether the judgment task is memory-based or on-line. *Psychological Review, 93,* 258–268.
    Johansson, P., Hall, L., Sikstrom, S. & Olsson, A. (2005). Failure to detect mismatches between intention and outcome in a simple decision task. *Science,* 310, 116–119.
    Wegner, D.M. (2002). *The illusion of conscious will.* Cambridge, MA: MIT Press.
    Wilson, T.D., Dunn, D.S., Kraft, D. & Lisle, D.J. (1989). Introspection, attitude change, and attitude-behavior consistency: The disruptive effects of explaining why we feel the way we do. In L. Berkowitz (Ed.), *Advances in experimental social psychology* (Vol. 23). New York: Academic Press.

35. Wegner, D.M. (2002). *The illusion of conscious will.* Cambridge, MA: MIT Press.
    Gazzaniga, M.S. (2008). *Human: The science behind what makes your brain unique.* New York: HarperCollins.

36. Kahneman, D. (2011). *Thinking, fast and slow.* New York: Farrar, Straus and Giroux.

37. For a complete review of how the adaptive unconscious works, including in the making of choices, see, Wilson, T.D. (2002). *Strangers to ourselves: Discovering the adaptive unconscious.* Cambridge, MA: Belknap Press.

38. Wegner, D.M. (2002). *The illusion of conscious will.* Cambridge, MA: MIT Press, p. 29.

39. Wegner, D.M. (2002). *The illusion of conscious will.* Cambridge, MA: MIT Press, p. 145.

40. Wegner, D.M. (2002). *The illusion of conscious will.* Cambridge, MA: MIT Press, p. 96.

41. Bargh, J.A. (1997). The automaticity of everyday life. In R.S. Wyer, Jr. (Ed.), *Advances in social cognition* (Vol. 10, pp. 1–62). Hillsdale, NJ: Erlbaum.
    Bargh, J.A. & Ferguson, M.J. (2000). Beyond behaviorism: On the automaticity of higher mental process. *Psychological Bulletin,* 126, 925–945.

42. What scientists would call an epiphenomenon.

43. Jaynes, J. (1976). *The origin of consciousness in the breakdown of the bicameral mind.* Boston: Houghton Mifflin.
    Scaruffi, A. (2006). *The nature of consciousness.* Retrieved June 27, 2013. www.scaruffi.com/nature/

44. If you don't believe this, try it yourself. See also, Scaruffi, A. (2006). *The nature of consciousness.* Retrieved June 27, 2013. www.scaruffi.com/nature/

# 4

# THE ORIGINS OF WELL-BEING SYSTEMS

In the previous chapter I provided an overview of how self-related needs provide the foundation of all Well-Being Systems. In this chapter I extend that idea to discuss the biological origins of those needs, beginning with seven basic and distinctive categories of need that define all human Well-Being Systems. Also covered in this chapter are the origins of Well-Being Systems and the trillions of historically hidden needs that animate the collective well-being of all humans.

## The Seven Modalities of Need

My separation of Well-Being Systems into seven basic categories is anything but arbitrary.[1] Drawing equally from research and theory in evolutionary biology, the social sciences and philosophy, these categories emerge as clearly distinguishable clusters of human need. They are distinguishable because each reflects a critical burst of evolutionary development; each cluster representing the by-product of a major transitional event in humanity's evolutionary history. Although it is likely that there were many more than seven critical evolutionary events in humanity's long evolutionary history, for example evolutionary biologists John Maynard Smith and Eors Szathmary hypothesized that there were at least eight such events,[2] these particular seven left an especially indelible footprint.

Each category of need arose in response to specific environmental events and selective pressures. Within each of these modalities, in particular those that are most recently evolved, it is also possible to identify entirely modern and uniquely human types of needs. But whether ancient or modern, all the Systems within a particular modality are designed to support well-being through satisfaction of very similar types of needs. From oldest to youngest, the seven modalities of need are:

1. *Continuity*—the cluster of Systems designed to actively maintain a constant and self-sustaining physiological state; a main goal is increased survivability through stability.[3]

2. *Individuality*—Systems designed to protect and defend the whole organism by recognizing, avoiding and when necessary attacking others perceived to be "non-self;" a main goal is increased survivability through security.

3. *Sexuality*—Systems primed to recognize and respond to other selves, either positively or negatively depending upon species-specific sexual characteristics; a main goal is increased survivability through reproductive success.

4. *Sociality*—the cluster of Systems that selectively foster associations with and cooperation between other entities perceived as part of the self; a main goal is increased survivability through belonging.[4]

5. *Relationality*—Systems of social awareness that enable conscious perception of the relative position of the individual in comparison to others within the group; main goals are increased survivability through enhanced status and esteem.

6. *Reflectivity*—Systems that utilize conscious awareness as a vehicle for projecting the self beyond immediate circumstances in time and space; main goals are improved survivability through an understanding of the past, consideration of alternatives and planning for the future.

7. *Creativity & Spirituality*—Systems that enable the highest levels of abstract thought, and with it the ability to purposefully and imaginatively project one's self into situations unfettered by immediate realities; main goals are increased survivability through personal fulfillment and development of an expanded identity.[5]

Needs related to each of these seven Well-Being Systems are apparent within Teresa's emigration narrative. The *Continuity* modality is seen in Teresa's description of the challenges she faced finding suitable food and shelter while waiting in the small, hot desert border town of Altar and in her need to stay hydrated during her walk through the desert. Although she does not dwell at length on any of these issues, clearly she was concerned about how she was going to satisfy her family's basic physiological needs and made choices accordingly. Ernesto's crying because of being stuck with thorns is also an example of the *Continuity* modality.

While in Altar, Teresa's main concern was not food or shelter, but actually her family's safety. She was afraid of being robbed or potentially even physically threatened or injured. Health and safety-related issues are reflective of a suite of Well-Being modalities designated as *Individuality*. Similarly, Teresa's concern that Ernesto's crying might compromise their need to avoid detection from the border patrol was reflective of this modality.

The needs and drives related to sex are representative of the third distinct Well-Being System modality—*Sexuality*. Although there is no evidence in her narrative that Teresa's own sexuality influenced her choice-making, clearly other people's sexual desires did. One of the things that Teresa feared the most in Altar was the possibility of sexual assault, "There's a lot of risk for the girls getting raped, older people getting raped," and her focus on keeping the family safe in one hotel room was specifically designed to prevent this from happening.

As illustrated in both the current and previous chapters, Teresa's narrative begins and ends with her desire to support or accommodate someone she cared about, either her children, her husband, her brother and his family or her friend; these all fall within the modality of *Sociality*. A disproportionate number of Teresa's recollections revolved around how a particular choice was influenced by, or would influence, one or more other people that she cared about.

Teresa's narrative also demonstrates an additional dimension related to the social sphere, a separate, fifth modality of Well-Being Systems I have called *Relationality*. This latter modality transcends the basic feelings, choices and actions one associates with *Sociality*, such as maternal love or needing to belong to a group. *Relationality*-related Well-Being Systems involve active, conscious comparisons between people. This is the modality of choices related to the needs of esteem and social position. It is the modality that was in evidence in the relationship Teresa had with the Coyotes. Although Teresa may not have liked or even respected the Coyotes, because of her social situation during the crossing, the Coyotes held a superior position and Teresa had no choice but to do whatever they told her to do. Although she managed to elude the border patrol, awareness of their authority and fear of what they would do animated much of Teresa and her fellow crossers' behavior during the journey through the desert.

Finally, Teresa's narrative includes abundant examples of the last two modalities— *Reflectivity* and *Creativity & Spirituality*. The first of these, *Reflectivity* Systems, enable individuals to consciously connect current information with both information about events that took place in the past and projections of how events might transpire in the future, allowing individuals to better deal with present challenges and opportunities. *Reflectivity* also is the modality that influences people to opt to make choices consistent with their interests and prior understandings of events. Teresa clearly spent time weighing the pros and cons of her current situation against an imagined future. By her telling, she did a great deal of thinking about what could or should happen if she stayed or went and attempted to act in ways appropriate to these conceptualizations of the future outcomes of particular choices. However Teresa, despite her desire to be deliberative, often made choices based more on the modality I have labeled as *Creativity & Spirituality* than on *Reflectivity*. Her religious beliefs in particular, and the complex principles and practices that underlie those beliefs, strongly influenced nearly all her conscious choice-making.

There are obvious similarities between these seven modalities of need and Abraham Maslow's Hierarchy of Needs.[6] However as outlined in detail in the End Notes, there is not a one-to-one relationship between the needs defined by Maslow's and the seven needs I have defined. Like Maslow, my categories are reflective of human behavior, but I have modified and extended Maslow's categories based on additional data, particularly data from biology, anthropology, psychology and the neurosciences.[7] However focusing on the superficial resemblance between my modalities and Maslow's ultimately detracts from the real differences between Maslow's and my theory. For starters, I assert these seven needs are nested and that people are not only capable of achieving well-being through satisfaction of *any* one of the seven Well-Being System modalities of need, in any order and at any time, but that people frequently strive to satisfy several or all of these needs simultaneously. In my model, there is no hierarchy, no value judgement. Achieving well-being by satisfying the *Creativity & Spirituality*-related needs, i.e., purposes, does not result in a higher state of well-being. Well-being feels good, whether achieved by listening to a Beethoven sonata or eating a meal when hungry. The inherent value of that state of well-being is totally relative and determined by the beliefs of the individual experiencing that well-being.[8]

However the single most important distinction between my conceptualization of needs and Maslow's is that I would argue that the basic underlying functioning of all these needs, whether *Reflectivity* and *Creativity & Spirituality* or *Continuity* and *Individuality* are biologically homologous. They may not be identical psychologically but they all share a high degree of biological similarity. This is because later evolving Well-Being Systems arose from the foundations of earlier evolved Well-Being Systems, with each new Well-Being System re-purposing earlier evolved biological pathways and processes in order to adapt to new challenges and opportunities.[9] All the different ways present-day humans have of achieving well-being arose through biological and cultural evolutionary elaborations of earlier Well-Being Systems; all share a common origin. This process of evolutionary complexification has been going on for a very long time, starting long before there were humans, in fact, starting long before there were even such things as brains. The origins of Well-Being Systems can be traced all the way back to the very beginnings of life itself more than 3.7 billion years ago.[10]

## Origins of Well-Being Systems

A fundamental need of all living things is the maintenance of an appropriate chemical balance between the inside and outside of an organism. All living things satisfy well-being in this way through processes biologists call homeostasis. The fact that all living things—bacteria, redwood trees, insects and humans—possess these homeostatic systems has led scientists to conclude that this capability must have already evolved very early in the evolution of life, at a minimum prior to the appearance of the last universal common ancestor.[11] Although life on earth shares a number of other common capabilities, the most famous example being DNA-based reproduction, some scientists believe that homeostasis was not only a critical first step on the road to life, but *the* critical step.[12] From the beginning of life, homeostasis has functioned using the following basic process (see Figure 4.1).

This diagram should look quite familiar by now: the similarity between this homeostasis diagram and my Well-Being Systems diagram is intentional.[13] Homeostasis and Well-Being Systems are one and the same; they just described biological processes at different scales. However, regardless of scale, both are systems that regulate the well-being of an organism by effecting appropriate responses to the perceived environment. Although the evolutionary origins of homeostasis are hypothesized to have been a mechanism for maintaining an appropriate balance

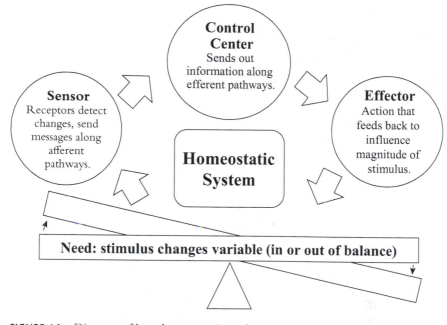

**FIGURE 4.1**   Diagram of how homeostasis works

*Source*: Based on a diagram in Marieb, E.N. (2006). *Essentials of human anatomy and physiology* (8th ed.). Retrieved March 14, 2014. www.google.com/search?q=Cummings,+B.+%282006%29.+Pearson+Ed ucational+Publishing.+homeostasis&biw=1368&bih=772&source=lnms&tbm=isch&sa=X&ved= 0ahUKEwje8LDLnZ3SAhUJ6WMKHciLArgQ_AUIBigB&dpr=2#imgrc=ZND6LDnTwMlm5M

of a single chemical,[14] life ultimately evolved a wide range of similar systems for dealing with ever more complex physiological needs; each new system functioning independently, yet interconnected within the larger complex of physiological regulating systems.[15] I assert that the evolution of homeostatic-like systems did not end with physiological processes. Through successive *exaptations*,[16] these Well-Being Systems evolved to support organismic regulation at every biological level—the molecular, cellular, organ, organism, social, community and potentially beyond.[17]

This means that even the simplest cell is comprised of hundreds, if not thousands of homeostatic/Well-Being Systems. Over evolutionary time, life utilized the basic genetic and biochemical machinery of homeostasis to build other well-being maintaining systems; each new system utilizing the same basic, multi-step process of sensing need states, making choices, effecting appropriate actions and then judging the consequences of that cycle again based upon the state of some self-related need variable such as temperature, safety, belonging or a new solution to a problem. The result is that life itself can be thought of as a complex adaptive system comprised of trillions upon trillions of highly interconnected, nested, functionally similar, but not identical Well-Being Systems.[18] The functioning of all such systems, from the simplest chemical regulation within a cell to the most complex control of an entire organism, is dynamic across time and space, constantly adapting to an ever-changing environment.[19] Although the conscious human mind is oblivious to the reality, within every human, at any given moment, vast numbers of Well-Being Systems are simultaneously cycling along, perceiving needs and enacting choices.

## Trillions of Well-Being Systems

The reason there is such a vast number of Well-Being Systems within every person is because every human body is made up of trillions of cells, including liver cells, heart cells, skin cells and brain cells, and each of these cells comes with its own set of Well-Being Systems. Every one of these trillions of cells, in addition to any other role it might play in the human body, also has to maintain its own cellular well-being. Thus, from this perspective each human is actually made up of not just multiple cells, but trillions and trillions of individually operating Well-Being Systems. A multicellular organism like a human is not just a random collection of cells though, but a tightly interconnected confederation of cells, with various cells combining to form tissues, organs and organ systems. These collaborations too result in additional Well-Being Systems. Each of these separate but interconnected Well-Being Systems makes choices and acts upon those choices in ways designed to maximize well-being, in this case not just individual well-being but the collective well-being of the larger entity. Humans are in this way made up of numerous nested sets of Well-Being Systems, variously working at maintaining multiple, increasingly complex levels of well-being.

If this alone was not such a mind-bogglingly complex and novel idea, add to this picture the realization that not all of the cells in the human body actually function as part of some human tissue or organ system; many are unattached, free-agents. In fact, a surprisingly large number of cells in the human body are not even human cells. Over the past few decades, scientists have determined that every person plays host to a massive array of genetically unrelated microbes living on and in the human body. This collection of human-inhabiting microbes has come to be called the microbiome.[20]

It is now estimated that there are more than ten times as many unrelated cells living within a person than genetically related ones, and although each of these denizens of the microbiome is tiny and weighs virtually nothing, if combined they would weigh about six pounds.[21] More amazing still is that scientists are only beginning to fully appreciate why these tens of trillions of microbial cells need to be taken seriously. It seems that individually and collectively the constituents of the microbiome exert a diversity of specific and highly important influences on their host human's Well-Being Systems.

Most of the initial research on the microbiome focused on how these myriad microscopic creatures influenced human physiology and health. For example, research suggests that the microbes living within a person's gut directly affect when that person feels the need to eat, as well as which foods she chooses to eat.[22] Increasingly though, scientists have come to realize that these microbes likely have other influences as well. For example, upon closer study it was revealed that the bacteria living inside a person were producing a wide range of chemicals, some that are widely known to act as important neurotransmitters, chemicals such as dopamine, serotonin and gamma-aminobutyric acid (GABA). Given that these are the exact same chemicals neurons use to communicate within and between themselves, it seems that the production and release of these chemicals by the microbiome may not be coincidental but rather a purposeful way for these microbes to impact a range of whole-human processes. For example, it has been shown that the presence of certain gut bacteria correlates with self-related mood disorders, such as depression and anxiety, both of which strongly influence how and why a person makes the choices they do. Furthermore, these findings are certainly just the tip of the proverbial iceberg since they only account for the non-related cells presumed to be "friendly" to humans. Research is also beginning to reveal that humans are likely host to a range of malign microbes as well.

Starting in the early 1990s, a Czech evolutionary biologist, Jaroslav Flegr, began to suspect that a single-celled parasite in the protozoan family was affecting his, and by extension other people's, personality and behavior, perhaps their very perception of self. The protozoan in question has long been known as a parasite of cats. Veterinarians typically diagnose the presence of the parasite by examining the animal's feces. Called *Toxoplasma gondii* (*T. gondii* or *Toxo* for short), the parasite has also been known to infect humans, though in both cats and humans there historically was little evidence that the parasite did any great harm. However, the same cannot be said for very young humans. In the 1920s doctors became aware that pregnant women who developed toxoplasmosis—the disease caused by the parasite—could transmit the disease to their fetus, resulting in cases of severe brain damage or death. As a result, it has become standard medical practice to advise pregnant women to avoid cat litter boxes. This makes great sense since it is now known that the parasite is quite common in both cats and humans. In fact, *Toxoplasma gondii* is the most common protozoan parasite in developed nations, comparable in prevalence to the malaria parasite *Plasmodium* in parts of the less developed world. Depending upon eating habits and exposure to cats, up to 80% of the human population in some areas may be infected.[23] With the rise of HIV/AIDS, researchers again started paying attention to *T. gondii* because it can be a major threat to people with weakened immune systems. However with the exception of immune-compromised individuals and neonates, it was observed that healthy children and adults generally experienced nothing more than brief flu-like symptoms before quickly fighting off the protozoan's effects, or that *was* the conventional medical wisdom.[24]

What Flegr discovered, and now has been confirmed by others, is that the parasite is not eradicated by the body, but rather moves on to its primary target, the brain. Once in the brain, the parasite begins its real work, altering many of the neural connections and in the process dramatically changing the way in which infected people respond to life situations. According to Flegr's research, infected men and women respond to events and make different choices than they typically would; interestingly many infected individuals become paranoid. As a consequence, Flegr observed that infected individuals were more than twice as likely as uninfected individuals to be involved in car accidents, suicides and mental disorders such as schizophrenia.[25] In an interview, Flegr said that when you add up all the different ways it harms people, *Toxoplasma* is as significant a parasite as malaria, potentially killing at least a million people a year.[26]

Once scientists learned about Flegr's research, they also began to see similar impacts caused by other parasites. For example, new research shows that the malaria parasite, *Plasmodium*, changes the behavior of not only its mosquito hosts, but potentially humans also. The parasite changes the body chemistry of an infected person in such a way that it gives off chemicals that attract mosquitoes, and by causing recurring fevers which incite its human host to throw off bed coverings and open windows, it makes the person behave in ways that make it more available to mosquitoes.[27] What is even more surprising is that many experts now suspect that *T. gondii* and *Plasmodium* may be far from the only microscopic puppeteers capable of manipulating human Well-Being Systems.

It seems that parasites such as *T. gondii* and *Plasmodium*, as well as likely a large number of the more benign denizens of the microbiome, have evolved their own ways of influencing their human hosts. Each has evolved strategies for getting their host to help them meet their *own* unique self-related needs and priorities. Given that self-related needs drive Well-Being Systems, and thus choices and actions, it is quite startling to consider the possibility that needs of the trillions of *other* selves silently living within a person might actually be driving much of what that person does in a given day. That literally and figuratively, each human self is actually an amalgam of selves with an army of alien microbes controlling a large percentage of what the mind perceives as self-related needs.[28]

Even though not all Well-Being Systems involve the mind and not all parts of every Well-Being System are comprised of nervous tissue, a disproportionate number are.[29] Brains evolved to support efficient and effective collection and processing of information related to needs and to support the making of choices and initiating of actions based on that information. Whether need-related signals are initiated by an unrelated microbe or a genetically related liver cell, whether designed to satisfy an internal need such as low blood sugar or oxygen levels, or triggered in response to some externally perceived threat such as seeing a stranger prowling outside of one's house, they are relayed to the brain for processing and triage. How this processing and triage work, the neural dimensions of Well-Being Systems, is the topic of the next chapter.

## Notes

1. These seven interconnected but functionally discrete modalities of need reflect my best effort to build on previous theory and synthesize available evidence. I particularly relied on four specific sources, each representing a synthesis of available data from a different perspective.

    I sought to accommodate the considered thinking of historian Jerrold Siegel's monumental analysis of 500 years of Western philosophical thought on the nature of the self in which he distinguished three basic types of self-perception—*bodily*, *relational* and *reflective* (Siegel, J. (2005). *The idea of the self: Thought and experience in Western Europe since the eighteenth century*. Cambridge: Cambridge University Press).

Psychologist Abraham Maslow's five levels of human need, often represented as a pyramid of well-being, has long been a dominant model for understanding human behavior (Maslow, A.H. (1943). A theory of human motivation. *Psychological Review*, 50(4), 370–396). Maslow's five stages of well-being, often referred to as Maslow's hierarchy of needs because each stage was thought to build upon the satisfaction of needs in the stage below, included: *physiological needs, safety, love/belonging, esteem* and *self-actualization*. In later years, Maslow subdivided "self-actualization" into four categories to include *knowledge and understanding needs, the need for aesthetics, self-actualization* and *transcendence* (Maslow, A.H. (1970). *Motivation and personality*. New York: Harper & Row). I include these categories in the table below in brackets.

I've also included for comparison a more recent version of Maslow's hierarchy of needs developed by evolutionary psychologists Douglas Kenrick, Vladas Griskevicius, Steven Neuberg and Mark Schaller (Kenrick, D.T., Griskevicius, V., Neuberg, S.L. & Schaller, M. (2010). Renovating the pyramid of needs: Contemporary extensions built upon ancient foundations. *Perspectives on Psychological Science*, 5, 292–314). Kenrick, Griskevicius Neuberg and Schaller argue that although basically sound, Maslow's hierarchy of needs was never accurately or appropriately anchored to evolutionary theory. They proposed a new hierarchy, primarily based on findings from evolutionary psychology, including needs such as *mate acquisition* and *retention* and *parenting*.

Finally, in what is now considered a classic work, evolutionary biologists John Maynard Smith and Eors Szathmary hypothesized that there were eight major transitions in the evolution of life, beginning with the *compartmentalization of molecules*, i.e., evolution of cell membranes, to the evolution of *societies and language* (Smith, J.M. & Szathmary, E. (1995). *The major transitions in evolution*. Oxford, UK: Oxford University Press).

A comparison of my model with these four other models follows:

| Falk | Siegel | Maslow | Kenrick, et al. | Smith & Szathmary |
|---|---|---|---|---|
| Continuity | Bodily | Physiological Needs | Immediate Physiological Needs | Populations of Molecules in Compartments Unlinked Replicators to Chromosomes |
| Individuality Sexuality | | Safety Physiological Needs | Self-Protection Mate Acquisition | Genetic Code Prokaryotes to Eukaryotes |
| | | | | Asexual Clones to Sexual Populations |
| Sociality | Relational | Love/ Belonging | Affiliation | Protists to Multicellular Organisms Solitary Individuals to Colonies |
| Relationality | | Esteem | Status/Esteem | Primate Societies to Human Societies/ Language |
| Reflectivity | Reflectivity | [Knowledge & Understanding Needs] | Mate Retention | |
| | | [Need for Aesthetics] | Parenting | |
| Creativity/ Spirituality | | Self-Actualization | | |
| | | [Transcendence] | | |

What should be apparent from this table is the close, though not perfect, alignment between the ways I categorize the human need-related Well-Being Systems and the major categories proposed by these other four models. Perhaps not surprisingly, given my focus on humans, my model, like that of Siegel and Maslow, adopts a more fine-grained view of later evolving modalities, while consolidating several of the important early evolutionary milestones noted by Smith and Szathmary, who were primarily focused on non-humans. At a minimum, these multiple lines of evidence drawn from philosophy of self, psychology of need and evolutionary biology support the basic premise that it is possible to distinguish categorical disjunctions in human evolutionary history; disjunctions I argue are reflected in the form and function of present-day human Well-Being Systems.

2. Smith, J.M. & Szathmary, E. (1995). *The major transitions in evolution.* Oxford, UK: Oxford University Press.

3. I selected the terms Individuality and Continuity to describe these first two fundamental Well-Being System modalities since they reflect what English philosopher David Wiggins described as the two foundational and complementary aspects of all human perceptions of self (Wiggins, D. (2001). *Sameness and substance renewed* (2nd ed.). Cambridge: Cambridge University Press).

4. Relationality is the generic term historian of philosophy Jerrold Siegel uses to describe this class of self-related perceptions (Siegel, J. (2005). *The idea of the self: Thought and experience in Western Europe since the eighteenth century.* Cambridge: Cambridge University Press.).

5. NOTE: I lump creativity and spirituality together into a single category because, as described in more detail in Chapter 13, I believe these are culturally different expressions of the same basic biological phenomenon.

6. Maslow, A.H. (1943). A theory of human motivation. *Psychological Review,* 50(4), 370–396.

7. e.g., Kenrick, D.T., Griskevicius, V., Neuberg, S.L. & Schaller, M. (2010). Renovating the pyramid of needs: Contemporary extensions built upon ancient foundations. *Perspectives on Psychological Science,* 5, 292–314.
   Zimmer, C. (2014). Secrets of the brain. *National Geographic,* 225(2), 28–57.
   Eagleman, D. (2015). *The brain: The story of you.* New York: Pantheon.

8. Of course each individual's beliefs about what constitutes quality well-being are shaped by that individual's personal, biological and cultural lived experiences. The belief that there are such things as higher/better needs/purposes is a strong Western bias, not one equally shared by many hunting and gathering peoples. A good meal and a story well-told are perceived by many peoples as fundamental reasons for being alive, and thus their satisfaction yield great sense of well-being.

9. Adami, C., Ofria, C. & Collier, T.C. (2000). Evolution of biological complexity. *Proceedings of the National Academy of Sciences (USA),* 97, 4463–4468.
   Torday, J.S. (2015). A central theory of biology. *Medical Hypotheses,* 85, 49–57.

10. Gramling, C. (2016). Hints of oldest life on earth. *Science.* Retrieved August 31, 2016. www.sciencemag.org/news/2016/08/hints-oldest-fossil-life-found-greenland-rocks

11. Woese, C. (1998). The universal ancestor. *Proceedings of the National Academy of Sciences (USA),* 95(12), 6854–6859.

12. Torday, J.S. (2015). Homeostasis as the mechanism of evolution. *Biology,* 4, 573–590.

13. NOTE: For the reasons specified in Chapter 1, I purposefully simplified the language used to describe the different parts of the model.

14. It is speculated that the first homeostatic mechanism was designed to regulate calcium concentrations in the primordial cell. Kamierczak, J. & Kempe, S. (2004). Calcium build-up in the Precambrian seas. In J. Seckbach (Ed.), *Origins* (pp. 329–345). Dordrecht, The Netherlands: Kluwer.

15. McEwan, B.S. & Wingfield, J. (2010). What is in a name? Integrating homeostasis, allostasis and stress. *Hormones and Behavior,* 57, 105–111.
    Giordano, M. (2013). Homeostasis: An underestimated focal point of ecology and evolution. *Plant Sciences,* 211, 92–101.

16. Exaptation is the term currently used by biologists, in place of the more teleologically-loaded term "pre-adapted," to describe how earlier evolving structures become re-purposed

or co-opted to support new traits or functions (cf., Gould, S.J. & Vrba, E.S. (1982). Exaptation—A missing term in the science of form. *Paleobiology*, 8(1), 4–15).

17. It should be noted that I am certainly not the first person to see a connection between homeostasis and higher order processes, including human psychological functioning (e.g., Cofer, C.N. & Appley, M.H. (1964). Homeostatic concepts and motivation. In C.N. Cofer & M.H. Appley (Eds.), *Motivation: Theory and research* (pp. 302–365). New York: Wiley). But most of these early applications of homeostatic processing to human behavior were based upon Behaviorist frameworks and assumed that humans mechanistically and rigidly respond to the environment analogous to the way a thermostat responds to changes in temperature. These early models also did not account for the diversification and radiation of these homeostatic-like processes into the wide array of new, evolutionarily connected but functionally novel forms that humans and other life-forms now display, including at the social and analytical levels.

18. It is not a stretch to think of Well-Being Systems as having fractal-like qualities, appearing as suggested by John Torday (Torday, J. (2016). The cell as the first niche construction. *Biology*, 5, 19–26) at every level of biological organization, subcellular to cellular to tissue to organ to organism to social system, potentially all the way up to the Gaia-like level of ecosystems.

19. Torday, J.S. (2015). Homeostasis as the mechanism of evolution. *Biology*, 4, 573–590.

20. cf., Miller, W.B., Jr. (2013). *The microcosm within: Evolution and extinction in the hologenome*. Boca Raton, FL: Universal-Publishers.

21. Wolfe, N. (2013). Small, small world. *National Geographic*, 223(1), 136–147.
    Smith, P.A. (June 23 2015). Can the bacteria in your gut explain your mood? *New York Times*. Retrieved June 27, 2015. www.nytimes.com/2015/06/28/magazine/can-the-bacteria-in-your-gut-explain-your-mood

22. Ridaura, V.K., Faith, J.J., Rey, F.E., Cheng, J., Duncan, A.E., Kau, A.L., Griffin, N.W., Lombard, V., Henrissat, B., Bain, J., Muehlbauer, M.J., Ilkayeva, O., Semekovich, C.F., Funai, K., Hayashi, D.K., Lyle, B.J., Martini, M.C., Ursell, L.K., Clemete, J.C., Van Treuren, W., Walters, W.A., Knight, R., Newgard, C.B., Heath, A.C. & Gordon, J.I. (2013). Gut microbiota from twins discordant for obesity modulate metabolism in mice. *Science*, 341(6150), 1214.

23. Tenter, A.M., Heckeroth, A.R. & Weiss, L.M. (2000). Toxoplasma gondii: From animals to humans. *International Journal of Parasitology*, 30, 1217–1258.

24. McAuliffe, K. (2012). How your cat is making you crazy. *The Atlantic*. Retrieved June 18, 2013. www.theatlantic.com/magazine/archive/2012/03/how-your-cat-is-making-you-crazy/308873/

25. Flegr, J. (2007). Effects of *Toxoplasma* on human behavior. *Schizophrenia Bulletin*, 33(3), 757–760.

26. McAuliffe, K. (2012). How your cat is making you crazy. *The Atlantic*. Retrieved June 18, 2013. www.theatlantic.com/magazine/archive/2012/03/how-your-cat-is-making-you-crazy/308873/

27. BBC. (2014). How parasites manipulate us. *BBC News Magazine*. Retrieved July 13, 2016. www.bbc.com/news/magazine-26240297

28. Miller, W.B., Jr. (2013). *The microcosm within: Evolution and extinction in the hologenome*. Boca Raton, FL: Universal-Publishers.

29. Although the nervous system, particularly the part that forms the brain, clearly plays a vital role in human Well-Being Systems, everything does not happen in the brain. The majority of Well-Being Systems are bigger than just neurons, having significant pieces residing outside the brain, e.g., the sense organs, all the various viscera and parts of the skeletal and circulatory systems and of course all the extended aspects of the self that exist beyond the body's physical boundaries. Important to remember too is that Well-Being Systems predate the evolution of nervous systems by billions of years, and nervous systems themselves initially evolved primarily to facilitate the challenges of internal communication and coordination faced by early multicellular organisms and only secondarily to support interactions with the external world (Schmidt-Rhaesa, A. (2007). *The evolution of organ systems*. Oxford: Oxford University Press).

# 5

# WELL-BEING SYSTEMS AND THE BRAIN

Much of the action in choice-making goes on in the mind. This chapter describes the neural mechanisms underlying choice-making, including how the brain selects between options, perceives needs and communicates those needs emotionally and linguistically to the conscious mind. As in earlier chapters, Teresa's emigration story provides a wealth of useful examples with which to explore these ideas.

We were inside the [canyon], and then the truck arrived. It was only a matter of crossing the highway [into the U.S.]. Yes, the highway was on the other side; we could see that we were finally to come over here [the U.S.]. I was so tired and weak, so weak, but we all climbed [out of the canyon] and ran across the street so we wouldn't be seen by the Immigration [border patrol]. Then we climbed into [a waiting] truck so we wouldn't be seen. We got on the truck, the [Coyote] went in the front, and I was [in the back] with Grandma and the children. It was very small and it was very hard for me, thinking that if I sat, I wasn't going to be able to stand [again]. I had lots of cramps, a lot. If I sat, I couldn't stand quickly.

And they had a mesh, so I had to hold the mesh. . . . They put [the mesh] over us to cover us people up from being seen. It was a mesh with holes, like those they put on [inaudible]. They just put it on top [of us]. And I [was told that I] had to hold the mesh with my hands, so that it didn't fly with the air [fly off when the truck was moving]. And I said "Oh!" [SHOWS DISCOMFORT]. I was so tired and sleepy because I hadn't slept. For a moment I was holding the mesh, and my eyes shut, and I was falling asleep despite the noise the truck was making and [the intense heat that was] beating down on us. The tiredness was huge and my eyes shut, and then I [suddenly] said, "No, I can't sleep, no." Because they told me, "It depends on you whether they catch us or whether we pass," that it depended on me. Because if I let go of the mesh [the border patrol] were going to find us. So that had me anxious and I couldn't help feeling sleepy. But lying there and with so much tiredness, I could feel [that my grip on] the mesh was loosening up, and I said, "God, please, keep me awake, I can't sleep." And I felt awake and we continued until a certain place, where they moved me to the front and left Grandma and the children in the back [holding the mesh], and that's how we got to the place where we could finally rest [and wait for the next leg of the journey].

People are regularly required to choose between conflicting signals. In the example above, Teresa says she had to decide whether to succumb to her body's demand for sleep or the Coyote's demand that she hold onto the mesh. Setting aside for the moment the reliability of Teresa's description of her thought process, what does neuroscience say about how she might have made this choice?

Scientists have yet to completely understand how the brain weighs all the welter of incoming signals, ultimately making the choices it does. There are many competing theories, but the one I (and many others) have found particularly persuasive is the one first postulated by Gerald Edelman in his 1978 book, *The Mindful Brain*,[1] and further extended in his subsequent writings.[2] Although Edelman was not a trained neuroscientist, people paid attention to his ideas because he was a Nobel Prize winner for his work in immunology, in particular, the discovery of the structure of antibodies. He proposed that the ways the components of the brain evolve over a lifetime to make sense of information and make choices is likely totally analogous to the ways he discovered that components of the immune system evolve over the life of an individual. He called his theory Neuronal Group Selection, more popularly referred to as Neural Darwinism.

A key premise of Edelman's theory of Neuronal Group Selection is that the basic organization of the brain, the way neurons are connected and function, is through a process of selective coupling of mechanical and chemical processes on a molecular scale. This process of selective coupling takes place primarily epigenetically; in other words, through a process of on-going interaction between genes and the environment. The critical idea is that although the basic blueprint for the brain is contained in the genes, the specifics of brain construction occurs in each individual over time, but particularly during the course of early development—both in and out of the womb—in response to events in the individual's internal and external environment. The net result is that the construction of each brain, comprised of billions of neuronal groups/Well-Being Systems, is a unique, diverse and highly "plastic" event which results in each individual's brain possessing an architecture unlike that of any other's.

Although the basic anatomical structure of the brain is developed early in a person's life, it does not permanently remain this way. Ongoing selective processes occur over the course of the typical day-to-day existence of a person, including particularly important social experiences. In this way, neuronal groups/Well-Being Systems are constantly shaped and reshaped by experience, as are the structures and strength of the connections within and between them.[3] The key aspect of Edelman's theory is not *that* these repertoires of experience differentially shape a person's neuronal structures, since this had been long assumed, but rather *how* these experiences shape and amplify neuronal Well-Being Systems.

The "big idea" of Edelman's theory is that each incoming signal, be it electrical, chemical or typically some combination of the two, *competes* against the other signals coming into the brain. The signal that is most likely to be "heard" and attended to is the one that is best adapted to the brain's existing network of Well-Being Systems.[4] This is the Darwinian aspect of this theory. The best "adapted" signals generally are of two kinds: 1) those that already have well-developed, large existing neuronal networks tightly connected to past feelings of well-being; and 2) those that are deemed as spectacular or important because of the strength, urgency or some other characteristic that demands that they be attended to. Examples of both types of signals are evident in the part of Teresa's story that starts this chapter.

Teresa was extremely fatigued. This would have been an example of the first category of signal: a well-developed, pre-existing network. Her body was unrelentingly signaling to her brain that she was exhausted, which caused her brain, specifically her thalamus, to release the neurotransmitter adenosine.[5] The typical response to elevated levels of adenosine is to curl up somewhere, close one's eyes and go to sleep. Well-Being Systems related to sleep are part of the *Continuity* modality. In general, messages from this modality are fundamental to human survival and physiological well-being and are difficult to ignore. Obeying the needs of Continuity-related Well-Being Systems, for example sleeping when one's body communicates it is tired, are highly correlated with feelings of well-being. These are classic examples of short-term well-being. For example, most people know from daily experience that not sleeping when exhausted will make one feel really crummy. As suggested in Chapter 2, people are disproportionately inclined to choose the short-term over the long-term; a history of good feelings of well-being when getting enough rest would have been a powerful motivator for Teresa. But her Sleep Well-Being System was getting other messages as well.

The Coyote did not ask, he demanded that Teresa hold onto the mesh, and backed it up with a threat. "It depends on you whether they catch us or whether we pass." This was clearly the second type of signal and would have been strongly connected to and activated additional neural networks in Teresa's brain; additional Well-Being Systems within the modalities of *Relationality, Individuality* and *Sociality*. This was an order by a feared authority figure; the consequences of disobeying were frightening since they were framed as being a risk to the welfare of both her and her loved ones (as well as all of the other people on the truck with whom presumably by this time Teresa would have formed some personal bond).

Both of these incoming signals of need were competing for neuronal time and attention within Teresa's mind at the very same instant, both the familiar, internal message of fatigue, and the threatening, external message from the Coyote. According to Edelman's theory, only the "fittest" of these messages would have been attended to. In this case the need to stay awake and hang onto the mesh won that competition. Teresa "decided" that holding onto the mesh was more essential than sleeping. Holding the mesh was chosen because Teresa deemed that this action would result in greater short term survival and well-being for her and her family (see Figure 5.1).

Some self-related signals and responses, for example learning to associate the internal feelings associated with fatigue with the act of physically lying down and closing one's eyes, become deeply ingrained in the individual's neural architecture. This is so much the case that later in life, it takes great conscious will to choose not to lie down, close one's eyes and fall asleep when one experiences fatigue, i.e., adenosine levels rise beyond their threshold. Some Well-Being Systems, such as those within the Creativity & Spirituality modality, also benefit from early learning and experience, but seemingly require continuous reinforcement and social support to remain primed for receptivity. But these signals also can assume great salience if properly catalyzed. For example, Teresa repeatedly relied upon her belief in God as the ultimate choice-making mechanism as she dealt with a never-ending series of challenges during her emigration ordeal.

Teresa's narrative reveals dozens of these conflicts between competing signals. However, at every moment of every day, even under typical circumstances, hundreds of external and internal signals in the form of self-related needs would have

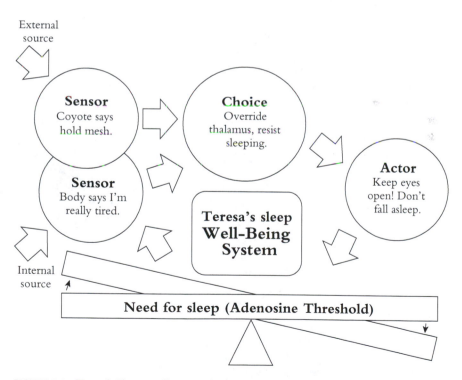

**FIGURE 5.1** Teresa's Sleep Well-Being System

flooded her brain, each need connected to a particular Well-Being System, each jostling for time and attention. The vast majority of these signals Teresa would have ignored because they did not have sufficient competitive "clout" to command her attention. Importantly though, the Well-Being Systems in Teresa's brain that were most likely to "win" and become activated were the ones that had won in the past, systems that had previously resulted in feelings of well-being. The brain is conservative, always preferring to make the same choices over and over again, particularly if those choices were successful before. In Teresa's case this was true of sleeping when she got tired, following orders from people in authority and praying to God and following what she perceived his response to be. Only very rarely, and then only in extreme situations, will novel signals override well-worn pathways.[6]

## The Neurobiology of Well-Being

The brain is both an electrical and chemical organ, thus both processes are at work. To date, science has developed an increasingly sophisticated understanding of the electrical wiring of the brain, particularly through a range of computer-driven 3D imaging technologies.[7] Though the wet chemistry of the brain is equally important, it is currently much less understood. Take for example the following two events shared by Teresa, both involving neural Well-Being processes.

> [In Altar] we had to go where we were going to meet the people who were going to cross us. . . . There are a lot of little houses, boxes where I imagine people go to sleep. When we arrived there one of the men [began] pushing my daughter towards one of the houses. She started crying . . . I said "Leave her alone, she doesn't want to sleep here."
>
> He said "Ok, ok, this is all I can offer to people, I can't offer you more unless you have money, [If you do] I can get you a room in a hotel, and if not, you have to stay here." So people who don't have any money, they stay there.
>
> I told him "Ok." He says "Do you have money to pay 500 pesos[8] per night?", and I said "Yes." All of us stayed in a [single] room. But it was safer. It was an ugly place, but thank God, we could stay in a room and be there the whole time we stayed before leaving to the desert.

Both of these events involved a situation in which Teresa perceived a threat to one or more of her children, but the neurochemistry of these two fear events would likely have been different. The first event would have sent signals to multiple brain regions, but seeing her daughter being directly threatened would have triggered Teresa's "fight or flight" mechanisms, instantly flooding her body with adrenaline, cortisol and noradrenaline.[9] The "thinking fast" parts of her brain would have taken precedent causing Teresa to immediately respond and attempt to prevent the man's actions.[10]

The latter event, the negotiation over a place to stay, likely involved an activation of her adrenal system with the related release of chemicals associated with anxiety and uncertainty, such as the adrenocorticotrophic hormone and cortico-trophin release factor, but importantly, events were unfolding at a pace in which she could consciously think through a response.[11] In other words, the "thinking slow" parts of her brain would have won the competition.[12]

Although neuroscience is now able to provide a general sketch of how Darwinian selection affects the brain-based parts of Well-Being Systems, the exact biological mechanisms are quite murky and much more complicated than this example would suggest. Current evidence suggests that there is not a single mechanism at work, but rather a mélange of mechanisms; the results of repeated evolutionary events all patched together into a single, if not entirely seamless, at least sufficiently integrated whole.[13]

The idea of how the brain operates as an integrated whole, while processing signals from myriad locations, has historically been one of the greatest challenges for neuroscientists to understand. Edelman's theory of Neuronal Group Selection provides an important clue to how this process works, but it does not solve the problem entirely because the actual step-by-step biology is highly complex and often quite convoluted. This complexity is why the vast majority of neuroscientists only work on one piece of brain activity at a time, for example, how information is processed during sight or how a person learns to read. But living people, like Teresa, do not use one system at a time. When the man in Altar grabbed her daughter and started pushing her towards one of the houses, Teresa was not only dealing with the safety and well-being of her child, she also was sizing up the man she was addressing, scoping out the environment for other opportunities and threats, while simultaneously plotting what her next course of action would be. But that is not all her brain was doing. While all this was going on, the flood of adrenaline, cortisol and noradrenaline in her blood would have caused Teresa's breath and heart rate to increase as she prepared her body for a potential fight. Meanwhile, the digestion of her food would have temporarily stopped in order to allow more blood to flow to her large muscle systems that she would need should physical action against the man be required. Although this is an extreme example, the idea of the simultaneous activation of multiple systems is not. There is always lots happening every second inside and outside a human's body. It is miraculous that every person seems to be able to effortlessly blend these widely disparate thoughts and sensations into a coherent whole in order to make a steady stream of life-supporting choices. Why is a person not paralyzed by indecision?

According to current neuroscience theory, the key appears to be that a person functionally has not just one brain, but many brains. Totally analogous to my idea of multiple modalities of semi-autonomous but interconnected Well-Being Systems, current brain science suggests humans have multiple brain systems, all variously interconnected and yet fundamentally discrete.[14] Each of the multiple modules of the brain, like the multiple modalities of Well-Being Systems, represent an evolutionary response to particular biological needs and realities. As humanity's ancestors faced new and ever more complicated self-related needs, one adaptive response was the evolution of new layers of the brain, each new layer containing additional Well-Being Systems. I am arguing that there is an evolutionary correlation between the main modules of the brain and the seven modalities of Well-Being. Over evolutionary time, each of these brain modules, and thus also their constituent Well-Being Systems, became integrated with proceeding modules in such a way that they functioned collaboratively, in order not to undermine the overall well-being of the individual. With the rise of consciousness, the activities of some but not consistently all of these modules would have become subject to awareness, with some modules being more consistently and closely connected to the neural machinery of consciousness than others.[15]

## Perceiving Well-Being

Thus it is that despite the never-ending flurry of activity within the brain, only a small fraction is actually consciously perceived, and an even smaller amount stored in the brain as memory. In his book *Synaptic Self,* neuroscientist Joseph LeDoux attempts to explain how people sort through this cacophony of activity, perceiving the world not as a disjointed welter of thousands of disconnected perceptions, but instead as a single integrated whole.[16] He proposes a series of key principles, or processes that underlie the mechanism by which the brain assembles and integrates all of the various messages coming into the multitudinous neural modules, creating a conscious perception of unity.[17] First among many though according to LeDoux are emotions; emotional feelings unify the mind.[18] Emotions make events salient. It comes as no surprise that out of thousands of events that occurred over the course of her journey one of the things that Teresa most vividly recalled was the man in Altar pushing her daughter and her immediate angry response.

Historically, it was thought that feelings such as anger "caused" certain behaviors. For example, seeing the man push Teresa's daughter made her angry, which in turn triggered her verbal reproach to the man to leave her daughter alone. But as originally proposed by William James in the late 19th century, and confirmed some hundred years later, feelings actually happen after these responses are initiated, not before.[19] Although the conscious perception of feelings of anger that arise when someone sees one's child threatened are interconnected with the Well-Being Systems that affect bodily responses to the threats, these feelings originate from different areas of the brain and have their own unique Well-Being loops.

Feelings are generated by many parts of the brain, but the core of feeling appears to reside in the most ancient part of the vertebrate brain, the brain stem.[20] The brain stem is physically located at the very bottom area of the brain, the part that connects with the spinal cord.[21] This area of the brain has also been found to be the coordination hub for all human choice-making.[22] This area of the brain includes the basal ganglia and much of the limbic system, including the *amygdala, thalamus, insula,* and *cingulate gyrus.* These limbic system structures support emotions, as well as virtually every action a person takes, from eating and sex, to social attachment and the processing of abstract ideas and conscious thought.[23] Is it a coincidence that both the seat of human emotion and the hub of human choice-making appear to be located in the exact same area of the brain?

## Emotion and Well-Being Systems

Historically philosophers and social scientists assumed that choice-making was an inherently rational process.[24] Over the last quarter century a range of studies have undermined this assumption, demonstrating that choice-making can never be cleanly divided between decisions made through rational thought and those made by emotion. Even though Teresa herself seems to consistently perceive that she consciously, and at least within her own mind, logically reflected upon her various choices, for instance when she deliberated between the desire to sleep and the imperative of staying awake so she could continue to hold onto the mesh in the back of the truck to avoid detection by the border patrol, it is clear that her choice-making was as much emotionally driven as it was logically driven. In fact, emotion figures prominently in virtually all of Teresa's choices, even those she characterized as being highly reasoned, particularly that most deliberative of her choices, whether or not to emigrate to the U.S. in the first place. Even in the retelling, evidence of Teresa's emotions is never far from the surface. It turns out that Teresa is not exceptional in this regard. Emotions are always part of human choice-making.

In what is now considered a classic study, neuroscientist Antonio Damasio studied a patient who had suffered damage to the emotional integration center of his brain.[25] Although this individual had lost the ability to perceive and relate emotions to his thoughts, the rest of his brain, including all the "intellectual" parts involved with rational thought, seemed to be perfectly normal. This individual could enumerate the factors involved in a choice, imagine the consequences of actions and even discuss the pros and cons of different choices, but he absolutely could not make a choice and decide upon an action. In the absence of emotion, deciding between choices was not possible. Extensive research has confirmed Damasio's findings and reinforced the essential role that emotions and other "intuitive" processes play in myriad neural processes, particularly choice-making.[26] In summarizing the past two decades of neuroscience research, researcher Mary Helen Immordino-Yang states, "It is literally neurobiologically impossible to build memories, engage complex thoughts or make meaningful decisions without emotion."[27] More importantly, it is not possible to perceive well-being without emotion.

Not only does most incoming perceptual information flow through the emotional areas of the brain, and in the process receive an emotional "read," but these areas also act as a relay for the brain, providing feedback to the various sensory organs telling them which and what signals to attend to. Meanwhile the *amygdala* and other parts of the limbic system also send out messages to other brain modules, alerting them to what, emotionally speaking, is happening in the world.

This is a great deal of responsibility for one part of the brain which is why it has evolved multiple systems for dealing with emotional regulation.[28] Damasio and others have shown that there are numerous inter-connected emotional systems, which collectively play a critical role in virtually all aspects of brain functioning.[29] Neuroscientist Jonathon Turner explains it this way, "Emotions give each alternative a value and, thereby, provide a yardstick to judge and to select alternatives. This process need not be conscious; and indeed, for all animals including humans, it rarely is. . . . One can't sustain cognitions beyond working [i.e., short-term] memory without tagging them with emotion."[30] The human brain stores choices as memories, and memories, in turn, are stored in networks of meaning, and emotions play a major role in whether an event is experienced as meaningful, thus whether and how it is remembered. If a contextually appropriate emotion is triggered, the brain marks the experience as meaningful, and stores memory of it in the networks activated by the emotion and similar experiences.[31] Human Well-Being Systems are always emotionally-driven processes.

The more emotionally rich an experience is, the more memorable it is.[32] And perhaps not surprisingly, what determines whether or not an experience has a high emotional value is whether or not it satisfies needs; emotion and perceived well-being are tightly interlinked. As described earlier, choices, actions and feelings of well-being do not exist in isolation, but rather are typically part of multiple inter-connected Well-Being Systems. Humans, as well as other organisms, are wired to maintain the stability of their Well-Being Systems; emotion is the mechanism vertebrates in particular have evolved to provide feedback on the success of that endeavor. In other words, what makes some parts of an overall experience emotionally arousing and thus memorable, and others not, is based on perception of need. When needs are satisfied, when the triggers of need are in balance, other Systems related to emotion are activated which result in the person feeling positive emotions. When needs are unsatisfied, when the trigger of need is out of balance, these interconnected Systems generate feelings of negative emotion. As has been discussed, the actual trigger can be as tangible as the concentration of adenosine in the brain, which determines whether or not one needs to sleep, or can be as abstract as a perception that God has given you a sign telling you to emigrate to the U.S.

Emotions act like the dashboard gauge that lets you know how much gas is in the tank; emotions are gauges of underlying processes, not the actual processes or even the causes. When things are in balance, neurotransmitters are released that generate feelings such as pleasure, happiness and serenity. The opposite is also true. When the trigger is out of balance, neurotransmitters are released that result in feelings such as fear, anger, unease and shame. Importantly, not only do emotions provide feedback on one's current state but they also tend to make things memorable. The more intense the emotion, positive or negative, the more salient the memory.[33] As several of the above examples illustrate, often the most highly emotional, salient and memorable life events involve not a single Well-Being System, but commonly, myriad interlocking Well-Being Systems.

## The Blending of Well-Being Systems

Most human choices and actions represent a blend of Well-Being Systems, often representing some combination of the seven modalities of Well-Being. Again Teresa's journey is illustrative.

> We promised to meet up with the [other groups] who went the other way. We set a place to meet at a certain hour with two other groups [at about] 3 hours after we have started walking. But they had already been caught, and so we kept walking. It was getting late, cold and dark when suddenly we came close to Immigration [Border Patrol], like 10 steps from them. [We could see] their motorcycles were there, and it was impossible that they didn't see us, a group of 10 people, right? But we saw them and we just turned around. The guide [Coyote] said, "Walk ten steps back, get into the canyon and wait for me there." That was also the hardest moment at the desert, because you don't know if the guide is coming back. Because that's why a lot of people die in the desert, because it could be that the guide gets caught, or he could just do as he wishes and leave you there, lost. At that time, we walked, we walked, and I told him, or I didn't tell him, I just thought, but I said, "Please Lord, may he come back." We were just praying, we were just asking God for this man not to leave us there. It was getting dark and for a moment I said, "Oh, if he goes and leaves us, it is better to shout at the Immigration officer that we are here, because the guide can leave and leave you there." That was very, very hard, because we didn't know if Immigration was catching the Coyote that is crossing you.

Apparent in this description are various combinations of six of the seven human modalities of Well-Being. Teresa clearly expressed concerns about her safety (Individuality), but she was also concerned about it getting cold and dark (Continuity). Meanwhile she contemplated what she and the rest of her group's (Sociality) best actions would be (Reflectivity), what the motivations of the Coyote might be (Relationality), while continually seeking direction from her faith (Creativity & Spirituality). Depending upon the situation and prior lived experience, every human is continuously mixing and matching his various core self-related needs, often quite creatively, in an effort to maximize perceived well-being. As a result, the seven core modalities of Well-Being allow an almost infinite variety of self-expressions to be possible.

To understand how this almost limitless variability can arise from a limited starting point, one can metaphorically think about how it is possible to create an enormous palette of colors by combining just a handful of primary colors. Anyone who has ever gone to the paint store to buy house paint can appreciate how this works. One starts by selecting a paint color from a selection of hundreds upon hundreds of color samples on little strips of paper, each with a number printed on it. The number is a code representing a specific ratio of red, blue, yellow and black pigments. With this color card in hand, the paint store personnel are able to create the selected paint color by using a special machine that adds the four primary pigment colors to a can of white paint according to the formula dictated by the code. Voila, custom color from a mixture of four core pigments into a white base!

Reinforcing how even small variations can result in immense variability, consider the challenge of reversing the process and matching a particular paint color. As anyone who has tried will attest, it is easy to get close to a color-match, but extremely difficult to perfectly match an existing color because even tiny variations result in noticeable deviations. Add to this the fact that in humans, the starting point is not seven identically manufactured pigments representing each of the core modalities of Well-Being, but rather living, constantly evolving networks of neurons and related bodily components. Also important to appreciate is that the seven Well-Being System modalities I have described are not monolithic; each modality is actually a conceptual place-holder for an entire suite of thousands or more evolutionarily—and culturally-related Well-Being Systems, all of which are constantly morphing and adapting to changing circumstances.[34] Hence, the number and variability of the base "pigments" humans use to create the "colors" of life in action are actually hundreds of orders of magnitude greater than seven. The total possible number of combinations is so astronomically large it exceeds the number of stars in the universe. Still, from a relatively small subset of basic modalities of well-being derived needs, an almost limitless number of possible choices and actions emerge. It is these end products that humans are most aware of, not the underlying processes that control the choices and actions they make.

Humans have the ability to consciously reflect upon and verbally describe some of their choice-making processes and actions, but clearly not all. Conscious awareness, and ultimately the language to describe that awareness, represents an important evolutionary advancement, but it is important to remember that these abilities were late add-ons. Long before the evolution of consciousness or language, living things were utilizing Well-Being Systems to support their survival.

## Consciousness

Although neglected as an area of study for much of the 20th century, research on consciousness became quite a hot topic over the last quarter century, with the result that there are now a number of compelling theories. As part of his theory of Neuronal Group Selection, Gerald Edelman also attempted to explain how organisms, in particular humans, come to experience constancy in their interactions with the world in both space and time. Edelman posited that each of the various neuronal groups in the brain became wired together, in the process forming one or more local "maps." Typically, there is considerable redundancy in these maps so that when a stimulus occurs, several maps in parallel are likely to be activated. Through a process Edelman called "reentrant signaling," the human brain integrates these widely distributed groups of neurons in the brain to achieve integrated and synchronized firing. Edelman theorized that this synchronized firing is how the brain becomes self-organizing and "intelligent." It is also arguably why neural functions are rarely localized in just one area of the brain but typically distributed through many regions. The reentry signaling process is also how humans can achieve higher mental functions, such as metacognition, that is, thinking about thinking. In theory, if multiple neuronal groups fire in parallel, one neuronal group can simultaneously be "thinking" about how another neuronal group is "thinking." This, according to Edelman, is the mechanism that allowed humans to achieve consciousness.[35]

Edelman and his neural scientist colleague, Giulio Tononi, proposed that consciousness evolved as a direct result of increasing brain complexity, and was a natural consequence of more and more neuronal groups becoming progressively combined and simultaneously activated. [36] As brain cells evolved to become ever more integrated, information could be combined more readily, and therefore the essence of complicated, conscious thought became possible.[37] However, this advance is determined not just by the size of the brain, but more importantly, by its complexity. According to Tononi, the quality of integration appears to go up not just because of the quantitative connection of more and more individual neurons, but also when large numbers of separate clusters of neurons become qualitatively integrated and organized. As Tononi metaphorically stated, "What you need are specialists who talk to each other, so they can behave as a whole,"[38]

Neurophysiologist John Eccles has argued that this interlinking ability is a characteristic of not just primates, but the mammalian brain in general, with origins that potentially go back at least 85 million years.[39] From this perspective, long before humans evolved, there were creatures running around the planet possessing a rudimentary form of consciousness. Work by Damasio in particular, but others as well, has shown that many other animals possess what Damasio calls core consciousness—the sense of the individual organism in the act of knowing.[40] Clearly, this capability had some kind of selective advantage since over evolutionary time these rudimentary forms of consciousness not only persisted, but continued to evolve, becoming reasonably acute in a range of organisms, including mammals such as whales and dolphins, but particularly acute in higher primates, such as chimpanzees, orangutans and humans. One of the key things all these diverse organisms have in common is that all are highly social. The challenges inherent in navigating complex social relationships was likely a major catalyst for this huge evolutionary leap in brain organization.[41]

## Consciousness as (Social) Attentional Awareness

Support for the idea that social awareness was the basis for the evolution of consciousness in general, and in humans, in particular, comes from new data and theories presented and proposed by neuroscientists Michael Graziano and Sabine Kastner.[42] They accept the idea that consciousness is an emergent property of the brain resulting from Edelman's notion of neuronal organization and complexity, but they argue that consciousness, at least in humans and apes, appears to arise from a particular area of the brain—the neocortex[43]—in a very specific way—through focused awareness and attention. This particular brain area also appears to be critical to social relationships. According to Graziano and Kastner, "Humans have specialized neuronal machinery that allows us to be socially intelligent. The primary role for this machinery is to construct models of other people's minds thereby gaining some ability to predict the behavior of other individuals."[44] Evidence for their theory comes from studies of brain-damaged individuals.[45]

Assuming Graziano and Kastner are correct, consciousness likely evolved initially, as is still evident in chimps and humans, for the purpose of navigating the social world. Graziano and Kastner suggest that these "social" areas of the brain were tied early on to other important social facilitating areas in the brain, in particular, the mirror neuron system. Mirror neurons are sets of neurons located in various parts of the brain that simulate the observed actions of others.[46] Quite literally, these special neuronal clusters allow a person to mentally "mirror" the actions and feelings of others. For example, brain scan studies of people watching someone crying and being sad showed that the areas in the imaged person's brain associated with crying and sadness "lit up," even though the person was not directly doing the crying or feeling sad.[47] Neuroscientists have speculated that the evolution of mirror neurons may have been a key neural breakthrough that allowed advanced primates to feel empathy towards others.[48] Important also, since mirror neurons are present in primates other than humans, in fact, were first discovered in macaques, is the idea that empathy also predates the evolution of the human brain.[49] According to Graziano and Kastner, the perceptual receptors in the neocortical region of the brain supply the necessary information to drive the mirror-neuron simulations, and these simulations in turn "have the potential to provide detailed, high quality feedback, resulting in a more elaborate, more accurate model of the other mind. In this proposed scheme, the mirror neuron system is an extended loop, adding to and enhancing the machinery that constructs models of minds."[50]

The key aspect of Graziano and Kastner's *Attention Schema* theory is that consciousness is at its core a capability to focus one's awareness and attention; capabilities that just happen to be tied to the areas of the brain that initially evolved to support social purposes. As stated by Graziano and Kastner, "awareness is a perceptual reconstruction of attentional state; and the machinery that computes information about other people's awareness is the same machinery that computes information about our own awareness."[51] The value of constructing an awareness of another person's actions, and attributing it to that person, is that it enables someone to usefully predict what another person might be doing and even thinking; general abilities I have lumped under the Well-Being System category of Relationality. But it has an additional consequence; it allows the person to create a focused and abstract representation of the world by creating an informational representation of reality, a representation that can be manipulated independently of the actual world. According to Graziano and Kastner, attention and awareness are two different and separate brain functions. The miracle of conscious awareness was the interconnection of these two historically separate brain activities.

Through conscious awareness the brain became capable of being aware of what it was attending to.[52]

In this view, conscious attention is a particular form of information processing in which the brain focuses its resources on a limited set of interrelated signals coming from the external world. These internalized signals are then converted into an internal depiction of that reality, and the individual then treats that internal representation as if it was indeed the real thing. Typically, a person's internal representations of the outside world bear a rough approximation to events and circumstances in the outside world, but not always. For example, a person might perceive that a person in her life hates her. Once she has constructed that perception of the other person, every action by that person, even friendly gestures, are interpreted by her as evidence that her internal, conscious perceptions are correct. What is important to note is that these consciously constructed perceptions may or may not accurately reflect how that person actually perceives the other. Most normal people constantly adjust their internal perceptions to fit the stimuli coming to them from the real world. So, for example the woman described in the previous few sentences may over time come to realize that this other person does not really hate her, that the initial event that prompted her to have these perceptions was a misunderstanding. Of course there are people who have difficulty making these adjustments, individuals whose internal perceptions of the world markedly differ from what others perceive as the real world, who consistently inaccurately read external cues. These people are typically diagnosed as being schizophrenic, delusional or having some kind of personality disorder. In general though, the notion of internalized awareness works quite well, since it allows a person to predict other people's intentions and actions.

Consciousness appears to have gone into hyper-evolution in humans, currently dominating how humans perceive the world.[53] Although the neural nets associated with conscious awareness, as well as those involved with language, interconnect with a vast number of the Well-Being Systems involved with actual choice-making and action, as described in Chapter 3 conscious awareness typically trails rather than precedes choice-making.[54] People can be aware of the functioning of their Well-Being Systems, and offer up descriptions of these systems, but neuroscience research suggests that such representations are merely artifacts, fragmentary clues suggestive of actual underlying processes. Still, even fragmentary evidence has value, if its importance as data is kept in perspective.

## Self-Aspects

People always see the world from the inside out, a fact that results in everyone being at least somewhat self-centered. People are born egocentric, and then only gradually develop the capacity, though not always the inclination, to view the world from someone else's perspective. The developmental nature of this basic human bias towards egocentrism was made famous by the psychologist Jean Piaget. Piaget observed that prior to the age of eight or so, children seemed cognitively incapable of taking the perspective of another person.[55] Only over time, after the necessary brain maturation has occurred, does it become physiologically possible for a person to think about how another person might perceive the world. Although all normal adults have the cognitive tools necessary to see the world through another's eyes, such perspectives only rarely happen. Even when they do, no one is ever capable of completely seeing the world from another's perspective. Not only do people generally frame their perceptions of the world, even their perceptions of other people and their motivations, through the lens of their own self, they really have no choice but to do so.[56] Each person has only this singular frame of reference on which to base their assessments. All memories and narratives at their core are framed through the lens of self-perception. This is also the case for verbalizations of these self-perceptions.

The psychologist Patty Linville is credited with being the first researcher to hypothesize that the ability of an individual to conceptualize and describe how they or someone else feels, in other words to have a self-perception of what at any given moment is happening in their or another person's life, must have a tangible, biological reality. In this view, every single one of the thousands of individualized and idiosyncratic roles, relationships, contexts, feelings or activities a person perceives and/or recalls needs to somehow directly connect with the underlying structure of the brain; each perception needing to be viewed not as some abstract psychological construct, but as a concrete and distinguishable physical neural entity. Linville called these cognitive neural entities *self-aspects*.[57]

Linville hypothesized that each person's multiple self-aspects were likely the result of a unique neural network or node of related networks, each in turn interconnected with associated networks of other neurons. In this way, every time a person perceived an association between an idea, emotion, relationship or behavior they would actually be drawing upon existing interconnections between neuronal nodes; each reflecting a specific cognitive, affective and/or evaluative memory. Linville went on to theorize that the strength of associations among these various self-aspect nodes should vary, with some self-representations being very important to the person, and thus highly interconnected with other nodes, and some less important and only weakly interconnected.[58] As summarized earlier in this chapter, brain research supports Linville's ideas.[59]

Whenever an individual consciously perceives a relationship between himself and some other entity, whether that entity is an object, idea or social relationship, that perception is reflective of both the actual neural structures within that individual's brain that represent a memory of that entity as well as the neural structures that permit a language-based description of those memories. Thus, Teresa's recollections of her journey to the U.S. represents not only an interesting story, but actually provides insights into the way her brain is wired. The underlying connections between her various Well-Being Systems are reflected in the self-aspects she used to describe her journey.

According to social psychologist Bernd Simon, people form self-aspects whenever they attempt to think about and rationalize their thoughts and behaviors in relation to the world. According to Simon, people make sense of their actions and roles by ascribing self-related qualities or descriptions to themselves within a specific situation according to generalized characteristics or traits (e.g., tenacious), physical features/attributes (e.g., defenseless woman), states (e.g., fatigued), roles (e.g., parent), abilities (e.g., capable of overcoming hardship), tastes (e.g., distaste for men who would make their living doing illegal things like the Coyotes), attitudes and beliefs (e.g., God will lead me), behaviors (e.g., I had to pretend to be positive and in control) and explicit group or category membership (e.g., Mexican).[60] Some self-aspects are generalizable across a wide range of situations, such as Teresa's self-image of herself as a committed parent, something that characterized her behavior from the start to finish of her ordeal. But many other self-aspects are quite narrow and only relate to very particular circumstances: "'ok, ok.' I repeated to myself, 'I have to be positive, because we already are in the field, we are in the desert and I can't be like this.'"

The key to Simon's approach is appreciating that self-aspects represent a mechanism by which an individual is able to convert otherwise vague and unknowable biological processes into language. The underlying firing of neurons is notoriously difficult to study, but the resulting self-aspects are amenable to study since they represent the operationalization of self-perception into a definable and observable entity. Simon begins with the assumption that "through self-interpretation, people achieve an understanding of themselves or, in other words, a [sense of self], which in turn influences their subsequent perception and behavior."[61] Quite literally, as situations arise, people address those situations by consciously, as well as unconsciously, responding on the basis of how they think about themselves. Of course, people do not actually perceive the biological/neural processes that affect the choices they make, but often they can represent those processes through self-aspects; revealing typically after-the-fact not only what they did but why they did what they did.

Building on this foundation, I have been able to both describe, and to a modest degree predict, the behavior of visitors to museums and other similar venues based on the self-aspects they use to describe their reasons for visiting in the first place. The key insight was that the self-aspects people used to describe their visit motivations revealed clues to the underlying self-related needs people were trying to satisfy. I theorized that since the purpose of the visit was satisfaction of these self-related needs, it stood to reason that these same needs should also influence choice-making during their visit.[62] The data that I and others have collected appears to support this theory.[63]

The process of constructing self-aspects to define and explain behavior appears to be something that humans do all the time,[64] though some individuals, and some cultures, do it more than others.[65] Individuals regularly construct in their heads self-related descriptions of themselves, descriptions that are specific to the event or situation they have just completed, as well as occasionally for those they are about to engage in. Not only do people create personal, autobiographical narratives using self-aspects in the present, much as Teresa did in her narrative, these self-aspect-driven narratives regularly serve as working models for the person, telling him why he did what he did in the past, as well as what to expect and how to behave in particular types of situations in the future.[66] A critical aspect of this understanding is that every individual's self-aspects are inherently idiosyncratic, resulting daily in individuals around the world generating billions upon billions of distinctive, self-related explanations for their actions. Self-aspects are always indicative, but never fully illustrative of Well-Being Systems.

## Notes

1. Edelman, G. (1978). *The mindful brain*. Cambridge, MA: MIT Press.
2. e.g., Edelman, G. (1989). *Neural Darwinism—The theory of neuronal group selection*. New York: Basic Books.
   Edelman, G. & Tononi, G. (2000). *A universe of consciousness*. New York: Basic Books.
3. LeDoux, J. (2002). *Synaptic self: How our brains become who we are*. New York: Penguin.
4. Edelman, G. (1989). *Neural Darwinism—The theory of neuronal group selection*. New York: Basic Books.
5. Clasadonte, J., McIver, S.R., Schmitt, L.I., Halassa, M.M. & Haydon, P.G. (2014). Chronic sleep restriction disrupts sleep homeostasis and behavioral sensitivity to alcohol by reducing the extracellular accumulation of adenosine. *Journal of Neuroscience*, 34, 1879–1891.
   Halassa, M.M., Florian, C., Fellin, T., Munoz, J.R., Lee, S.Y., Abel, T., Haydon, P.G. & Frank, M.G. (2009). Astrocytic modulation of sleep homeostasis and cognitive consequences of sleep loss. *Neuron*, 61, 216–219.
6. Duhigg, C. (2012). *The power of habit*. New York: Random House.
7. e.g., Zimmer, C. (2014). Secrets of the brain. *National Geographic*, 225(2), 28–57.
8. 500 pesos is roughly equivalent to $25.
9. Eagleman, D. (2015). *The brain: The story of you*. New York: Pantheon.
10. Kahneman, D. (2011). *Thinking, fast and slow*. New York: Farrar, Straus and Giroux.
11. Grupe, D.W. & Nitschke, J. (2013). Uncertainty and anticipation in anxiety. *National Review of Neuroscience*, 14(7), 488–501.
    Armony, J. & Vuilleumier, P. (Eds.). (2013). *Cambridge handbook of human affective neuroscience*. Cambridge: Cambridge University Press.
12. Kahneman, D. (2011). *Thinking, fast and slow*. New York: Farrar, Straus and Giroux.
13. LeDoux, J. (2002). *Synaptic self: How our brains become who we are*. New York: Penguin.
    Eagleman, D. (2015). *The brain: The story of you*. New York: Pantheon.
14. LeDoux, J. (2002). *Synaptic self: How our brains become who we are*. New York: Penguin, p. 307.
15. LeDoux, J. (2002). *Synaptic self: How our brains become who we are*. New York: Penguin, p. 307.
16. LeDoux, J. (2002). *Synaptic self: How our brains become who we are*. New York: Penguin.
17. LeDoux's first principle is that the different modular systems of the brain all experience the same world, and thus have a shared "sense" of reality. Although each neural system is focused on a different function, they are all part of the same organism which is experiencing the same world, thus each system encodes the same life events, albeit in a different way. So while one set of systems focuses on sights and another set on sounds and still others on the emotional or conceptual aspects of an event, they are all treated by the brain as a conceptual whole. Consequently, "as a result of parallel encoding by, and parallel plasticity within, neural systems, a shared culture develops and persists among the systems, even if they never communicate directly" (p. 310). But typically, the systems of normal brains are not totally isolated. Which is principle number two, that synchronous firing of the parallel systems reinforces the relationship between what were separately encoded experiences. Since all of the systems are contained within a single

person, and thus are at some level interconnected, the person's brain perceives each of these simultaneously occurring and separately encoded events as interconnected parts of a single event. So that although a person actually encodes the words on this page in multiple places of the brain—the shapes of the letters, the feel of the book or e-reader, the meanings of the individual words as well as emotional responses felt—that person still perceives the experience of the book as a unified whole, and thus ultimately remembers it that way as well.

Most of the processes involved in synchronous encoding happen within the brain electrically through changes in the action potentials of neurons, but the interactions between modules are also supported chemically. Another key process is that a whole range of chemicals help to stimulate and coordinate the actions of different brain modules; collectively these chemicals are called "modulators." The cells that produce neural modulators—chemicals like dopamine, norephinephrine, epinephrine, serotonin and acetylcholine—are located in the brain stem but have branches connected to nearly all parts of the brain. The actions of these chemicals are widespread and seemingly help to coordinate the brain's activity. These modulators along with electrical impulses help the brain coordinate and synchronize perceptions, and in so doing enable all of the disparate parts of the brain to function as a unified self. As described by LeDoux, "The modulator system functions somewhat like an alarm sounded by the firehouse in the center of a small town. The alarm is very effective in alerting all the town's firemen to the fire, and summoning them to the station, but it doesn't tell them whose house is on fire. This they have to learn by other means, just as brain areas have to determine precisely what it is that's causing the arousal by other means" (p. 310). Unlike the brain's electrical signals that operate on time frames of milliseconds, the brain's chemical modulator effects last for seconds—thousands of times longer. Thus, although different parts of the brain might be electrically stimulated at different times and rates, the chemical modulators help to bring all of the various brain systems together and enables them to remain stably focused and synchronized over relatively long periods of time.

Seemingly all of these parallel mechanisms—both electrical and chemical—are necessary but not sufficient to insure that a single, perceptual unity exists within the brain. For this to happen, according to LeDoux, requires yet another major process; a process especially prevalent in humans and other primates. This process is the presence of what are referred to as convergence zones, regions in the brain where information from diverse systems can be collected and integrated. It seems that many vertebrates possess multiple, parallel systems that can learn simultaneously by synchronous firing and modulatory chemicals, but only mentally more "advanced" mammals have convergence zones in their brains. Humans seem to have more such convergence zones than any other organism studied. Basically, what these convergence zones do is take loosely integrated information from independent modules and connect and package them into more coherent forms of information. According to LeDoux, it's sort of like the Federal Express hub that collects all of the packages going to a general geographic area and then re-bundles them into discrete, related groupings. In FedEx's case these secondary groupings are again based on geography and designed to insure that all of the packages can be divided into manageable routes that make it possible for one driver to deliver them all in one day. In the brain's case, the convergence zones bundle information in a number of ways, including based upon an idea, emotion or even a particular image. The result is that events are perceived and memories are stored in ways that favor coordination over randomness, unity over chaos.

However, not all of these self-awareness coordinating areas of the brain appear to be unique to humans or even primates. Reinforcing the idea that the foundations of conscious self-perception almost certainly existed long before the evolution of humans, neuroscientists have discovered that certain kinds of brain damage, occurring deep within some of the evolutionarily oldest parts of our brains, can disrupt certain basic kinds of conscious self-perception and awareness. Neuroscientist Antonio Damasio (Damasio,

A.R. (1999). *The feeling of what happens: Body and emotion in the making of consciousness.*
New York: Harcourt Brace & Company) describes these as follows:

> Nearly all the sites of brain damage associated with significant disruption of core
> consciousness share one important trait: they are located near the brain's midline,
> in fact, the left and right sides of these structures are like mirror images, looking
> at each other across the midline. At the level of the brainstem and diencephalon
> (the region that encompasses the thalamus and hypothalamus), the damaged sites
> are close to the long set of canals and ventricles that define the midline of the
> entire central nervous system. . . . None of them can be seen when we inspect
> the lateral (external) surfaces of the brain, and all of them occupy an intriguingly
> "central" position. These structures are of old evolutionary vintage, they are pres-
> ent in numerous nonhuman species, and they mature early in individual human
> development.
>
> *(p. 106)*

All of the processes described so far operate automatically, bottom-up as it were. Thus,
an individual's memories are bundled-up in ways that include not just perceptions of
events gleaned from the outside world but also impressions and feelings bubbling up
from within. Because of the influences of neuronal group selection outlined earlier,
a person's brain also filters and selects which information to attend to, and in process
organizes and stores presently perceived experiences based upon past experiences. In this
way, past thoughts and memories can and do directly shape and influence what a person
attends to in the present, the way she sees things, how she mentally packages what she
perceives, and ultimately how she chooses to act upon that information—this is LeDoux's
next principle. According to LeDoux and most other cognitive scientists, these top-down
processes are an extremely important aspect of human cognition. In both subtle and
often very direct ways, a person's past experiences create the foundation on which all of
present experiences are built. Recent neuroimaging studies suggest that several relatively
recently evolved brain areas—the *medial prefrontal cortex*, located right behind the eyes,
the *precuneus*, an area near the top and middle of the brain, and the *anterior insula*, an area
right behind the ears—might be particularly important for packaging and processing
conscious perceptions of self in humans. Although some of this top-down cognitive
organization is conscious, much of it operates below the level of awareness.

LeDoux's final principle is also quite interesting and important. It is that although the
various connections and checks and balances of these various brain modules generally
work really well, they are not perfect. Sometimes the things a person thinks about doing
are not the things she actually does. Sometimes a person perceives that they are acting in
a consistent way when in fact they are not. According to LeDoux the most likely cause
of these "glitches" is that the connections within the brain are good but not perfect; the
interconnections between the various modules are not always up to the task. After all,
the numerous neural modules in the human brain evolved over different time frames
and often originally for different purposes. For example, there's good evidence that the
large parts of the brains people utilize for processing speech was only relatively recently
rewired and repurposed—perhaps as recently as 100,000 years ago or so and potentially
some of the areas of the brain used for reason and planning might be even younger. As
a consequence, the neural modules a person uses for reasoning are not perfectly connected to some of the older brain modules, like for example those used for sex. This is
why an individual might rationally know that adultery is a bad thing but still act upon
the strong emotional tug of having sexual relations with a person other than his spouse;
at least in the short-term the actual well-being derived from the sexual act overwhelms
the potential loss of well-being that infidelity is likely to engender.

18. LeDoux, J. (2002). *Synaptic self: How our brains become who we are.* New York: Penguin.
19. cf., James, W. (1884). What is an emotion? *Mind*, 9(34), 188–205.
20. Emotions have been playing this focusing role for vertebrates a long time, seemingly
    for as long, or nearly as long as there have been vertebrates (Leliveld, L., Langbein, J. &

Puppe, B. (2013). The emergence of emotional lateralization: Evidence in non-human vertebrates and implications for farm animals. *Applied Animal Behaviour Science*, 145(1–2), 1–14.

21. Damasio, A.R. (2011). Neural basis of emotions. *Scholarpedia*, 6(3), 1804. Retrieved December 8, 2016. www.scholarpedia.org/article/Neural_basis_of_emotions

22. Damasio, A.R. (2010). *Self comes to mind*. New York: Vintage.

23. Eagleman, D. (2015). *The brain: The story of you*. New York: Pantheon.

24. Philosophers, at least from the time of Socrates and Plato and likely earlier, have asserted that humanity's uniqueness stems from our ability for conscious, rational thought, as opposed to unthinking, instinctive reaction. However, this idea only gained significant traction beginning about 400 years ago during the Age of Enlightenment when it was championed by such notable philosophers as the German Immanuel Kant; Englishmen Francis Bacon, Thomas Hobbes and John Locke; and Frenchmen Rene Descartes, François-Marie Arouet (better known by his *nom de plume* Voltaire) and Henri Rousseau. The Enlightenment might best be characterized as the time in human history when the idea that everything in the universe could be rationally demystified and cataloged first arose and gained widespread acceptance; the supreme example of that maxim was human behavior itself, perhaps best exemplified by Descartes' famous statement, "Except our own thoughts, there is nothing absolutely in our power" (Descartes, R. (1960). *Discourse on method and meditations*. L. J. Lafleur (trans). New York: The Liberal Arts Press).

   Many hundreds of years later, most debates in contemporary philosophy of the mind continue to revolve around a foundational belief in the conscious, deliberative nature of human thought (e.g., Stein, E. (1996). *Without good reason: The rationality debate in philosophy and cognitive science*. Oxford: Oxford University Press; Lyons, W. (1995). *Approaches to intentionality*. Oxford: Oxford University Press). Likewise, some of the most important theories in moral and political philosophy have been based explicitly on these kinds of rational choice assumptions (cf., Gauthier, D. (1986). *Morals by agreement*. Oxford: Oxford University Press; Rawls, J. (1971). *A theory of justice*. Cambridge: Belknap Press of Harvard University; Nozick, R. (1990). *A normative model of individual choice*. New York: Garland Press). With some recent exceptions (e.g., Dennett, D. (1978). *Brainstorms: Philosophical essays on mind and psychology*. Cambridge, MA: MIT Press; Dennett, D. (2013). *Intuition pumps and other tools for thinking*. New York: W. W. Norton & Company), most philosophical theories about mind and language operate under the assumption that individuals communicate with one another with the goal of entering into purposeful, cooperative exchanges, which by extension assumes that all the relevant actors are rational (see discussion by Chai, S.K. (2001). *Choosing an identity*. Ann Arbor, MI: University of Michigan Press).

   However it is not just philosophers who have emphasized conscious and deliberate decision-making. Social scientists too, including psychologists, sociologists, economists, political scientists and anthropologists, have long championed this perspective; with the major proponents of this view following one or more versions of what is known as *rational choice theory* (cf., Friedman, M. (1953), *Essays in positive economics, Part I—The methodology of positive economics*. Chicago: University of Chicago Press; Blume, L.E. & Easley, D. (2008). Rationality. In S. N. Durlauf & L. E. Blume (Eds.). *The New Palgrave Dictionary of Economics* (2nd ed.) (pp. 884–893). London: Macmillan; Sen, A. (2008). Rational behavior. In S. N. Durlauf & L. E. Blume (Eds.). *The New Palgrave Dictionary of Economics* (2nd ed.) (pp. 68–76). London: Macmillan; also Fishbein, M. & Ajzen, I. (1975). *Belief, attitude, intention, and behavior: An introduction to theory and research*. Reading, MA: Addison-Wesley; Ajzen, I. (1991). The theory of planned behavior. *Organizational Behavior and Human Decision Processes*, 50(2), 179–211; Ortner, S.B. (1984). Theory in Anthropology since the Sixties. *Comparative Studies in Society and History*, 151. Retrieved July 14, 2016. http://mysite.du.edu/~lavita/anth-3135-feasting-13f/_docs/ortner_theory_in_anthropology.pdf; Scott, C. (2000). Rational choice theory. In G. Browning, A. Halcli & F. Webster (Eds.), *Understanding contemporary society: Theories of the present*. Beverly Hills, CA: Sage Publications. Retrieved July 14, 2016. www.soc.iastate.edu/sapp/soc401rationalchoice.pdf).

25. Damasio, A.R. (1994). *Descartes' error: Emotion, reason, and the human brain.* New York: Avon Books.

26. cf., Plutchik, R. (2003). *Emotions and life: Perspectives from psychology, biology and evolution.* Washington, DC: American Psychological Association.
    Dolan, R.J. (2002). Emotion, cognition, and behavior. *Science,* 298(5596), 1191–1194.
    LeDoux, J. (2002). *Synaptic self: How our brains become who we are.* New York: Penguin.

27. Immordino-Yang, M.H. (2015). *Emotions, learning, and the brain: Exploring the educational implications of affective neuroscience.* New York: W. W. Norton & Co.

28. e.g., Karama, S., Armony, J. & Beauregard, M. (2011). Film excerpts shown to specifically elicit various affects lead to overlapping activation foci in a large set of symmetrical brain regions in males. *PLoS ONE,* 6(7), e22343. Retrieved September 19, 2013. www.ncbi.nlm.nih.gov/pmc/articles/PMC3144904/

29. Damasio, A.R. (1999). *The feeling of what happens: Body and emotion in the making of consciousness.* New York: Harcourt Brace & Company.

30. Turner, J.H. (2000). *On the origins of human emotions: A sociological inquiry into the evolution of human affect.* Stanford, CA: Stanford University Press, p. 59.

31. Lazarus, R.S. (1966). *Psychological stress and the coping process.* New York: McGraw-Hill.

32. McGaugh, J.L. (2003). *Memory & emotion: The making of lasting memories.* New York: Columbia University Press.

33. Schacter, D.L. (1996). *Searching for memory.* New York: Basic Books.
    Eagleman, D. (2015). *The brain: The story of you.* New York: Pantheon.

34. Torday, J.S. (2015). Homeostasis as the mechanism of evolution. *Biology,* 4, 573–590.

35. Edelman, G. & Tononi, G. (2000). *A universe of consciousness.* New York: Basic Books.

36. Edelman, G. & Tononi, G. (2000). *A universe of consciousness.* New York: Basic Books.

37. Tononi, G. (2008). Consciousness as integrated information: A preliminary manifesto. *Biological Bulletin,* 215(3), 216–242.

38. Zimmer, C. (2010). Sizing up consciousness by its bits. *New York Times.* Retrieved August 11, 2013. www.nytimes.com/2010/09/21/science/21consciousness.html?pagewanted=all&_r=1&

39. Eccles, J.C. (1992). Evolution of consciousness. *Proceedings of the National Academies of Science USA,* 89, 7320–7324.

40. Damasio, A.R. (1999). *The feeling of what happens: Body and emotion in the making of consciousness.* New York: Harcourt Brace & Company.

41. Dunbar, R. (1998). The social brain hypothesis. *Evolutionary Anthropology,* 6, 178–190.
    Graziano, M. (2013). *Consciousness and the social brain.* Oxford, UK: Oxford University Press.

42. Graziano, M.S.A. & Kastner, S. (2011). Human consciousness and its relationship to social neuroscience: A novel hypothesis. *Cognitive Neuroscience,* 2, 98–113.
    Graziano, M. (2013). *Consciousness and the social brain.* Oxford, UK: Oxford University Press.

43. In particular the superior temporal sulcus and the temporo-parietal junction.

44. Graziano, M.S.A. & Kastner, S. (2011). Human consciousness and its relationship to social neuroscience: A novel hypothesis. *Cognitive Neuroscience,* 2, 99.

45. In particular important areas of the brain involved in social processing, the superior temporal sulcus and the temporo-parietal junction.

46. Rizzolatti, G. & Sinigaglia, C. (2010). The functional role of the parieto-frontal mirror circuit: Interpretations and misinterpretations. *Nature Reviews Neuroscience,* 11, 264–274.

47. Decety, J. & Chaminade, T. (2003). Neural correlates of feeling sympathy. *Neuropsychologia,* 41, 127–138.

48. Decety, J. & Chaminade, T. (2003). Neural correlates of feeling sympathy. *Neuropsychologia,* 41, 127–138.

49. Di Pellegrino, G., Fadiga, L., Fogassi, L., Gallese, V. & Rizzolatti, G. (1992). Understanding motor events: A neurophysiological study. *Experimental Brain Research,* 91, 176–180.

50. Graziano, M.S.A. & Kastner, S. (2011). Human consciousness and its relationship to social neuroscience: A novel hypothesis. *Cognitive Neuroscience,* 2, 107.

51. Graziano, M.S.A. & Kastner, S. (2011). Human consciousness and its relationship to social neuroscience: A novel hypothesis. *Cognitive Neuroscience*, 2, 98.
52. Graziano, M.S.A. & Kastner, S. (2011). Human consciousness and its relationship to social neuroscience: A novel hypothesis. *Cognitive Neuroscience*, 2, 98–113.
53. In fact, I'm inclined to believe that the Well-Being Systems involved in conscious awareness have become almost parasitically within humans, crowding out other important systems for neural space and resources. Humans, particularly modern humans, have come to see consciousness as the quintessential human capability, as the most important function of mind, but arguably that's just the consciousness modules acting as puppet master, insuring that their own self-related well-being needs are given priority.
54. Wegner, D.M. (2002). *The illusion of conscious will*. Cambridge, MA: MIT Press.
55. Whitbourne, S. (2012). It's a fine line between narcissism and egocentrism. *Psychology Today*. Retrieved December 28, 2016. www.psychologytoday.com/blog/fulfillment-any-age/201204/it-s-fine-line-between-narcissism-and-egocentrism
56. Bem, D.J. (1972). Self-perception theory. In L. Berkowitz (Ed.), *Advances in Experimental Social Psychology* (Vol. 6, pp. 1–62). New York: Academic Press.
57. Linville, P.W. (1985). Self-complexity and affective extremity: Don't put all your eggs in one cognitive basket. *Social Cognition*, 3, 94–120.
    Linville, P.W., (1987). Self-complexity as a cognitive buffer against stress-related illness and depression. *Journal of Personality and Social Psychology*, 52, 663–676.
58. Linville, P.W. (1985). Self-complexity and affective extremity: Don't put all your eggs in one cognitive basket. *Social Cognition*, 3, 94–120.
    Linville, P.W. (1987). Self-complexity as a cognitive buffer against stress-related illness and depression. *Journal of Personality and Social Psychology*, 52, 663–676.
59. Eagleman, D. (2015). *The brain: The story of you*. New York: Pantheon.
60. Simon, B. (2004). *Identity in modern society: A social psychological perspective*. Oxford, UK: Blackwell, p. 46.
61. Simon, B. (2004). *Identity in modern society: A social psychological perspective*. Oxford, UK: Blackwell, p. 45.
62. Falk, J.H. (2006). An identity-centered approach to understanding museum learning. *Curator*, 49(2), 151–166.
    Additional discussion of these ideas can be found in Chapters 14 and 15.
63. Falk, J.H. (2009). *Identity and the museum visitor experience*. Walnut Creek, CA: Left Coast Press.
    Falk, J.H. (2016). Museum audiences: A visitor-centered perspective. *Loisir et Société/ Leisure and Society*, 39(3), 357–370.
64. Cantor, N., Mischel, W. & Schwarz, J. (1982). A prototype analysis of psychological situations. *Cognitive Psychology*, 14, 45–77.
    Schutte, N.S., Kenrick, D.T. & Sadalla, E.K. (1985). The search for predictable settings: Situational prototypes, constraint, and behavioral variation. *Journal of Personality and Social Psychology*, 51, 459–462.
65. Diamond, J. (2012). *The world until yesterday*. New York: Viking.
    Schutte, N.S., Kenrick, D.T. & Sadalla, E.K. (1985). The search for predictable settings: Situational prototypes, constraint, and behavioral variation. *Journal of Personality and Social Psychology*, 51, 459–462.
66. McAdams, D.P. (2008). Personal narratives and the life story. In O. John, R. Robins & L.A. Pervin (Eds.), *Handbook of personality: Theory and research* (3rd ed., pp. 242–262). New York: Guilford Press.
    NOTE: Although a person is likely to perceive their own self-aspects as accurate representations of their reality, others might not agree with this assessment. For example research on the dietary disease anorexia nervosa has shown that people with this illness perceive themselves to be fat, which drives them to avoid eating. This behavior happens despite the fact that everyone else in the person's world judges that person to already be well beyond a normal state of thinness and in need of food (Passi, V., Bryson, S. & Lock, J. (2003). Assessment of eating disorders in adolescents with anorexia nervosa: Self-report

questionnaire versus interview. *Eating Disorders*, 33(1), 45–54.). In another example of the importance of such self-aspects on motivations, choice and behavior, psychologist Carol Dweck and her colleagues have shown that individuals who self-describe themselves as persistent learners consistently achieve better in school than individuals who self-define themselves as smart. According to Dweck, those who thought of themselves as persistent learners were able to overcome short-term failures, and as self-described, persevere through to success. Self-defined smart kids were often afraid of failure, and thus failed in the face of adversity. Both types of self-aspect—persistent learner and smart—were perceptions rather than reality, for example both were independent of the actual intelligence of the individuals as measured by standard IQ tests (Dweck, C. (2000). *Self-Theories: Their role in motivation, personality and development.* New York: Psychology Press.). These are but two examples that show how a person's self-perceptions directly influence choices and behaviors, frequently in profound and even predictable ways.

# 6

# THE WELL-BEING SYSTEMS MODEL

This final, synoptic chapter in this first section of the book covers three broad topics: 1) what optimal well-being looks like in people; 2) the affordances and constraints of language-based descriptions of Well-Being Systems; and finally, 3) a summarizing of the key assumptions underlying my Well-Being Systems model. As in previous chapters in this section, Teresa's story is used to illustrate key points.

This model affords not only new and deeper understandings of the nature of human choice-making but of all human behavior as well. The key premise of my Well-Being Systems model is that all human choices and actions are designed to satisfy underlying self-related needs, the satisfaction of which support feelings of well-being, which evolved as a way for living things to maximize fitness and insure survival. When the system is in balance, when choices and actions result in enhanced short-term fitness, people feel good. When the system is out-of-balance, when choices and actions fall short and a person's immediate fitness is diminished, people feel bad.

Judging fitness and survivability in this way is extremely difficult, particularly since the judgements are continuously made on a moment-to-moment basis while the consequences might take hours, days or even years to manifest themselves. My model postulates that the emotional states which people perceive as well-being, or not, have evolved to correlate with these long-term outcomes. The operative term is correlate, which means there can and often are errors. For example, gorging on foods with a high sugar content whenever and if ever they appeared was historically a great strategy since these types of food bestowed significant short-term energetic benefits and typically were quite limited in availability. In the modern world, these types of food are now readily and continuously available and this once "adaptive" behavior no longer correlates very well with fitness.[1] However, this example is the exception. On the whole, long-standing Well-Being Systems continue to work quite well for humans and other life forms. Arguably the best researched and most complete social science description of what a human Well-Being System looks like when it is optimally functioning comes from psychologist Mihaly Csikszentmihalyi's theory of "Flow."[2]

## Flow as Well-Being Systems at Peak Functioning

Over many years, and through hundreds of interviews and surveys with individuals from many countries representing individuals engaged in a wide range of activities, Csikszentmihalyi and his associates discovered an amazingly consistent pattern in the ways people described experiences of peak personal satisfaction and happiness. It did not matter if the person was an artist, rock climber or chess player, scientist or street sweeper, professional dancer or amateur naturalist, when in a state of peak well-being the person's experiences seemed to converge on a state that Csikszentmihalyi called *flow*. When in a flow state, Csikszentmihalyi observed that individuals became completely absorbed in what they were doing and felt a great sense of control as they perceived that everything in the world functionally seemed to shrink down to just those things they were choosing to focus on. According to Csikszentmihalyi and his colleague Jeanne Nakamura, the six key characteristics of a flow experience are as follows:[3]

- Intense and focused concentration on the present moment;
- The merging of action and awareness;
- A loss of reflective self-consciousness;
- A sense of personal control or agency over the situation or activity;
- A distortion of the subjective experience of time;
- The experience of the activity as intrinsically rewarding.

All of these qualities also describe what happens when a person perceives that their self-related needs are in positive balance. For as long as these perceptions last the individual will strive to keep doing what he is doing; he will strive to maintain this flow state for as long as possible. During flow, whether engaged in romantically kissing another person or singing in a performance, the body is producing a host of neurotransmitters and hormones, including dopamine, oxytocin, serotonin, endorphins and adrenaline, which are collectively perceived by a person as "pleasurable."[4]

Traditionally, the concept of flow has not been applied to things like kissing. However, arguably this is because Csikszentmihalyi and his colleagues have always focused on flow as an example of "higher" human experience, i.e., experiences typically associated with Maslow and other positive psychologists' notions of "self-actualization."[5] Csikszentmihalyi began his work investigating individuals who were highly successful and displayed extreme skill and inventiveness while playing music, dancing or playing chess; individuals presumed to be functioning at the top of Abraham Maslow's hierarchy of needs. However even the more basic Well-Being Systems, for example satisfying physiological needs such as urinating and satiating appetitive drives like hunger and sex can result in well-being. When it comes to well-being, humans are always mixing and matching the needs from each of the seven Well-Being modules. Typically, the more basic, bodily modalities of Well-Being have been viewed from a deficit perspective, ala Maslow, as things that need to be obtained in order to climb higher. As discussed previously, I disagree with this perspective and would argue from an asset-based perspective that each module of Well-Being—Continuity, Individuality, Sexuality, Sociality, Relationality, Reflectivity and Creativity & Spirituality—affords its own opportunities for achieving a sense of well-being, as do all of the unique blends of these modalities that humans typically express. Well-being occurs any time one or more of a person's needs can be maximally satisfied, presumably without unduly sacrificing the well-being of all the rest of the self-perceived needs a person has. In fact, one of the reasons well-being, whether it is called flow or something else, is always ephemeral is that a person begins with so many self-related needs to satisfy, and the world is constantly imposing new ones.

People don't live in a bubble where they can forever keep the vicissitudes of the world at bay. Whether it is the dehydration of cells creating an over-powering thirst or someone entering the room and asking a distracting question, eventually some other need will arise that makes it impossible to remain single-mindedly focused on satisfying the current flow-causing need. For this reason, flow states are always transient. However brief, flow states elicit strong positive emotions, creating strong feelings of well-being. This is why individuals find them extremely satisfying, memorable and highly meaningful. It is also why people repeatedly strive to reproduce their previously experienced flow states again and again.[6]

## Meaning, Memory and Narrative

According to anthropologist Clifford Geertz, meaning is the mind's way of making sense of the world, the translation of existence into conceptual form.[7] Meaning provides a framework for helping someone assess what is important and supports their understanding and actions. All living things are expert meaning-makers, i.e., selectively attending to those things most likely to facilitate well-being. Humans are no exception.

Every human, every day attempts to make meaning of their life experiences. Each and every time an individual engages in an action, they bring to bear on that action their prior knowledge, life-experiences, interests and values in order to actively, though not necessarily consciously, determine which parts of the event are worth focusing on. In other words, people always preferentially attend to the aspects of an action or experience which they perceive to be most meaningful; virtually everything else is ignored. Let me make this point crystal clear, again using Teresa's journey as example.

Over the several months encapsulated by her narrative, Teresa would have had tens of thousands of experiences, but she actually only attended to some of those experiences, and even fewer were stored in her memory and thus available as the foundation of her tale. As described to this point, the actual events that underlie Well-Being Systems are quite complex and only partially available to conscious awareness. Memories typically contain pieces of each of the key components of these systems—the feelings of well-being, the choices made and the key self-perceptions that modulated the system. Once again, Teresa's narrative provides a useful anchor for discussion.

> I felt very discouraged [during much of the journey] but at the same time, when we entered the desert, watching Ernesto, the youngest boy, saying "Oh, I'm almost there with my parents." Then I said to myself, "Ok, ok." I repeated to myself, "I have to be positive, because we already are in the field, we are in the desert and I can't be like this." Even if I was, even if I couldn't [help being scared], I needed to be positive for the children. It was a lot of pressure. And since I didn't sleep, I didn't sleep, I was awake there, taking care of them in the desert while they were sleeping. Throughout this whole time I felt unwell, I felt weak.

Teresa still has vivid memories of her journey, despite the events in question having occurred roughly a decade before. Her narrative focuses on the significant events and choices she perceived she needed to make in order to insure the success of her crossing. For example, in this excerpt she describes her own state of fatigue and feelings of ill health, but how she was compelled despite her own challenges to reinforce and support the enthusiasm of her young nephew Ernesto. Although language-based awareness and recollections cannot reveal all of the hidden dimensions of human Well-Being Systems, they typically can and do provide important clues. Human language-based conscious awareness, even if not playing the central, controlling role so long assumed by philosophers and social scientists, can provide an important window onto the workings of human Well-Being Systems. The first important clue that all personal narratives like Teresa's afford are insights into Teresa's psyche and beliefs. Teresa's entire tale, like all autobiographical tales, was framed entirely through the lens of her own self-perceptions, narrated through Self-Aspects.

The use of language to communicate thoughts, motivations, needs and beliefs is quintessentially human. Most social scientists assume that the ability to linguistically organize one's thoughts is a pre-requisite for these latter human behaviors. Although I have argued that this is not always or even typically the case, it clearly is true that narratives, both thought and spoken, are fundamental to how most humans make sense of, and thus navigate their world. Narrative skills, the ability to develop intelligible stories involving human or humanlike characters who act in the world over time,[8] develop early in the life of a human.

Research has shown that already by the end of the first year of life, human infants recognize that other human beings are intentional agents who act in a goal-directed manner,[9] and by the second year of life children evidence the ability to create their own stories, populated by a range of characters, including themselves.[10] The two-year-old human self is thus already illustrative of William James' ideas of a subjective "I" that observes and begins to construct an objective "me."[11] This kind of development of the narrative mind continues on through childhood and appears to be particularly critical for enabling the child to navigate the social world.[12] Also not surprising is that this kind of social awareness, supported by autobiographical memory and self-storytelling, is socially constructed. Parents typically encourage children to talk about their personal experiences as soon as children are verbally able to do so.[13] As children move through the first dozen years of life, they increasingly come to narrate their personal experiences in ways that conform to their observed understandings of how good stories should be structured and what they should include, i.e., they begin to "internalize their culture's norms and expectations concerning what the story of an *entire human life* should contain."[14]

However it is only during adolescence that individuals begin to be able to comprehend other people's actions as independent of their own,[15] as well as begin to be able to craft causal narratives to explain how different events are linked together in the context of their own personal biography.[16] At this time in life, humans start to regularly develop narrative accounts of their life that explain how one event caused, led up to, transformed or in some way was/is meaningfully related to other events in their life. This use of what cognitive psychologists call *autobiographical memory* to frame one's experience continues to develop and mature as the individual ages such that by late adolescence and into adulthood the development of coherence and consistency in these narratives becomes a central part of the individual's sense of themselves as a person,[17] or what social scientists often call "identity-work."[18] Young adults use these newly developed tools to make critical life decisions, including what kind of job/career to pursue, whom to marry and where to live.[19] On through midlife and into old age adults continue to refashion and refine their narrative understandings of themselves and others.[20]

Throughout life, then, humans create this personal as well as shared autobiography as a way to communicate their prospective choice-making as well how they retroactively understand and justify previously made choices and actions. These narratives always take the form of self-aspects. The ability to tap into memory and utilize self-aspects as a way to share with one's self and others otherwise hidden motivations and understandings almost certainly influenced the course of human evolution. It obviously accelerated the rate at which humans could reflect on their situation and make increasingly thoughtful choices. But it also had other, "unintended" consequences. One of the interesting by-products of this neurological process is that envisaged, self-initiated memory recall is inherently creative. As was observed roughly a century ago by one of the pioneers of cognitive psychology, Frederick Bartlett, each act of recall is distinct from every other because it always entails the active reconstruction of memory.[21] Autobiographical memories are stitched together when and as they are needed; each memory "built" by connecting together information stored in different Well-Being Systems. The result is that autobiographical memories are highly susceptible to revision and distortion.[22]

When building an autobiographical memory, a person's brain combines fragments of sensory memory with a more abstract knowledge about events and reassembles them according to the demands of the present; all with the goal of simultaneously trying to keep the memory both true to what actually happened as well as ensuring that the emerging story coherently fits with the individual's well-being needs.[23] Because of the constructive nature of memory recall, where every reflection represents a unique event, memory and the narratives people use to share their memories are fundamentally creative acts designed to support and as necessary invent a person's relationship with the world.

The creative and constructed nature of autobiographical self-aspects means that extreme caution needs to be used when interpreting what they actually mean. As suggested previously, one should not confuse conscious awareness of behavior with behavioral agency. Human explanations of a choice always, or nearly always, represent *post-hoc* justifications rather than the actual drivers of the choice.[24] However, even beyond this caveat, the self-aspects a person uses to describe their underlying Well-Being Systems suffer from two additional and highly problematic biases. Historically the scale and scope of virtually all social science explanations of choice-making have been framed within specific and limited dimensions of time and space; what scientists would call a "grain size" issue. Second, since all human narratives are constructed using the unique personal, social and cultural context of the teller it stands to reason that similarly all interpretations of that spoken narrative, as well as the meanings made of the specific self-aspects that comprise that narrative, must also be filtered through an individual, social and cultural filter; the filter of the listener.

## Grain Size Biases

As a whole, social science investigations of self-perception and choice have focused on a fairly narrow subset of human experience. Like all humans, social scientists tend to almost exclusively find salient those phenomena occurring within a fairly narrow range of time and space. For example, most social scientists would be comfortable with the focus of Teresa's narrative on her social interactions with friends, family and the Coyotes. They would be unconcerned that she neglected to mention how and when she took bathroom breaks during the long truck ride to Altar or that a lack of physical preparation and cardiovascular fitness might have contributed to her fatigue during her long walk through the desert. In fact, had she included such details the typical social scientist would have wondered why she felt the need to do so. But why should this be? Why when talking about humans is it acceptable to discuss at length some Well-Being System modalities and their influences on choice-making and totally ignore others? The obvious answer is that the selection of a particular grain size on which to focus is based on assumptions of importance; assumptions typically unspoken and unchallenged.

Like all sensory apparatus, human self-perception works best at certain "bandwidths" of "reality." The human eye, for example, is only capable of perceiving electromagnetic radiation in the [human] visible spectrum—390 nanometers to

700 nanometers—despite the existence of light waves at both shorter and longer wavelengths. In a similar fashion, although Well-Being Systems operate along a continuum from the subatomic to the galactic, and from timescales of nanoseconds (Seconds$^{-9}$) to eons (Years$^9$), humans generally only perceive events within a fairly narrow sphere of experience.[25] I have labeled this sphere the "language sphere" because everyday language evolved specifically to describe the self-perceptions and choices, events and feelings occurring within this grain size of human experience (see Figure 6.1). Events occurring within this sphere are what most social scientists, what most modern peoples, would typically think of as the big questions of life such as whether to emigrate to the U.S. This sphere would also typically include some of the daily details of life, such as feeling like one's feet are sore, determining what clothes to wear depending upon the weather and the social situation and whether or not one's immediate social group approves of one's clothing choices. But for all the reasons discussed previously, only some of these events are deemed sufficiently salient to merit encoding in long-term memory or relating as part of a narrative.[26]

Favored within the Language Scale are events occurring disproportionately within certain modalities of Well-Being. Most languages are rich in vocabulary related to needs, choices and actions falling within the Sociality and Relationality-related Well-Being Systems. And though words obviously exist to describe needs,

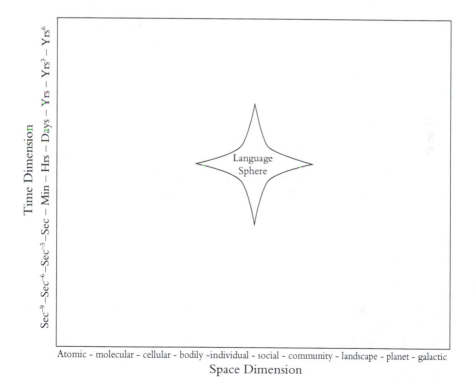

**FIGURE 6.1**   The scope and scale of human experience

choices and actions falling within the other four Well-Being System modalities, they typically get less space in people's normal discourse. By way of example, in Teresa's narrative she found particularly salient what the impact of crossing to the U.S. would have on her children's lives, her conversations with her husband and friend in Mexico and interactions with the Coyote and other people she encountered along the way. Mentioned, but given relatively little space, were discussions about bodily needs. And despite being consistently queried by the interviewer about why she chose to make the decisions she did, these reflective issues accounted for only a modest percentage of Teresa's descriptions of events. As suggested in the previous chapter, the evolutionary origins of conscious awareness insure that social relationships are particularly salient and thus memorable. Only rarely, and typically only when something is very wrong, very unusual or when specifically prompted as was Teresa, do most people attend to events happening within these "outlying" modalities of Well-Being.[27]

As suggested by my term "language sphere," humans in every culture have developed rich and varied self-aspects for describing their everyday experiences within this delimited time and space dimension, but relatively few outside this dimension. Occasionally a word or two from the world of science or technology slip into the popular vernacular; descriptions of events occurring at the scale of the very small or very big, very quick or very slow. Examples include words like "microbe," "ecology" or "light years." In general though, the public possesses only the vaguest sense of what even these commonly used words really imply since they fall outside the realm of their normal perceptual reality. Meanwhile, scientific investigation of the very small and the very large, the very fast and the very slow continue to reveal not only the occurrence but importance of these "imperceptible" events. Although people totally lack the perceptive abilities to sense ionizing radiation, it is now known that exposure to too much short wavelength radiation causes cancer. Similarly, only recently was it determined that the chemicals (e.g., hydrocarbons) created by the burning of fossil fuels was affecting the climate of the planet. Getting people to respond appropriately to this type of information, though, is challenging. Humans, like all organisms, evolved to respond to and treat as real only those things they can perceive. Anything that is imperceptible is treated as functionally non-existent.

Many scientists possess this same perceptual bias. As a consequence, social scientists in particular have tended to be blind to a whole host of naturally occurring events, almost exclusively focusing their analytic lens on events occurring within the language sphere.[28] Thus social scientists frequently ask questions like why would someone emigrate to the U.S., buy this product or vote a certain way in the upcoming election, but only rarely ask questions like how did what Teresa ate on the morning of her departure into the desert influence her feelings and stamina or how did walking through the desert for 17 hours influence the behavior of her children ten years later. It takes considerable effort to step outside historical ways of thinking to appreciate that Well-Being Systems occur at all of the spatial and temporal scales shown in Figure 6.1. Not only do Well-Being Systems occur across all of these dimensions, each exerting an influence on well-being, but the vast majority, including most of those within the language sphere, operate without the individual ever being fully consciously aware of their happening. And even when a person or social scientist is aware of an event or description, they invariably interpret that event or description through their own specific sociocultural lens.

## Sociocultural Biases

Obviously, everyone has their own particular cultural lens and sense of how the world works, one strongly informed by not only their sociocultural context but equally their own unique personal experience. These beliefs cannot but affect how a person interprets what someone says and does. And despite scientists' best efforts to view the world objectively, it has long been understood that all interpretations are inherently subjective and to a degree relative.[29] According to social scientists Joseph Henrich, Steven Heine and Ara Norenzayan, sociocultural bias is not a minor issue to be acknowledged in a footnote but rather a serious and persistent problem. So much so, they believe that most current social science theory is significantly flawed due to sociocultural bias. Nearly all social science theory about humans is based on the data derived from a very rarified and unusual group of people.

Henrich, Heine and Norenzayan coined the acronym WEIRD—*W*estern, *E*ducated, *I*ndustrialized, *R*ich and *D*emocratic—to describe this bias.[30] Virtually all of the work that has been done in the human sciences in general, and on the topic of human choice-making in particular, derive from this single sociocultural context.[31] Although the protagonist of this chapter, Teresa arguably would not be classified as "WEIRD"; the research I have used to build my model and understand her choice-making—including psychological, neural science and even physiological research—were all created by WEIRD people based on experiments conducted with WEIRD subjects. So how much of what I have postulated thus far can really be generalized to all humanity?

Although Teresa's belief in the powers of an all-powerful God seem slightly out of place in the over-rational, secular world of WEIRD Western social science, it is still far more consistent with and comprehensible by people living in the WEIRD world than are most of the hundreds of different belief systems practiced by various hunter-gathering peoples around the world, belief systems where much of a person's daily activity revolves around his relationship with assorted supernatural spirits, ancestors, deities and the magic they weave.[32] And in general, individuals believe that their particular view of the world, whatever that might be, represents "reality." For example, Teresa describes, with derision, her perceptions of the belief system of her Coyotes.

> I think [the Coyotes] use witchcraft a lot. People who think . . . I don't know, I don't know what they think. They believe, they believe that water has power. So I remember they told us "If you don't put this water on your skin, I'm not taking you." At the beginning, before entering the desert,

[One of the Coyote's] said "Everybody has to put on this water or I won't take anyone who doesn't."

So then I told my children, "Look, this water will not get us crossed, I have no faith in this water, but put it on. If they say that's the only way they are taking us, well, put the water on. But you know who is the one you are going with; we know who is leading us? God is leading us."

Although most social scientists would bend over backwards to accommodate this kind of diversity in belief systems, the fact that so much research is conducted with culturally homogeneous populations is not only common, but endemic to most of the human sciences. As Henrich, Heine and Norenzayan report, "Behavioral scientists routinely publish broad claims about human psychology and behavior in the world's top journals based on samples drawn entirely from WEIRD societies. Researchers—often implicitly—assume that either there is little variation across human populations, or that these 'standard subjects' are as representative of the species as any other population."[33] Henrich, Heine and Norenzayan's review of a large database of experiments from a variety of disciplines and topics including visual perception, fairness, cooperation, spatial reasoning, categorization and inferential induction, moral reasoning, reasoning styles, self-concept and related motivations, as well as the heritability of IQ, strongly suggested that not only was there considerable variability across populations but that WEIRD subjects were decidedly unusual when compared with the rest of the human species; WEIRD subjects' responses across a variety of dimensions emerged as frequent outliers from the rest. They concluded that members of WEIRD societies, including young children, are actually among the *least* representative populations on earth, and thus represent a poor choice of population on which to base generalizations about humans.[34] If the phenomena of human choice-making, as well as the mechanisms that underlie the choice-making process, are to be understood, than clearly explanations that transcend the unique realities of the WEIRD world need to be considered.[35]

The roughly 7 billion people alive today comprise an amazing diversity of social and cultural traditions. However most of this amazing diversity exists in the margins of the planet. Nearly 99% of all people alive on earth today live within agriculture-based societies. The demands of agriculture and influence of trade and globalization have had significant homogenizing affects. As a consequence, these 6.9+ billion individuals collectively account for less than 1% of the world's complement of social and cultural traditions.[36] For most of the last roughly 150,000 to 200,000 years of modern human existence, not to mention the several millions of years of hominin evolutionary history that preceded the emergence of *Homo sapiens sapiens*, humans and their ancestors lived within small semi-isolated groups of nomadic hunters and gatherers. Over the past several thousands of years, these groups diverged into tens of thousands of unique social and cultural communities; each with their own norms and behaviors, and potentially unique mechanisms for expressing Well-Being Systems both in action and self-aspect. The differences and idiosyncrasies of these various groups are indeed of great interest, but so too are the similarities. It stands to reason that if choice-making is truly a pan-human trait, then there should not just be differences, but great commonalities across human groups, and many, if not most of such commonalities in Well-Being Systems, might well be assumed to have at least some degree of a biological basis. And so it seems to be.

I would claim that my Well-Being Systems model, with its focus on the seven key modalities of Well-Being, is indeed socioculturally neutral. All people need to eat, breathe, sleep and excrete wastes. All humans worry about their health and security. All people are sexually attracted to others and act in ways designed to support those attractions. All people have social relationships that they care about and seek to manage. All people reflect on their situation and envisage alternatives. And all people are at times motivated by creativity and spiritual beliefs and ideas. Thus even when the expressions of choice-making both in language and self-aspect appear to vary dramatically between peoples, the driving, well-being-related needs that underlie those choices and verbal descriptions arguably are common to all people. Although how these needs are prioritized and expressed vary, not so the well-being drivers of Well-Being; these are universal to all humans.[37]

## The Well-Being Systems Model

So recapping, the key assumptions underlying the Well-Being Systems model I propose are as follows:

- People constantly make choices in an effort to satisfy needs; collectively choices and needs and the sensing and acting that mediate between the choices and needs combine to form a Well-Being System.
- Well-Being Systems were selected for over evolutionary time because perceptions of well-being correlated with enhanced fitness.
- Creating well-being is challenging, as is maintaining well-being. As a consequence, choice-making on behalf of well-being is primarily designed to achieve short-term well-being and is assessed, moment by moment.
- Well-being is always framed through the lens of self-perception. Self-perceptions allow a person to distinguish and judge the quality of his reality relative to his surroundings, which in turn provides a concrete frame of reference for making actionable choices.
- Every human is comprised of not just a single Well-Being System, but trillions upon trillions of Well-Being Systems.
- Although these myriad Well-Being Systems all have distinct characteristics they all share a common, ancient origin and generally reflect seven broad underlying modalities of need—Continuity, Individuality, Sexuality, Sociality, Relationality, Reflectivity and Creativity & Spirituality.
- Every human choice and every resulting action represents an individually unique response originating from a desire to satisfy one or frequently some combination of these seven core self-related needs, i.e., purpose.

- Human Well-Being Systems come in a wide range of forms and sizes with some located entirely within the brain, some entirely within individual cells and others distributed across large areas of the body.

- Despite their varied size and distribution, signals from the vast majority of Well-Being Systems find their way to the brain where they are monitored and processed. The millions of competing signals coming from both internal and external sources vie for dominance, the "fittest" are selected, resulting in choices and actions, which in turn are monitored to determine whether or not well-being is enhanced and maintained.

- Emotion evolved as a device for facilitating the maintenance of Well-Being Systems. Signals with high emotional valence are deemed worth attending to. High emotional valence also makes choices and actions more likely to be memorable (and consciously discernable) and thus likely to influence future perceptions of self and need.

- Most of the activity involved in the functioning of Well-Being Systems operates below the level of conscious awareness. Individuals typically become aware of these processes through secondary, parallel processes, e.g., emotions. Thus a person's verbal descriptions about the nature and functioning of their Well-Being Systems, as expressed through Self-Aspects, can provide useful clues about underlying processes but should never be viewed as fully accurate representations of these processes.

## Conclusion

So as I bring this first section of the book to a conclusion, I would assert that my Well-Being Systems model provides a theoretically sound and plausible way to effectively describe the fluidity and complex adaptability of life in general, and humans in particular. The Well-Being Systems model offers a comprehensive way to understand the macro processes affecting observable human behaviors and accompanying narrative explanations of how and why individuals choose to act in the ways they do. Equally, if not more importantly, the Well-Being Systems model offers an explanation for the micro processes as well, with fractal-like commonalities occurring at each biological level, starting at the biochemical level. However considerable caution needs to be used when interpreting either macro or micro processes since the tools currently available for deciphering the immense complexity of interlocking and synergistic Well-Being Systems is limited and often subject to perceptual bias. This is particularly true with regard to the standard tool of social science, interpretations of verbalized narratives such as the one used as an example throughout this first section of the book—Teresa's description of her emigration-related experiences.

So before delving in more detail in the final section into how this Well-Being Systems model might actually be utilized as an analytical tool across differing grain sizes of experience, the next section explores the origins and workings of Well-Being Systems.

# Notes

1. Lieberman, D.E. (2013). *The story of the human body*. New York: Pantheon.
2. Csikszentmihalyi, M. (1990). *Flow: The psychology of optimal experience*. New York: Harper Perennial.
3. Nakamura, J. & Csikszentmihalyi, M. (2009). Flow theory and research. In C.R. Snyder & S. Lopez (Eds.). *Handbook of positive psychology* (pp. 195–206). Oxford: Oxford University Press.
4. Kirshenbaum, S. (2011). *The science of kissing*. New York: Grand Central Publishing.
   Keeler, J., Roth, E., Neuser, B., Spitsbergen, J.M., Waters, D.J. & Vianney, J.-M. (2015). The neurochemistry and social flow of singing: Bonding and oxytocin. *Frontiers of Human Neuroscience*, 9, 518–525. Retrieved December 31, 2016. www.ncbi.nlm.nih.gov/pmc/articles/PMC4585277/
5. Maslow, A.H. (1943). A theory of human motivation. *Psychological Review*, 50(4), 370–396.
   Privette, G. (1983). Peak experience, peak performance, and flow: A comparative analysis of positive human experiences. *Journal of Personality and Social Psychology*, 45(6), 1361–1368.
6. Csikszentmihalyi, M. (1990). *Flow: The psychology of optimal experience*. New York: Harper Perennial.
7. Geertz, C. (1973). *The interpretation of cultures*. New York: Basic Books.
8. Bruner, J. (1986). *Actual minds, possible worlds*. Cambridge, MA: Harvard University Press.
9. Kuhlmeier, V., Wynn, K. & Bloom, P. (2003). Attribution of dispositional states by 12-month olds. *Psychological Science*, 14, 402–408.
10. Howe, M.L. & Courage, M.L. (1997). The emergence and early development of autobiographical memory. *Psychological Review*, 104, 499–523.
11. McAdams, D.P. (2008). Personal narratives and the life story. In O. John, R. Robins & L.A. Pervin (Eds.), *Handbook of personality: Theory and research* (3rd ed., pp. 242–262). New York: Guilford Press.
12. Baron-Cohen, S. (1995). *Mindblindness: An essay on autism and theory of mind*. Cambridge, MA: MIT Press.
13. Fivush, R. & Nelson, K. (2004). Culture and language in the emergence of autobiographical memory. *Psychological Science*, 15, 573–577.
14. McAdams, D.P. (2008). Personal narratives and the life story. In O. John, R. Robins & L.A. Pervin (Eds.), *Handbook of personality: Theory and research* (3rd ed.). New York: Guilford Press, p. 251.
15. Piaget, J. (1957). *Construction of reality in the child*. London: Routledge & Kegan Paul.
16. Habermas, T. & Bluck, S. (2000). Getting a life: The emergence of the life story in adolescence. *Psychological Bulletin*, 126, 748–769.
17. Habermas, T. & Bluck, S. (2000). Getting a life: The emergence of the life story in adolescence. *Psychological Bulletin*, 126, 748–769.
   Habermas, T. & Paha, C. (2001). The development of coherence in adolescents' life narratives. *Narrative Inquiry*, 11, 35–54.
18. Seigel, J. (2005). *The idea of the self: Thought and experience in Western Europe since the seventeenth century*. Cambridge: Cambridge University Press.
19. McAdams, D.P. (2008). Personal narratives and the life story. In O. John, R. Robins & L.A. Pervin (Eds.), *Handbook of personality: Theory and research* (3rd ed., pp. 242–262). New York: Guilford Press.
20. Bluck, S. & Gluck, J. (2004). Making things better and learning a lesson: Experiencing wisdom across the lifespan. *Journal of Personality*, 72, 543–572.
   Pasupathi, M. & Mansour, E. (2006). Adult age differences in autobiographical reasoning in narratives. *Developmental Psychology*, 42, 798–808.
   See also Erikson, E.H. (1963). *Childhood and society* (2nd ed.). New York: Norton.
21. Bartlett, F. (1932). *Remembering*. Cambridge: Cambridge University Press.

22. Eagleman, D. (2015). *The brain: The story of you.* New York: Pantheon.
23. Conway, M.A. & Loveday, C. (2015). Remembering, imagining, false memories & personal meanings. *Consciousness and Cognition, 33,* 574–581.
    Wells, C., Morrison, C.M. & Conway, M.A. (2014). Adult recollections of childhood memories: What details can be recalled? *Quarterly Journal of Experimental Psychology, 67*(7), 1249–1261.
24. Wegner, D.M. (2002). *The illusion of conscious will.* Cambridge, MA: MIT Press.
25. NOTE: Although related, events in time and space are not linearly related. In other words, although many things happening for example at the molecular or cellular level happen over short periods of time, sometimes molecular events can play out over much longer time frames such as when an ionizing radiation can cause cells to mutate, but the mutations may only happen years after the fact. Similarly, although one typically thinks of galactic events happening over long time frames, like light years, many of the most significant events in the history of our universe happened in the first fractions of a second after the Big Bang.
26. Worth noting is that what is considered salient, memorable and worthy of mention varies as a function of cultural norms. Thus what might be included within the narrative of someone like Teresa may or may not be deemed salient, memorable and noteworthy in the narratives of other cultures.
27. The exception to this rule is when an individual possesses considerable education or training that makes them attend to these events, for example how a physician, athlete, artist or psychologist might approach daily human experience.
28. In fact, there are many social scientists who insist that all choices, learning and behavior are mediated through language, either spoken language or internal language, e.g., socioculturalists who base their theories on the work of Russian psychologist Lev Vygotsky (Vygotsky, L.S. (1978). *Mind in society: The development of higher psychological processes.* Cambridge, MA: Harvard University Press); this despite evidence that clearly a wide assortment of choices, learning and behavior happen beyond outside the realm of language.
29. e.g., Raven, D., Van Vucht Tijssen, L. & de Wolf, J. (Eds.). (1992). *Cognitive relativism and social science.* Piscataway, NJ: Transaction Publishers.
30. Henrich, J., Heine, S.J. & Norenzayan, A. (2010). The weirdest people in the world? *Behavioral and Brain Sciences, 33*(2–3), 61–83.
31. For example, not only do most social scientists, neuroscientists, physiologists and philosophers work in universities located in major, industrialized urban communities but also they were born and live in those same types of communities. Also problematic is the fact that most of the subjects used in human research come from these very same socioeconomic pools, often drawn from a single demographic since they are disproportionately university students. The assumption that Creativity-Spirituality-related purposes should be privileged over Continuity or Sexuality-related purposes is an example of WEIRDness.
32. e.g., Caldarado, N. (2007). Caching, money, magic, derivatives, mana and modern finance. *Journal of World Anthropology: Occasional Papers, 3*(2), 1–47.
    Peoples, H., Duda, P. & Marlowe, F. (2016). Hunter-gatherers and the origins of religion. *Human Nature, 1,* 1–22. doi:10.1007/s12110-016-9260-0
33. Henrich, J., Heine, S.J. & Norenzayan, A. (2010). The weirdest people in the world? *Behavioral and Brain Sciences, 33*(2–3), 61.
34. Henrich, J., Heine, S.J. & Norenzayan, A. (2010). The weirdest people in the world? *Behavioral and Brain Sciences, 33*(2–3), 61.
35. Brooker, L. & Woodhead, M. (2008). *Developing positive identities.* London: The Open University.
36. Diamond, J. (2012). *The world until yesterday.* New York: Viking.
37. Schacter, D.L., Wegner, D. & Gilbert, D. (2007). *Psychology.* New York: Worth Publishers, pp. 26–27.

# PART II

# Evolution and Workings of Well-Being Systems

# 7

# CONTINUITY (ORIGINATING MORE THAN 3.7 BILLION YEARS AGO)

The roots of Well-Being Systems, in particular Continuity-related needs, reach all the way down to the beginnings of life itself. I begin this chapter by providing a thumbnail sketch of the evolutionary origins of life and Continuity-related Well-Being Systems and some basics about how these Systems work. Next, in an effort to better illustrate what Continuity-related choice-making looks like, I fast-forward to the present and provide two examples of human Continuity-related Well-Being Systems in action. The first example focuses on the extreme situation when the needs of a single Continuity-related Well-Being System dominate the life of the individual while the second example highlights how all Well-Being Systems, even those related to the most basic physiological processes, can and do adapt to the demands and realities of environmental conditions.

## Origins of Life and the Evolution of Well-Being

Although there are many hundreds of creation myths, and dozens of scientific origin theories, the following represents the current best scientific guess about the origins of life. The Earth is over four and a half billion years old. Massive asteroids and other extra-terrestrial objects likely bombarded the planet almost continuously over the first 500 million years or so. The largest of these impacts would have created such huge heat storms and disturbances that they would have functionally sterilized the planet of any early life forms, should they have existed. As the solar system settled down and these bombardments began to subside, conditions on earth would have begun to stabilize, particularly in the vast seas that covered the planet. However, almost certainly occasional impacts would have still occurred, each one heating up the ocean to near or over the boiling point. It is probable that life evolved numerous times on the early earth, but it is thought that it is highly likely for there to have been one or more hot-ocean "bottlenecks"—periods when only hyperthermophiles (organisms who prefer living in water at or near the boiling point) would have survived.[1] Close relatives of these earliest hyperthermophilic life forms can still be found today, living near deep-sea, hydrothermal vents. From these extreme beginnings it is believed that life evolved, diversified and spread so that by about at least 3.7 billion years ago life was well established on earth and most of the principal biochemical pathways that sustain the modern biosphere had evolved and were global in scope.[2]

The primordial earth of roughly 4 billion years before the present was an immense maze of ponds, lakes and warm, shallow seas exposed to cycles of heat and cold, ultraviolet light and rain.[3] As has now been replicated numerous times in laboratories around the world, conditions such as these lead to a wide range of spontaneous chemical reactions. Consequently, it is assumed that the waters of the primordial earth became increasingly stocked with a vast assortment of chemicals. Combinations of molecules formed, broke up, and reformed, their energy links formed by the constant energy input of sunlight and intermittent lightning strikes. Scientists have speculated that under these conditions, and in the absence of oxygen, increasingly complex molecule chains would have formed, and remained intact for ever longer periods of time. At some point, a critical boundary was crossed and these various molecules began to interact in ways that were "auto-catalyzing"—cyclical processes that not only consumed but replaced key elements and created self-perpetuating systems characteristic of life. The more protected and concentrated the chemicals were the longer and more complex and self-reinforcing it is assumed their activities would have become.[4]

Chemicals naturally flow from areas of high concentration to areas of low concentration; this is called diffusion. Although passive diffusion probably generally worked in the favor of proto-life forms in replacing depleted chemicals and moving noxious chemicals away from them, it ultimately would have been too slow or too haphazard to fully meet the needs of the burgeoning proto-organism population. Sometimes needed chemicals were either not sufficiently plentiful or were too plentiful to depend upon diffusion to insure a suitable environment. Seemingly very early in the history of life, perhaps by as early as 3.7 billion years ago, some of these proto-living things evolved the ability to sidestep the slow process of diffusion and became capable of moving chemicals against a gradient, as and when needed.[5] In other words, early life forms evolved the ability to make choices. They possessed the ability to detect an imbalance of specific atoms or molecules and act upon that perceived imbalance; this was the earliest Well-Being System. Some scientists believe the need to lower concentrations of the potentially toxic, positively charged calcium atom was the first need achieved by these first Well-Being Systems;[6] others have argued the goal was manipulation of sodium concentrations.[7]

Maintaining a chemical imbalance, whether with calcium, sodium or some other atom or molecule, would have required some kind of semi-permeable barrier; a barrier that kept the "good" stuff in and the "bad" stuff out but had "gates" that could selectively be opened to allow the movement of these stuffs if and when needed. It is seemingly impossible to have a permeable membrane without possessing what are known as membrane proteins and translocases (a general term for a protein that assists in moving another molecule) to shuttle essential materials in and out of the cell. But the reverse is equally true. It is unlikely that very specialized membrane proteins were able to form without some kind of a membrane already being initially present within which to function. Thus it has been hypothesized that over the course of repeated natural "experiments" an initially permeable, porous membrane eventually evolved that integrated specialized proteins into its structure such that the whole structure ultimately was capable of being a single, highly specialized and efficient membrane system—capable of being both permeable and impermeable, depending upon need.[8] The evolution of a permeable membrane surrounding the internal biochemical machinery of life appears to have been a very early and key event in the history of life.[9] Then as now, the relationship between a living organism and some element of its environment is determined primarily by how that element is "perceived" by the living organism relative to its needs.[10]

Over time living things evolved the ability to distinguish between whole sets of atoms or molecules, under different conditions and in different locations both inside and outside the organism. Given the diversity of strategies used by extant organisms for this kind of chemical recognition process, it seems likely that there was not a single evolutionary event, but several convergent evolutionary events.[11] The net result though was consistent. All living things evolved the ability to selectively recognize and respond to a wide range of chemicals and molecules in a self-referential manner, and act upon those chemicals differently depending upon their needs in the moment; all in order to achieve and as best as possible maintain organismal well-being. As always, by well-being is meant a state that more often than not improves the organism's chances of survival by insuring a positive balance of everything from nutrients to thermoregulation. These Continuity-related Well-Being processes, what biologists call homeostasis, make life possible.

Not only are Continuity-related choice-making processes ubiquitous among living things, these processes designed to insure the smooth physiological functioning of the organism represent a significant focus of every organism's daily life, including humans. This statement might strike many readers as odd since most affluent 21st century people only occasionally, and then only in terms of nuance rather than in terms of necessity, give much thought to these Continuity-related needs. However, should someone find herself in extremis, such as when deprived of food, water, warmth, sleep or clean, oxygenated air to breathe, her thoughts would be totally focused on Continuity. Extreme situations provide a useful lens through which to more deeply probe the nature of the Continuity modality. Few situations are as extreme as war.

## Continuity-Related Well-Being Systems: An Overview

Dear Mother,

War is Hell. That is a summary of my life right now, but I'm sure you and the children would not be satisfied with a one sentence letter. So here is what I've been up to.

We have been spending the past few months in the trenches. I highly doubt that these trenches are any safer than normal warfare. There is constant disease and death. The smells are putrid. If you really need an idea, imagine dead bodies, human waste, and men who haven't showered in months. There are many times where we are ankle deep in mud for weeks on end. Many of us have trench foot (a horrible condition where our feet become waterlogged and frozen).

Under all these conditions, sometimes I wonder if it's really worth it to serve our country. Many fellows decided it wasn't. They shot themselves "accidentally" so that they may go home instead of serving.

I must go now. Take care of yourselves and pray for me and my comrades.

Your loving son,<br>Karl

P.S. If it isn't any trouble, could you please send me some socks? All of mine are in horrid condition.[12]

War is hell, and World War I was particularly hellish. Most World War I soldiers willingly enlisted, at least early on, filled with a patriotic fervor that made them feel like they were part of something much larger than themselves. They had no idea what they were getting themselves into. Most believed the propaganda that the war would be over quickly, and they enthusiastically volunteered to fight for the glory and honor of their country. But as the war dragged on, conditions deteriorated, and for most, getting through each day was a challenge with the chief enemy typically being environmental conditions rather than the opposing side's soldiers. World War I was particularly hard on soldiers on the Western Front since most spent months on end in sordid trenches living without clean water, dry clothes or sufficient food. As described above, under these conditions the role of Well-Being Systems involved with basic physiological needs became front and center in a soldier's mind. Although all people (like the soldier above) have the ability to describe their physiological needs using self-aspects, they have no real ability to accurately perceive or describe the actual events going on inside of their body that make them feel so physically miserable.

However because Continuity-related Well-Being Systems have been long understood to be central to the functioning of life, biologists have spent years attempting to fill this void so that they can accurately describe how these internal processes work.[13] As described in the previous section, Well-Being Systems are not a single process, but a series of interlocking processes, beginning with the ability to perceive internal or external changes, which are "processed" by some mechanism and result in a response. The response results in changes, which are again perceived and monitored. The key is the feedback mechanism that monitors events and triggers an action if some pre-determined threshold is violated. In the language of systems theory, there are two main ways that an organism could theoretically respond to a perceived threshold imbalance, either through a negative feedback system or a positive feedback system. Negative feedback is a reaction in which the system responds in such a way as to reverse the direction of change. For example, when the concentration of glucose in the body falls below an ideal level, the cells of the body signal the brain that it is necessary to increase the intake of food. Positive feedback systems are responses designed to amplify changes in a particular variable in order to achieve a prospective balance. In other words, if the organism perceives some critical chemical is enhancing an experience, it can trigger mechanisms to increase that critical chemical. An example of a positive feedback mechanism is the contractions that accompany child birth. During labor, a hormone called oxytocin is released that intensifies and speeds up contractions. The increase in contractions causes more oxytocin to be released and the cycle goes on until the baby is born. The birth ends the release of oxytocin and ends the positive feedback mechanism.

Since both of these types of feedback systems produce the same result— maintenance of continuous state—evolution could and seemingly has selected for both approaches. However investigators have discovered that the vast majority of Continuity-related processes operate by negative feedback.[14] It is speculated that the reason for this is that although positive feedback strategies work, they are harder to control and thus have been less frequently selected for over evolutionary time.[15] However, natural selection does not necessarily result in the most "efficient" or "elegant" solutions; evolution selects survival-oriented processes without design.[16]

Although there is always variation, both between individuals and even within individuals, these kinds of Continuity-related Well-Being Systems have evolved to insure that a person's various physiological processes are maintained within very narrow ranges. These systems often have been conceptualized as having a fixed "set-point" like a thermostat, but in fact Well-Being Systems are always dynamic and self-correcting, with the capacity to change and modify as circumstances demand.[17] When a system is perceived to be in balance, the choice-making is straightforward—continue doing whatever one has been doing in the past moment. However, when a system is perceived to be out of balance, then choices and actions need to be undertaken in order to return the system back to what is perceived to be optimal for survival. The perceived urgency is totally dependent upon the intensity of signals arriving in the brain; the more intense the signals the more crucial and immediate is the need for corrective action. Hunger provides a useful case study for how this works.

## Hunger: An Example of a Continuity-Related Well-Being System in Action

> We've been without rations for days. Finally got some food tonight, no bread, I'm still hungry.[18]

Food shortages are a common problem during wartime. For example, it is estimated that as many, if not more, Turkish soldiers died during World War I from hunger and malnutrition-related diseases than died from direct combat.[19] Even among the Allied forces, tens of thousands of soldiers died of starvation and many thousands more from diseases associated with poor nutrition.

In the years following WWI considerable research was conducted to better understand both the physiology and psychology of starvation. But the classic study on how dietary restriction can influence human behavior was an experiment conducted during the Second World War known as the Minnesota Starvation Experiment.[20] In November 1944, 36 young men took up residence in the corridors and rooms of the University of Minnesota football stadium. They were not members of the football team. Rather, they were volunteers preparing for an almost yearlong experiment on the effects of starvation. Although there were numerous anecdotal reports of the effects of famine and starvation prior to this time, there was little in the scientific literature that described its physiological and psychological effects.

As summarized by psychologists David Baker and Natacha Keramidas,

> Subject selection was stringent. Subjects had to be male, single and demonstrate good physical and mental health (largely based on the newly developed Minnesota Multiphasic Personality Inventory). They also had to show an ability to get along well with others under trying circumstances and interest in relief work. The final 36 men were selected from more than 200 often volunteers and in November 1944 made their way to the University of Minnesota to begin their service.
>
> The research protocol called for the men to lose 25 percent of their normal body weight. They spent the first three months of the study eating a normal diet of 3,200 calories a day, followed by six months of semi-starvation at 1,570 calories a day (divided between breakfast and lunch), then a restricted rehabilitation period of three months eating 2,000 to 3,200 calories a day, and finally an eight-week unrestricted rehabilitation period during which there were no limits on caloric intake. Their diet consisted of foods widely available in Europe during the war, mostly potatoes, root vegetables, bread and macaroni. The men were required to work 15 hours per week in the lab, walk 22 miles per week and participate in a variety of educational activities for 25 hours a week. Throughout the experiment, the researchers measured the physiological and psychological changes brought on by near starvation.[21]

Changes in behavior and interest happened rapidly as the men experienced near-starvation. They would dream and fantasize about food, read and talk about food and savor the two meals a day they were given. Much of the day was now spent planning how they would eat their allocated food. The subjects of the study were often caught between conflicting desires to gulp down their food ravenously or to consume it so slowly that the taste and smell of each morsel of food would be fully appreciated. The latter approach seemed to win out. In order to prolong their enjoyment of the food eaten, the amount of time spent eating a meal incrementally increased over the course of the experiment. The men would eat in silence and would devote their total attention to the consumption of their food. By the end of the starvation period of the study, the men would dawdle for almost two hours over a meal that they previously consumed in a matter of minutes.

Irritability and frequent outbursts of anger became increasingly common, although the men had quite tolerant dispositions prior to the beginning of the experiment. The men became reluctant to plan activities and to make decisions and they would spend more and more time alone. They claimed it became "too much trouble or too tiring" to have contact with people. For most subjects, anxiety became more evident. As the experiment progressed, many of the formerly even-tempered men began biting their nails or smoking because they felt nervous. Apathy also became common, and some men who had been quite fastidious neglected various aspects of personal hygiene. During semi-starvation, two subjects developed disturbances of "psychotic" proportions. The extraordinary impact of semi-starvation was reflected in the social changes experienced by most of the volunteers. Although originally quite gregarious, the men became progressively more withdrawn and isolated. Humor and the sense of comradeship diminished amidst growing feelings of social inadequacy. The volunteers' social contacts with women also declined sharply. Those who continued to see women socially found that the relationships became strained. Referring to his relationship with his girlfriend, one volunteer stated, "It's almost too much trouble to see her even when she visits me in the lab. It requires effort to hold her hand. Entertainment must be tame. If we see a show, the most interesting part of it is contained in scenes where people are eating."[22] It was not just social interest that deteriorated, sexual interest also was drastically reduced.

Although outward signs of normality did return to most of the men once they were again provided sufficient calories, some things, including sexual interest, took a surprisingly long time to return to pre-experimental levels. Even after three months, the men judged themselves to be far from normal in this area. However, after eight months of re-nourishment, virtually all of the men had recovered their interest in sex.

The profound effects of starvation clearly illustrate how the needs of Continuity can dominate choice-making, totally overwhelming other need-driven Well-Being Systems, even other Continuity-related Systems. This makes complete evolutionary sense. Over billions of years of evolution, a major threat to the survival of all living things was starvation. The same is true for human evolution. If the body weight of humanity's early ancestors had not been carefully modulated and controlled, they would have died. The Minnesota Starvation Experiment clearly illustrates how lack of food can and does dramatically influence choice-making and behavior. A hungry person will subordinate most choice-making to the singular goal of obtaining and consuming food, including normal social and sexual functioning.

People have long understood the behavior altering effects of physiological deprivation, including and particularly food deprivation, and have used this knowledge during wartime in efforts to control other's behaviors. A notable and long-standing example being the wartime tactic of the siege, where an entire population, soldier or civilian is surrounded and prevented from leaving or restocking their provisions. If the siege is successful, the resulting desperation caused by starvation eventually leads the surrounded population to accept whatever terms the sieging army demands.

Many people, including many social scientists, begin with the assumption that the needs related to Continuity-related Well-Being Systems are "hard-wired" and thus not really choice-making systems. A few Well-Being Systems, such as the Systems associated with the need to breathe, do seem to be inalterably locked in, but surprisingly most Continuity-related Choice-Well-Being Systems, like virtually all Choice-Well-Being Systems evolved to be adaptive systems and thus, to a surprising degree, nearly all are susceptible to modification under the right conditions.

## The Responsiveness of Well-Being Systems to Environmental Conditions

Take for example the Well-Being System-controlled need to stay alive. Presumably no Well-Being System should be more hard-wired than those involved with avoiding behaviors that result in one's own death. Yet the entire machinery of war depends upon soldiers who are willing put themselves in harm's way. Although getting soldiers to willingly choose to place themselves in deadly situations is never an easy task, for centuries armies have managed this feat, taking almost any young (historically) male civilian and turning him into a soldier with all the right reflexes and attitudes. And perhaps most amazingly, this transformation can be achieved in only a matter of a few weeks or months. The key, according to historian Gwyn Dwyer is in who the army selects and the environment to which they are subjected.[23]

Armies very selectively recruit young people, ideally with no more than 17 to 20 years' experience of the world, most of it as children. You can try and re-condition older individuals to the ideals of army life but they never really fully adapt to or like it. Adolescents are more malleable, plus they possess enthusiasm and naiveté. Historically, most recruits came from well-being impoverished situations. Once in the army, job number one is building up an initial sense of well-being. New recruits are given new clothes, quality meals (often better than they have ever experienced growing up) and a sense of comradery and purpose (again something that was often lacking from most of their earlier experience). Then, in a totally controlled environment, individuals go through a ritualized conversion process, what is currently referred to as basic training. Basic training is nothing short of psychological manipulation on a grand scale, the essentials of which have been perfected over centuries,[24] as the following quote attests:

> Just think of how the soldier is treated. While still a child he is shut up in the barracks. During his training he is always being knocked about. If he makes the least mistake he is beaten, a burning blow on his body, another on his eye, perhaps his head is laid open with a wound. He is battered and bruised with flogging. On the march . . . they hang heavy loads round his neck like that of an ass.
>
> *(Egyptian, ca. 1500 B.C.E.)*[25]

The goal of basic training involves a brief but intense period of indoctrination within a highly controlled environment whose sole purpose is to change the recruits' perceptions of self and need; revising values, loyalties and norms so as to "retool" the individual's Well-Being Systems. Interestingly, the teaching of basic military skills like how to shoot a rifle come along for the ride. Although learning military skills during training is valuable, it is not a necessity, since these are things that can and are learned "on the job." Not so the conditioning necessary to overcome a person's innate survival instincts in the face of threat.

Over weeks and months incipient soldiers are totally isolated from their normal civilian environment and placed under enormous physical and mental pressure, with only one right way to think and behave. The trainee is required to learn to follow new schedules and procedures, reinforced by lots and lots of repetition. They are subjected to harsh physical conditions, such as wallowing through the mud, and an ever-present sense of risk, such as bullets flying over their head and explosions occurring all around them. The goal is always the same though, to insure that the incipient soldier's perceptions of self-related need, choice and action become remolded in ways consistent with what the military deems appropriate. A key element of training is learning that their well-being depends upon them sublimating all of their past learned motivations and choices to those of their commanding officer.

> I can motivate a recruit and in third phase, if I tell him to jump off the third deck, he'll jump off the third deck. Like I said before, it's a captive audience and I can train that guy; I can get him to do anything I want him to do. . . . But as far as motivation—here, we can motivate them to anything you want, in recruit training.
>
> *(U.S. Marine Corps drill instructor, Parris Island, Georgia)*[26]

Basic training works. After training, the newly minted soldiers have rewired most of their Well-Being Systems to conform to the military's version of well-being. Supported by an entire infrastructure, the soldier has learned to redefine his every need and response. The soldier chooses to sleep, eat and exercise on a military schedule, to treat as family individuals who were total strangers a mere month or so earlier. More fundamentally, new soldiers have learned that physiological hardship can and should be endured. They have learned not to flinch or retreat when an explosion happens right next to them. And they have learned to unquestionably obey their commanding officers, even when commanded to do things that seem likely to put them in extreme danger. Obviously basic training is not fool-proof, and the fear engendered by the extreme horrors of war can cause some soldiers to revert to previous Well-Being System patterns. But over millennia, basic training has worked sufficiently well at rewiring Well-Being Systems to insure that not only do large numbers of individuals regularly accept physiological discomforts and life-threatening circumstances that normal people would find unbearable, but large percentages opt to keep doing it year after year.[27]

People clearly respond to their environment and adapt their perceptions of need to the realities imposed by their surroundings, including even the most basic physiological needs associated with the modality of Continuity. The same is true for the needs of the equally basic and almost as ancient set of Well-Being Systems associated with the modality of Individuality.

## Notes

1. Nisbet, E.G. & Sleep, N.H. (2001). The habitat and nature of early life. *Nature*, 409(6823), 1083–1091.
2. Nisbet, E.G. & Sleep, N.H. (2001). The habitat and nature of early life. *Nature*, 409(6823), 1083–1091.
3. I have relied heavily for this description on Margulis, L. & Sagan, D. (1986). *Microcosmos*. New York: Summit Books.
4. Margulis, L. & Sagan, D. (1986). *Microcosmos*. New York: Summit Books.
   Torday, J.S. & Miller, W.B., Jr. (2017). A systems approach to physiologic evolution: From micelles to consciousness. *Journal of Cellular Physiology*. https://www.unbound medicine.com/medline/citation/28112403/A_systems_approach_to_physiologic_ evolution:_From_micelles_to_consciousness. Retrieved June 7, 2017.
5. Margulis, L. & Sagan, D. (1986). *Microcosmos*. New York: Summit Books.
   Deamer, D.W. (1986). Role of amphiphilic compounds in the evolution of membrane structure on the early earth. *Origins of Life and the Evolution of the Biosphere*, 17, 3–25.
   Deamer, D., Dworkin, J.P., Sandford, S.A., Bernstein, M.P. & Allamandola, L.J. (2002). The first cell membranes. *Astrobiology*, 2, 371–381.
6. Martin, W. & Russell, M.J. (2003). On the origin of cells: A hypothesis for the evolutionary transitions from abiotic geochemistry to chemoautotrophic prokaryotes, and from prokaryotes to nucleated cells. *Philosophical Transactions of the Royal Society of London, B-Biological Sciences*, 358(1429), 59–85.
   Making the case for calcium regulation as key to nearly all life processes, evolutionary medicine researcher John Torday stated, "Biochemically, [calcium/lipid homeostasis] is the operating principle that lies at the bottom of the balancing selection for vertebrate physiology, beginning with the first instantiation of life, all the way to consciousness and thought because both paramecia and we utilize the same calcium fluxes for integrating physiology and the environment. If you expose yeast to 0 x gravity they lose their ability to regulate calcium because they've lost their orientation to the environment (they also cannot reproduce, which is probably a consequence of the loss of calcium flow through the cell) so they're comatose. In slime molds the absence of food in their environment forces them from an amoeboid locomotor form to a colonial sessile form due to a fundamental change in calcium flux too. In us, when sperm meets egg there's a calcium burst that doesn't stop till we die. . . . Bottom line is that when choices are made, if they align calcium fluxes effectively it results in optimal adaptation." (J. Torday, Personal Communication, January 30, 2017).
7. Mulkidjanian, A.Y., Galperin, M.Y., Makarova, K.S., Wolf, Y.I. & Koonin, E.V. (2008). Evolutionary primacy of sodium bioenergetics. *Biology Direct*, 3, 13–32.
8. Mulkidjanian, A.Y., Galperin, M.Y. & Koonin, E.V. (2009). Co-evolution of primordial membranes and membrane proteins. *Trends in the Biochemical Sciences*, 34(4), 206–215.
9. Margulis, L. & Sagan, D. (1986). *Microcosmos*. New York: Summit Books.
10. Falk, J.H. (1981). *The origin of self*. Unpublished Manuscript.
    Varela, F. (2000). Four batons for the future of cognitive science. In B. Wiens (Ed.), *Envisioning Knowledge*. Cologne: Dumont.
    Varela, F. (1999). Steps to a science of Interbeing: Unfolding the Dharma implicit in modern cognitive science. In S. Bachelor, G. Claxton, & G. Watson (Eds.), *The psychology of awakening*. New York: Rider/Random House.

Torday J.S. & Miller, W.B., Jr. (2017). A systems approach to physiologic evolution: From micelles to consciousness. *Journal of Cellular Physiology*. https://www.unbound medicine.com/medline/citation/28112403/A_systems_approach_to_physiologic_ evolution:_From_micelles_to_consciousness. Retrieved June 7, 2017.

11. Soyer, O.S. (2010). The promise of evolutionary systems biology: Lessons from bacterial chemotaxis. *Science Signals*, 3(128), 23–48.

12. Letters from a German Soldier in WWI to his mother. Retrieved March 3, 2014. www.teenink.com/fiction/historical_fiction/article/517658/Letters-From-a-German-Soldier-in-WWI-to-his-mother/

13. Typically, all of these processes have been described using the generic term "homeostasis."

14. Berntson, G.G. & Cacioppo, J.T. (1990). From homeostasis to allodynamic regulation. In J.T. Cacioppo, L.G. Tassinary & G.G. Berntson (Eds.), *Handbook of psychophysiology* (2nd ed., pp. 459–481). Cambridge: Cambridge University Press.

15. Berntson, G.G. & Cacioppo, J.T. (1990). From homeostasis to allodynamic regulation. In J.T. Cacioppo, L.G. Tassinary & G.G. Berntson (Eds.), *Handbook of psychophysiology* (2nd ed., pp. 459–481). Cambridge: Cambridge University Press.

16. Dawkins, R. (1986). *The blind watchmaker: Why the evidence of evolution reveals a universe without design*. New York: Norton.

17. Damasio, A.R. & Damasio, H. (2016). Exploring the concept of homeostasis and considering its implication for economics. *Journal of Economic Behavior & Organization*, 126, 125–129.

18. Personal diary of William J. 'Bill' Schira in World War I. Retrieved March 4, 2014. http://net.lib.byu.edu/estu/wwi/memoir/Schira/Schira.htm

19. Zürcher, E.J. (1999). The Ottoman conscription system in theory and practice, 1844–1918. In Erik Jan Zürcher (Ed.), *Arming the state: Military conscription in the Middle East and Central Asia*, London: I.B. Tauris, 88.

20. Keys, A., Brožek, J., Henschel, A., Mickelsen, O. & Taylor, H.L. (1950). *The biology of human starvation* (2 Vols). St. Paul, MN: University of Minnesota Press.

21. Baker, D. & Keramidas, N. (2013). The psychology of hunger. *Monitor on Psychology*, 44(9), 66–67.

22. Cited in: Garner, D.M. & Garfinkel, P.E. (Eds.). (1997). *Handbook of treatment for eating disorders* (2nd ed., chapter 8, pp. 145–177). New York: Guilford Press, p. 160.

23. Dwyer, G. (1985). *War*. New York: Crown.

24. Dwyer, G. (1985). *War*. New York: Crown.

25. Cottrell, L. (1968). *The warrior pharaohs*. London: Evan Brothers.

26. Dwyer, G. (1985). *War*. New York: Crown, p. 110.

27. Though rates vary as a function of branch of service, race, gender and years of service, recent data show that year in and year out, roughly half of all U.S. soldiers reenlist (Military Leadership Diversity Commission. (2010). *Reenlistment rates across the services by gender and race/ethnicity*. Issue paper #31, Retention. Retrieved February 12, 2017. http://diversity.defense.gov/Portals/51/Documents/Resources/Commission/docs/Issue%20 Papers/Paper%2031%20-%20Reenlistment%20Rates%20Across%20the%20Services.pdf

# 8

# INDIVIDUALITY (ORIGINATING MORE THAN 3.5 BILLION YEARS AGO)

Individuality as a modality of Well-Being is nearly as ancient as Continuity, having also originated early-on in the history of life. I begin this chapter by describing the selection forces that propelled life to expand on the Well-Being foundations of Continuity and evolve larger, more complex Systems related to Individuality. As in the previous chapter, I follow this up with two examples demonstrating both how Individuality functions in general as well as specifically in humans. Building on the idea presented in the last chapter suggesting that all Well-Being Systems are inherently adaptive and malleable, I show how this inherent quality of Well-Being Systems has made possible the evolution of life forms capable of solving ever more complex life-challenges, at ever more complex levels of organization.

## Evolution of Individuality as a Modality of Well-Being

The earliest Well-Being Systems were focused on the needs of physiological Continuity. These Systems evolved to discriminate and make well-being-related choices at the atomic or molecular level. Seemingly from the very beginnings of life, life forms were able to recognize chemicals that were potentially harmful to them and if their internal concentration exceeded some threshold, remove them from the cell. Likewise, living things evolved the ability to recognize self-defined beneficial chemicals and selectively harvest them from the environment. Over time, life also evolved the ability to sense and actively respond to its environment. If the cell came in contact with a potentially harmful chemical in the external environment, the organism could enact some kind of avoidance behavior. But these types of Well-Being Systems were minimally effective in deterring an attack by a hostile organism such as a pathogen since a pathogen was not just a single atom or molecule endangering the organism but a larger entity, which in the broadest sense was often remarkably similar in general shape and content to the organism itself. Pathogens represented an entirely different class of need and required a whole different level of self-perception and choice-making. It was the ability to enact Well-Being Systems at this level of discrimination that I have characterized as falling within the *Individuality* modality.

On the early earth, as now, a host of organisms would have existed which were capable of capitalizing on the rich concentration of nutrients represented by early forms of life. It is not unreasonable to assume that these early pathogens/predators could have actually become quite numerous; so numerous that they threatened to totally overwhelm the early life forms who were doing all the "work" of converting free-floating molecular bits into concentrated, energy-rich packets of sugars, fats and proteins. These early pathogenic/predatory creatures were the ancestors of all the various pathogenic/predatory bacteria, worms, protists and viruses that still prey on microscopic life forms as well as collectively cause all the millions of types of diseases that afflict every form of life alive today. Numerous strategies ultimately evolved for combating these voracious scourges, in particular pathogens.

Given that all extant life share many of the same strategies for dealing with pathogens, it is likely that ancestral forms of both the pathogens and defenses against these pathogens had already evolved by the time of the last universal common ancestor.[1] Collectively, biologists refer to these various strategies as immune systems. This unique nomenclature has tended to obscure the fact that immune systems, like the homeostatic systems they evolved from, are fundamentally all variations of Well-Being Systems.

Over evolutionary time four distinct types of immune system have evolved: 1) cell membranes; 2) gene mutations; 3) innate immune systems; and 4) adaptive immune systems.[2] Humans, for example, possess all four of these types of immune systems. But even the simplest creatures, including bacteria and their even more ancient cousins the Archaea, possess and deploy multiple versions of these same immune strategies.[3] Each of these immune strategies is effective only up to a point. Like any defensive system, no immune system is 100% failsafe; all can ultimately be circumvented. As a consequence, all immune systems are involved in a never-ending arms race with their potential invaders. Natural selection always favors individuals with better ways to detect and eliminate invaders, but natural selection also favors invaders that possess better ways to avoid detection and elimination by their host. In this way, immune systems are in some ways always playing catch-up to the ever-evolving and changing invaders, who in turn are always playing catch-up with their ever-evolving hosts.[4]

All major organismal groups, including primitive single celled organisms, have evolved some form of adaptive or acquired immunity.[5] These Well-Being Systems are often quite unique and highly elaborate such that sponges have one kind of immune system, earthworms another and spinach still another. Each of these specific Well-Being Systems evolved to meet the needs of perceiving and responding to the specific type of pathogens attacking that type of organism. Some plants for example when invaded by a parasite will create poisonous chemicals that the parasite eats as it chews on the plant, but these same chemicals are also emitted to the outside world, attracting other parasites—parasites of the parasites. The attracted "hyper-parasites" follow the scent and attack the plant's parasites. Amazingly, there's evidence that plants are able to perceive and discriminate between the various species of parasite attacking them and selectively respond by emitting different chemicals for different parasites, which in turn attracts only the appropriate species of hyper-parasite needed to kill their attacker.[6]

Scientists have only just begun to unravel all of the twists and turns involved in how immune systems work; many of which seemingly represent several independent lines of evolution.[7] However the best current understanding of immune systems is that they all seem to operate in a totally analogous way.[8] The key is an ability to distinguish "self" from "non-self." Organisms learn to recognize and accept as their self those pieces and occasionally wholes of organic life that they grow up with and regularly encounter. By contrast, any pieces not recognized as self are treated as non-self. These latter new or unfamiliar pieces are typically treated with great malice.[9] Although all living things are fundamentally open systems, they have by necessity evolved to act as if they are closed systems. As will be discussed later, this simple reality turns out to have had profound implications for life. The evolution of life forms capable of perceiving themselves as a whole, as unique individuals, separate and distinct from all others, was a momentous event and appears to have arisen as a series of elaborations of earlier Well-Being Systems.[10] As a result, these new *Individuality* self-perception-based Well-Being Systems, like their predecessor *Continuity* self-perception-based Well-Being Systems, tended to operate through negative feedback processes.

Periodically new threats would emerge, presenting life forms with ever more novel and elaborate ways to disguise themselves from detection, often with devastating effects. Even today, new pathogens emerge capable of evading detection by highly evolved and successful immune systems. Recent human examples include Ebola, AIDS and most recently Zika, while historic examples include the Black Plague and Spanish Flu which killed millions upon millions of people incapable of either detecting or fighting off the pathogen. However, at least normally, there are always a few individuals who seem to be pre-adapted to surviving these outbreaks, and their descendants inherit the Well-Being Systems that enable new generations to detect and fight off the pathogen. Such has been the case since the beginning of life on earth. The result is that every living thing, including humans, inherit a vast collection of nested Individuality-activated Well-Being Systems, each keyed to recognizing and responding to molecules or configurations of molecules deemed to be foreign. Over evolutionary time, the presence of foreign entities has been perceived as diminished well-being, what humans would linguistically describe as being sick, while having no or minimal foreign entities has been perceived as feeling good or healthy, i.e., having well-being. Again over evolutionary time, being sick, low well-being, strongly correlates with reduced survival and reproductive success while being healthy, high well-being, positively correlates with enhanced survival and reproductive success.

## Health, Well-Being and Fitness

> Last week I came down with dysentery. It was dreadful, I got so weak that I was crawling about, my trousers round my feet, my backside hanging out, everything soiled. When the Sargent gave us an order to muster out, I just looked at him. I couldn't even walk.[11]

When a soldier became sick or injured they ceased to be fit for fighting. In fact, a sick or injured individual is not very good at much. When the individual's defenses are shattered, and he becomes sick or injured, life turns inward. Much like individuals suffering from malnutrition, sickness directly affects choice and behavior. More than a quarter century of research has shown that even minor illnesses such as the common cold directly influence the cognitive functioning and behavior of those afflicted.[12] In one major study, scientists compared mental functioning before and after head colds in 189 men and women from the U.K. When the subjects were healthy, they completed tests assessing reaction time, verbal-reasoning skills, memory and mood. Cold symptoms, such as sore throat and sneezing, were rated on a five-point scale. Sleep duration was assessed. Of the subjects, 48 developed upper respiratory tract infections and were retested when the illness had been present 24 to 96 hours. The remaining 141 stayed healthy and were used as controls; they were retested after 12 weeks. There were significant differences between the cold and healthy subjects on a range of measures. Colds were found to selectively affect measures of psychomotor performance, encoding of new information and memory speed and accuracy. In general, cold sufferers not only had reduced alertness and information processing capabilities, they also had a lowered perception of well-being.[13] Sick individuals make different choices than do healthy people.

Typically, when a person falls sick or gets injured, her focus tends to become narrower than normal, and the sicker or more severe the injury, the tighter the focus. Even the common cold makes it harder to concentrate, with attention continually drawn to whatever ails a person—a sore throat, running nose or rasping cough. The acute pain of an injury is particularly interesting, since even a relatively modest injury like a splinter in a finger can make it impossible to think of anything else; a person's highest priority becomes stopping the pain. When a person falls ill, he is inclined to forgo previous plans in deference to trying to rest or take whatever medicines might help alleviate the symptoms. Gone are normal desires and interests; what awareness there is shifts almost entirely to the challenges of the body. The person just wants to lie down, close his eyes, and if possible, go to sleep. In short, a person's self-perception is that they are not the same person as normal, although people cannot generally directly perceive that some other thing or being has invaded their body, the self-aspects ascribed to this state like, "I don't quite feel myself today," often reflect this reality.

Infections are literally invasions of the body by alien lifeforms; lifeforms committed to their own rather than the host's well-being. Take for example what happens when one is infected with a typical flu virus. The virus usually enters through the nose or eyes, migrates up the air passage and burrows into the airway cells. The virus is able to evade the body's immune system because in its present form it is not recognized as a non-self by the millions of circulating antibodies. Once inside the body's cells the virus hijacks the cell's genetic machinery, causing the cell to begin churning out thousands upon thousands of new virus cells. When the human cell has produced a sufficiently large number of new viruses, the virus causes the cell to break open (lyse) so that the newly replicated viruses can leave in search of new human cells to infect. Lysis effectively kills the infected human cells. This process goes on for days. The first symptoms of the flu begin to appear only after a day or two, including sneezing and wheezing, by which time the virus has created sufficient copies of itself that it is able to spread the virus beyond the person.

After several days the person begins to feel serious symptoms. The infected person is not only rapidly using up her nutrient resources in support of the virus's reproduction but she also is being debilitated because an increasing number of her cells are being destroyed as cell after cell bursts open. More importantly, her immune system is furiously trying to keep up with the now perceived invasion. The perceptible consequences of these events are the traditional flu symptoms of fever, chills, headache and aching muscles. Other symptoms can include coughing, vomiting, bleeding and diarrhea. Much of the misery stems from inflammation, the result of an immune system working full-on. All of the body's energy is being used to slay the flu viruses, which means there is precious little left over for any other activity. To keep all of the dead cell debris from clogging up the lungs, the body develops a dry cough. The throat starts to ache from the irritation, which can trigger a release of mucus. As the internal disasters going on inside the person magnify, the individual shunts more and more of her blood resources to fight against the flu virus. In extreme types of flu, the person can actually turn blue from lack of external blood supply. In really extreme cases, the redeployment of blood to fight the invasion can result in blood being diverted from the brain, causing the person to lapse into unconsciousness.

Ultimately, the only thing that prevents the flu from killing the person is the adaptive response of the immune system. Eventually the immune system learns to recognize the virus and develops antibodies and killer T-cells that lock onto and destroy the virus. More often than not, in healthy individuals, the immune system eventually finds and eliminates all of the flu viruses living inside the body, and in the process builds up a permanent store of antibodies capable of remembering this particular invader in the future. This is the essence of adaptive immunity. Unfortunately for humans, and other creatures plagued by flu-like viruses, the virus is constantly mutating and recombining with other similar viruses. The result is that by the following year, when the next strain of flu virus invades the person, she will be presented with an entirely different "appearing" virus, one likely to once again evade the immune system. Today, the basic biochemistry of how the immune system "recognizes" pathogens is relatively well understood.[14] The essence of the process is that the body is designed to recognize same and different—things that are the same are accepted and things that are different are destroyed. Some of this sense of individuality is innate, but the big insight that new immune theories afforded is that much of what determines whether something is considered "self" or "non-self" is, like basic training, learned.

Few things are more fundamental to a person's long-term survival and well-being than insuring safety from attack, and the Well-Being Systems that originally evolved as mechanisms for insuring safety from microscopic invaders at the cellular level ultimately evolved into Well-Being Systems capable of detecting and responding to self-non-self relationships at successively higher and more complex levels of organization—the tissue, organ, organismic levels, and even beyond including the social levels of the family and community. At each level, maintaining well-being involves multiple steps, but it always begins with awareness; a perception that one's Individuality has somehow been threatened. As discussed above, the reason for this is that breaches in a person's Individuality nearly always result in diminished fitness, which in turn is correlated with reduced survivability.

## Individuality: A Window Into the Workings of Well-Being Systems

Individuality-related Well-Being Systems were historically assumed to be totally rigid. It was assumed that the ways organisms defined and distinguished their "self" from others was essentially "baked-in" at birth; or if not birth very early in life. It was assumed this rigidity was true at all levels of Individuality-related need, from immune systems to social systems. A familiar example of the latter is the comfort people naturally feel towards those considered to be social "intimates" and the discomfort they feel towards those they consider social "outsiders."

Humans appear to readily recognize as part of their extended "self" that small group of individuals they regularly encounter while growing up, typically their immediate family and friends. Anyone outside this immediate social group is considered a stranger, or as anthropologists usually call these individuals who are "non-self," the "other." Seemingly this process begins to happen as early as seven to nine months after birth. At this age, babies will cry if someone they do not recognize comes into the room or they become separated from their mother or father. Although over time infants learn to tolerate strangers, from this age on trust is something that needs be earned, not something that is just automatically given. Racism and xenophobia are legacies of this evolutionary tendency of humans to early on develop strong, individuality-related responses towards people who are perceived as "different."[15]

Throughout history, humans have exhibited a knee-jerk, often violent reaction to those they consider the other. However, in many modern societies, including the one I live in, such historic aversions to individual difference are considered to be societal ills caused by inadequacies in a person's upbringing. However, all people possess a visceral distrust of difference, in large measure for reasons related to their evolutionary history. This is not to excuse those who hold racist or xenophobic views but rather to suggest that these tendencies arise from an innate need to separate and protect self from non-self. The characteristics of individuals a person comes to recognize as familiar and associated with one's immediate self, as opposed to those that do not accord with that pattern and are thus associated with strangeness, the other, are learned early in development and once learned are hard to reverse. Like all human Well-Being Systems, this System too is a product of biology, culture and lived experience. That is why even the most egalitarian upbringing is not a guarantee of racial and ethnic tolerance. Every person is likely to possess some hidden biases and have a tendency to stereotype and categorize people even if it does not rise to the level of outright prejudice.[16] Although putting people into a category is generally considered to be a negative thing, this natural human tendency evolved for basically positive reasons.[17] These types of generalizations enabled people to interact quickly and effectively with those they encountered. Every individual has to have some idea of what people are likely to be like and how they will likely behave towards them. More often than not these decisions are based on a quick, unconscious appraisal of that person's similarity and differences relative to a learned sense of self.[18] Of course the wonder of the system is that it can change; even long and deeply held beliefs can change.

Although all perceptions of self, including perceptions of Individuality, have a genetic basis, they are ultimately not directly controlled by genes. Perceptions of individual self, whether physiological, psychological or social, are always an emergent, learned process and thus at some level adaptable. Direct, personal experiences play a significant role in how these perceptions are ultimately formed. Take for example a person's relationship to their appendages. Infants are not born knowing that their hands and feet are part of them; that understanding develops over the first months after birth.[19] By the time a child leaves the crib though, they have learned to recognize that the various parts of their body are part of themselves. They know that the hands connected to their arms belong to them, not someone else. Similarly, the hands connected to someone else's arms are not their own. But what about artificial limbs? Much as with racism and xenophobia it would not be surprising to discover that over time a person could come to learn that an artificial limb is part of their unique individual self. What turns out to be surprising though is just how quickly this learning process can happen; not over days, weeks or months but seemingly in seconds.

In the 1990s a then neural science graduate student by the name of Matthew Botvinick conducted an experiment with a group of undergraduate students. In the experiment Botvinick hid one of the hands of a subject behind a screen and then placed a fake rubber hand in the subject's line of sight, positioned where their real hand would have been had it normally extended out from the body. He then simultaneously stroked both the real and the fake hands with a paint brush. Participants reported "feeling" the brush strokes on the fake hand as if it was real.[20] Subsequent research by Botvinick and others have confirmed this effect and shown that subjects respond to a range of stimuli, from pleasurable stroking to threatened stabbing, as if the fake hand was truly their own.[21] In all cases, even though the experimental subjects were clearly aware of what was going on and intellectually knew the hand was fake they involuntarily responded psychologically, physically and physiologically to actions on their fake hand as if it was real. In other words, within seconds the subject's brain had subsumed the fake hand into their sense of self; the rubber hand was perceived to be part of the person's Individuality-related Well-Being Systems, and the person responded to pleasure or threat accordingly. Collectively, what these kinds of experiments suggest is that humans, and likely other organisms as well, have the ability to adjust their perception of Individuality to an ever evolving array of life situations. Although a person acts as if his Individuality is fixed and discrete, in reality the perceptions of Individuality are far from fixed. Although this example of the malleability of Individuality seems bizarre, it at least seems credible because it is a perceptual phenomenon, a manipulation of a mental construct. But what about at the physiological level of organs or cells?

Working at the time of WWI, the pioneering plastic surgeon Harold Gillies is credited with achieving the very first successful tissue transplants.[22] Responding to the devastating effects that high impact explosives had on soldiers' faces and bodies during the war, Gillies developed a technique for successfully grafting skin from healthy parts of a soldier's body onto parts seriously damaged or disfigured and in the process is credited with allowing many of these men to live a more-or-less normal life as civilians. Following WWI, donating skin from one part of a person's body to another place on the body became common ways to treat burns and other similar ailments; though because of immune responses it was always a challenging operation.

These successes led others to dream about even broader possibilities. If it was possible to transplant a tissue or even an organ from one part of a person to another part of them, why not a transplant to an entirely different person? Despite repeated attempts over the next fifty years, almost without exception efforts to transplant tissue or organs from one person to another failed. The body treated the tissues of other people in the same ways as it did an invading pathogen. In every situation, the body always recognized the foreign body part as non-self and mounted an immune response and rejected the new part. Tissue/Organ transplantation did not become fully successful until the discovery of the powerful immunosuppressant drug cyclosporine in 1970.[23] Even then, it still took many more years of trial and error before doctors successfully learned how to consistently circumvent the problems of rejection. Unfortunately, in these early days of transplantation, the only way patients could be prevented from rejecting their new tissues or organs was to take these immunosuppressive drugs for the rest of their lives, but cyclosporine and other such drugs have very nasty side effects.

As more and more was learned about how the immune system actually works, in particular the role that natural selection and learning play in the process,[24] new techniques were developed that took an entirely new approach to the challenge of tissue rejection. It was discovered that rather than trying to prevent rejection by shutting down the immune system, greater success could be achieved by "training" the immune system to recognize the new organ as part of self.[25] In other words, even something seemingly as "hardwired" as the body's immune system was capable of changing how it perceived Individuality.

Collectively these and other examples of how life comes to build Well-Being Systems yield very interesting insights in the workings of not just Individuality-related Well-Being Systems, but all Well-Being Systems. Clearly organisms are not born with totally fixed Well-Being Systems; even the perceptions of self-related need, the key threshold variables that regulate all Well-Being Systems, are subject to adaptation. Although frequently the general structure and characteristics of perceived needs are inherited, these appear to almost always be amenable to modification based on environmental conditions and history.[26] This adaptive capacity, the ability to learn and change, appears to be built into Well-Being Systems at every level, from the molecular, cellular, tissue and organ, all the way up to the organismic and social levels. The key insight is that all Well-Being Systems, regardless of level, whether brain-based or not, are dependent upon sensing and maintaining the equilibrium of some kind of threshold-dependent need.

Importantly, these threshold-dependent needs are always "constructed." Whether that need is signaled by the presence or absence of a particular molecule or through the presence or absence of some perceivable visual cue, the threshold of well-being is always fundamentally arbitrary and is ultimately determined by lived experience. Except in very rare cases where a chemical is so toxic that its mere presence at any concentration causes immediate negative consequences, all of the critical needs on which Well-Being Systems depend represent a learned state, a state that life has come to recognize as critical. In vertebrates for example, the intracellular concentration of ionized calcium is roughly 100 nm, but can be increased anywhere from 10 to 100 times that concentration during various cellular functions.[27] These concentrations of ionized calcium are ultimately an arbitrary product of evolution, not some pre-ordained absolute. Life has evolved to recognize higher concentrations of ionized calcium as a critical signal, as triggers indicative of some preferred alternative state.[28] Fundamentally, though, the exact concentration that serves as a trigger is always just an arbitrary construction of life determined by a range of both historic evolutionary events as well as individually unique and often idiosyncratic factors. And for this reason, all self-related needs, and the Well-Being Systems that they help to regulate, are capable of varying from individual to individual, and even within an individual from situation to situation.

However, life systems are not built on uncertainty, in fact exactly the opposite is true. To act upon one's perceptions of need and make choices requires certainty; it requires knowing with certainty whether a specific threshold of need is exceeded or not. Hence the irony of Well-Being Systems is that life has evolved to perceive self-related needs as if they were constant, concrete realities; the more discrete and black and white, the better.

For example, every person perceives himself as bounded, essentially a closed entity. Something that can be defined in space and time, something a person can point to and describe as, "this is where I begin and this is where I end." In actuality though, each individual is an open system, with quite fuzzy boundaries.[29] I would assert that the evolutionary reason for this illusion of boundedness is that it is selectively advantageous to perceive the existence of a 100% tangible and closed life-boundary, even if reality is otherwise.[30] A tangible, closed self-boundary is capable of being defended against the depredations of others, while an open undif-ferentiated space is not. So, although in reality every lifeform is indeed indiscrete and at some level continuous with its surroundings, people like all other types of life prefer to see themselves as discrete and separate from the world, defin-able by simple self-non-self dichotomies—inside-outside, me-not me, good-bad, safe-unsafe. In this way organisms have evolved to impose boundaries on the ephemeral and open-ended nature of life and act as if there was permanence and continuity. Organisms interpret the dissimilarities and discontinuities inherent in all systems as evidence of uniqueness and individuality. In this way, life has been able to impose order on the otherwise cacophonous patterns and events in the world. Life perceives that a state of well-being exists when the relative abundance of patterns and events it associates with itself exceed some threshold of patterns and events it associates with those things that are not itself.

The innate tendency for every organism to perceive itself as an individual and remain independent from every other organism is deeply embedded within the make-up of life. In fact, for billions of years and still today, the vast majority of liv-ing things were single-celled, autonomous creatures; each with the capacity to not only distinguish between itself and that which is non-self but with the ability to act on those things perceived as non-self with great prejudice. Still the fundamen-tally abstract and metaphoric nature of individual self-perception has proved to be amazingly important for the evolution of life on earth. Because the self-perception of Individuality is a learned, subjective response, an imposition of tangible order on an inherently chaotic, abstract reality, all of the Well-Being Systems based on those perceptions have a built-in flexibility; need thresholds based on perceptions of self can be adjusted to accommodate changing environmental realities. Well-Being Systems have evolved to be dynamic, modifiable processes, susceptible to significant individual differences, not only on evolutionary time scales but also on individual and developmental time scales.[31]

This quirk of evolution has meant that from the beginning, an organism's self-perceived needs, and the resulting choices those perceptions precipitated, had the potential to change not only through genetic evolution but over shorter time frames through learning and development.[32] This inherent flexibility in how an organism perceived itself relative to the world was exploited by life, likely numerous times, and has resulted in some of earth's most amazing evolutionary changes. The flexibility around what it means for something to be perceived as an individual made it possible for life to, figuratively speaking, bend the rules suf-ficiently to become increasingly larger and more complex—initially through colo-nies of nearly identical individuals but ultimately through symbiotic relationships between unrelated entities.[33] This stretching of the definition of Individuality made possible the evolution of eukaryotes with their organelles and made possible sexual reproduction—where two unrelated and thus theoretically antagonistic bodies could join together to form a new organism. If the perception of the Indi-vidual were truly discrete and inflexibly perpetuated from one generation to the next, such momentous evolutionary events could arguably have never happened. Although self-perceived need does indeed possess the ability to adapt and change as a function of experience and learning, the basic blueprint for self-perception in humans and their immediate relatives is encoded and perpetuated through a DNA-based hereditary system,[34] a hereditary system involving the sexual union of genes from two separate and unique individuals.

## Notes

1. Litman, G.W., Cannon, J.P. & Dishaw, L.J. (2005). Reconstructing immune phylogeny: New perspectives. *Nature Reviews: Immunology*, 5(11), 866–879.
2. Litman, G.W., Cannon, J.P. & Dishaw, L.J. (2005). Reconstructing immune phylogeny: New perspectives. *Nature Reviews: Immunology*, 5(11), 866–879.
3. Makarova, K.S., Wolf, Y.I., Snir, S. & Koonin, E.V. (2011). Defense islands in bacterial and archaeal genomes and prediction of novel defense systems. *Journal of Bacteriology*, 193, 6039–6056.
   Blower, T.D., Short, F.L., Rao, F., Mizuguchi, K., Pei, X.I., Finneran, P.C. & Luisi, B.F. (2012). Salmond GP identification and classification of bacterial Type III toxin-antitoxin systems encoded in chromosomal and plasmid genomes. *Nucleic Acids Research*, 40, 6158–6173.
   Makarova, K.S., Wolf, Y.I. & Koonin, E.V. (2013). Comparative genomics of defense systems in archaea and bacteria. *Nucleic Acids Research*. Retrieved July 30, 2013. http://nar.oxfordjournals.org/content/early/2013/03/06/nar.gkt157.full
4. Dawkins, R. & Krebs, R.J. (1979). Arms races between and within species. *Proceedings of the Royal Society Biological Sciences Series B*, 205, 489–511.
5. The discovery and now exploitation of one of the more ancient forms of these systems—CRISPR-Cas (Koonin, E.V. & Makarova, K.S. (2013). CRISPR-Cas: Evolution of an RNA-based adaptive immunity system in prokaryotes. *RNA Biology*, 10(5), 679–686) is on the cusp of revolutionizing how humans deal with the world.
6. DeMoraes, C.M., Lewis, W.J., Pare, P.W., Alborn, H.T. & Tumlinson, J.H. (1998). Herbivore-infested plants selectively attract parasitoids. *Nature*, 393, 570–573.
7. Cooper, M.D. & Herrin, B.R. (2010). How did our complex immune system evolve? *Nature Reviews Immunology*, 10, 2–3.
8. Perdue, S.S. (2015). Immune system. In *Encyclopedia Britannica*. Retrieved February 7, 2016. www.britannica.com/science/immune-system/Evolution-of-the-immune-system
9. Although the self-non-self model remains at the core of most theories of immunology, some have questioned whether it should continue to be so. Critiques by Alfred Tauber (Tauber, A.I. (1994). *The immune self: Theory or metaphor?* New York and Cambridge: Cambridge University Press) and Thomas Pradeu and Edgardo Carosella (Pradeu, T. & Carosella, E.D. (2006). The self model and the conception of biological identity in immunology. *Biology and Philosophy*, 21, 235–252) have specifically framed their concerns around the metaphoric nature of the self-non-self dichotomy, which they argue when applied to real biological events does not always work. Although these authors raise some interesting issues, ultimately these and other critiques are predicated on the argument that self-perception cannot exist because it would require that living organisms, including simple one-celled creatures like bacteria, be capable of dealing with abstractions rather than the actual concrete realities of real life, in other words chemistry and physics.

   I would argue that rather than trying to force living things into a mechanistic mode where all processes are based on absolutes, we should accept that life is actually quite creative and that flexible adjustments to an ever changing and variable world are not exceptions but the rule for living things. So rather than seeing the metaphoric nature of self-perception as a fundamental flaw in how we think about biological processes, we should see it as a fundamental strength. The metaphorical and open-ended nature of the model of Well-Being Systems I have proposed actually quite accurately reflects the realities it is attempting to explain. The fact is, the perceptual distinction between self and non-self is always a self-referential abstraction, but the ways in which life acts upon these perceptions are by necessity always concrete. *The essence of life is its ability to operationalize the metaphorical; the ability to make abstract realities sufficiently concrete and tangible to be able to act upon them.* Living things impose boundaries on the ephemeral and open-ended nature of life and act as if there was permanence and *continuity*. Living things interpret the dissimilarities and discontinuities inherent in all systems as evidence of uniqueness and *individuality*. Living things regularly make choices by taking the inherent chaos and noise of the world and perceiving order and relationship. They do this by imposing species and individual-specific patterns on their perceptions, connecting these patterns to innate and learned relationships to their perceptions of themselves. Actions are initiated when the threshold between perceived reality falls below some tolerable level of the ratio of self-beneficial and other-harmful. In other words, life is constantly constructing perceived relationships between the state of self and non-self, despite the fact that functionally no such relationship actually exists.

10. Torday, J.S. & Rehan, V.K. (2012). *Evolutionary biology, cell-cell communication, and complex disease.* New York: John Wiley & Sons.

11. www.dailymail.co.uk/news/article-271509/The-haunting-account-trenches.html#ixzz40AmwCwo6

12. Smith, A.P. (2013). Twenty-five years of research on the behavioural malaise associated with influenza and the common cold. *Psychoneuroendocrinology*, 38(6), 744–751.

13. Smith, A. (2012). Effects of the common cold on mood, psychomotor performance, the encoding of new information, speed of working memory and semantic processing. *Brain, Behavior, and Immunity*, 26(7), 1072–1076.

14. Over the years, various models had been proposed to describe how the human immune system worked. Currently the most widely accepted version involves an internal process of natural selection. Building on ideas originally proposed by Neils Jerne in the mid-1950s, immunologists Frank Burnet with input from David Talmage posited that the way antibodies proliferate in the body in response to a microbial invasion is through a process they called the *clonal selection theory*. According to this theory, the human body normally possesses a vast array of immune cells which are constantly circulating in the body, prior to any infection. When an alien/other molecule/cell enters into the body and by chance bumps into one of the pre-existing array of antibodies that possesses connectors on its surface that match with the connectors on the other molecule/cell, the match-up will cause the immune cell to produce a corresponding antibody to destroy the other molecule. The contact with a non-self molecule/cell will also stimulate the body to start reproducing this particular kind of immune cell. Through this process, the body "remembers" these foreign invaders because the more often an immune cell bumps into and binds with an invading molecule/cell, the greater the number of immune cells generated by the body and the greater number of corresponding antibodies that will be circulating in the body ready for a future attack. For this and additional work, Burnet and Medawar shared the Nobel Prize for physiology and medicine in 1960. Jerne in turn built upon Burnet and Medawar's ideas, and further proposed that the immune system functions as a network that is regulated via interactions between the variable parts of these various immune cells and their secreted antibody molecules. *Immune network theory*, as this Jerne model came to be known, also resulted in a Nobel Prize, this time won by Jerne himself.

15. Reynolds, V., Falger, V.S.E. & Vine, I. (Eds.). (1987). *The sociobiology of ethnocentrism: Evolutionary dimensions of xenophobia, discrimination, racism and nationalism.* London: Croom Helm.

16. Burgess, H. (2003). Stereotypes/characterization frames. In G. Burgess & H. Burgess (Eds.), *Beyond Intractability*. Boulder, CO: Conflict Information Consortium, University of Colorado. Retrieved July 24, 2014. www.beyondintractability.org/essay/stereotypes

17. e.g., Reynolds, V., Falger, V.S.E. & Vine, I. (Eds.). (1987). *The sociobiology of ethnocentrism: Evolutionary dimensions of xenophobia, discrimination, racism and nationalism.* London: Croom Helm.
18. Kahneman, D. (2011). *Thinking, fast and slow.* New York: Farrar, Straus and Giroux.
19. Sears, W. (2016). *Month-to-month guide to baby's milestones.* Retrieved January 7, 2017. www.parenting.com/article/month-by-month-guide-to-babys-milestones
20. Botvinick, M. & Cohen, J. (1998). Rubber hands 'feel' touch that eyes see. *Nature*, 391, 756.
21. Crucianelli, L., Metcalf, N.K., Fotopoulou, A. & Jenkinson, P.M. (2013). Bodily pleasure matters: Velocity of touch modulates body ownership during the rubber hand illusion. *Frontiers of Psychology*, 4, 1–7.
22. Wikipedia. Retrieved March 14, 2014. https://en.wikipedia.org/wiki/Harold_Gillies
23. Wikipedia. Organ transplantation. Retrieved March 14, 2014. http://en.wikipedia.org/wiki/Organ_transplantation
24. Notably Gerald Edelman played a key role in these discoveries, cf., Retrieved January 7, 2017. https://en.wikipedia.org/wiki/Gerald_Edelman
25. Contie, V. (2012). Organ transplants without lifelong drugs. *NIH Research Matters.* Retrieved March 14, 2014. www.nih.gov/researchmatters/march2012/03192012transplants.htm
26. An interesting example is the recently discovered inter-relationship between sex and immunity; specifically the fact that frequent sex primes the immune system in ways that make successful conception possible (Reynolds, G. (October, 25, 2015). A sexually aware immune system? *Well: New York Times Magazine.* New York: New York Times). Examples of learned immunity have now been found for a variety of sexual interactions, including kissing and oral sex. The exchange of bodily fluids during heavy kissing and oral sex, in particular the act of a woman eating a man's sperm, also appear to increase the chances of conception. Again, the critical finding appears to be that the ingestion of these bodily fluids leads to a decreased negative immune response by the woman for that individual's sperm (Moalem, S. (2009). *How sex works: Why we look, smell, taste, feel, and act the way we do.* New York: Harper Perennial).
27. Brini, M., Call, T., Ottolini, D. & Carafoli, E. (2013). Chapter 5 Intracellular calcium homeostasis and signaling. In L Banci (Ed.), *Metallomics and the cell: Metal ions in life sciences* (Vol. 12, pp. 119–168). Dordrecht: Springer.
28. Krebs, J. & Carafoli, E. (2016). Why calcium? How calcium became the best communicator. *The Journal of Biological Chemistry*, 29(40), 20849–20857.
29. Pradeu, T. & Carosella, E.D. (2006). The self model and the conception of biological identity in immunology. *Biology and Philosophy*, 21, 235–252.
30. And nature is definitely not bounded; all elements of the world are "fuzzy" and not perfectly bounded. Whether that entity be an atom, a molecule, a cell, an organism or an ecosystem, all are fundamentally open systems, possessing only approximately tangible and discrete boundaries.
31. Torday, J.S. & Miller, W.B., Jr. (2016). Phenotype as agent for epigenetic inheritance. *Biology*, 5, 30–36.
32. According to Jabonka and Lamb (Jablonka, E. & Lamb, M. (2014). *Evolution in four dimensions: Genetic, epigenetic, behavioral and symbolic variation in the history of life.* Cambridge: MIT Press), changes caused by learning also have the ability to become transmitted over time and thus be part of the hereditary system of an organism.
33. Bonner, J.T. (2006). *Why size matters.* Princeton: Princeton University Press.

# 9

# SEXUALITY (ORIGINATING MORE THAN 2 BILLION YEARS AGO)

The desire for sex, as well as the decision to act upon that desire, stems from one of the most basic of all life needs, the largely unconscious need to persist beyond the moment, to cheat entropy and death by perpetuating some part of one's self into the future. The ultimate purpose of sex may be buried deep within the unconscious but not the desire. Sexually-related desires take a vast array of forms, animating directly or indirectly a large percentage of human choices and behavior.[1] This chapter begins with a section on the evolutionary history of sex and follows with two additional sections highlighting the importance of Sexuality-related Well-Being Systems in human affairs.

## Origins of Sex

Virtually every plant or animal that people can see and are aware of practices sex of some kind. Though sexual reproduction is widespread, it is actually unique to only one of the three major branches of life, the groups of organisms collectively known as Eukaryotes. To appreciate how unique this process is one needs to understand how sexual reproduction starkly differs from asexual reproduction.

The two other major kingdoms, the Prokaryotes—Archaea and Bacteria—all reproduce in basically the same way, using a process that has changed little over the past nearly 4 billion years. The key aspect of asexual reproduction is that each individual reproduces by forming two matching copies of itself; each with a full complement of genetic material and an equal share of the cellular constituents of the mother cell (including cell membranes for example).[2] The genetic and cellular material in each of the two new cells created is identical, or in the modern parlance clones of each other. I mention all of this because nowhere in this process is there a need to counteract Individuality-related Well-Being Systems. Prokaryotic reproduction is all a process of one individual dividing into two totally equivalent individuals, which then divide into two more totally equivalent individuals, and so on forever until death of a lineage intervenes. Prokaryotic reproduction is the quintessence of sameness—each daughter cell persists as a clone of the mother cell, generation after generation in an unending sequence. Of course this does involve a form of self-recognition since each DNA molecule within the cell rebuilds itself by matching itself exactly from the raw materials floating around inside the cell; a process that involves each nucleotide base binding with its corresponding mate.[3] Although a similar DNA splitting process occurs in Eukaryote reproduction it is much more elaborate, and rather than creating identical daughter cells, each new Eukaryote is actually a unique recombination of two closely related but unlike strands of DNA. Eukaryotic reproduction differs from Prokaryotic reproduction in a number of ways, but the most striking difference, and one of particular interest here, is that Eukaryotic reproduction requires *sex*. Sex is always challenging given that it entails the union in time and space of two similar but fundamentally unlike cells.

Sexual reproduction always involves the fusing of two unrelated cells to form a single new cell with similar but not identical genetic material to the parent cells. Rather than merely a division, sexual reproduction represents a merger, and a lot can go wrong in a merger. Biologists have long debated the pros and cons of these two reproductive systems—asexual and sexual—and generally agree that sex has thrived as a reproductive strategy because it overall improves the long-term chances for survival. That said, in the short term, in a stable environment, asexual reproduction, which is energetically relatively cheap and preserves the parent's well-adapted combination of genes, is likely always a better solution.

Biologists currently believe that sexual reproduction theoretically has four big benefits over asexual reproduction. The first and most widely accepted is that sex creates genetic variability that enables the offspring resulting from sexual reproduction to be better adapted to a variable and changing world.[4] Two additional benefits have been suggested for sex, both of which occur at the molecular level and result from the elaborate Eukaryotic process of chromosome division. The first of these relates to the quality of replication. Every time DNA divides there is a chance for mistakes, for mutations to creep into the process. Although mutations can lead to improvements, the chances of benefit are miniscule as compared to the chances of harm; most mutations are lethal. There is evidence that the eukaryotic process of chromosomal division has better DNA repair mechanisms built into it than those used by Prokaryotes.[5] There is also evidence that sexual reproduction provides some benefits to the offspring in escaping disease.[6] In addition to these potential benefits, the eukaryotic chromosomal division process also increases the heterogeneity of the genes—matching chromosomes from two similar but not identical partners; this process increases the chances for benign variation, a process known as "hybrid vigor." The advantage of gene heterogeneity is that it allows for both the expression of new traits as well as masking of the negative consequences of potentially harmful mutations.[7] Despite these seeming clear advantages, asexual reproduction is clearly successful since Prokaryotes have been successfully reproducing this way for billions of years.

Whatever the downsides of asexual reproduction, from an energetic perspective it is clearly superior to sexual reproduction. Sex is an expensive and wasteful way to reproduce since each organism is actually reducing the number of offspring it can produce—with asexual reproduction one organism produces two as compared with sexual reproduction which requires two organisms to yield only one. Also problematic is that each contributing organism is actually only perpetuating half of itself. An asexually reproducing organism produces two genetically identical clones of itself every time it divides, while those creatures committed to sexual reproduction get only half of themselves replicated every time there is a union of egg and sperm. Biologists (and more importantly nature) have concluded that the added success of the offspring created through sexual reproduction yield benefits that more than compensate for the added costs.[8]

Typically missing from these discussions of cost-benefit ratios has been one additional cost related to sex. That is the cost of overcoming the strong inhibitions created by the cell's Individuality-related Well-Being Systems; Systems that would have already been in place long before the evolution of sexuality. At the core of sexual reproduction is an inequality. Although each of the combining cells contributes half of the genetic material, one of the cells is relatively large (biologists call the large cell the female or egg) and contains lots of extra "goodies" essential to life,[9] while the other is relatively small (biologists call this small cell the male or sperm) and contributes virtually nothing except the genetic material.[10] Across evolutionary time this discrepancy between the female egg and the male sperm have grown and resulted in a whole range of diverse and at time perverse relationships.[11] In this arrangement males function more like the parasites described in an earlier chapter, reprogramming the female egg in ways that benefit the reproductive goals of the male.[12] Not only does the sperm use the female's cellular machinery to nurture and utilize its genetic material, it also fundamentally changes the behavior of the egg. To do this though requires overcoming the female cell's strong aversion to invasion by a foreign entity.

Sexual reproduction seemingly evolved around 2 billion years ago amongst the early proto-ancestors of Eukaryotes; although long after the onset of life, this event still happened relatively early in the history of life on earth. By this time these cells would have already possessed highly refined self-perceptive abilities capable of recognizing themselves as unique individuals in order to prevent parasitism or attack by other cells. All of these Individuality-related Well-Being Systems would have created significant barriers to a successful sexual merger at both the cellular and molecular levels, frequently resulting in the death of both the sperm and the egg. Clearly at some point early in the history of sexually reproducing organisms the two germ cells would have needed to evolve strategies for overcoming the barriers of Individuality sufficient to permit sexual reproduction to occur. However even today it appears that most sexual unions overcome Individuality-induced resistance only with great difficulty.

For example, at the cellular level the encounter between sperm and egg is rarely simple. The sperm needs to implement a suite of strategies that allows it to overcome the egg's defenses so that it can penetrate the cell membrane and another set of actions once inside the egg to avoid destruction by the egg's immune system. Alternatively, the female cell needs to sufficiently lower its barriers to allow one, but only one, entering sperm cell to co-exist within her. Typically, both of these solutions need to operate for successful union to occur. These clashes of Individuality-related Well-Being Systems occur not only at the cellular level though.

Sexuality also precipitates clashes at the organismal level. All sexually reproducing organisms but particularly those such as arthropods and vertebrates that have evolved to reproduce through internal insemination have been forced to directly address the inherent challenges created by mate selection and reproduction.[13] The result has been the evolution of all manner of bizarre appendages and rituals, virtually all designed to allow males to overcome the intrinsic diffidence of females to allowing another creature to violate their perceived Individuality for the purposes of copulation. The fact that there is always an inherent inequality in the outcome of this act does not make it any easier.[14]

Humans too have been subject to similar evolutionary challenges with the result that people have evolved, both biologically and particularly culturally, a vast array of mating systems and strategies.[15] The fact that sexuality has existed for more than 2 billion years has seemingly only marginally minimized the challenges of sexual union, as any sexually active adult can attest. Although all peoples have invested considerable time and energy in constructing elaborate social and cultural practices and norms to overcome the inherent tensions of sexual union, the barriers created by Individuality-related Well-Being Systems remain an obstacle to Well-Being Systems associated with sex. After all, sexual union ultimately requires extreme intimacy and trust.

In spite of the challenges, humans regularly engage in sex. And unlike in most mammals, both male and female humans are capable of achieving orgasm,[16] and both males and females find sex extremely pleasurable;[17] a fact that significantly contributes to why people choose to have sex. Sex it seems yields significant short-term feelings of well-being.

## Sexual Needs

It has been suggested that prostitutes and arms merchants have long been the principal commercial beneficiaries of war.[18] Not unlike those who peddled ever improved ways to kill people during the first World War, the women who tended to the sexual needs of the soon to be killed soldiers discovered that fear was a potent stimulant to their business. Though many would argue that prostitution is an inherently exploitive and unequal expression of sex, the choice-making nature of prostitution makes it an interesting case study. For example, Nell Kimball, who was a celebrated "Madam" at one of New Orleans' most popular whorehouses, described in primarily psychological terms the sudden boom in her business that coincided with the U.S.'s entry into WWI in the spring of 1917,

> Every man and boy wanted to have one last fling before the real war got him. One shot at it in a real house before he went off and maybe was killed. I've noticed it before, the way the idea of war and dying makes a man raunchy, and wanting to have it as much as he could. It wasn't really pleasure at times, but a kind of nervous breakdown that could only be treated with a girl and a set-to.[19]

Meanwhile, over in France, the prostitution trade was brisk. One snap-shot study carried out by British medical officers counted 171,000 visitors to the brothels in just one street, of just one port town, in but a single year of the war.[20] But French brothels were rarely if ever restricted to one street within a town, and there were hundreds of French towns engaged in serving the sexual needs of soldiers over the many years of the war. In other words, there were likely hundreds of millions of visits to French brothels made by soldiers during the war.

At the peak of hostilities, it was estimated that a junior officer lived an average of just six weeks. It was common for these men to feel that they needed to squeeze an entire life's worth of experiences into just a few days. Lieutenant James Butlin was one of those men. Shortly after the outbreak of war, he gave up his college career at Oxford University for life in the trenches. Immediately before Butlin was shipped to the front, he spent a few days in the French town of Rouen. He revealed to a confidante how the town had been "ruinous to my purse, not to mention my morals. From what I heard out here I decided quickly that life must be enjoyed to the full—and so it has been, without judicious selection or moderation."[21]

But these were the easy sex-related statistics to accumulate. During wars it is not just prostitution that increases; it is sexual flings of all kinds that flourish. Sex during wartime ranges along a continuum from women voluntarily participating at one end (sometimes becoming "war brides"), to their implicit or explicit trading of sex for money or food in the middle, all the way to rape at the other extreme.[22] What one researcher referred to as "war aphrodisia" is common amongst not just soldiers but civilians as well. Under these kinds of stressful situations, "sexual restraint . . . [was] suspended for the duration." As one [WWII-era] British house-wife put it, "We were not really immoral, there was a war on."[23]

Although there have been many attempts to analyze the physiological and psychological benefits of sex,[24] perhaps, as already discussed in the first section of this book, the best language-level explanation for why people repetitively engage in experiences they find satisfying comes from the theory of "flow" developed by the psychologist Mihaly Csikszentmihalyi.[25] Just to recap, when in a flow state, Csikszentmihalyi observed that individuals became completely absorbed in what they were doing and felt a great sense of control as they perceived that everything in the world functionally seemed to shrink down to just those things they were choosing to focus on. In other words, individuals in a state of flow feel a high sense of well-being.

This is exactly what happens, even if briefly, when two individuals have positive sexual relations.[26] During good sex,[27] for example, the selves of two individuals become as one, time stands still and all other distractions melt away. It is an intense experience where the individual is primarily conscious of pleasure and almost totally unaware of any other internal or external reality. Although the moment of orgasm itself is often quite brief, it feels so good that a person finds it intensely rewarding and wants to replicate that experience again. Research suggests that even "bad sex" can result in positive associations.[28] Research has shown that, as hypothesized for flow, making love stimulates the body to produce a host of neurotransmitters and hormones, including dopamine, oxytocin, serotonin, endorphins and adrenaline; most of which are perceived by a person as "pleasurable."[29] These feelings of well-being commonly become associated with sex and thus once experienced, sex is assiduously pursued by all peoples. However due to the cultural biases of most WEIRD[30] scientists relative to sexuality, virtually all of the prevailing models of well-being and happiness totally ignore the importance of human sexuality.[31]

However as I have described, well-being occurs any time one or more of a person's self-perceived needs can be maximally satisfied, presumably without unduly sacrificing the well-being of all the rest of the self-perceived needs a person has. Sex is clearly one of those times. Research suggests that people pursue sex for multiple reasons, and accordingly perceive well-being based on the satisfaction of multiple needs. The most commonly cited analysis is based on the groundbreaking research of psychologists Cindy Meston and David Buss.[32]

Meston and Buss asked hundreds of people aged 17 to 52 to answer one question, *"Please list all the reasons you can think of why you, or someone you have known, has engaged in sexual intercourse in the past."* They concluded, and subsequent research has confirmed, that people perceive thirteen major reasons for having sex that can be grouped into four major categories:

> *Physical Reasons*: 1) tension relief; 2) pleasure; 3) physical desirability; and 4) experience-seeking.
> *Goal attainment*: 5) resources (trying to obtain the objects of our desires); 6) social status; 7) revenge; and 8) utilitarian (using sex to gain an advantage in a relationship or life domain).
> *Emotional reasons*: 9) love and commitment; and 10) expression (one of the ultimate ways of communicating, at least with one's romantic partner).
> *Insecurity*: 11) self-esteem boost (a strategy to gain a modicum of strength and power); 12) duty/pressure (anything from obligation or coercion by another person); and 13) mate guarding (doing the deed to ward off poachers).

There were significant gender differences. Meston and Buss reported that men were significantly more likely than women to endorse reasons centering on the physical appearance and physical desirability of a partner, such as "The person had a desirable body," or "The person's physical appearance turned me on."[33] These findings support the evolution-based hypothesis that men tend to be more sexu-ally aroused by visual sexual cues than are women, since physical appearance pro-vides a wealth of cues to a woman's fertility and reproductive capacity.[34] Men were also more significantly likely than women to give reasons related to experience-seeking and mere opportunity. Examples included "The person was 'available,'" or "The opportunity presented itself."

By contrast, women exceeded men in endorsing certain of the emotional motivations for sex, such as "I wanted to express my love for the person" and "I realized that I was in love." These findings support the evolution-based theory that women, more than men, prefer sex within the context of an ongoing com-mitted relationship, and feelings or expressions of love provide signals of that commitment.[35] Also supporting the theory that evolutionary forces underlie these gender-based differences in sexual motivations were the findings suggesting that sex without emotional involvement was a more powerful motivator for men than for women.[36] However a key finding of the study was that there were NO gender differences in the perception that emotional motivations were a major reason for engaging in sex. Men and women were equally likely to express sentiments like "I wanted to feel connected to the person" or "I desired emotional closeness." In fact, Love and Commitment and Expression emerged as the only two of the thirteen broad reasons for sex where both men and women were in total agreement. This finding supports a growing body of clinical evidence suggesting that both men and women at times desire intimacy and emotional connectedness from sexual activity.[37] That said, given the WEIRD bias in this particular study caution needs to be exercised in assuming results are totally generalizable to all peoples.

The bottom line is that people choose to engage in sex because it is a powerful source of human well-being. Sex invariably feels so good that individuals who experience it, no matter how fleeting or for whatever reason, desire to try and replicate the experience again and again. However, it is possible for a person to become unduly fixated on satisfying just this, or some other singular dimension of well-being at the expense of all others.

## When Perception of Need Undermines Well-Being

I have argued that the pursuit of well-being is not merely an important driver of human choice and behavior, it is THE major driver. Every person spends their time striving to keep the needs of as many of their Well-Being Systems in a posi-tive state as possible, be that through accumulation of money, friends, possessions, ideas, food, sufficient sleep or sexual relations or by avoiding people they don't trust or dislike, dark alleys, foods they think will make them sick, sleepless nights or unpleasant sex. Although as stated above, Sexuality is not often included in most models of well-being, sex clearly seems to be a particularly strong need. Even though each person's perceptions of what constitutes sexual well-being are clearly influenced by their culture and personal experience, those perceptions cannot be totally detached from older, more innate systems. Thus despite the fact that social and cultural norms can and often do play an important role in minimizing Sexuality-related Well-Being Systems, it is clear that these deeply felt Systems and their incumbent needs play an important role in human affairs, even amongst presumably satisfied, already paired off individuals.

Incidents of infidelity between heterosexual married couples is quite common. One of the most consistent data sources on infidelity derives from the General Social Survey sponsored by the U.S. National Science Foundation which has tracked the opinions of Americans about their social behaviors since 1972. The survey data shows that in any given year, about 10% of married couples (12% of men and 7% of women) have engaged in sex outside their marriage. However over the 15-year period 1991 to 2006 the rate of lifetime infidelity for men over 60 increased nearly 50%, with 28% of older men in 2006 saying they had sex outside of their marriage. For women over 60, this rate increased from 5% in 1991 to 15% in 2006.[38] Despite apparent gender differences in these rates, other studies have found that women are as likely, if not more likely, to engage in infidelity as men.[39] Infidelity is of course more complicated than just sex, often involving a host of complicating social and personal causes, but sex consistently emerges as the single most important contributing motivation.[40] Sexual desires can cause people to make many seemingly irrational choices, often with devastating consequences. Although a majority of individuals who become involved in sexually-motivated extra-marital experiences end up remaining married and regret their lustful decision, it is estimated that 90% of all divorces involve infidelity.[41]

Arguably, these examples of sexuality fall within the norm, at least for those living within typical Western societies. However sometimes the pursuit of well-being through sexuality can go beyond these bounds, and behaviors that normally bring feelings of well-being can become an obsession. The obsessive pursuit of well-being through satisfaction of a single type of need has a name, and that name is addiction. Like a lot of pathologies, sexual addiction provides a useful window into underlying mechanisms.

The basic neurobiology of sexual desire is relatively well understood. The seat of the sex drive is the hypothalamus. When it is removed, the individual loses all interest in sex as well as the ability to perform sexually.[42] The hypothalamus in turn is linked to the pituitary gland, which produces the hormones that fuel sexual arousal. However, in humans, sex, like everything else, is more complicated. Neuroscientists have identified two brain regions that seem particularly important in romantic love, in particular the caudate nucleus and the right ventral tegmental area (VTA); both of which are very old parts of the vertebrate brain, both of which are involved in reward processing and feelings of euphoria.[43] These brain regions are all interconnected into a major, dopamine-fueled pathway within the brain called the mesocortical limbic system.

Interestingly, these exact same neural pathways have been observed to be in play across a wide range of addictions, including addictions to substances such as alcohol, opiates or cigarettes or behaviors such as sex, gambling, shopping, making money or eating.[44] In all cases, these dopamine-fueled pathways provide the addict with a compelling sense of well-being that they disproportionately indulge in satisfying at the expense of other forms of well-being. Clinically, addiction is characterized by loss of control, preoccupation, compulsivity, narrowing of interests, dishonesty, guilt and chronic relapse.[45] However, addiction is not merely a mental phenomenon.[46] In fact brains may not even be required, or at least not brains in the typical human sense of a brain, since research suggests that addiction likely predates the evolution of the vertebrate brain. For example, there's growing evidence that invertebrates too, even simple creatures like worms with virtually no brain to speak of can display signs of addiction.[47]

Based on the theory proposed here, regardless of the exact mechanisms involved, addiction represents an effort by an organism to repeatedly engage in acts it has found to maximize one particular Well-Being System, often in the process neglecting others. So pervasive is the feeling of well-being that a particular substance or behavior creates, the addicted individual finds it difficult to choose not to use the substance or indulge in the behavior again and again, even when such behaviors threaten alternative forms of well-being, including fundamental life processes. Compulsive gamblers describe the act of gambling as a "high" or euphoric state, terms usually associated with drug use.[48] The following description by a sex therapist is illustrative: "Just as a heroin addict chases a substance-induced high, sex addicts are bingeing on chemicals—in this case, their own hormones."[49]

In general, the addict when choosing to engage or about to choose to engage in her addictive experience feels good because she perceives positive signals coming from one or more of her sexuality-related Well-Being Systems. Although most addictions do deliver the actual "good" that the resulting perceptions of well-being were meant to signal, those feelings never last and must be continually repeated. Still, the fact that they are perceived as so pleasurable as to prevent engagement in other potentially pleasurable acts reinforces the idea that perceptions of pleasure and well-being evolved as a way for living things to regulate events going on within themselves that they could not otherwise perceive. If it feels good, it must be good for you.

Addiction of any kind occurs when somehow one particular proxy stimulus, i.e., feeling of well-being, comes to dominate the perceptive apparatus of the organism. It is as if the organism "believes" that as long as that particular proxy stimulus is satisfied, everything else in its life will be well. Typically, addicted individuals are less fit, in an evolutionary sense, than "normal" individuals and are weeded out of the population through natural selection. However, one can equally imagine that every once in a while an addiction might be adaptive and spread through the population, particularly if it results in more descendants. This insight helps clarify why the perception of well-being has been such a major engine of natural selection.

People cannot directly detect the firing of their neurons nor the state of their internal chemistry, but they can perceive the feelings of well-being that result when a Well-Being System is working well. Since life has evolved to utilize perceptible feelings of well-being, or not, as proxies for the internal processes that cannot be perceived, it is no surprise that, on average, the strongest feelings should be associated with Well-Being Systems that yield the highest survival payoff. Sexuality certainly qualifies as a high-payoff Well-Being System.[50] In other words, over evolutionary time perceived states of high well-being have become strongly correlated with high levels of organism health, longevity and reproductive success, while perceived states of low well-being have become strongly correlated with sickness, death and lack of reproductive success. Feelings of sexual satisfaction in particular have over evolutionary time had highly significant benefits. Organisms that were able to maintain high levels of perceived well-being through positive sexual experiences were on average more likely to leave more offspring than those whose sexual well-being was continually compromised. This feedback loop would have resulted in the selection for generation after generation of men and women who perceived sexual desires, and who sought to positively satisfy those desires. It also would have opened the door to potential distortions and/or actual malfunctions in this basic system. Many cultures view sexual infidelity and addiction as deviant and thus incidents of these behaviors are typically under-reported. Research by evolutionary psychologists would suggest that these incidents are actually more common than reported, and often the consequences are not as negative as cultural norms might suggest.[51]

## Summing Up the Well-Being Systems of Continuity, Individuality and Sexuality

Collectively the Well-Being Systems of *Continuity*, *Individuality* and *Sexuality* influence how and why people behave the way they do by mediating a host of humanity's choice-making. Under extreme circumstances they can even dominate how and why choices are made. But even under normal conditions, their influence cannot be denied. According to the U.S. Bureau of Labor Statistics, American adults spend roughly half of their day exclusively attending to the body's various self-perceived needs such as sleeping, eating, drinking and eliminating.[52] But even when these self-perceptions are not overtly directing choice-making, the brain is being made aware of bodily needs and responding accordingly. Nearly all human choices involve some accommodation to these fundamental needs, e.g., "yes I'll continue shopping, but only if I can sit down for a minute."

Advertisers have long understood the critical influence these bodily needs have on choice-making. Most advertising includes images of healthy, attractive people (Continuity) within familiar, safe settings (Individuality) engaging implicitly or explicitly in Sexuality-related behaviors. The goal is to connect, in the minds of the consumer, a relationship between the product and the person's perceptions of bodily Well-Being-related needs; between use of a particular product and feelings of well-being. These advertising-influenced perceptions of well-being influence the choices of food a person eats, the clothes he wears, the car he drives, the things he buys for his house and the health choices he makes.[53] Advertisers were also amongst the earliest social scientists to appreciate the relationship between demographic factors like age and gender on choice-making.

As has been documented through numerous social science investigations, the influence of *Continuity*, *Individuality* and *Sexuality*-related variables like age, genetic similarity (sometimes defined as "race/ethnicity") and gender influence far more than consumer-related choices. These most basic of lived experience variables to a greater or lesser extent influence virtually every choice a person makes, including social relationships. Research has shown that the self-related perceptions of *Continuity*, *Individuality* and *Sexuality* directly influence who a person chooses as a partner or friend,[54] who gets hired or fired in the workplace[55] and who gets elected to public office.[56] The point is that these three Well-Being System modalities significantly influence virtually every facet of a person's daily life, sometimes in ways that are apparent but more often in ways that are more subtle or often totally submerged below the level of conscious awareness.

## Notes

1. Abramson, P.R. & Pinkerton, S.D. (1995). *With pleasure: Thoughts on the nature of human sexuality*. New York: Oxford University Press.
   Diamond, J. (1997). *Why is sex fun? The evolution of human sexuality*. New York: Basic Books.
   Sukel, K. (2012). *This is your brain on sex*. New York: Simon & Schuster.
2. For more than half a century, biologists have considered genes to be at the heart of all biological functioning, as well as the drivers of evolution. This latter idea was most clearly articulated by the biologist Richard Dawkins, initially in his landmark book *The Selfish Gene* (Dawkins, R. (1976). *The selfish gene*. New York: Oxford University Press). I'm not inclined to agree with this reductionist view of self or for that matter genes. Clearly, the genome plays an essential role in the process of life since DNA is fundamental to the building and regulation of life processes as well as the perpetuation of the species information over time. Where I deviate from the current selfish gene dogma is that I believe the real action, where life meets natural selection, is not within the genes but in the epigenetically manufactured products of the genes, including and particularly self-perception. Self-perception is an emergent property of life processes. Although the building blocks for these life processes are encoded within the genes, it is only when they become assembled and expressed that they become active and able to be adaptive and acted upon by evolution.

   In this regard I subscribe to the view of the late Stephen Jay Gould who argued that genes are not directly "visible" to natural selection and thus are unlikely to be the direct agents of evolution. Rather, "the unit of selection is the phenotype, not the genotype, because it is phenotypes which interact with the environment at the natural selection interface" (Gould, S.J. (1990). *The Panda's Thumb: More reflections in natural history*. Harmondsworth: Penguin Books, p. 72). Summarizing Gould's view, biologist Kim Sterelny states, "Gene differences do not cause evolutionary changes in populations, they register those changes." (Sterelny, K. (2007). *Dawkins vs. Gould: Survival of the fittest*. Cambridge: Icon Books, p. 83). Our genes are the memory stores that permit the body to perpetuate these activities day after day, generation after generation. Our genes are not the actors on the stage of life, they are more like the scripts that tell the actors what to say. And like good actors, organisms occasionally modify the script based upon the context, the audience or the other actors on the stage with them. Self-perception and the actions it precipitates is one of the key genetic expressions of genes that allow organisms to respond adaptively to the external world. This adaptive capability, which apparently was part of the early repertoire of life, has been preserved and perpetuated down through the ages by genes. However, these abilities to perceive and respond to the world are epigenetic expressions of the genes, not the genes themselves.

As biologists are now discovering, most of the interesting aspects of life are in the expression of genes rather than the genes themselves (Goldman, D. (2012). *Our genes our choices: How genotype and gene actions affect behavior*. Amsterdam: Elsevier). Through a process called epigenetics, the basic underlying messages of genes become changed as the proteins and other structures encoded within the genes are built by the body (Berger, S.L., Kouzarides, T., Shiekhattar, R. & Shilatifard, A. (2009). An operational definition of epigenetics. *Genes Development*, 23(7), 781–783). It turns out that the environment in which a gene is expressed is as important to the ultimate result as is the fundamental arrangement of nucleotides with the gene. That is why life is so variable; even identical genes will yield slightly different results. Take for example the most fundamental self-perception-action processes, such as homeostasis. Although the structures and functioning of human homeostasis are tightly scripted by our genes, these structures and functions too are always expressed through interactions with and within the organism's internal environment. So despite strong pressures to keep this internal environment constant, creating minimal opportunity for deviation from the basic script, variation between individuals does exist. On average the normal human internal temperature is 37.0°C (98.6°F), but everyone's normal temperature is actually slightly different—some slightly warmer and others slightly cooler. Given that even something as unvarying across individuals as human internal temperature is subject to epigenetics, we should not be surprised to find that a quality as variable and individualized as individuality or sexuality would be strongly epigenetic, molded not just by genetics but environment and culture as well. Our genes dictate that we should have a sense of ourselves as individuals or sexual beings, but the way that individuality or sexuality is perceived and acted upon depends upon the biological, cultural and personal context in which it develops. Because those contexts are constantly changing, it was adaptive for life to have the ability to accommodate those changes. The genes are fixed, but the epigenetic expression of self-perception of need and the choices life make in response to those needs are not.

3. A full explanation of how the basic processes of DNA division, replication and transmission work can be found in any basic biology textbook.

4. Maynard Smith, J. (1978). *The evolution of sex*. Cambridge: Cambridge University Press.

5. Burt, A. (2000). Perspective: Sex, recombination, and the efficacy of selection—Was Weismann right? *Evolution*, 54(2), 337–351.

6. Moalem, S. (2009). How sex works: Why we look, smell, taste, feel, and act the way we do. New York: Harper Perennial.

7. Burt, A. (2000). Perspective: Sex, recombination, and the efficacy of selection—Was Weismann right? *Evolution*, 54(2), 337–351.

8. "Since there are both potential advantages and disadvantages to sexual reproduction, it is not surprising that it is used to different extents and in different ways in different species. What we see today is a whole spectrum of modes of reproduction and modifications of the sexual process." Jablonka and Lamb, p. 82.

9. The large female reproductive cell not only contains half of the DNA but virtually all of the nutrients and a significant percentage of the cellular machinery needed for the resulting embryo to mature and lead a successful life (for example the cell membrane, ribosomes, chloroplasts (if a plant) and mitochondria) (cf., Cavalier-Smith, T. (2004). The membranome and membrane heredity in development and evolution. In R.P. Hirt & D.S. Horner (Eds.), *Organelles, genomes and eukaryote phylogeny: An evolutionary synthesis in the age of genomics* (pp. 335–351). Boca Raton, FL: CRC Press).

10. Notably sperm do carry an enzyme that creates nitrous oxide which seems to be the universal signal for the egg to start maturing. The nitrous oxide also causes the egg cell to release a wave of $Ca^{2+}$ ions to the egg surface. The presence of the $Ca^{2+}$ ions makes the surface of the egg's cell membrane impenetrable to other sperm (Kuo, R.C., Baxter, G.T., Thompson, S.H., Stricker, S.A., Patton, C., Bonaventura, J. & Epel, D. (2000). No is necessary and sufficient for egg activation at fertilisation. *Nature*, 406, 633–636).

11. Jones, S. (2003). *Y: The descent of men*. New York: Houghton Mifflin.

12. Jones, S. (2003). *Y: The descent of men*. New York: Houghton Mifflin, p. 28.

13. e.g., Williams, G.C. (1975). *Sex and evolution*. Princeton: Princeton University Press.
    Edward, D.A (2014). The description of mate choice. *Behavioral Ecology*, 26, 301–310.
    Kokko, H., Brooks, R., Jennions, M. & Morley, J. (2003). The evolution of mate choice and mating biases. *Proceedings of the Royal Society B.*, 270(1515), 653–664.
14. cf. review by Jones, S. (2003). *Y: The descent of men*. New York: Houghton Mifflin.
15. cf., Darwin, C. (1871). *The Descent of man, and selection in relation to sex*. London: John Murray.
    Miller, G.A. (2000). *The mating mind: How sexual choice shaped the evolution of human nature*. London: Heineman.
    Schmitt, D.P. (2005). Sociosexuality from Argentina to Zimbabwe: A 48-nation study of sex, culture, and strategies of human mating. *Behavioral and Brain Sciences*, 28(2), 247–274.
    Gangestad, S.W., Haselton, M.G. & Buss, D.M. (2006). Evolutionary foundations of cultural variation: Evoked culture and mate preferences. *Psychological Inquiry*, 17(2), 75–95.
16. Puts, D.A., Dawood, K. & Welling, L.L. (2012). Why women have orgasms: An evolutionary analysis. *Archives of Sexual Behavior*, 41(5), 1127–1143.
17. Diamond, J. (1997). *Why is sex fun? The evolution of human sexuality*. New York: BasicBooks.
18. Costello, J. (1985). *Love sex and war: Changing values, 1939–45*. London: William Collins.
19. Costello, J. (1985). *Love sex and war: Changing values, 1939–45*. London: William Collins.
    From *Chapter 14: The Girls They Met 'Over There'*. Retrieved February 10, 2016. www.heretical.com/costello/14govert.html
20. Makepeace, C. (2011). Sex and the Somme: The officially sanctioned brothels on the front line laid bare for the first time. *Daily Mail*. Retrieved February 10, 2016. www.dailymail.co.uk/news/article-2054914/Sex-Somme-Officially-sanctioned-WWI-brothels-line.html#ixzz3znAdTiqM
21. Makepeace, C. (2011). Sex and the Somme: The officially sanctioned brothels on the front line laid bare for the first time. *Daily Mail*. Retrieved February 10, 2016. www.dailymail.co.uk/news/article-2054914/Sex-Somme-Officially-sanctioned-WWI-brothels-line.html#ixzz3znAdTiqM
22. Goldstein, J.S. (2001). *War and gender: How gender shapes the war system and vice versa*. Cambridge: Cambridge University Press. Retrieved February 11, 2016. www.warandgender.com/wggensex.htm
23. Goldstein, J.S. (2001). *War and gender: How gender shapes the war system and vice versa*. Cambridge: Cambridge University Press. Retrieved February 11, 2016. www.warandgender.com/wggensex.htm
24. cf., Sukel, K. (2012). *This is your brain on sex*. New York: Simon & Schuster.
25. Csikszentmihalyi, M. (1990). *Flow: The psychology of optimal experience*. New York: Harper Perennial.
26. Regardless of whether that sex is heterosexual or homosexual.
27. By good sex I mean sex that is non-coercive, e.g., rape or other forms of nonconsensual sex would not be considered good sex.
28. Tolman, D.L. & Diamond, L. (Eds.). (2014). *APA handbook of sexuality and psychology*. Washington, DC: American Psychological Association.
29. Kirshenbaum, S. (2011). *The science of kissing*. New York: Grand Central Publishing.
    Sukel, K. (2012). *This is your brain on sex*. New York: Simon & Schuster.
30. WEIRD is an acronym standing for Western, Educated, Industrialized, Rich and Democratic.
31. Kashdan, T.B. (2016). 13 reasons why people have sex. *Psychology Today*. Retrieved January 8, 2017. www.psychologytoday.com/blog/curious/201601/13-reasons-why-people-have-sex
32. Meston, C. & Buss, D. (2007). Why humans have sex. *Archives of Sexual Behavior*, 36(4), 477–507.
33. Meston, C. & Buss, D. (2007). Why humans have sex. *Archives of Sexual Behavior*, 36(4), 477–507.

34. cf., Buss, D.M. (2003). *The evolution of desire: Strategies of human mating* (rev. ed.). New York: Basic Books.
35. cf., Buss, D.M. (2003). *The evolution of desire: Strategies of human mating* (rev. ed.). New York: Basic Books.
36. Kashdan, T.B. (2016). 13 reasons why people have sex. *Psychology Today*. Retrieved January 8, 2017. www.psychologytoday.com/blog/curious/201601/13-reasons-why-people-have-sex
37. Kashdan, T.B. (2016). 13 reasons why people have sex. *Psychology Today*. Retrieved January 8, 2017. www.psychologytoday.com/blog/curious/201601/13-reasons-why-people-have-sex
38. Zare, B. (2011). Reviews of studies on infidelity. *3rd International Conference on Advanced Management Science IPEDR*, 19, 182–186. Retrieved February 11, 2016. www.ipedr.com/vol19/34-ICAMS2011-A10054.pdf
39. Brand, R.J., Markey, C.M., Mills, A. & Hodges, S. (2007). Sex differences in self-reported infidelity and its correlates, *Sex Roles*, 57, 101–109.
40. Omarzu, J., Miller, A.N., Schultz, C. & Timmerman, A. (2012). Motivations and emotional consequences related to engaging in extramarital relationships. *International Journal of Sexual Health*, 24(2), 154–162.
41. Zare, B. (2011). Reviews of studies on infidelity. *3rd International Conference on Advanced Management Science IPEDR*, 19, 182–186. Retrieved February 11, 2016. www.ipedr.com/vol19/34-ICAMS2011-A10054.pdf
42. Sukel, K. (2012). *This is your brain on sex*. New York: Simon & Schuster.
43. Sukel, K. (2012). *This is your brain on sex*. New York: Simon & Schuster.
44. e.g., Berke, J.D. & Hyman, S.E. (2000). Addiction, dopamine, and the molecular mechanisms of memory. *Neuron*, 25(3), 515–532.
    Koob, G.F., Ahmed, S.H., Boutrel, B., Chen, S., Kenny, P., Markou, A., O'Dell, L., Parsons, L. & Sanna, P. (2004). Neurobiological mechanisms in the transition from drug use to drug dependence. *Neuroscience and Biobehavioral Reviews*, 27(8), 739–749.
45. http://psychcentral.com/lib/an-introduction-to-compulsive-gambling/000360 Retrieved May 16, 2014.
46. e.g., Crabbe, J.C. (2002). Genetic contributions to addiction. *Annual Review of Psychology*, 53, 435–462.
    Nestler, E.J. (2001). Total recall—The memory of addiction. *Science*, 292(5525), 2266–2267.
47. Wolf, F.W. & Heberlein, U. (2003). Invertebrate models of addiction. *Journal of Neurobiology*, 54, 161–178.
48. http://psychcentral.com/lib/an-introduction-to-compulsive-gambling/000360 Retrieved May 16, 2014.
49. Alexandra Katehakihttp. Retrieved February 11, 2016. www.goodreads.com/quotes/tag/sex-addiction
50. Gray, P. & Garcia, J. (2013). *Evolution and human sexual behavior*. Cambridge, MA: Harvard University Press.
51. Gray, P. & Garcia, J. (2013). *Evolution and human sexual behavior*. Cambridge, MA: Harvard University Press.
52. U.S. Bureau of Labor Statistics (2014). Table A-1 Time spent in detailed primary activities . . . 2014 annual averages. Retrieved February 11, 2016. www.bls.gov/tus/tables/a1_2014.pdf
53. e.g., Tanner, J. & Raymond, M.A. (2012). *Marketing Principles, Chapter 3 Consumer behavior: How people make buying decisions*. Retrieved February 11, 2016. http://2012books.lardbucket.org/books/marketing-principles-v1.0/s06-consumer-behavior-how-people-m.html. Steptoe, A., Pollard, T.M. & Wardle, J. (1995). Development of a measure of the motives underlying the selection of food: The food choice questionnaire. *Appetite*, 25, 267–284; Heikkila, R., Mantyselka, P. & Ahonens, R. (2011). Price, familiarity, and availability determine the choice of drug—A population-based survey five years after generic substitution was introduced in Finland. *BMC Clinical Pharmacology*, 11, 20–24; Mennecke, B.E., Townsend, A.M., Hayes, D.J. & Lonergan, S.M. (2007). A study

of the factors that influence consumer attitudes toward beef products using the conjoint market analysis tool. *Journal of Animal Science*, 85, 2639–2659; Murray, P. (2013). How emotions influence what we buy: The emotional core of consumer decision-making. *Psychology Today*. Retrieved February 11, 2016. www.psychologytoday.com/blog/inside-the-consumer-mind/201302/how-emotions-influence-what-we-buy

54. e.g., Little, A.C., Jones, B.C. & DeBruine, L. (2011). Facial attractiveness: Evolutionary based research. *Philosophical Transactions of the Royal Society London B: Biological Sciences*, 366(1571), 1638–1659; Andersson, M. (1994). *Sexual selection*. Princeton: Princeton University Press; Elder, G.H. J. (1969). Appearance and education in marriage mobility. *American Sociological Review*, 34, 519–533.

55. e.g., Desrumaux, P., De Bosscher, S. & Leoni, V. (2009). Effects of facial attractiveness, gender, and competence of applications on job recruitment. *Swiss Journal of Psychology*, 68(1), 33-43; Bardack, N. & McAndrew, F. (1985). The influence of physical attractiveness and manner of dress on success in a simulated personnel decision. *Journal of Social Psychology*, 125, 777–778; Hosoda, M., Stone-Romero, E. & Coats, G. (2003). The effects of physical attractiveness on job-related outcomes: A meta-analysis of experimental studies, *Personnel Psychology*, 56, 431–434.

56. e.g., Little, A.C., Burriss, R.P., Jones, B.C. & Roberts, S.C. (2007). Facial appearance affects voting decisions. *Evolution and Human Behavior*, 28, 18–27; Olivio, C. & Todorov, A. (2009). The look of a winner: The emerging—and disturbing—science of how candidates' physical appearances influence our choice in leaders. *Scientific American*. Retrieved February 11, 2016. www.scientificamerican.com/article/the-look-of-a-winner/#; Bailenson, J., Yengar, S., Yee, N. & Collins, N. (2008). Facial similarity between voters and candidates causes influence. *Public Opinion Quarterly*, 72(5), 935–961.

# 10

# SOCIALITY (ORIGINATING MORE THAN 600 MILLION YEARS AGO)

People are quintessential social creatures, and as a range of humanists and social scientists of all stripes have observed, understanding humans requires an understanding of relationships. People are born into relationships and then spend the rest of their lives making relationship-related choices. However most aspects of present-day human Sociality are built on Well-Being Systems that pre-date the emergence of human-like organisms. Exploring the evolutionary foundations of Sociality is a major focus of this chapter. Also considered is the evidence that satisfying Sociality-related needs, more than the satisfaction of any other type of need, leads to long-term well-being.

## Origins of Sociality-Related Well-Being

Sociality-driven behavior must be a good thing since it has independently evolved numerous times, appearing in virtually every major grouping of life, with examples occurring even amongst primitive bacteria.[1] But the social behaviors of single-celled creatures like bacteria pale in comparison to those of more complex organisms with the evolution of multicellularity amongst plants and animals particularly significant. The latter event, the evolution of multicellularity in animals, is believed to have happened around a half billion years ago. It was so momentous that it has been dubbed the "Biological Big Bang" (in reference to the cosmic "Big Bang" that created the universe),[2] or alternatively, the "Cambrian Explosion." For billions of years, there was seemingly nothing but single celled, microscopic life. Then in an evolutionary blink of the eye, the fossil record is suddenly filled with macroscopic, multicellular animals of all shapes and sizes, many of which seemed to be living in relation to each other. Some have argued that the same processes that enabled the earliest single-celled animals to become multicellular through the evolution of internal symbiotic coalitions of formerly independent cells also enabled Sociality, the evolution of symbiotic coalitions of formerly independent animals.[3]

We humans take for granted that living things can be large, multicellular and live within complex social structures. We assume that it is normal for millions of cells, let alone millions of organisms, to live together as if they were one, but this was a huge evolutionary leap; a leap made highly unlikely given the importance to life of Individuality-related Well-Being Systems. For the first two billion years of life on earth, living things actively and aggressively preserved their individuality; rejecting anything deemed to be non-self was a matter of life and death. No doubt the earliest forms of life, with their leaky cell membranes and asexual form of reproduction, would have found themselves living cheek to jowl with their neighbors. Most of those neighbors would have been close relatives, perhaps even identical clones. However due to random mutations some genetic diversity would still have been present amongst these neighbors. Interestingly, there's considerable speculation that these early life forms regularly swapped their genetic material in a process known as Horizontal Gene Transfer.[4] Modern day bacteria still swap their genes and many still live in vast colonial "mats." Some of the earliest evidence of life on earth comes from the fossil remains of these large, ancient mats of bacteria.[5] But making the leap from a mat of genetically similar bacteria to a true multicellular, social creature was huge. To provide some perspective on this event, even today hundreds of millions of years after the Biological Big Bang, the vast majority of life on earth still tenaciously clings to its single-celled, independent life style. The exact circumstances that allowed the breakdown of the Individuality-related Well-Being Systems sufficient to allow this burst of evolution into multicellularity and sociality has been a topic of deep debate ever since the time of Darwin.

Sociality has been an area of particular focus over the past fifty years, as well as one of the most contested.[6] Literally hundreds of theories have been put forward and as many rejected to account for the rise of social systems and socially motivated choice-making.[7] One of the challenges of understanding the choices people make in an effort to satisfy relational needs is that such choices are inherently more complex than those made in order to satisfy individual needs. The following quote from renowned biologist Edward O. Wilson highlights this complexity.

> What is good for the individual can be destructive to the family, what preserves the family can be harsh on both the individual and the tribe to which the family belongs; what promotes the tribe can weaken the family and destroy the individual; and so on upward through the permutations of levels of organization.[8]

From a very human perspective, the forces that would have resulted in life evolving in the direction of Sociality, including the value of cooperation, seem obvious. Seen from the vantage point of a highly evolved, super social species, nothing seems more self-evident than the fact that cooperating with others has survival value since it insures that all members of the group are more likely to survive. Or to put it in the framework of my model, the choice to cooperate is predicated on the assumption that doing so, even if temporarily, increases the odds that good things will happen, i.e., that well-being will be enhanced. Certainly the human experience would suggest that on average, this is true; and thus natural selection would have increasingly favored this mode of behavior. The evolutionary biologists who have pondered this phenomenon over the past half century are not universally convinced that the evolution of Sociality was quite this straightforward. This is because most evolutionary biologists operate from the perspective that the engines of evolution are exclusively the genes within an individual and that no organism acts in a way which is not in the best interest of those individual, inherently selfish genes.[9] In other words, the only way cooperative behaviors can end up persisting in a population is if those behaviors directly benefit one or more genes, independent of what they do for the organism as a whole.

Although I do not fully subscribe to this view of how evolution works, considerable thought and research have gone into these ideas, and the considerable data on which these ideas are based are almost certainly valid. Whether the underlying theory is true or not, after much discussion and fifty years of debate, most evolutionary biologists seem to have finally agreed that there are three basic circumstances in which social cooperation emerges, with presumably each circumstance resulting in a unique set of Sociality-related Well-Being Systems.[10,11]

## The Three Key Sociality-Related Well-Being Systems

Implicit in discussions about these three circumstances which supported the evolution of sociality is that they represent a gradation, with the first of these forms evolving first and subsequent forms building upon and evolving from earlier ones. I will introduce each of these three separate types of Sociality-related Well-Being Systems initially using non-human examples since these are what are most frequently used in the evolutionary biology research literature.

The first and most common form of sociality is one where the benefits of cooperation immediately and directly accrue to the individual performing the cooperative act. In other words, by being cooperative with another individual, the individual initiating the cooperative act will be more reproductively successful and leave more offspring independently of any benefit to others. Although it is possible that as a consequence of cooperating, others too might benefit, that is not what drives the individual to cooperate nor was such shared benefit the driver for evolving the appropriate Sociality-related Well-Being Systems. A classic example of this principle is the schooling behavior of fish. Research has shown that one fish swimming by itself has a much higher chance of being attacked and consumed by a predator than does a similar fish swimming amongst a school of hundreds of fish.[12] Although a predator is more likely to see a large school of fish than an individual fish and is even more likely to catch a fish under these conditions, by cooperating as part of a school, each fish in the school significantly decreases its individual risk of being the victim of predation. Hence a cooperative schooling behavior directly increases each fish's overall genetic fitness, so each fish "selfishly" swims as part of the school for its own, not other fish's benefit. Under these conditions, cooperation is evolutionarily advantageous and Sociality-related Well-Being Systems supporting this type of cooperation would have been selected for.

A second form of sociality involves cooperative behaviors where an individual's helping of another alters the behavioral response of its partner such that the second individual ends up doing something that directly or indirectly increases the genetic success of the first. This is the basic "if I scratch your back, you'll scratch mine" idea. A common example of this might be cooperative feeding in birds. Sometimes food resources are more or less evenly distributed within the environment. When this happens typically birds can and do stake out territories, particularly during the breeding season, and defend these territories so that they can be guaranteed that no other bird will poach their food supply. But in other situations food only occurs in unpredictable patches, often in great abundance where it does occur. The challenge in these situations is finding the food. So rather than waste time and energy defending territories with limited resources, birds which depend upon patchy food resources travel in flocks in which each individual can cooperatively help to locate food. At any given time, only one individual is likely to locate a food source, but collectively and over time each member of the group is better off because of sharing. Hence the genetic fitness of the individual is enhanced and these types of Sociality-related Well-Being Systems would evolve.

The third and final form of sociality involves more altruistic relationships, typically discussed in the literature as the preferential interactions between related individuals. It was long observed that highly social animals ranging from bees and ants to herds of buffalo and troops of baboons tended to be closely related genetically. Still why these related organisms would risk their lives for each other was unclear. British theoretical biologist William Hamilton is credited with developing the first really satisfactory explanation for how this could have evolved (that is satisfactory as defined by the selfish gene explanation for evolution). Hamilton's model was called "kin selection" and predicted that the level of cooperation between related organisms should be directly proportional to the percentage of shared genes. In other words, brothers who share half their genes should be more likely to cooperate than cousins who share only one eighth of their genetic material; in fact, brothers should be four times more likely to cooperate than cousins. A wide range of studies have found evidence in support of this pattern. The closer the genetic relationship of group members, the more stable and intricate are their social bonds.[13] This, according to the theory of kin selection, is why social insects like bees and ants are so tightly organized since all members of the colony are genetically sisters, with half of all their DNA in common. Following from these arguments, most evolutionary biologists have questioned whether altruism actually ever occurs outside of kin-selection type circumstances,[14] this despite widespread evidence for the presence of altruism amongst humans, even in cases of limited genetic relatedness.[15] Nonetheless, it can be assumed that evolution of Sociality-related Well-Being Systems based on kin selection also likely has evolved amongst some species.

The world of business and commerce provides a particularly rich source of human examples of Sociality. Scholars and practitioners of the business world have for nearly a century recognized that cooperation is a key component of business success, in particular defining business organizations like corporations as systems of cooperative effort and coordinated activity.[16] In these systems, leaders and members of work groups are judged by how well they cooperate to deliver the results the organizations and their business environments demand. "Those who adeptly develop and help others to develop cooperative relationships are poised for success, as are the organizations that employ them."[17] However not all cooperation within the business world shares the same motivation, in fact examples of not one but all three of the above Sociality-related Well-Being Systems can be found.

Not so many years ago, a very successful business investor by the name of Charlie Munger gave a talk at Harvard Business School called the "The Psychology of Human Mismanagement."[18] Munger's goal was to describe how management could get workers to act in ways that were in the best interest of the company. He talked about how the huge package delivery company FedEx could not get its night shift to finish on time despite trying everything to speed things up. That is until they stopped paying night shift workers by the hour and started paying them by completion of their shift. He also talked about how technology company Xerox created a new, better, faster copier machine, but after a year they were dismayed to see that it had sold fewer units than their inferior, older machine. That is when they figured out that their sales staff got a bigger commission for selling the older machines. Once they corrected that problem, the new machine sold better. Munger concluded his talk by saying that basically all a manager needed to know about motivating workers was that workers were motivated by incentives. In other words, workers are not actually working for the good of the company; they are working for their own good. According to Munger, as long as you reward them properly, in fact only if you reward them properly, will they do what is necessary to make the collective, i.e., the corporation, work better.

Although considerable evidence exists that individuals work for a wide range of reasons,[19] making money (and having benefits) is clearly one of them. And clearly there is evidence, anecdotal as above as well as empirical, to suggest that by and large the greater the personal benefit, e.g., the more money and benefits an individual receives, the more likely it is that employees will choose to work in ways that benefit the group.[20] In other words, this is a clear example of the evolutionary biologist's first type of Sociality, where an individual's action has the potential to benefit the group, but the main motivation is insuring the individual's own perception of success and thus, presumably, that individual's well-being and fitness. In fact, the entire science of economics is built on the assumption that this type of "me-first" behavior is the norm for people, that all human choice-making is inherently selfish in nature. Two hundred and forty years ago, Adam Smith, considered one of the founders of the discipline of economics, described it this way:

> Every individual necessarily labours to render the annual revenue of the society as great as he can. He generally neither intends to promote the public interest, nor knows how much he is promoting it . . . He intends only his

own gain, and he is in this, as in many other cases, led by an invisible hand to promote an end which was no part of his intention. Nor is it always the worse for society that it was no part of his intention. By pursuing his own interest he frequently promotes that of the society more effectually than when he really intends to promote it. I have never known much good done by those who affected to trade for the public good.[21]

However, the rise of industrialization in the 18th and 19th centuries caused others in the business community to rebel against this selfish view and advocate for alternative forms of collaboration. Samuel Gompers, one of the leaders of the fledgling American labor movement, gave the following speech in the spring of 1890.

My friends, we have met here today to celebrate the idea that has prompted thousands of working-people of Louisville and New Albany to parade the streets . . .; that prompts the toilers of Chicago to turn out by their fifty or hundred thousand of men; that prompts the vast army of wage-workers in New York to demonstrate their enthusiasm and appreciation of the importance of this idea; that prompts the toilers of England, Ireland, Germany, France, Italy, Spain, and Austria to defy the manifestos of the autocrats of the world and say that on May the first, 1890, the wage-workers of the world will lay down their tools in sympathy with the wage-workers of America, to establish a principle of limitations of hours of labor to eight hours for sleep, eight hours for work, and eight hours for what we will.[22]

Perhaps there is no better business example of the evolutionary biologists' second condition—"if I scratch your back, you'll scratch mine" than the labor movement. Labor unions were created based on a belief in the value of solidarity, the sense that each individual should look out for the interests of the group, and in so doing the interests of the individual would be better served. The assumption was that each individual had limited power or security when working within a large organization. Jobs were scarce and the number of individuals wanting to work was great. The owners could treat workers as interchangeable parts; if one individual was unhappy or unproductive, they could easily be replaced by someone else. However, if the workers bound together, then each individual's risk could be mitigated by the strength of the collective. Replacing an entire workforce was not so easy. Taking this kind of unified position obviously required that each individual had to potentially be willing to contribute to the whole, to make some kind of individual sacrifice—be that a part of their wage, a reduction in their individual connection to management, or potentially the risk of a strike—in return for collective benefits such as higher wages, better working conditions and ultimately, job security. The history of the labor movement is the history of those assumptions being played out, sometimes confirming the benefits of collective action and sometimes not. Over the past several hundred years, millions of workers have chosen to give this idea a try, by and large for the better.

Not always, but occasionally, labor unions have also attempted to advocate for an even "higher" form of collaboration, cooperation just for the sake of cooperation, i.e., altruism.

> Labor News, 1/14/2010: The AFL-CIO Thursday called for the United States and the entire international community, including the global union movement, to "do our utmost to aid our Haitian sisters and brothers in their moment of extraordinary need."[23]

After a massive earthquake struck Haiti in 2010, not just labor unions but people from all walks of life attempted to come to the island's aid. Among those who responded were countless doctors and nurses from every part of the world who left their jobs and flew to Haiti to provide assistance to the injured. One such person was Eugenia Millender. Both a nurse and a Ph.D., Millender had experienced multiple hurricanes as a Florida resident and Panama native, and knew firsthand what it was like to have such a major natural disaster strike. But even she was struck by the scale of the disaster as it unfolded on television. "As a human being, I couldn't imagine how a person could one day have their whole family, friends, and neighbors, and the next day, lose them all," she said. "Day after day, the stories I heard got worse to the point that I just couldn't watch anymore. I wanted to do more than pray."[24] So she decided to leave her job and travel to Port-au-Prince to see how she could help.

Millender, like many others who responded to the Haitian and other similar disasters, justified her actions as one of personal commitment to the well-being of others. Millender was not related to anyone in Haiti, in fact prior to the disaster she could not name a single individual who lived in Haiti. Still she made a significant sacrifice of her own time and livelihood in order to volunteer in service to these individuals. Hers was an act that can only be described as altruistic. And this is where the evolutionary biologists' agreed on conditions get problematic. Although this is indeed an example of their third condition, an individual choosing to cooperate when there is no clear immediate benefit for the individual, i.e., altruism, what is missing is any evidence that the selfish gene/kin selection model explains the behavior. As stated above, there was no evidence that any of the individuals Millender was seeking to help were genetically closely related to her. She was choosing to cooperate with individuals who were total strangers with no expectation that there would be any reciprocal benefit to her other than her own self-perception of well-being.

The idea, and mathematics, of kin selection works really well for organisms like social insects such as bees and ants or even social mammals like prairie dogs because all the animals in the colony are indeed genetically closely related (in the extreme case of social insects all the workers are genetic sisters). The same does not seem to apply to most human examples of altruism, including and particularly within the business world; here genetic relatedness is the exception rather than the rule. Although historically nepotism was common practice within companies, it is currently strongly frowned upon. Yet, there are many examples of apparent altruistic behavior ranging from extreme examples such as individuals risking their lives to save their co-workers during an emergency to the almost daily occurrence of unrelated colleagues happily sharing their ideas and time, often at the expense of their own personal benefit. Why would this be the case? As suggested by a number of recent social science studies, it seems that the evolutionary biologists got it partly but not totally right. Humans are only willing to altruistically cooperate when they perceive, consciously or not, relatedness, but perceived relatedness need not be genetic.

## Learning to Cooperate

In a recent blog post, industrial engineer Jeffrey Matthius describes how he learned the value of being a sharing workmate through his participation in a series of free workshops conducted by a group of programmers, the Ruby community, committed to fostering cultures of sharing within the workplace.

> It was an intense 10 weeks, and during that time I got steeped in the sharing culture of the Ruby community. I had two professional mentors who volunteered for no other reason than they wanted to help spread the knowledge. It was a breath of fresh air.[25]

He went on to describe how week after week, individuals for no apparent reason other than wanting to help others gave "away the secrets of an awesome skill or tool they've spent years honing or creating. Even better, contrary to the beliefs of the entire industrial design community, these speakers, who aren't paid for their presentations, are considered pillars of the community. And their careers thrive because of it." [26] This experience was transformational for Matthius. He now goes out of his way to "give back." When he discovered that a group of his co-workers were interested in programming but did not know where to begin, he offered to teach them, and has been doing so ever since.

One of the benefits of sharing something with others is the development of stronger personal bonds, and stronger personal bonds become self-reinforcing. The more a person shares with someone, the more likely that second person will share back with the first person, which in turn will cause the first person to want to share again with the second. This is an example of a learned positive feedback loop, and it is the essence of most of the Sociality-related Well-Being Systems that exist in the workplace and beyond.

Although social scientists have documented a wide range of reasons for why individuals within organizations might cooperate, including reasons of personal gain, power, trust and resource interdependence,[27] one of the most powerful reasons is the development of strong relationships. Co-workers with a shared sense of values, interests and concerns are more likely to cooperate than are those with a limited sense of shared values, interests or concerns. In other words, co-workers with a shared perception of self are most likely to collaborate, a sense of one-ness fosters collaboration. Evidence for this conclusion comes from work done by business psychologists Laurie Milton and James Westphal who investigated the motivations for collaboration of workgroups in two unrelated divisions of a large, diversified public organization. In total Milton and Westphal surveyed nearly all the employees, 261 members in all, of these organizations involved in emer-gency response groups that sent and coordinated support services in emergency situations (e.g., fires, riots, accidents, assaults) and of construction groups that worked on roads and bridges.[28] Based on an extensive survey that was designed to test a variety of possible reasons for cooperation, their results suggested that co-worker collaboration, particularly under stressful and at times dangerous situ-ations, ultimately depended upon whether or not an individual perceived that another co-worker shared his sense of personal identity, and that this perception was reciprocated.

This learned relatedness influences human choice-making and behavior across a wide swath of situations. Research by communications scientist Daniel Kahan has shown that perceptions of social relatedness, and the desire/need for maintain-ing those bonds, can and in many cases does override conventional notions of rationality when it comes to choice. For example, it has been shown that many of the individuals who actively deny that humans are significantly contributing to global climate change, a finding supported by virtually all scientists, take this position not because of a lack of awareness of the scientific data but rather due to their need to remain in tune with the beliefs of their social network, what Kahan calls "identity protective cognition."[29] In other words, the key reason two individuals cooperate or even choose to act in comparable ways was indeed as pre-dicted by evolutionary biologists, due to perceptions of relatedness, but in this case perceived relatedness is a learned rather than an inherited condition.

Historically, perceptions of relatedness, even in humans, was almost exclu-sively something that occurred between genetically related individuals—parents and their children; brothers, sisters and cousins growing up together; related adults living together within a single tribal village. Under the conditions that prevailed over most of human history the evolutionary biologist's ideas of kin selection probably applied—those individuals most likely to exhibit altruism towards each other were indeed those individuals most closely related to each other since these were the people a person grew up with and lived with daily. But these historic patterns reflected correlations rather than causality; genetic relatedness it appears does not really cause humans to make these kinds of choices. At least for an intel-ligent vertebrate like humans, the causative factor appears to be learned related-ness. As discussed in the previous chapter with regard to immune reactions, the body learns to perceive as "self" those entities it begins life associated with. More often than not, these self-related entities are genetically very similar, but they need not be. Over the years, evidence of human altruistic forms of Sociality, in which an individual risks life or limb for another, have been shown to involve both genes and learning.[30,31] However as human societies have become more mobile, families more fluid and people are spending an increasing percentage of their lives interacting with non-related individuals, the importance of learned relatedness as opposed to genetic relatedness has become ever more apparent.

One of the more interesting pieces of evidence supporting the learned nature of relatedness comes from people and their pets. There is a growing propensity amongst modern, urban humans to treat their pets like family members; to basically ascribe the same attention and even perception of relatedness to these non-human "children" as someone might to their own biological children. This behavior was vividly demonstrated in the wake of Hurricane Katrina when thousands of New Orleans residents were stranded by flooding for days without food or clean water. Despite being desperate to be saved, many individuals refused to be rescued when help arrived. The reason was that when the National Guard arrived in boats and helicopters, they were under orders to rescue only people. The rules stated that no pets were be evacuated. Hundreds of people refused to be evacuated when they realized it meant leaving their pets behind.[32] The image of people having to decide between their own and their pet's welfare caused such an uproar that in the aftermath of the storm, the U.S. Congress rewrote federal emergency management policies so that pets too would be rescued in event of future such catastrophes.[33]

Although some might argue that this is an example of modern values running amok, it demonstrates the principle that if a person spends sufficient time around another organism, and that organism is perceived to provide the attributes associated with relatedness, e.g., affection and social support, then that organism is likely to trigger the same Sociality-related Well-Being Systems as would a child or other close relative. This is seemingly not just a quirk of human learned relatedness; there are numerous anecdotal examples of pet dogs risking their lives in order to help/save their genetically unrelated owners. These altruistic behaviors make absolutely no sense if relatedness is defined solely by genetics but make perfect sense if the operative principle is that the self-perceptions of relatedness for humans are primarily learned. In fact, the trigger for an altruistic act does not even have to be animate. Humans will rush into a burning house to save family pictures or objects once owned by a loved one.

The examples point out another aspect of Sociality-related Well-Being Systems. They are clearly important to people, or why would someone risk their life in order to preserve them? Evidence for just how important comes from many sources. According to psychologists who study well-being, the healthiest, longest lived and also happiest people on earth are those who perceive that their Sociality-related needs are well satisfied.[34]

## Sociality and Well-Being

Data supporting the strong positive correlation between Sociality-related well-being and fitness comes from many sources, but arguably one of the most persuasive comes from the longest study of human development ever conducted, the Harvard University "Grant Study."[35] Beginning in 1938, the Grant Study set out to follow the lives of a group of Harvard University students—among them President John F. Kennedy and former Washington Post editor Ben Bradlee—and it has been tracking every aspect of these individual's lives ever since. In the 1970s, the study began collaborating with a similar longitudinal study of young men from the inner-city Boston tenements; that study had been going on since the 1940s. The result of these combined studies is an unprecedented compendium of long-term data of individuals (though all are white males) of varying social status and upbringing. At regular intervals, all of the men's physical and emotional well-being was assessed, including the addition in recent years of genetic testing. Robert Waldinger, a Harvard psychiatrist, assumed the project's leadership in 2003. Although there is a wealth of data and many conclusions that have been gleaned from monitoring these many lives from young adulthood through old age, Waldinger believes that there is but one clear takeaway: The happiest and healthiest participants in both groups were the ones who made the decision that maintaining close, intimate relationships was their highest priority.

Many in both study groups, but particularly the men from Harvard, were very success oriented and chose to invest their time and energy in building careers and wealth. In no small measure due to the social advantages they began life with, many did achieve significant fame and amass great fortunes. However, the process of acquiring fame and wealth often resulted in these same individuals becoming quite socially isolated. According to Waldinger, "people who are more isolated than they want to be from others find that they are less happy, their health declines earlier in midlife, their brain functioning declines sooner and they live shorter lives than people who are not lonely. . . . good, close relationships seem to buffer us from some of the slings and arrows of getting old."[36] According to Waldinger, wealth, fame and career success, long assumed to be vital to personal well-being, did not correlate with long-term health or happiness; what did correlate with long-term health and happiness was having close connections with other human beings.

Corroborating evidence for this conclusion comes from situations where an individual feels lonely,[37] or where social bonds break down and individuals feel socially adrift, for example when an individual decides to leave a social group in which she has been a long time member,[38] or when someone decides to change jobs.[39] These disruptions to social relationships have been shown to precipitate a range of negative effects, including decreased blood flow and breathing, negative moods such as fatigue and depression, and weakening of the immune system.[40]

It is interesting to ponder why social relationships, Sociality-related needs, should be so particularly central to perceived well-being. One possible explanation could be related to persistence. Feelings of well-being are notoriously difficult to attain and maintain. This is true whether the needs being satisfied are Continuity-related such as satiation or temperature regulation, Individuality-related such as good health, Sexuality-related such as sexual arousal and satiation, or even the more intellectual modalities of Reflectivity or Creativity & Spirituality.

By contrast, once established, the positive feelings associated with a good friendship can last a lifetime; so too the feelings associated with love for a child. By this hypothesis, the high salience of Sociality-related well-being may only partially be due to the quality of well-being it affords, but equally the quantity of well-being it affords. Other drivers of well-being continually wax and wane, and constantly require considerable time and energy. Strong social bonds persist for long periods of time and, relatively speaking, require less time and energy to maintain. From a cost/benefit perspective, Sociality delivers significant pay-off.

Alternatively, it could just be that humans have evolved to value the needs of social relationships above all else. Regardless of the reason why Sociality-related needs are so important, one thing is clear: people have a fundamental need to have relationships and feel like they belong to a group.[41] And whether the actual time and energy required to support Sociality is actually greater or less than other modalities, an incredibly large percentage of most people's daily thoughts, actions and feelings are motivated by these types of social needs, so much so, that the lived experience variables related to Sociality disproportionately influence how and why people make the choices they do. In this respect, humans are not so dissimilar from a whole host of other social species, including most mammals and birds, which hone to the "herd" when faced with choice-making.[42] What sets humans apart from nearly all other species though is the ability to mentally ponder their social relationships and consciously and strategically attempt to align their actions with those individual(s) deemed most advantageous.

## Notes

1. Wilson, E.O. (1975). *Sociobiology: The new synthesis.* Cambridge, MA: The Belknap Press.
2. Koonin, E.V. (2007). The Biological Big Bang model for the major transitions in evolution. *Biology Direct*, 2, 21–30. Retrieved July 5, 2013. www.biology-direct.com/content/2/1/21
3. With some favoring a process called endosymbiosis, e.g., Margulis, L. (1998). *Symbiotic planet: A new look at evolution.* New York: Basic Books, and others favoring a process known as colonial symbiosis, e.g., Wolpert, L. & Szathmáry, E. (2002). Multi-cellularity: Evolution and the egg. *Nature*, 420(6917), 745–751.
   Hall, B.K., Hallgrímsson, B. & Strickberger, M.W. (2008). *Strickberger's evolution: The integration of genes, organisms and populations* (4th ed.). Sudbury, MA: Jones and Bartlett Publishers.
4. Woese, C. (1998). The universal ancestor. *Proceedings of the National Academy of Sciences, USA*, 95(12), 6854–6859.
5. Awramik, S.M. (1983). Filamentous fossil bacteria from the Archean of Western Australia. *Precambrian Research*, 20(2–4), 357–374.
   Achenbach, J. (2016). 3.7-billion-year-old fossils may be the oldest signs of life on Earth. *Washington Post*. Retrieved August 31, 2016. www.washingtonpost.com/news/speaking-of-science/wp/2016/08/31/3-7-billion-year-old-fossils-may-be-the-oldest-signs-of-life-on-earth/?utm_term=.a2c769c27e3f
6. A particular area of contention has been theories about cooperation and altruism.
7. Lehman, L. & Keller, L. (2006). The evolution of cooperation and altruism: A general framework and a classification of models. *Journal of Evolutionary Biology*, 19, 1364–1375.
8. Wilson, E.O. (1975). *Sociobiology: The new synthesis.* Cambridge, MA: The Belknap Press, p. 4.

9. These ideas were most clearly expressed in Richard Dawkins' seminal book *The Selfish Gene* (Dawkins, R. (1976). *The selfish gene.* Oxford: Oxford University Press).

10. Lehman, L. & Keller, L. (2006). The evolution of cooperation and altruism: A general framework and a classification of models. *Journal of Evolutionary Biology*, 19, 1364–1375.

11. Actually, evolutionary biologists have proposed at least two additional possible conditions for supporting cooperation. According to evolutionary biologists, another possible condition is what is known as the "green beard" hypothesis. This is a special form of kin selection in which a specific "altruistic" gene occurs in a population, but to be effective it not only needs to be shared by all members, it also needs to be clearly recognized by all members of a community. The idea was originally hypothesized by W.D. Hamilton (Hamilton, W.D. (1964). The genetical evolution of social behaviour. I. *Journal of Theoretical Biology*, 7, 1–16), but it was given its colorful name by Richard Dawkins a decade later when speculating that because of the deleterious consequences of cheating, which would undermine the cooperation, any such cooperative gene would need to be accompanied by some really obvious physical trait, e.g., a green beard, that allowed others to readily distinguish between those who possessed the cooperative gene and those who did not. Thus, green beards would only cooperate with other green beards and could avoid cooperating with non-green bearded free-loaders (Dawkins, R. (1976). *The selfish gene.* Oxford: Oxford University Press, p. 96–97). For many years the idea of a green beard gene was considered a hypothetical possibility but unlikely to actually occur in real organisms. However in recent years there have been claims that green beard genes have been found in some species of yeast, slime molds, ants, lizards and wood mice (cf., Grafen, A. (6 August 1998). Green beard as death warrant (PDF). *Nature*, 394(6693), 521–522; Keller, L., Ross, K. & Kenneth, G. (6 August 1998). Selfish genes: A green beard in the red fire ant. *Nature*, 394(6693), 573–575; Queller, D.C., Ponte, E., Bozzaro, S. & Strassmann, J. (3 January 2003). Single-gene greenbeard effects in the social amoeba Dictyostelium discoideum (PDF). *Science*, 299(5603), 105–106; Sinervo, B., Chaine, A., Clobert, J., Calsbeek, R., Hazard, L., Lancaster, L., McAdam, A.G., Alonzo, S., Corrigan, G. & Hochberg, M.E. (May 2006). Self-recognition, color signals, and cycles of greenbeard mutualism and altruism. *Proceedings of the National Academy of Sciences of the USA*, 103(19), 7372–7377.

    Prakash, S. (18 December 2008). Yeast gone wild. *Seed*. Retrieved 29 November 2009; Smukalla, S., Caldara, M., Pochet, N., Beauvais, A., Guadagnini, S., Yan, C., Vinces, M.D., Jansen, A. & Prevost, M.C. (14 November 2008). FLO1 is a variable green beard gene that drives biofilm-like cooperation in budding yeast. *Cell*, 135(4), 726–737; Moore, H., Dvoráková, K., Jenkins, N. & Breed, W. (1 March 2002), Exceptional sperm cooperation in the wood mouse. *Nature*, 418, 174–177). However, to the best of my knowledge there is currently no evidence nor much discussion suggesting that cooperation in humans is primarily driven by the presence of one or more green beard genes.

    There is one final condition that has been proposed as a possible evolutionary mechanism for Relationality. This condition is what is known as "group selection," a situation in which natural selection acts on whole groups of organisms as opposed to individual genes, favoring some groups over others, leading to the evolution of traits that are group-advantageous. Originally proposed by individuals like V.C. Wynne-Edwards and Konrad Loren, as well as later championed by none other than E.O. Wilson (1975). *Sociobiology: The new synthesis.* Cambridge, MA: The Belknap Press, one of the leading figures in sociobiology, it is generally disavowed by main-stream evolutionary biologists.

    Given the controversies surround these two mechanisms, I will not deal with either of these "conditions" for social collaboration in this chapter.

12. Wilson, E.O. (1975). *Sociobiology: The new synthesis.* Cambridge, MA: The Belknap Press, p. 38.

13. Wilson, E.O. (1975). *Sociobiology: The new synthesis.* Cambridge, MA: The Belknap Press, p. 73.

14. e.g., Trivers, R.L. (1971). The evolution of reciprocal altruism. *The Quarterly Review of Biology*, 46(1), 35–57.

Foster, K.R., Wenseleers, T. & Ratnieks, F.L.W. (2006). Kin selection is the key to altruism. *TRENDS in Evolution and Ecology,* 21(2), 57–59.

15. cf., Fehr, E. & Fischbacher, U. (2003). The nature of human altruism. *Nature,* 425, 785–791.

16. Barnard, C.I. (1938). *The functions of the executive.* Cambridge, MA: Harvard University Press.

17. Milton, L.P. & Westphal, J.D. (2005). Identity confirmation networks and cooperation in work groups. *Academy of Management Journal,* 48(2), 191–212.

18. Lewis, M. (2011). *The big short.* New York: Norton.

19. e.g., Why people work. Retrieved March 10, 2016. http://davetgc.com/Why_People_Work.html

20. It is also worth noting that recent research has shown that the benefit that has the greatest long-term payoff for companies is actually not giving monetary rewards to workers but praise and encouragement (cf., Ariely, D. (2016). *Payoff: The hidden logic that shapes our motivations.* New York: Simon & Schuster).

21. Smith, A.P. (1776). *An inquiry into the nature and causes of the wealth of nations* (1st ed.). London: W. Strahan. Retrieved March 10, 2016. www.investopedia.com/terms/i/invisiblehand.asp#ixzz42WpCoL7O

22. Gompers, S. (1890). Retrieved March 10, 2016. www.historymuse.net/readings/GompersWhatdoestheworkingmanwant.htm

23. Motion Picture Editors Guild. (2010). Retrieved March 10, 2016. www.editorsguild.com/labornews.cfm?LaborNewsid=2926

24. Minority Nurse (2011). Retrieved March 10, 2016. http://minoritynurse.com/nursing-volunteer-efforts/

25. Matthius, J. (2013). Why I teach programming to my co-workers. *SendGrid.* Retrieved July 21, 2016. https://sendgrid.com/blog/why-i-teach-programming-to-my-co-workers/

26. Matthius, J. (2013). Why I teach programming to my co-workers. *SendGrid.* Retrieved July 21, 2016. https://sendgrid.com/blog/why-i-teach-programming-to-my-co-workers/

27. cf., Lundin, M. (2007). Explaining cooperation: How resource interdependence, goal congruence, and trust affect joint actions in policy implementation. *Journal of Public Administrative Research Theory,* 17(4), 651–672.

28. Milton, L.P. & Westphal, J.D. (2005). Identity confirmation networks and cooperation in work groups. *Academy of Management Journal,* 48(2), 191–212.

29. Kahan, D.M. (2017). The expressive rationality of inaccurate perceptions. *Behavioral and Brain Sciences,* 40. https://www.cambridge.org/core/journals/behavioral-and-brain-sciences/article/expressive-rationality-of-inaccurate-perceptions/0B7D1B92F41B5408FBA7EFFFD78CD25E Retrieved June 11, 2017.

30. Holland, M. (2004). *Social bonding and nurture kinship: Compatibility between cultural and biological approaches.* Unpublished Doctoral Dissertation. London School of Economics, London.

31. Perhaps the best evidence for the role of learning in issues of Relationality comes from studies related to incest aversion. All humans seem to have some kind of innate aversion to incest, typically expressed as an aversion to incest with a sibling. However research has shown that individuals of different genetic origins, if raised together, have the same incest aversion as do genetically related siblings. Thus the expression of incest aversion is based on learning to avoid those one grows up with rather than based upon some innate sense of actual genetic relatedness (Biello, D. (2007). Evolving a mechanism to avoid sex with siblings. *Scientific American.* Retrieved February 7, 2014. www.scientificamerican.com/article/evolving-mechanism-avoid-sibling-sex/).

32. Glassey, S. (25 October 2010). Owners willing to risk lives for pets—Survey. *News.com.au.* Retrieved February 7, 2014. www.news.com.au/breaking-news/owners-willing-to-risk-lives-for-pets-survey/story-e6frfku0-1225834438263

33. Bea, K. (2007). *Federal emergency management policy changes after Hurricane Katrina: A summary of statutory provisions.* Washington, DC: Congressional Research Service. Retrieved February 10, 2014. www.fas.org/sgp/crs/homesec/RL33729.pdf

34. Diener, E. & Biswas-Diener, R. (2008). *Happiness: Unlocking the mysteries of psychological wealth.* Malden, MA: Blackwell.

Cha, A.J. (2016). People on the autism spectrum live an average of 18 years less than everyone else study finds. *Washington Post*. Retrieved March 18, 2016. www.washingtonpost.com/news/to-your-health/wp/2016/03/18/people-on-the-autism-spectrum-live-an-average-of-18-years-less-than-everyone-else-study-finds/?hpid=hp_hp-cards_hp-card-national%3Ahomepage%2Fcard

35. Itkowitz, C. (2016). Harvard researchers discovered the one thing everyone needs for happier, healthier lives. *The Independent*. Retrieved March 2, 2016. www.independent.co.uk/life-style/harvard-researchers-discover-the-one-thing-everyone-needs-for-happier-and-healthier-lives-a6907901.html

36. Waldinger, R. (2015). *What makes a good life? Lessons from the longest study on happiness*. Retrieved March 2, 2016. www.ted.com/talks/robert_waldinger_what_makes_a_good_life_lessons_from_the_longest_study_on_happiness?language=en

37. Hawkley, L.C. & Cacioppo, J.T. (2007). Aging and loneliness: Downhill quickly? *Current Directions in Psychological Science*, 16, 187–191.

    Hawkley, L.C., Thisted, R.A., Masi, C.M. & Cacioppo, J.T. (2010). Loneliness predicts increased blood pressure: Five-year cross-lagged analyses in middle-aged and older adults. *Psychol Aging*, 25, 132–141.

    Jaremka, L.M., Fagundes, C.P., Glaser, R., Bennett, J.M., Malarkey, W.B. & Kiecolt-Glaser, J.K. (2012). Loneliness predicts pain, depression, and fatigue: Understanding the role of immune dysregulation. *Psychoneuroendocrinology*, pii: S0306–4530(12)00403–9. doi:10.1016/j.psyneuen.2012.11.016.

38. e.g., Harris, K.J. (2015). *Leaving ideological social groups behind: A grounded theory of psychological disengagement*. Retrieved March 13, 2016. http://ro.ecu.edu.au/theses/1587

39. e.g., Faragher, E.B., Cass, M. & Cooper, C.L. (2005). The relationship between job satisfaction and health: A meta-analysis. *Occupational & Environmental Medicine*, 62, 105–112.

40. Goleman, D. (2006). *Social intelligence: The new science of human relationships*. New York: Bantam Books.

41. Baumeister, R. & Leary, M. (1995). The need to belong: Desire for interpersonal attachment as a fundamental human motivation. *Psychological Bulletin*, 117, 497–529.

42. e.g., Raafat, R. M., Chater, N. & Frith, C. (2009). Herding in humans. Trends in Cognitive Sciences. 13(10), 420–428.

# 11

# RELATIONALITY (ORIGINATING MORE THAN 16 MILLION YEARS AGO)

Nearly all mammals exhibit Sociality, but only a tiny few possess the Well-Being module of Relationality. Relationality is being able to consciously anticipate the consequences of one's actions, to possess social awareness such that one understands how what one does is likely to influence the behavior of others; this ability has potential to yield immense personal benefits.[1] It is in this modality that the social scientist's concept of *agency*—the process of actively pondering alternatives, making plans and carrying out actions in response to desires—first appears as an essential need-satisfaction tool.[2] Given how important relationships are to most mammals, this ability would have been transformative. This chapter will focus on when and how Relationality arose in humans and how it is used by humans to advance their individual and collective well-being.

## The Evolution of Relationality

Nearly all primates are social; most spend their lives in large social groups. For individuals living in such a highly social world, few choices are more important than one's social choices—choices of friends, choices of groups to hang out with, choices of sexual partners and life-mates, and choices as to how best to interact with each of these social partners. Even small choices can make a huge difference to one's social status within the group. Thus it is no surprise that socially conscious individuals regularly exercise this ability. Take for example the description below of two adolescent females.

> The [two females] led . . . the whole crowd of eager males. They regularly liked to [duck into inaccessible places] for no other reason [than to tease the males], thus provoking much tension amongst [them] . . . It resembled an elaborate cat and mouse play between the males mediated by the females.

This very purposeful sexual game sounds familiar, and easily could be a description of a group of teenagers at the local shopping mall. Actually, it is a description of the behavior of a group of forest chimpanzees.[3] Just as with humans, the better a chimp's ability to understand, empathize and, to the degree possible, anticipate what her fellow chimps are going to do, the greater her selective advantage. Those individuals with better social skills move higher up in the chimp social order than do those who lack sufficient social awareness. Chimps with poor social awareness not only end up lower on the chimp social hierarchy, but they die younger and produce fewer offspring.[4] Not unlike modern humans, it is others of their kind, other chimpanzees, that represent the greatest source of hazard and distress in a chimp's life, but also represent the greatest source of well-being. Chimps are notorious for their complex social repertoires. Individuals will engage in endless plots and schemes; at various times ruthlessly abusing, bribing or teasing and at other times tenderly loving and caring for each other. According to those who study them, the life of a chimpanzee is marked by a seemingly never-ending set of political alliances and betrayals; without exaggeration, a chimp's life is a veritable soap opera.[5]

The fact that chimpanzees' social-sexual shenanigans sound so remarkably familiar strongly suggests that the brains of both humans and chimpanzees possess similar capacities for conscious self-awareness and social agency. In fact considerable evidence exists to support this idea.[6] It appears that chimpanzees, just like humans, possess conscious social awareness; also just like humans, they exercise agency in order to successfully navigate the complexities of their social world.[7]

Given that both chimpanzees and humans share conscious self-awareness, most anthropologists and primatologists believe that this modality of Well-Being likely evolved at least 5 to 7 million years ago, sometime before the split between the human and chimpanzee lines. However, it is now known that other members of the great ape family also possess similar abilities, including bonobos, gorillas and orangutans. Likely then, the evolutionary beginnings of human Relationality must date back to at least 15 or 16 million years ago, the time of the last common ancestor between all these species. Of course, the Relationality modality could be even older than that since it has been discovered in other species of primates, for example rhesus macaques. However current thinking is that it arose independently on several occasions within highly social species, which would explain why a version of the Relationality modality of Well-Being has been found in a variety of totally unrelated species including whales and dolphins, elephants and even some birds like the European Magpie and likely dogs, crows and other creatures as well.[8] Thus to understand the human modality of Relationality it is best to focus on the evolution of these abilities specifically within the primate line.

A variety of monkeys and apes have been found to react in strikingly similar ways in the laboratory to experiments designed to test social and self-awareness. Psychologist Julie Neiworth conducted a review of nonhuman primate research and concluded that the common denominator across all species showing evidence of social awareness was a keen attentiveness to other animals like themselves, a mirror neuron system that responded in the same way to actions made by the self and by others, and cooperative behaviors that predispose organisms towards a foundation for social thinking.[9] Let me briefly review each of these elements.

The first of these attributes, an attentiveness to others like one's self, is the most basic and is not unusual in social animals of all kinds. However, those primates with tendencies towards social awareness took this attentiveness to new heights. Monkeys who showed this ability were likely to not only observe but mimic the actions of others. They also observed and mimicked the use of objects used by others, although not necessarily the goals for which those objects were used.[10]

The second of these attributes, mirror neuron systems, is particularly interesting. As described in Chapter 5, mirror neurons are sets of neurons located in various parts of the brain that simulate the observed actions of others.[11] Quite literally, these special neuronal clusters allow an individual to mentally "mirror" the actions and feelings of others. To reiterate my earlier description, brain scan studies of people watching someone crying and being sad showed that the areas in the imaged person's brain associated with crying and sadness "lit up" even though they were not directly doing these things or having these feelings.[12] Mirror neurons have now been found a wide range of primates, including macaques where they were originally discovered.[13] Neuroscientists have speculated that the evolution of mirror neurons many have been one of the key neural breakthroughs that allowed for the development of intraspecific social awareness.[14]

An important aspect of the finding that mirror neurons are key contributors to Relationality is that this system predates conscious awareness. Mirror neurons are motor neurons, and they act by stimulating awareness through direct activation of feelings, allowing organisms to enact awareness directly without the need for any intervening cognitive processes.[15] This fact reinforces one of the core premises of the model proposed in this book. Although it is theoretically possible for the separate components of well-being—sensing, deliberating/choosing, acting and regulating—to evolve as separate, totally independently functioning structures, that would not have been the most likely solution. Evolutionary history has dictated that the path of least resistance would have been for each newly evolving component to become integrated with pre-existing Well-Being Systems and in the process forming a single, larger and ever more complexly integrated Well-Being System.[16] In the case of Relationality, mirror neurons would have been one such component, which ultimately in humans and other great apes would have been subsumed into an even larger and even more complex Relationality-related Well-Being System that included conscious awareness.[17]

The final attribute pointed out by Neiworth is a history of cooperative behaviors. Again, a wide range of primate species exhibit some minimal level of cooperative behavior, but these are often quite limited. The key threshold behavior according to Neiworth seems to be cooperative breeding.[18] All of the most highly cooperative primate species are species that have evolved the ability, and in some cases ultimately the need, to socially support each other in raising young.[19]

In summary, it appears that the evolution of the mental tools required for Relationality-related Well-Being Systems did not just suddenly appear with the emergence of humans, but rather evolved progressively through the primate line, with new lineages adding ever more sophisticated and effective links to existing Relationality-related Well-Being Systems. Although a human-sized brain was clearly not necessary for Relationality to evolve in the first place, it appears that both the demands and the selective benefits of Relationality favored the evolution of ever-larger, ever-more complex brains.[20]

## Relationality and Brain Size

Some 50 years ago a behavioral biologist by the name of Alison Jolly hypothesized, based on studying lemurs, a relatively primitive group of primates, that brain size and intelligence were directly related to social complexity.[21] The same conclusion was independently reached by another biologist, Nicholas Humphrey, who stated, "I argue that the higher intellectual faculties of primates have evolved as an adaptation to the complexities of social living."[22] In essence, the necessity of interacting with increasingly complex social relations resulted in ever-larger brains evolving. And in general, this does indeed appear to be the case. As worked out by anthropologist Robin Dunbar, each type of primate species tends to have a consistent social group size; and the bigger the social group, the bigger the neocortex. Before definitively making this conclusion, Dunbar attempted to determine if some other factor might be equally if not more important. He looked at diet, home range size, day journey length and how the primate species acquired its food, but there was no correlation between any of these factors and brain size. However, dealing with more individuals socially did matter.[23] He concluded that the number of individuals a primate can keep track of is "a direct function of relative neocortex size, and that this in turn limits group size . . . the limit imposed by neocortical processing capacity is simply based on the number of individuals with whom a stable inter-personal relationship can be maintained."[24] By way of example, our nearest cousin the chimpanzee typically lives in social groups of around 55 individuals—not just the immediate family, but the basic network of family groups a single individual is likely to interact with over a year or two. Based on a statistical analysis of the neocortex size of 38 species of primate, Dunbar estimated that humans should have a "mean group size" of about 150, which with sampling error probably meant, he reasoned, group sizes somewhere in the neighborhood of 100 to 200 or so individuals.

Dunbar then compared this prediction with observable group sizes for humans. Since the ancestors of modern humans were all hunter-gatherers, and he was an anthropologist, that is where he started. Along with a colleague he searched the anthropological and ethnographical literature for census-like group size information for various studied hunter-gatherer societies, the closest approximations, anthropologists assume, to what ancient Pleistocene societies of humanity's ancestors were like. Most hunter-gather groups exist(ed) in small bands with size ranges of 30 to 50 individuals, but all of these periodically coalesce into cultural lineage groups of 100 to 200 individuals that gather(ed) together annually for traditional ceremonies. Of course around 10,000 years ago, some humans began giving up the hunter-gather existence and started settling down and raising animals and crops. Dunbar's surveys of village and tribe sizes also appeared to approximate this predicted value. For example, about 150 individuals was the estimated size of most Neolithic farming villages.

More impressive was his discovery that 200 is generally the upper bound on the number of academics in a discipline's sub-specialization; 150 is the basic unit size of professional armies in Roman antiquity as well as again in modern times. It also turns out that 150 to 200 is the average size of most people's Christmas card list (back when people did such things), and it is also the upper size that a company can grow to without developing significant hierarchical management structures.[25] Although most humans now live in cities, many with more than a million inhabitants, people do not actually deal with all these millions of people; they only deal with a relatively small number. Over the course of days, weeks and months a person is likely to meet many new people, and some of these are likely to become part of that person's social network. Over that same time period, other individuals with whom that person previously had a social relationship are likely to be dropped. Amazingly, over time, the total number of individuals in a modern person's social network is likely to remain relatively constant and hover at around 150 individuals +/- about 50. This number it seems is based on a capacity for relationships that has remained virtually unchanged for hundreds of thousands of years and is defined not by culture but by the neural limitations of the human brain.[26]

However, limitations aside, neuroscientists are beginning to appreciate just how central to neural functioning is the ability to perceive and navigate social relationships. The brain has traditionally been studied in individuals, in isolation, typically preforming some active task, like doing a math problem or building with blocks. But these types of experiments tend to ignore two important realities. The first is that an enormous amount of what happens within an individual's brain directly relates to what is happening within other peoples' brains. It seems that once the ability to perceive and process social relationships evolved, attention to social relationships between friends, family, co-workers and associates increasingly came to dominate much of human thought.[27] The second is that much of the time the brain is not actually performing a specific task but functionally operates on a sort of "idle." Neuroscientists have begun looking more closely at what the brain does during these non-active, "neural idling" moments, when a person is at rest. The results have been surprising.

It turns out that every time a person is not engaged in an active task, like when she takes a break from doing that math problem or building with blocks, the brain falls into a neural configuration called the "default network." In fact, any time a person mentally pauses, even if it is just for a second, this brain system comes on automatically.[28] What neuroscientist Matthew Lieberman discovered is that the default network looks almost identical to another brain configuration, the configurations involved with Relationality-related Well-Being. According to Lieberman, when pausing, the brain kicks into a mode designed to make sense of other people and one's self.[29] In essence, he has found that this default human network directs the human mind to think about other people's minds, their thoughts, feelings, and goals.[30] It appears that the Relationality-related Well-Being Systems involved with insuring positive social relationships are always active within humans, always responsive to the on-going need to be noticed, loved or otherwise appreciated by others.

## Variability in Relationality and the Consequences of That Variability

Not all people are equally adept at perceiving and navigating social relationships. Some people just seem to naturally pick-up and understand social cues, while others regularly miss those cues. These differences in ability end up having highly significant consequences for choice-making and well-being. The more socially aware a person is, the greater is her ability to successfully navigate the intricacies of social relationships and the more likely she is to rise in the social pecking order; and generally the higher in the pecking order a person perceives themselves to be, the greater is their well-being.[31] For example in the business world, it has been observed that 90% of top performers score high on measures of social awareness.[32]

> On his desk Golomb has a row of five gold stars, given to him by his dealership in honor of his performance. In the world of car salesmen, Golomb is a virtuoso. . . . Someone you never met walks into your dealership, perhaps about to make what may be one of the most expensive purchases of his or her life. Some people are insecure. Some are nervous. Some know exactly what they want. Some have no idea. Some know a great deal about cars and will be offended by a salesman who adopts a patronizing tone. Some are desperate for someone to take them by the hand and make sense of what seems to them like an overwhelming process. A salesman, if he or she is to be successful, has to gather all that information—figuring out, say, the dynamic that exists between a husband and a wife, or father and a daughter—process it, and adjust his or her behavior accordingly, and do all of that within the first few moments of the encounter. Bob Golomb is clearly the kind of person who seems able to do that kind of thing effortlessly.[33]

All normal humans have the ability to "read" and process social information, but individuals as socially gifted as Bob Golomb are rare. This kind of social awareness was first described by the psychologist Edward Thorndike in 1920[34] and more recently framed by the educational psychologist Howard Gardener in his theory of multiple intelligences as *interpersonal intelligence*.[35] Either way, the gist is that there clearly is a spectrum of social abilities within the population, ranging from those with little to no ability to read and act upon the social cues of others, e.g., autistic individuals, to gifted individuals like Golomb with highly attuned abilities.

The benefits of possessing well-developed Relationality skills is apparent, so too the consequences of lacking Relationality. Recent research on Autism Spectrum Disorder (ASD) reinforce the devastating consequences of deficiencies in Relationality-related Well-Being Systems. Commonly individuals with ASD find it difficult to perceive or exhibit emotions and they lack the ability to understand why others do what they do, to basically "read" other people. As a consequence of these deficiencies in their Relationality-related Well-Being Systems, individuals with ASD characteristically have few if any friends, rarely participate in social activities and generally receive none of the basic social supports that other, more normal individuals take for granted; all of which have consequences for well-being. Research has consistently shown that individuals with ASD suffer significantly diminished health, lower incomes and lower reproduction rates.[36] And interestingly, the challenges of ASD usually are not restricted to the affected individual; typically the families of ASD sufferers also have diminished well-being.[37]

As evidenced by those with ASD, a lack of Relationality almost always compromises a person's ability to fit in, which in turn always compromises an individual's chances for survival.[38] But survival is not merely dependent upon fitting in and getting along, but equally upon getting ahead. Invariably, human societies always operate from a position of scarcity—limited food, shelter, jobs or prospective mates—attaining some degree of status with the group increases the likelihood of securing one's needed share of those limited resources.[39] Thus all humans utilize Relationality-related Well-Being Systems in making choices designed to both gain acceptance from others as well as for achieving social status, for garnering the group's esteem.[40]

## Esteem

Esteem is an important motivator, and the need for esteem acts as a significant Well-Being trigger.[41] All humans have a need to feel respected and valued by others, to be appreciated as someone who makes a contribution. Not surprisingly, people often associate their jobs or hobbies with a sense of esteem; these endeavors both build and sustain many people's sense of self-efficacy and value; beliefs that fuel greater feelings of well-being.[42] People who perceive they lack esteem often make choices designed to heighten their sense of esteem. The need for esteem is so great that in order to achieve esteem people often engage in unnecessarily risky behaviors, self-aggrandizement or even aggression or other forms of anti-social behavior.[43]

Unlike many of the bodily Well-Being Systems described in previous chapters, esteem appears to be regulated primarily by positive rather than negative-feedback mechanisms.[44] The more one does things that garner esteem, the greater the sense of pleasure one feels and the more one wants to keep doing those things. Studies have shown that individuals who perceive that others respect them for exercising increase their levels of exercise.[45] Similarly, if a person perceives that being healthy garners respect then that person is more likely to report feeling less depressed and having fewer aches and pains.[46]

Conscious awareness appears to be a particularly critical aspect of this modality of Well-Being Systems. One can feel a sense of well-being as a consequence of satisfying all manner of needs, many of which do not require conscious awareness. Not so it seems the needs of Reflectivity. Over all, individuals who perceive they are better off than most people are happier than people who perceive they are worse off than others.[47] Individuals who perceive that they have high esteem self-report that they are happier, have more cheerful memories and generally higher levels of life-satisfaction than do individuals who perceive they have low esteem.[48]

As discussed in this chapter and in earlier chapters, the roots of most of humanity's Well-Being Systems go back millions if not billions of years and pre-date the emergence of conscious self-awareness. In fact, even consciousness itself, or at least social consciousness, appears to predate the evolution of humans as a unique species since consciousness appears to be integral to both chimpanzees' and humans' Relationality-related Well-Being Systems. Yet clearly the differences between chimpanzees and humans are stark, including how the two species wield their Relationality tools. The evolutionary trajectory of humans suggests that something remarkable happened very soon after the chimpanzee and human lines diverged some 5 to 7 million years ago. The story of those changes and their impacts on the evolution of Well-Being Systems and choice-making is the topic of the two final chapters in this section of the book.

## Notes

1. Leotti, L.A., Iyengar, S.S. and Ochsner, K.N. (2010). Born to choose: The origins and value of the need for control. *Trends in Cognitive Sciences*, 14(10), 457–463.
2. Lewis, M. (1990). Intention, consciousness, desires and development. *Psychological Inquiry*, 1, 278–283.
3. Boesch, C. (2009). *The real chimpanzees: Sex strategies in the forest*. Cambridge: Cambridge University Press, p. 11.
4. Constable, T. (2001). *Chimpanzees: Social climbers of the forest*. New York: Dorling Kindersley.
5. Constable, T. (2001). *Chimpanzees: Social climbers of the forest*. New York: Dorling Kindersley.
6. Barrett, L., Henzi, P. & Dunbar, R. (2003). Primate cognition: From 'what now?' to 'what if?' *Trends in Cognitive Science*, 7(11), 494–497.
7. As will be discussed more fully in the next chapter, unlike humans, social navigation appears to be the main use chimpanzees make of their conscious abilities.
8. Bekoff, M. (2001). Observations of scent-marking and discriminating self from others by a domestic dog (Canis familiaris): Tales of displaced yellow snow. *Behavioural Processes*, 55(2), 75–79.
   Gallup, Jr., G.G., Anderson, J.R. & Shillito, D.J. (2002). The mirror test. In M. Bekoff, C. Allen, & G.M. Burghardt (Eds.) *The cognitive animal: Empirical and theoretical perspectives on animal cognition* (pp. 325–333). Cambridge, MA: MIT Press.
   Griffin, D.R. & Speck, G.B. (2004). New evidence of animal consciousness. *Animal Cognition*, 7(1), 5–18.
   Hampton, R.R. (2001). Rhesus monkeys know when they remember. *Proceedings of the National Academy of Sciences*, 98(9), 5359–5362.
   Harland, D.P. & Jackson, R.R. (2004). Portia perceptions: The Umwelt of an araneophagic jumping spider. In F.R. Prete (Ed.) *Complex worlds from simpler nervous systems* (pp. 5–40). Cambridge, MA: MIT Press.
   Hart, B.L., Hart, L.A., McCoy, M. & Sarath, C.R. (2001). Cognitive behaviour in Asian elephants: Use and modification of branches for fly switching. *Animal Behaviour*, 62(5), 839–847.

Hunt, G.R. & Gray, R.D. (2003). Diversification and cumulative evolution in New Caledonian crow tool manufacture. *Proceedings of the Royal Society of London B: Biological Sciences*, 270(1517), 867–874.

Plotnik, J.M., de Waal, F. & Reiss, J. (2006). Self recognition in an Asian elephant. *Proceedings of the National Academy of Sciences of the USA*, 103(45), 17053–17057.

Prior, H., Schwarz, A. & Güntürkün, O. (2008). Mirror-induced behavior in the magpie (Pica pica): Evidence of self-recognition. *PLoS biology*, 6(8), e202.

Tennesen, M. (2003). *Do dolphins have a sense of self?* Reston, VA: National Wildlife. World Edition.

9. Neiworth, J. (2009). Thinking about me: How social awareness evolved. *Current Directions in Psychological Science*, 18(3), 143–147.

10. cf., Tomasello, M. & Call, J. (1997). *Primate cognition*. New York: Oxford University Press.

11. Rizzolatti, G. & Sinigaglia, C. (2010). The functional role of the parieto-frontal mirror circuit: Interpretations and misinterpretations. *Nature Reviews Neuroscience*, 11, 264–274.

12. Decety, J. & Chaminade, T. (2003). Neural correlates of feeling sympathy. *Neuropsychologia*, 41, 127–138.

13. Di Pellegrino, G., Fadiga, L., Fogassi, L., Gallese, V. & Rizzolatti, G. (1992). Understanding motor events: A neurophysiological study. *Experimental Brain Research*, 91, 176–180.

Rizzolatti, G., Camarda, R., Fogassi, L., Gentilucci, M., Luppino, G. & Matelli, M. (1998). Functional organization of inferior area 6 in the macaque moneky. II. Area F5 and the control of distal movements. *Experimental Brain Research*, 71, 491–507.

14. Icobani, M. (2008). *Mirroring people: The new science of how we connect with others*. New York: Farrar, Stuaus and Giroux.

15. Ferrari, P.F. & Rizzolatti, G. (2014). Mirror neuron research: The past and the future. *Philosophical Transactions of the Royal Society B*, 269, 169–173.

16. The term biologists' use for this evolutionary "path of least resistance" is expated (cf., Gould, S.J. & Vrba, E.S. (1982). Exaptation—A missing term in the science of form. *Paleobiology*, 8(1), 4–15.

17. Graziano, M.S.A. & Kastner, S. (2011). Human consciousness and its relationship to social neuroscience: A novel hypothesis. *Cognitive Neuroscience*, 2, 98–113.

18. Neiworth, J. (2009). Thinking about me: How social awareness evolved. *Current Directions in Psychological Science*, 18(3), 143–147.

19. Although not dwelled on by Neiworth, this also raises the possibility that the evolution of social awareness might have had a gender bias. A finding not out of line with current evidence amongst humans that, on average, females are more socially aware than are males (e.g., Goleman, D. (2011). Are women more emotionally intelligent than men? *Psychology Today*. Retrieved January 11, 2017. www.psychologytoday.com/blog/the-brain-and-emotional-intelligence/201104/are-women-more-emotionally-intelligent-men).

20. Gazzaniga, M.S. (2008). *Human: The science behind what makes your brain unique*. New York: HarperCollins.

21. Jolly, A. (1966). Lemur social behavior and primate intelligence. *Science*, 153, 501–506.

22. Humphrey, N.K. (1976). The social function of intellect. In P. Bateson & R. Hinde (Eds.), *Growing points in ethology*. Cambridge: Cambridge University Press.

23. Dunbar, R. (1998). The social brain hypothesis. *Evolutionary Anthropology*, 6, 178–190.

24. Dunbar, R. (1992). Neocortex size as a constraint on group size in primates. *Journal of Human Evolution*, 22(6), 469–493.

25. Hill, R. & Dunbar, R. (2003). Social network size in humans. *Human Nature*, 14, 53–72.

26. Gazzaniga, M.S. (2008). *Human: The science behind what makes your brain unique*. New York: HarperCollins.

27. Eagleman, D. (2015). *The brain: The story of you*. New York: Pantheon.

28. Lieberman, M. (2013). *Social: Why our brains are wired to connect*. New York: Crown.

29. Lieberman, M. (2013). *Social: Why our brains are wired to connect*. New York: Crown.

30. Lieberman, M. (2013). *Social: Why our brains are wired to connect*. New York: Crown.

31. Haught, H.M., Rose, J., Geers, A. & Brown, J.A.J. (2015). Subjective social status and well-being: The role of referent abstraction. *Social Psychology*, 155(4), 356–369.
32. Bradberry, T. (2015). Do you have emotional intelligence? Here's how to know for sure. *Inc.* Retrieved March 15, 2016. www.inc.com/travis-bradberry/are-you-emotionally-intelligent-here-s-how-to-know-for-sure.html
33. Gladwell, M. (2006). *Blink: The power of thinking without thinking.* New York: Little, Brown, p. 42.
34. Thorndike, E.L. (1920). Intelligence and its use. *Harper's Magazine*, 140, 227–235.
35. Gardner, H. (1983). *Frames of mind: The theory of multiple intelligences.* New York: Basic Books.
36. Knapp, M., Romeo, R. & Beecham, J. (2007). *The economic consequences of Autism on the U.K.* London: Foundation for People with Learning Disabilities.
37. Knapp, M., Romeo, R. & Beecham, J. (2007). *The economic consequences of Autism on the U.K.* London: Foundation for People with Learning Disabilities.
38. Hogan, R., Jones, W.H. & Cheek, J. (1985). Socioanalytic theory: An alternative to armadillo psychology. In B.R. Schlenker (Ed.), *The self and social life* (pp. 175–198). New York: McGraw-Hill.
39. Hogan, R., Jones, W.H. & Cheek, J. (1985). Socioanalytic theory: An alternative to armadillo psychology. In B.R. Schlenker (Ed.), *The self and social life* (pp. 175–198). New York: McGraw-Hill.
40. McAdams, D.P. (2013). The psychological self as actor, agent, and author. *Perspectives in Psychological Science*, 8(3), 272–295.
41. Lester, D. (1990). Maslow's hierarchy of needs and personality. *Personality and Individual Differences*, 11, 1187–1188.
42. Bandura, A. (1977). Self-efficacy: Toward a unifying theory of behavioral change. *Psychological Review*, 84(2), 191–215.
43. Bonnellan, M.B., Trzesniewski, K.H., Robins, R.W., Moffitt, T.E. & Caspi, A. (2005). Low self-esteem is related to aggression, antisocial behavior, and delinquency. *Psychological Sciences*, 16(4), 328–335.
44. Zahn, R., Moll, J., Paiva, M., Garrido, G., Krueger, F., Huey, E. & Grafman, J. (2009). The neural basis of human social values: Evidence from functional MRI. *Cerebral Cortex*, 19, 276–283.
45. Sapolski, R.M. (2004). Social status and health in humans and other animals. *Annual Review of Anthropology*, 33, 393–418.
46. Sapolski, R.M. (2004). Social status and health in humans and other animals. *Annual Review of Anthropology*, 33, 393–418.
47. Haught, H.M., Rose, J., Geers, A. & Brown, J.A.J. (2015). Subjective social status and well-being: The role of referent abstraction. *Social Psychology*, 155(4), 356–369.
48. Diener, E. & Biswas-Diener, R. (2008). *Happiness: Unlocking the mysteries of psychological wealth.* Malden, MA: Blackwell.

# 12

# REFLECTIVITY (ORIGINATING MORE THAN 5 MILLION YEARS AGO)

As skilled reflective thinkers, every human intuitively understands what conscious agency feels like; what it means to be aware of someone strange walking into a room, what it feels like to feel sick, what it means to make choices based on one's interests and preferences, and at the extreme of Reflectivity, what it is like to mindfully ponder intellectual topics like how and why people make the choices they do. One of the defining characteristics of Reflectivity is the ability to, at will, retrieve from memory relevant bits and pieces of past experience and creatively reassemble them into a perceptually coherent whole that can be used to both explain past actions as well as guide future actions. It is an ability that enables an individual to not only react to challenge or threat but anticipate challenge or threat and proactively make choices. In short, Reflectivity has proven to be the quintessential tool for understanding and to a degree controlling daily life. Without question, Reflectivity is fundamental to what is currently considered human well-being.

Reflectivity, though, is a capability only rarely practiced, and then in only the most rudimentary way by chimpanzees, our closest living relative. Both chimpanzees and humans possess conscious awareness, but humans use their conscious abilities more consistently, more flexibly and in many more ways than do chimpanzees. In this chapter I discuss when and why this difference might have arisen and how Reflectivity-related Well-Being Systems became central to the evolution of humans. Also discussed are the evolution and significance of culture, expectations and language.

## Reflectivity and Human Evolution

For most of human history, people actually knew next to nothing about the origins of humanity. It is only within the past half century that the basic rudiments of the human evolutionary story have begun to emerge. A spate of new discoveries in recent years has complicated the picture, leading to a number of competing theories on the timing and exact course of human evolution.[1] What is widely accepted, though, is that somewhere between 5 and 8 million years ago[2] a relatively modest-sized population of forest-living, chimpanzee-like primates moved out of their ancestral habitat and adapted to the challenges of living in more open, savanna-like environments—an environment filled with totally new and largely unfamiliar food resources as well as large numbers of fast and aggressive new predators like lions, wild dogs, cheetahs, leopards and hyenas. The choice to move into this new environment was almost certainly not made because it seemed like a great opportunity, but out of dire necessity. Happy, contented populations do not generally move from where they are into new and hostile lands; that is the behavior of those on the margins, those who are desperate and have no other choice. So it seemed was the case of humanity's distant ancestors. Human evolution is a story of remarkably rapid changes, not only in habitat and food preferences but also in posture, locomotion, social system and of course intelligence.

Over just a few short million years, humanity's early ancestors—collectively known as *hominins*—changed from creatures equally at home in a tree or on the ground, who when on the ground traveled on four legs, presumably by knuckle walking like humanity's modern-day relatives the gorillas and chimpanzees, into organisms that lived almost exclusively on the ground, standing upright and walking on just two legs. In the process, humanity morphed from primarily herbivores into omnivores with a distinct taste for meat.[3] Hominins also went from an ancestral mating system of polygynandry (both males and females have more than one mate) to one of primarily (semi-permanent) monogamy (both males and females have only a single mate). And importantly, hominins also evolved from a lineage of smart, social apes who primarily foraged individually into a lineage of very smart social apes who primarily foraged within groups.[4]

These changes—from a chimpanzee-like ancestor to human—were not a linear process though. Perhaps most improbably, from the loins of these earliest proto-hominins evolved not one, but perhaps as many as several dozen species, all within the span of a few million years.[5] For this burst of evolution to have occurred, this new form of savanna-dwelling creature must have possessed a skill-set that enabled it to be more than just marginally successful in this new environment; it needed to possess some capabilities that allowed it to be highly successful. Needless to say, many theories have been put forth to explain why and how human-like creatures achieved this remarkable success. But as suggested at the beginning of this chapter, my preferred explanation involves the adaptive advantages that conscious awareness afforded to these pioneering apes; a capability they already possessed but extended and re-purposed. The key to hominin success was the ability to voluntarily retrieve information and make "informed" choices in the service of perceived well-being. If true, all of the various other anatomical, neural and social adaptations were pulled along over time in response to the opportunities afforded by this one fundamental neural adaptation.

Historically, most theories about how and why early human-like creatures achieved their dramatic success assumed that it was because of the superior intelligence and increased brain size of hominins. However, the exponential increase in hominin fossil evidence discovered over the past quarter century has shown that increases in brain size only came relatively late in the development of the hominin line. Many other distinctive hominin attributes, such as upright posture and an opposable thumb, evolved early-on, but not so significantly a larger brain.[6] The best available evidence seems to suggest that early hominins had almost exactly the same size and same shaped brains as their chimpanzee relatives, and that over the first couple of million years of hominin evolution, brain size increased barely at all.[7]

It is almost certain that some neural changes were occurring that allowed these early chimp-like creatures to dramatically tilt the evolutionary scales in their favor. However, these changes would have had to have been in how the existing brain anatomy of these creatures was wired rather than the evolution of whole new structures. In other words, the changes that occurred that enabled the leap into the new and challenging world of the savanna, which in turn resulted in the evolution of multiple species of hominins, appears to have initially been driven by a qualitative rearranging of existing brain capabilities rather than a quantitative increase in brain size or anatomy.

Evolutionary psychologist Merlin Donald has speculated that self-initiated recall of memory initially arose as part of the ability to recall how to do things, physical skills like finding a particular food source or using a tool.[8,9] I am inclined to believe that these cognitive abilities arose from pre-existing conscious self-awareness capabilities that initially appeared in the common ancestors of chimps and humans in service to enhanced social relationships. Specifically, Reflectivity-related Well-Being Systems evolved from Relationality-related Well-Being Systems. Both systems enabled an individual to focus its attention outside of itself, either on another creature or some event in the environment, and infer, based upon its own lived experiences, some level of causality and prediction to that creature or environmental event. In both cases, the capacity to voluntarily reflect on one's behavior and repeat or modify it as necessary, whether in the social or physical realm, was a capability that required conscious awareness and the ability to envisage alternative possibilities. Arguably, it was the evolution of such reflective behaviors, and in particular the extension of these envisaging capacities to an increasing suite of situations and challenges, that critically contributed to the ability of ancestral hominins to move beyond the familiarity of the forest and exploit the new opportunities and challenges represented by life in the savanna.

Life for a relatively large,[10] long-lived organism is always precarious, in large part because of the challenges inherent in being able to regularly find and exploit sufficient resources to meet its significant metabolic needs. Even the most consistent of resources are likely to vary considerably in both space and time, e.g., season to season and year to year.[11] Five to eight million years ago, geologically known as the beginning of the Pliocene, the time period when hominins were splitting from chimpanzees. The Pliocene was one of those times in evolutionary history when a rapidly changing world made resources temporally and spatially even more variable than normal.

The world at the beginning of the Pliocene era has some striking parallels to the present world. Worldwide climate was changing. Unlike today, temperatures were falling rather than rising, but similar to today the result was a world in which weather became much more erratic. As a consequence of these changes the African continent began to undergo major environmental changes as falling temperatures and diminished rainfall led to significant shrinking of the vast rain forests that had covered much of continent. Vast stretches of semi-arid savanna replaced the rapidly disappearing rain forests. This was the place, the time and the situation in which these ancestral apes first began to evolve into human-like creatures—the hominins. As speculated above, presumably it was not just curiosity and a sense of adventure that pushed one or more bands of these early hominins out onto the savannas but rather a desperate need to survive in a rapidly changing world.

The climate changes at the beginning of the Pliocene represented an evolutionary opportunity for an increasingly sophisticated player capable of turning a bad situation into something positive. In a world where historical resources were no longer dependable, an organism capable of reflectively envisioning these changes, not just in present but anticipatorily into the future, would have created a huge adaptive advantage. It appears that early hominins were pre-adapted for this ability. Imagine the adaptive advantage that would accrue to an organism if rather than merely depending upon historic behavioral patterns to determine where good food and water are likely to be one could actually anticipate the location of these resources based on in-the-moment clues such as the presence or absence of particular kinds of animal droppings or the color of leaves. From the current human intellectual vantage point, after many millions of years of brain evolution, this act of reflective prognostication does not appear to be a huge intellectual leap. But it is hard to imagine your average hyena or antelope making this kind of intellectual connection. Arguably the earliest hominins were able to make this mental leap, and because of this capacity, a relatively frail and vulnerable primate was able to venture out into and survive within a wholly foreign and otherwise hostile environment; again not because it seemed a good choice but rather because it likely was a better choice than the alternative—stay put and starve.

The ability to project one's attentional self beyond the moment or even beyond the relatively limited range of other members of your social group, to envision the problems and realities of a complex physical and temporal environment and voluntarily retrieve relevant memories that could be applied to the problem was huge. Even a small deviation in attentional focus and retrieval capabilities, the ability to form new Well-Being Systems and access them at will, would have arguably been sufficient to catalyze the enormous cascade of evolutionary changes that supported the rise of hominins.

Five to eight or so million years ago, both the ancestors of chimpanzees and the ancestors of humans possessed the precursor neural abilities to consciously analyze and predict events into the future. The difference was that ancestral chimpanzees continued to live within the relatively stable and bountiful boundaries of the closed tropical rain forest. This environment then as now is a place of relative certainty—in general the same species of plants fruit every year, at the same time and in the same locations. Although the extent of African rain forest has expanded and shrunk numerous times over the past 10 million years or so, and the nature and variety of lifeforms within that system undoubtedly evolved, the demands of life within the rain forest have remained pretty much constant. For those organisms well-adapted to forest life, although not without challenges, food and water are generally plentiful and reasonably predictable; the places and resources that supported well-being last year are highly likely to continue to support well-being this year. As a consequence, the ancestral chimp's conscious agency could and seemingly did remain primarily focused on the one important part of its world that was consistently unpredictable—its social-sexual world. Meanwhile, the ancestors of humans found themselves in a decidedly unstable and unpredictable world. Although it is almost certain that these ancestral Pliocene hominins retained the need and capability for social agency, they also turned their acute self-awareness capabilities to other tasks as well, including the demands of finding food, water and shelter, and increasingly the making and using of tools to augment their limited physical prowess.

Even the slightest ability to make self-initiated predictions about weather, food and safety would have paid huge survival dividends for these early ancestors, allowing them to maintain some measure of well-being in the face of huge challenges. Even minimal changes in their ability to build Reflectivity-related Well-Being Systems would have been selected for. Unfortunately, changes in neural re-wiring are not preserved when the bones of the skull become fossilized. What fossilized bones do reveal, though, is the early and complete shift to bipedalism, an adaptation that supported the need for these early hominins to travel considerably greater distances in search of food than was required of their forest-living relatives.[12] Bipedalism has an additional, not insignificant benefit: it frees up the hands for tool use.

Early hominins would have become increasingly efficient tool users, which turned out to be less of a nicety and more of a necessity. Extracting food on the savanna was not as easy as it was in the forest. Savanna food sources were disproportionately in the form of roots and tubers rather than the fruits and leaves of the ancestral forest; roots and tubers are much harder to harvest and tougher to eat and digest than fruit and leaves.[13] More inferential is the assertion that difficulties of finding food on the savanna also selected for the strengthening of social bonds. As discussed in the chapter on Sociality, a group is more effective at searching for hard to find, patchily distributed food and then keeping an eye out for predators while others engage in the time-intensive task of digging out and extracting these scarce resources.[14]

The fossil record suggests that this suite of adaptations—bipedalism, tool use and Reflectivity—fostered the evolution of numerous species of hominin. Some early hominins became specialists in eating large nuts and tubers, while others became more generalists eating a wide array of roots, nuts and animal proteins. All likely possessed a keen ability to reflect, plan and predict; certainly keen as compared to most of the other denizens of the savanna. Over time, it makes sense that this mental capacity to separate one's self from that of another, to envision one's self in multiple scenarios and be able to select a course of action that will likely lead to better results, not only persisted but was increasingly selected for. However, changes in conscious capabilities no doubt came about quite slowly. As is typically the case, natural selection seems to operate on the theory "if ain't broke, don't fix it."[15] So several millions of years would go by with only limited change or improvement occurring. However the fossil record does reveal that changes did keep coming and that, over time, hominins became ever better at bipedal locomotion, the hand evolved to be ever better for grasping and manipulating tools, and ever so slowly, the size and presumably the complexity of the brain increased; a brain endowed with ever more elaborated Reflectivity-related Well-Being Systems.

According to the fossil record, the biggest leaps in hominin brain size occurred beginning about 2 million years ago, accelerating between 800,000 to 200,000 years ago. Interestingly, these latter changes in brain size match up almost exactly with further dramatic changes in world climate and also with evidence of changes in the way hominins gathered food. Although climatic instability was the norm for the Pliocene period, the greatest fluctuations during this epoch occurred between 800,000 and 200,000 years ago.[16] Paleontologists believe this correlation is not accidental.[17] Seemingly once again, the ability to adaptively respond to a complex, unstable environment resulted in greater survival for individuals with greater cognitive (Reflectivity) abilities. Greater Reflectivity abilities helped fuel the rise in a hunting and gathering lifestyle where social cooperation was essential. And these changes in turn led to selective pressures for accelerated evolution of ever more intelligent and adaptable species of hominin.

The beginnings of this rapid evolutionary burst are signaled by the appearance of a new genus of hominin that arose at this time, the genus called *Homo*—our direct ancestors. Also emerging during this period was the proto-human known as *Homo erectus*. First appearing around 2 million years ago, *Homo erectus* was very much like a modern human. In particular, he was a highly adept hunter and gatherer.[18] *Homo erectus* is also the first hominin that is known to have moved out of Africa. And move he did; over time this species eventually spread throughout much of Africa, Asia and Europe.

There's no question that modern humans were planners, but likely so too were these pre-humans. Around the time of *Homo erectus* is the first evidence of big game hunting. It is hard to hunt animals that are much bigger and fiercer than you without planning and social cooperation. Well before 2 million years ago fossil finds suggest that early hominins were hunting or scavenging for meat, but by the time of *Homo erectus* there is evidence suggesting that these human-like ancestors were eating virtually every and any species of animal they deemed worth eating.[19] Though it is possible, even probable, that most of the bigger species of animals these early human hunters were eating were scavenged rather than hunted, new evidence based on fossil *Homo erectus* bones discovered in East Africa from around 1.8 million years ago suggests that these early human ancestors already had evolved the anatomical ability to throw with speed and accuracy—necessary prerequisites for large game hunting.[20]

Being able to throw stones at a big beast like a rhinoceros or elephant is no guarantee of success. To be consistently successful at hunting a large, dangerous animal requires strategy, planning and group effort. Based on the anatomy of fossil shoulder bones, this ability was already present at around 400,000 years ago when the immediate ancestors of modern humans, *Homo heidelbergensis*, first appear in the fossil record. In addition to a similar shoulder structure, this very closely related species to modern humans also possessed a brain of very similar size and proportion. A great deal of evidence supports the hypothesis that *Homo heidelbergensis* hunted large game animals. Evidence from *Homo heidelbergensis* fossil sites show cut marks on the bones of wild deer, elephants, rhinos and horses.[21] The fossil record also suggests group hunting and group living; also associated with *Homo heidelbergensis* fossil sites is evidence of sophisticated tool use. Coordinated hunting, tool-making and fire use, and presumably a family social structure involving division of labor where men hunt and women gather and relatives help to take care of offspring suggests an additional evolutionary force; all are hallmarks of cultural evolution.

## Culture

Writer Malcom Gladwell in his best-selling book *The Tipping Point* suggests that cultural change is like an *epidemic*; just as a virus can rapidly spread through a susceptible population, so too an idea, song or practice.[22] Gladwell was not the first person to suggest this idea, just the most recent. The basic ideas underlying Gladwell's book were first laid out by a pair of agriculture extension agents named Bruce Ryan and Neal Gross who analyzed the spread of hybrid seed corn sales in Greene County, Iowa, in the 1930s.[23] Roughly a quarter century after they published their work and a quarter century before Gladwell, the noted evolutionary biologist Richard Dawkins had suggested quite a similar idea in the final chapter of his influential book, *The Selfish Gene*.[24] Dawkins did not talk about the transfer of ideas in terms of tipping points or epidemics but rather as the ability of ideas to pass from person to person, replicating as they go, acting very much like genes. In a play on words, Dawkins called these "sticky" ideas *memes*.

The critical idea behind all of these notions is that human choices are strongly influenced by other people; people behave in ways that mimic the behavior of other people. This influence on choice, and behavior, through non-genetic means is what is typically referred to as culture. Although most social scientists primarily study cultural influences through the lens of language, in actual fact, much as with the spread of Hush Puppies as described by Gladwell, cultural change originally evolved as a non-verbal process.[25] To this day, propagation of ideas by individuals watching and modelling the behavior of others remains a dominant mechanism of human cultural exchange.[26]

Children regularly observe the people around them behaving in various ways and imitate those behaviors. Social scientists call the individuals that are observed "models." Children grow up surrounded by many influential models, such as parents, siblings, friends and relatives. These days, children also model the characters they see on television and in the movies, and as they grow up their peer group becomes increasingly influential as models. The influence of modeling has been shown to range from gender identity and sense of the other to individual likes and preferences for everything from food to leisure.[27] Modeling is the most basic and arguably the most pervasive mechanism by which Reflectivity-related Well-Being Systems are created and perpetuated.

Take for example food preferences. A major determinant of why people choose to eat the foods they do has been shown to be social modeling, whereby people use others' eating as a guide for what they themselves should eat.[28] In a major review of experimental studies on eating behavior, psychologists Tegan Cruwys, Kirsten Bevelander and Roel Hermans reviewed 69 experiments (with over 5,800 participants) that systematically investigated the causality of eating preferences and found that 64 of these studies found a statistically significant modeling effect, despite substantial diversity in methodology, food type, social context and participant demographics. In reviewing the key findings from these studies, they conclude that there was "limited evidence for a moderating effect of hunger, personality, age, weight or the presence of others (i.e., where the confederate is live vs. remote)."[29] They concluded that food modeling, although primarily an unconscious act, still involved considerable planning. In short, food choices like other forms of cultural modeling involve Reflectivity-related Well-Being Systems and are designed to maximize well-being.

This type of cultural modeling almost certainly played a key role in human evolution. There is ample evidence that culture, the ability to accumulate and pass along behaviors and experiences from one generation to another, evolved long before the existence of hominins, since rudimentary forms of culture exist in virtually every group of animals from slime molds to penguins.[30] However the integral and direct connections between culture and the architecture of the brain that appears to have accompanied hominin evolution appears to have been unprecedented.[31] Supported by ever-longer and more delayed neural maturation, the forming of neural connections in the hominin brain was determined increasingly by culture and experience rather than genes. The success of this initial small connection between biological and cultural development was reinforced and extended generation after generation, ultimately setting off a cascade of both genetic and cultural evolutionary changes.

Although it is almost certain that both *Homo erectus* and *Homo heidelbergensis* possessed some form of culture, the first evidence of really modern human culture was found at fossil sites of our closest extinct cousins *Homo sapiens neanderthalensis*. Neanderthals first appear some 290,000 years ago and persisted until around 29,000 years ago. Not only did Neanderthals make tools, skin animals, make structures and control fire, they also showed evidence of communal camp sites. In addition, evidence from Neanderthal grave sites shows evidence of ritual burials. Alongside the buried bodies of Neanderthals are remains of game animals, the pigment ochre, flowers and tools.[32] Clearly these people possessed the ability to be self-reflective and evidenced highly evolved Reflectivity-related Well-Being Systems.

Thus by the time modern humans, *Homo sapiens sapiens* evolved sometime between 350,000 and 100,000 years ago, it is fair to assume that the basic capabilities we associate with conscious planning and reflection were not only present but already highly developed. Implicit in the ability to envisage, and presumably the Reflectivity-related Well-Being Systems that evolved to support this capability, is expectation. As individuals increasingly thought through their past actions, they increasingly would have formed expectations of what would happen in the future, which in turn influenced how they chose to act in the future. Over time, expectations of outcomes would have increasingly driven not only choice-making and actions, but even perceptions of need.

The psychological relationship between expectation, action and perceived need has long been understood. Nearly a half century ago psychologist Victor Vroom formulated a model of action which he called *Expectancy Theory*. *Expectancy Theory* states that an individual will act in a certain way based on the expectation that the act will be followed by a given outcome and on the attractiveness of that outcome to the individual.[33] Vroom's motivational model was later modified and elaborated on by several people,[34] but the basics of the model remain that what a person expects to find in an environment also affects how an individual responds to it.[35] This confluence between self-related need and perceived affordance, when combined with prior experience, results in more than just a choice; it results in a self-reinforcing need-choice-action *trajectory*.

## Expectations and Well-Being

Evidence of just how powerful the relationship between expectations and behaviors (and outcomes) can be comes from an unlikely place, medical research on drugs. A common phenomenon amongst medical researchers is what is known as the "placebo effect."[36] A placebo is usually an experimental "control" used by researchers to mimic the "intervention" but is designed to be something that actually has no "real" value. For example, an experimental drug might be injected or given as a pill to a group of patients and a matching set of patients are given a placebo injection of sugar water or given a similar sized and colored sugar pill. The idea is that if the treatment group has any positive or negative effects relative to the control group, those effects can be assumed to be caused by the "real" drug rather than just the process of having some kind of medical intervention. However, much to the dismay of medical researchers, an amazingly large number of people have positive effects just by virtue of being part of the study. It is not uncommon for as many as half of all participants receiving the placebo treatment to show the same improvements as those being treated with the actual medicine.[37] The expectation of receiving benefit seems sufficient to cause benefit.

Evidence for the benefits engendered by placebo effects go beyond just self-reports but can include actual changes in patients' physiological condition. For example, in one set of studies involving antidepressant medications, brain-scans of patients who were benefited by the medication showed significant changes in a particular area of the brain; roughly half of all patients receiving placebo medications also showed similar changes in activity in these exact same areas of the brain.[38] Further, there is additional evidence that the placebo effect is not just a human "psychological" phenomenon as placebo effects have been shown to regularly occur in experiments with laboratory animals like rats. In other words, expectations strongly influence behavior, and not only just those behaviors primarily under conscious control but underlying, unconsciously controlled dimensions of behavior as well.

Expectation-related positive feedback systems are not just a clinical research artifact though, they are increasingly being found to be a norm of human behavior. For example, leisure researchers have found a strong positive correlation between the expectations a person has for a leisure experience, the activities a person engages in during that experience and the resulting satisfaction that experience has for the individual.[39] Every choice, leisure or otherwise it seems, is ultimately informed by an expectation, which in turn is formed by that individual's collective experience—both biologically and lived. The underlying basis of those expectations is the probability that a particular action will result in an enhanced sense of well-being, or at a minimum, a decreased chance of decreased well-being. In others words, an individual engages in activity because she expects that it will satisfy a particular need, which in turn will result in an enhanced perception of well-being. From past experience she forms an expectation that this behavior will in fact satisfy this need and result in increased feelings of well-being. But even more importantly, these expectations actually shape perceptions of what she finds salient and how she actually acts. Her expectations mold her actions in ways that increase the likelihood of need satisfaction, which of course reinforces the idea that her expectations were accurate.

In this way, people's choices are driven by their desire to satisfy their self-related needs, which create a series of self-fulfilling prophecies—a situation where a prediction of what is to happen becomes true because of the desire of the individual to make that prediction come true. First proposed more than 50 years ago by the sociologist Robert Merton,[40] the effects and impact of self-fulfilling prophecies have been documented across an amazingly large number of contexts and situations and include everything from how teachers' expectations affect student learning, how real estate buyers' expectations influence the houses they purchase, how research scientists' expectations can and often do influence what results they choose to report, and how parental expectations directly impact children's behaviors for things such as underage drinking and drug use.[41] The reason self-fulfilling prophecies occur is because personal expectations are subjective and work at the level of emotions rather than conscious reason; therefore, the influence of expectations undermines building an objective knowledge base. A self-fulfilling prophecy is simply a cause-and-effect scenario that has been repeatedly proven true, e.g., "in the past, I've gone to places like this and this happened so there's no reason to believe it won't happen again. Even if it doesn't quite turn out that way, it was probably some quirky event that I can ignore since it was supposed to turn out that way.'[42]

A key tipping point, if not THE key tipping point, to use Gladwell's term, in these intellectual expectation, self-fulfilling prophecy loops was the development of language. Although expectations can and do operate unconsciously and without language, language enables these processes to operate more efficiently. Language enabled early humans to maximize the benefits afforded by Reflectivity at not only the individual cognitive level but also at the sociocultural level. Dating the origin of language is extremely difficult because there is no direct fossil evidence—language is a skill, not a thing, and even the basic anatomical components of language like the larynx, tongue and brain regions associated with language are made up of soft-tissue and do not fossilize. Still, most accept the conclusion of statistical linguists that language had evolved by the time of modern humans, somewhere between 350,000 and 100,000 years ago.[43]

Perhaps because of this lack of hard evidence, the number of theories put forward on how, when and even why language evolved are numerous;[44] in fact too numerous to review here. It is worth noting, though, that one particularly interesting theory ties the evolution of language to the same neural networking processes that resulted in the evolution of conscious, Reflectivity-related Well-Being Systems.[45] Critical in this view of the evolution of language is the close connection between language and sociality; that language basically evolved as a means for sharing, through performance, previously hidden motivations and understandings about why people did what they did. Because the performance of language is fundamentally a social act, it requires a deep understanding of the social context, which in turn suggests, as appears to be true, that Relationality-related Well-Being Systems, Reflectivity-related Well-Being Systems and language all need to be neurologically tightly interconnected.[46] It is reasonable to assume that by the time of our early modern human ancestors, much as in modern human societies today, daily life would have been largely language-driven. Although by 100,000 years ago changes in human behavior and adaptation would have become ever-increasingly culturally driven, it is important to appreciate that human biological evolution did not cease at this time. Biology and culture, then as now, continually co-evolve.[47]

## The Role of Narrative in Reflectivity-Related Well-Being Systems

> If you prick us, do we not bleed? If you tickle us, do we not laugh? If you poison us, do we not die? And if you wrong us, shall we not revenge?
>
> (William Shakespeare, *The Merchant of Venice*)

> Life's but a walking shadow, a poor player, that struts and frets his hour upon the stage, and then is heard no more; it is a tale told by an idiot, full of sound and fury, signifying nothing.
>
> (William Shakespeare, *Macbeth*)

> Neither a borrower nor a lender be; for loan oft loses both itself and friend, and borrowing dulls the edge of husbandry.
>
> (William Shakespeare, *Hamlet*)

Few have been more facile with language than the late 16th century English bard William Shakespeare. His narratives consistently and eloquently captured the full sweep of human thoughts, motivations, needs, beliefs and actions. Although undoubtedly Shakespeare had a gift for language, the use of language to communicate thoughts, motivations, needs, beliefs and actions is quintessentially human.

The social science literature on language in general, and narrative in particular, is arguably as vast and multifarious as any, rivaling the literature on choice and self which it of course overlaps with. Although I have argued in this book that language is not always or even typically required for people to make choices and act on those choices, it clearly is true that narratives, both thought and spoken, are fundamental to how most humans make sense of these choice-making processes. As outlined in Chapter 5, narrative skills, the ability to develop intelligible stories involving human or humanlike characters who act in the world over time,[48] begin developing early in childhood and typically reach full development by late adolescence.[49] Throughout life, then, humans create these personal as well as shared language-driven autobiographies as a way to support and communicate choice-making. Also as described in Chapter 5, these narratives always take the form of self-referential Self-Aspects.

The ability to tap into memory and actively share through linguistic performance information that could be used by others to construct new understandings and conceptualizations of the world almost certainly influenced the course of human evolution. It obviously accelerated the rate at which humans could reflect on their situation, learn from past successes and failures and reflectively initiate future actions. But so too did the fact that all memories and all language are fundamentally creative processes. Unless a person actually tries to consciously be consistent, for example by memorizing a speech, the ways in which she puts together a sentence to describe an idea will vary from situation to situation, depending upon context and recent experience.[50] As a consequence, early hominins would have often come up with novel and unexpected explanations for why they did what they did. This lack of fidelity to actual experience, this inherent creativity, would have been maladaptive at times, particularly in a constant environment. But arguably it would have been exceedingly useful for individuals living in a world with a high degree of unpredictability; and such was the world inhabited by early modern humans.

But it is not just memory recall and language that are inherently creative; so too are mental processing and memory formation. The constructed Well-Being Systems of two people are never exactly identical, even when based on the same piece of information. Every person builds his Well-Being Systems using his own unique prior knowledge and experience; each System is constructed to insure that all incoming signals are personally meaningful.[51] As ancestral peoples became increasingly dependent upon autobiographical memory and language for making choices, this quirk in the way Well-Being Systems are assembled and work would have resulted in the rise and increasing dominance within human cultural repertoires of the final modality of human Well-Being Systems—Creativity & Spirituality.

## Notes

1. e.g., Landau, E. (2013). Rare skull sparks human evolution controversy. *CNN*. Retrieved July 24, 2016. www.cnn.com/2013/10/17/world/europe/ancient-skull-human-evolution/#

   Shreeve, J. (2015). This face changes the human story: But how? *National Geographic*. Retrieved July 24, 2016. http://news.nationalgeographic.com/2015/09/150910-human-evolution-change/

   Zimmer, C. (2017). Oldest fossils of Homo Sapiens found in Morocco, altering history of our species. Science. New York Times (June 7). Retrieved June 7, 2011. https://www.nytimes.com/2017/06/07/science/human-fossils-morocco.html?emc=eta1

2. The exact date is disputed.

3. Recent evidence suggests that chimpanzees are actually more omnivorous than originally thought, though they still subsist on mainly a vegetable diet. www.janegoodall.ca/about-chimp-behaviour-diet.php Retrieved March 20, 2016.

4. Lieberman, D.E. (2013). *The story of the human body*. New York: Pantheon.

5. Stringer, C. (2011). *The origin of our species*. London: Allen Lane.

6. http://humanorigins.si.edu/human-characteristics/brains Retrieved August 9, 2013.

   In 2000, Martin Pickford and Brigitte Senut discovered in the Tugen Hills of Kenya a 6-million-year-old bipedal hominin which they named Orrorin tugenensis. And in 2001, a team led by Michel Brunet discovered the skull of Sahelanthropus tchadensis which was dated as 7.2 million years old, and which Brunet argued was a bipedal, and therefore a hominin.

7. http://humanorigins.si.edu/human-characteristics/brains Retrieved August 9, 2013.

8. Donald, M. (2012). Evolutionary origins of autobiographical memory systems: A retrieval hypothesis. In D. Berntsen & D.C. Rubin (Eds.), *Understanding autobiographical memory: Theories and approaches* (pp. 269–289). Cambridge: Cambridge University Press.

9. Utilizing the mental system cognitive scientists call procedural memory.

10. Although the ancestral hominins were not huge, maybe standing around 1 to 2.5 meters (3 to 5 feet) in height and weighing 25 to 44 kilograms (55 to 100 pounds), compared to most creatures on earth that is pretty large.

11. My late colleague Jim Lynch and I wrote a paper more than 30 years ago; although it was accepted for publication pending revisions, we unfortunately never made those revisions and to this day it remains unpublished (Falk, J.H. & Lynch, J.F. (1981). *The evolution and ecology of information*. Unpublished Manuscript). In this paper we argued that much of the diversity of life now seen on earth is the result of life evolving the ability to be more situationally flexible, and thus able to exploit ever scarcer resources within an increasingly complex world. In that paper we speculated that over evolutionary time, the "easy" resources in the "best," i.e., most stable, places would have been successfully commandeered by existing forms of life, resulting in the selection for organisms best able to successfully find and take advantage of the "crumbs" falling from the table of life—in essence selecting for ever more sophisticated players capable of playing ever more sophisticated games. However, despite becoming ever larger, more complex and increasingly "sophisticated," all of these newly evolved life forms were at some level always living at the margins. It is rarely appreciated that the myriad "higher" plants and animals that have evolved in the last half billion years, including us, have yet to dislodge the comparatively "simple" one-celled organisms like bacteria, fungi, blue-green and green algae from their bio-energetic supremacy. These simple one-celled creatures effectively, and early-on,

pre-empted most of the "quality" ecological niches on earth. The only resources left for exploitation would have been increasingly "difficult" resources—whether those resources be sunlight or the calories contained in some other organism. By difficult I mean they were resources that existed in either less than optimal situations (e.g., too dry, too hot, too ephemeral, too hard to catch, too dispersed, etc.) or came in some nasty package (e.g., too big, too toxic) making them energetically not worth the bother or beyond the reach of the dominant creatures, who were small and relatively immobile. Even today, most of the earth's biomass is created or consumed by one-celled creatures with ancient evolutionary pedigrees, and virtually all that biomass when it dies is ultimately re-processed by one-celled decomposer organisms. Accordingly, it is not a misnomer to refer to the resources exploited by recently evolving life forms as unexploited "crumbs." But just because much of life exists on crumbs doesn't mean there aren't lots of big "crumbs" lying around. Brains in general, and the vertebrate brain in particular, evolved in large part in order to capitalize on these difficult to find and/or capture high resource prizes.

12. Lieberman, D.E. (2013). *The story of the human body*. New York, Pantheon.
13. Lieberman, D.E. (2013). *The story of the human body*. New York, Pantheon.
14. Lieberman, D.E. (2013). *The story of the human body*. New York, Pantheon.
15. Gould, S.J. & Vrba, E.S. (1982). Exaptation—A missing term in the science of form. *Paleobiology*, 8(1), 4–15.
16. Smithsonian Institution. (2016). *What does it mean to be human?* Retrieved July 24, 2016. http://humanorigins.si.edu/human-characteristics/brains
17. Smithsonian Institution. (2016). *What does it mean to be human?* Retrieved July 24, 2016. http://humanorigins.si.edu/human-characteristics/brains
18. Lieberman, D.E. (2013). *The story of the human body*. New York: Pantheon.
19. http://anthro.palomar.edu/homo/homo_4.htm Retrieved August 11, 2013.
20. Roach, N.T., Venkadesan, M., Rainbow, M.J. & Lieberman, D.E. (2013). Elastic energy storage in the shoulder and the evolution of high-speed throwing in Homo. *Nature*, 498(7455), 483–486.
21. Brown, G., Fairfax, S., Sarao, N. & Anonymous, S. (2013). *Human evolution*. Retrieved August 11, 2013. http://tolweb.org/treehouses/?treehouse_id=3710
22. Gladwell, M. (2000). *The tipping point: How little things can make a big difference*. New York: Little, Brown and Company.
23. Ryan, B. & Gross, N. (1950). Acceptance and diffusion of hybrid corn seeds in two Iowa communities. *Research Bulletin*, 372. Ames, IA: Agricultural Experiment Station, Iowa State College of Agriculture and Mechanic Arts.
24. Dawkins, R. (1976). *The selfish gene*. Oxford: Oxford University Press.
25. Jablonka, E. & Lamb, M. (2014). *Evolution in four dimensions: Genetic, epigenetic, behavioral and symbolic variation in the history of life*. Cambridge: MIT Press.
26. Bandura, A. (1986). *Social foundations of thought and action: A social cognitive theory*. New York: Prentice-Hall.
27. Bandura, A. (1986). *Social foundations of thought and action: A social cognitive theory*. New York: Prentice-Hall.
28. Cruwys, T., Bevelander, K.E. & Hermans, R. (2015). Social modeling of eating: A review of when and why social influence affects food intake and choice. *Appetite*, 86, 3–18.
29. Cruwys, T., Bevelander, K.E. & Hermans, R. (2015). Social modeling of eating: A review of when and why social influence affects food intake and choice. *Appetite*, 86, 3.
30. Bonner, J.T. (1980). *The evolution of culture in animals*. Princeton: Princeton University Press.
31. Donald, M. (2012). Evolutionary origins of autobiographical memory systems: A retrieval hypothesis. In D. Berntsen & D.C. Rubin (Eds.), *Understanding autobiographical memory: Theories and approaches* (pp. 269–289). Cambridge: Cambridge University Press.
32. Brown, G., Fairfax, S., Sarao, N. & Anonymous, S. (2013). *Human Evolution*. Retrieved August 11, 2013. http://tolweb.org/treehouses/?treehouse_id=3710
33. Vroom, V. (1964). *Work and motivation*. New York: Jon Wiley & Sons.

34. e.g., Porter, L.W. & Lawler, E.E. (1968). *Managerial attitude and performance*. Homewood, IL: Irwin-Dorsey.

    deCharms, R. (1968). *Personal causation: The internal affective determinants of behavior*. New York, NY: Academic Press.

    Pinder, C.C. (1984). *Work motivation: Theory, issues, and applications*. Glenview, IL: Scott, Foresman and Company.

35. Oliver, R.L. (1980). A cognitive model of the antecedents and consequences of satisfaction decisions. *Journal of Marketing Research*, 17, 460–469.

36. The same phenomenon goes by the name "Hawthorne Effect," a term coined in 1955 by Henry A. Landsberger when analyzing older experiments from 1924–1932 GE's Hawthorne Works.

37. Moerman, D.E. (2002). *Meaning, medicine and the 'placebo effect'*. Cambridge, UK: Cambridge University Press.

    Price, D.D., Chung, S.K. & Robinson, M.E. (2005). Conditioning, expectation, and desire for relief in placebo analgesia. *Seminars in Pain Medicine*, 3(1), 15–21.

    Thompson, W.G. (2005). *The placebo effect and health—Combining science and compassionate care*. New York: Prometheus.

38. Leuchter, A.F. (2002). Changes in brain function of depressed subjects during treatment with Placebo. *American Journal of Psychiatry*, 159, 122–129.

    Also Mayberg, H., Silva, A., Brannan, S.K., Tekell, J.L., Mahurin, R.K., McGinis, S. & Jerbek, P. (2002). The functional neuroanatomy of the placebo effect. *American Journal of Psychiatry*, 159, 728–737.

39. del Bosque, I.R. & Martin, H.S. (2008). Tourist satisfaction: A cognitive-affective model. *Annals of Tourism Research*, 35(2), 551–573.

40. Merton, R.K. (1957). *Social theory and social structure* (rev. ed.). New York: Free Press.

41. e.g., Finn, P. (2006). Bias and blinding: Self-fulfilling prophecies and intentional ignorance. *The ASHA Leader*, 11(8), 16–17, 22.

    Jussim, L. & Harber, K.D. (2005). Teacher expectations and self-fulfilling prophecies: Knowns and unknowns, resolved and unresolved controversies. *Personality and Social Psychology Review*, 9, 131–155.

    Madon, S., Guyll, M., Spoth, R.L., Cross, S.E. & Hilbert, S.J. (2003). The self-fulfilling influence of mother expectations on children's underage drinking. *Journal of Personality and Social Psychology*, 84, 1188–1205.

    Wong, J.T. & Hui, E.C.M. (2006). Power of expectations. *Property Management*, 24, 496–506.

42. cf., Falk, J.H. (2009). Identity and the museum visitor experience. Walnut Creek, CA: Left Coast Press, pp. 120-127.

43. Nichols, J. (1998). The origin and dispersal of languages: Linguistic evidence. In N. Jablonski & L.C. Aiello (Eds.), *The origin and diversification of language* (pp. 127–70). (Memoirs of the California Academy of Sciences, 24.) San Francisco: California Academy of Sciences.

    Perreault, C. & Mathew, S. (2012). Dating the origin of language using phonemic diversity. *PLoS ONE*, 7(4), e35289.

44. cf., Stam, J.H. (1976). *Inquiries into the origins of language*. New York: Harper and Row.

    Christiansen, M. & Kirby, H. (2003). Consensus and controversies. *TRENDS in Cognitive Sciences*, 7(7), 300–307.

    Tallerman, M. & Gibson, K.R. (2012). *The Oxford handbook of language evolution*. New York: Oxford University Press.

45. Donald, M. (2012). Evolutionary origins of autobiographical memory systems: A retrieval hypothesis. In D. Berntsen & D.C. Rubin (Eds.), *Understanding autobiographical memory: Theories and approaches* (pp. 269–289). Cambridge: Cambridge University Press.

46. Donald, M. (2012). Evolutionary origins of autobiographical memory systems: A retrieval hypothesis. In D. Berntsen & D.C. Rubin (Eds.), *Understanding autobiographical memory: Theories and approaches* (pp. 269–289). Cambridge: Cambridge University Press.

47. Jablonka, E. & Lamb, M. (2014). *Evolution in four dimensions: Genetic, epigenetic, behavioral and symbolic variation in the history of life.* Cambridge: MIT Press.
48. Bruner, J. (1986). *Actual minds, possible worlds.* Cambridge, MA: Harvard University Press.
49. Habermas, T. & Bluck, S. (2000). Getting a life: The emergence of the life story in adolescence. *Psychological Bulletin*, 126, 748–769.
50. Chomsky, N. (2002). *On language and nature.* Cambridge: Cambridge University Press.
51. Bransford, J.D., Brown, A.L. & Cocking, R.R. (1999). *How people learn: Brain, mind, experience, and school.* Washington, DC: National Academy Press.
    Falk, J.H. & Dierking, L.D. (2000). *Learning from museums.* Lanham, MD: Altamira Press.

# 13

# CREATIVITY AND SPIRITUALITY (ORIGINATING MORE THAN 350,000 YEARS AGO)

Current society extols the virtues of creativity, often bestowing the moniker of "creative genius" on those who have achieved distinction because of their originality and societal impact. Over the decades society has variously proclaimed people like Pablo Picasso, Albert Einstein, Bill Gates, Steve Jobs and Stevie Wonder as creative geniuses, but I would make the case that this is too narrow a view. Although some people are certainly more adept than others, the core propensities of creativity, as well as spirituality, are the capacity to apply one's intellect to the purpose of understanding and uniquely solving problems. These capacities are not merely characteristic of a few exceptional people but aptly describe an entire species—*Homo sapiens sapiens.* All humans have the ability to perceive a situation, reflect on it, and arrive at a thoughtful, often non-obvious and original solution. This chapter describes when, how and why this very special capability evolved. Discussed is the necessary and somewhat ironic role that repetition and routine play in the fostering of Creativity and Spirituality. This discussion leads into a single, potentially controversial case study on religion which describes how Creativity & Spirituality-related Well-Being Systems uniquely support choice-making and feelings of well-being.

## The Rise of Creativity and Spirituality-Related Well-Being Systems

September 12, 1940. A warm afternoon in Dordogne, in southwestern France. Four boys and their dog, Robot, walk along a ridge covered with pine, oak and blackberry brambles. When Robot begins digging near a hole beside a downed tree, the boys tell each other that this might be the entrance to a legendary tunnel running beneath the Vézère River, leading to a lost treasure in the woods of Montignac. The youngsters begin to dig, widening the hole, removing rocks—until they've made an opening large enough for each to slip through, one by one. They slide down into the earth—and emerge into a dark chamber beneath the ground.

They have discovered not merely another place, but another time.

In the cool dark beneath the sunlit world above, the boys found themselves in "a Versailles of prehistory"—a vast series of caves, today collectively known as Lascaux, covered with wall paintings that, by some estimates, are close to 20,000 years old.[1]

The Lascaux caves contain more than 2,000 spectacular paintings and engravings. Throughout the multiple sections of the caves are depictions of horses, cattle, bison, cats, a bird, a bear, a rhinoceros, a human and various abstract signs; some of the markings are quite small and many of the images are enormous. Among the most famous images are four huge, black bulls or aurochs, an extinct relative of cattle. Each of the bulls appears to be in motion, one of which is over five meters in length (17 feet). Each of the different sections of the cave contains different groupings and types of creatures. Most have been painted onto the walls using mineral pigments although some designs have also been incised into the stone. Everyone who has ever seen the full extent of Lascaux is struck by its sheer scale and beauty. It is universally considered one of the greatest artistic achievements of all time, a work of creative genius.

Although the hominin line diverged from their common ancestry with chimpanzees 5 or more million years ago there is little fossil evidence of either creativity or spirituality for most of those millions of years. It is known that present-day chimpanzees are capable of creatively using tools to enhance their survival, fashioning sticks to probe into termite hills, selecting the right rock with which to crack nuts and or refashioning leaves to act as sponges,[2] and no doubt early hominins too employed some of these creative uses of objects to support their well-being, but these kinds of behaviors are not prone to evidence by fossilization. But the objects associated with human creativity and spirituality can be found. The first such "hard" evidence for human creativity appears in the fossil record at a little over 2 million years ago in the form of a constructed stone tool.

First attributed to the earliest member of the human genus, *Homo habilis*, hominins started flaking water-worn cobblestones with other stones to deliberately fashion a new type of stone, one that could be used as an effective cutting tool. This amazing invention was a creative breakthrough, but little new innovation seemed to follow. This same basic style of hand ax appears repeatedly in the fossil record, fundamentally unchanged, for the following 1.6 million years.[3] The capacity for creativity obviously was present early on, but the evidence seems to indicate that a complex mix of biological and social factors was required in order for it to become fully expressed, something that clearly had happened by the time of the Lascaux cave art. So what were these factors?

As described in the previous two chapters, one of the obvious evolutionary changes that happened during the time period in question—1.6 million to 20,000 years ago—is the significant increase in the size of the hominin brain. But size alone is not the issue; it matters equally where those increases in size occur. One of the areas that anthropologists have found that shows particular increases is the front, outer area of the brain known as the prefrontal cortex. This is the brain area associated with thought and action to accomplish goals. Examining this region in modern humans and in both chimpanzees and bonobos, physical anthropologists have discovered that several key subareas underwent a major reorganization during hominin evolution.[4]

A human's prefrontal cortex area is nearly twice the size and width of a chimpanzee's and by inference the size and width of the common ancestor of humans and chimpanzees. This enlargement creates more room for the kind of neural processing that is associated with complicated and novel interconnection between memories and thoughts, which in turn are the type of abstract thought cognitive scientists argue lie at the heart of Creativity & Spirituality-related Well-Being Systems.[5] A bigger neocortex enabled early hominins to more successfully free-associate, to connect disparate ideas together in new and useful ways.

Most psychologists agree that intelligence, in particular the special kind of intelligence involved in putting together seemingly unrelated ideas, is an essential quality of creativity. There are other important factors also thought to contribute to creativity and spirituality, including factors related to the social environment such as support and interaction with others.[6] Chimpanzees are social organisms and share their innovations with others, i.e., have culture. But what separates chimps from people seems to be the nature of that cultural exchange. While chimps seem quite capable of mimicking behaviors they observe in other chimps, they almost never seem to build on those behaviors, inventing new variations on the behavior. Instead, chimps will keep doing the same thing over and over, as faithfully replicated as possible.[7] Modern humans by contrast often not only try to improve upon a behavior, they will typically do so socially, comparing notes and talking through possible solutions. Anthropologists call this process *cultural ratcheting*.[8] Obviously for this process to happen an organism needs to have the right mental equipment, an evolutionary advance that appears to have happened as early as 2 million years ago with the evolution of *Homo erectus*. However, as suggested above, having the mental equipment to be creative does not mean that creative acts will spread through a population; that requires the appropriate social environment, including it seems the right social density.

A group of evolutionary geneticists have speculated that creativity is group-size dependent. The larger the social group size, the greater the chances are that one member will dream up an idea that could advance a technology.[9] Moreover, individuals in a large group who frequently interact with neighboring groups have a greater probability of learning a new innovation than do those living in small, isolated groups. To test these ideas, Thomas Griffiths, Brian Christian and Michael Kalish developed a computer model to simulate the effects of demographic distribution on the cultural ratcheting process.[10] Using genetic data from modern Europeans, the team estimated what the size of modern human populations in Europe would have been at around 50,000 B.C.E., the time period when archaeological evidence from Europe suggests human creativity started to spike. They also projected what African hominin populations would have looked like, simulating their growth and patterns of migratory activity. Their model showed that African populations would have reached the same population density as 50,000-year-old Europeans at roughly double that age, around 101,000 years before the present. This time period exactly aligns with the time period, according to archaeological evidence, when creativity as well as spirituality seemed to blossom in sub-Saharan regions of Africa, particularly those at the southern tip of Africa. *Homo sapiens sapiens* populations in Southern Africa dramatically increased in size at around this time period and for the first time so too did a number of significant, previously unseen advances in technology as evidenced by the material culture left behind.

In both cases, Europe and Africa, the simulations suggest that social networks needed to reach a critical size before human creativity (and spirituality) could flourish. Slowly at first, but with increasing rapidity, increases in population size led to advances in creativity (and spirituality), which (presumably) led to greater survivability, which led to increased population size, which led to further advances in creativity (and spirituality), with each cycle feeding upon the other in a continuous, positive feedback cycle. And there is no evidence that this positive feedback system between creativity and population size has stopped; if anything it appears to be accelerating.

Despite ups and downs, for thousands of years human populations have continued to grow, fueled by as well as stimulating advances in Creativity & Spirituality-related Well-Being Systems. As suggested by how I named this modality of needs, creativity was not the only expression of this virtuous co-evolutionary expansion of neural and social networks. At around the same time that advances in technologies like stone and bone tools were occurring, also appearing were advances in other seemingly non-utilitarian forms of creative expression such as art, body adornment and what archaeologists collectively call spirituality.

The earliest evidence of human spirituality is typically considered to be ritualized burial. Evidence of ritualized burial has been shown for hominin sites as old as 300,000 years,[11] and there is suggestive but controversial evidence that one of the earliest members of the genus Homo, *Homo naledi*, practiced a form of ritualized treatment of the dead as long ago as 2 million years before the present.[12] By 100,000 years ago, both Neanderthals and modern humans were regularly practicing ritual burial of the dead. By this time there is also consistent evidence that humans were creating a variety of ritual objects not associated with burial.[13] Meanwhile, the oldest evidence of a space dedicated to ritualized spirituality is in the Tsodilo Hills of Botswana. Deep inside this southern African cave, archaeologists discovered a rock that appeared to be carved into the shape of a python. Artifacts and carving tools unearthed near the snake-like rock date from about 70,000 years ago. Further suggesting that this was a place for some kind of spiritual practice is the fact that there was no evidence of any human settlement found associated with the site.[14] In addition, the Tsodilo Hills are to this day considered sacred by the ancient, indigenous San people, or Bushmen, who believe these hills and caves are the home of the gods and that humans descended from the sacred python.[15] Collectively these discoveries suggest that the roots of Spirituality, like Creativity, run very deep within the human lineage; and presumably so too the well-being related needs that Creativity and Spirituality support.

I would argue that it is highly likely that Spirituality and Creativity co-evolved, since their development has been tightly intertwined for most of human history. So much so that for most extant human cultures, the boundaries between things like art, music, dance, technology and spirituality are nearly impossible to discern. The idea that these two practices are actually distinct, separable types of human activity is actually quite recent and localized only within certain cultural contexts. The most notable examples are the cultural traditions that arose in Eurasia some 3,000 to 2,500 years ago.[16] These cultural traditions gave rise to not only the current dominant world culture, but also the current dominant intellectual traditions, one of which is the widely accepted distinction between creative acts like art and science and creative acts like spirituality and religion. There are many people alive that likely find such distinctions WEIRD.[17]

But all of the above primarily relates to when creativity and spirituality evolved, not really how and why. The challenge is understanding how the Well-Being Systems associated with creativity and spirituality could have become so well established with human populations that they would not only sporadically, but consistently show up in the fossil and archaeological record. These Systems are not simple, they are substantial. Creativity & Spirituality-related needs, and the Well-Being Systems that service those needs, are always quite complex. They involve the forming of new behavioral combinations and associations, typically requiring substantial learning and long-term cultural support.[18]

## Why Creativity and Spirituality-Related Well-Being Systems Evolved

Like so many of the ideas central to this book, various theories have been put forward for how and why both creativity and spirituality arose, with no single model currently totally accepted. Since these two human activities have only rarely been considered as variations on the same principle, there is little convergence in the various theories related to creativity and spirituality.[19] The model I will propose derives from the Well-Being Systems model developed in this book, pulling evidence as appropriate from research on both creativity and spirituality.

The first thing that needs to be established is what I actually mean by creativity and spirituality in general and Creativity & Spirituality-related Well-Being Systems in particular. Creativity research provides an important first principle. Creativity and spirituality always have two parts: originality and functionality.[20] Novelty is important, but equally important is that the act satisfies some need. Whether it is the creation of a physical object such as a new stone cutting tool or a work of spiritual art such as a cave painting, or something intangible such as a strategy for hunting large game or the telling of a creation story around the campfire, the essence of the creative or spiritual act is not merely coming up with something new, it is coming up with something new that has value, either to the individual or to others.[21] When viewed in this way it might be reasonable to suggest that the second part of creativity likely lagged behind the first. Early humans, like their chimpanzee cousins, probably regularly created new things, but the evolution of a culture of noticing and adopting innovation, of building on-going Creativity & Spirituality-related Well-Being Systems in order to satisfy needs, took longer to emerge.[22]

Creativity psychologists further distinguish between what is referred to as "little-c" creativity and "big-C" creativity.[23] Little-c creativity, which is often used as an indicator of mental health, includes everyday problem-solving and the ability to adapt to change. Big-C creativity, on the other hand, is far rarer and occurs when a person solves a problem or creates an object that has a major impact on how other people think, feel and live their lives. This latter form of creativity is usually associated with the term genius and, perhaps not surprisingly, a disproportionate amount of the research has focused on this type of creativity. The analog in spirituality might be "little-s" spirituality reflecting the various individual belief systems and practices people daily invent to deal with everyday life situations as opposed to the "big-S" spirituality of religion involving established and ritualized belief systems and practices followed by whole communities.

Over human evolutionary history both types of creativity and spirituality have evolved, but it seems reasonable to assume that big-C/S likely evolved out of little-c/s. Although in hindsight one can see how big-C/S creative/spiritual individuals might be valuable to the group or species, from antiquity to the present the individuals responsible for this type of creativity or spirituality would have more likely than not been marginal, eccentric and often unstable characters,[24] and the clear benefits of the changes proposed hard to grasp by others.[25] Not-so-little-c/s creative/spirituality. The threshold for achieving well-being through little-c/s type Creativity & Spirituality-related Well-Being Systems would have been quite low and would have acted primarily at the level of the individual as opposed to the level of the group.

The key factor appears to be that little c/s Creativity & Spirituality-related Well-Being Systems appear to increase well-being by effecting small scale, often immediate feelings of health and happiness, which would have primed the pump as it were for the possibility that big-C/S Creativity & Spirituality-related Well-Being Systems might ultimately also beneficially support needs. Little-c/s Creativity & Spirituality-related Well-Being Systems seemingly early on became associated with the bodily modalities of Well-Being, including Systems related to Continuity and Individuality; acts of little-c/s Creativity & Spirituality-related Well-Being appear to help people to deal with stress and uncertainty.

For example, there is considerable evidence that creative acts like singing, doing art or dancing reduce stress.[26] So too does spirituality. For example, studies of modern urban-dwellers find that individuals invoke their religion most when they experience difficult and trying circumstances.[27] Studies of hunter gatherers show similar results; individuals use religion to help them deal with trying circumstances, such as a string of unsuccessful hunts or the fears associated with voyaging in a small boat during times of bad weather.[28] Researchers have also found that individual as well as group prayer reduces blood pressure; high blood pressure being a reliable index of psychological stress and a precursor to a range of illnesses.[29]

As living systems became increasingly complex, so too did the perceived needs that regulated the Well-Being Systems essential to behavior and survival. Early in life's history, the boundaries of perceived self were constrained to the individual's singular cellular bits bounded by a single cell membrane, but with the evolution of multicellularity, symbiotic microbiomes and complex brains, the boundaries of self-perception came to encompass an increasingly diverse and abstract range of physical and mental well-being-related triggers. For example as discussed in earlier chapters, the well-being of a pet or even an inanimate object such as a framed picture could come to be perceived as just as integral to one's well-being as one's own physical body. Starting maybe a million or more years ago, but certainly by 100,000 years ago, humanity's ancestors would have evolved the cognitive capacities to interconnect the neural networks involved with Creativity & Spirituality-related Choice-Well-Being Systems and those involved with all other modalities, including Continuity, Individuality, Sexuality, Sociality and Relationality-related Choice-Well-Being Systems; and by virtue of these linkages between Systems people would have been able to infer cause-and-effect-type relationships. Engaging in specific creative and spiritual actions appeared to directly correlate with satisfaction of important needs; creative and spiritual acts appeared to influence one's health, or hunting or reproductive success (with sometimes the perceived correlations having an actual basis in fact and other times not). Of course, such linkages did not just emerge, they required time and learning to arise.

Although it is possible for a perceived connection between Creativity & Spirituality-related Choice-Well-Being Systems and Continuity, Individuality or other need-related Choice-Well-Being Systems to arise spontaneously, it is most likely for these connections to emerge through repeated experience. This idea is well encapsulated in a quote from one of the great geniuses of the late 19th and early 20th century, Thomas Alva Edison: "Genius is one percent inspiration, ninety-nine percent perspiration."[30]

Although new research has called into question Malcom Gladwell's oft repeated claim that with 10,000 hours of practice anyone can become an expert,[31] no one would dispute that most experts, and by extension most geniuses, have considerable training and practice in their area of expertise.[32]

## The Curious Relationship Between Creativity and Spirituality and Habit

The individuals who come up with new, innovative and useful ways to do something are typically already expert in the old ways of doing things. It requires a reasonably high level of expertise to be able to overcome the tried and true and see the potential that a slight variation or even a large variation in practice might afford. The innovations most novices come up with are not actually innovations; they either do not work or they have been tried and rejected before. Some insight into why this is true comes from cognitive research on novices and experts.

An active area of research for decades,[33] it has been found that the differences between novices and experts is not simply general abilities, such as memory or intelligence or even the use of more sophisticated strategies. Instead, the main difference is that experts have acquired extensive knowledge, often acquired over thousands of hours of practice, that affects what they notice and how they organize, represent and interpret information. This, in turn, affects their abilities to remember, reason and solve problems; often in creative ways.[34] People's abilities to retrieve relevant knowledge can vary from being "effortful" to "relatively effortless" (fluent) to "automatic."[35] The expert's knowledge retrieval in their domain is always fluent and typically automatic; it is habitual. Habit is a consequence of lots and lots of repetition.

Habit may seem the total opposite of creativity and spirituality but it is not. There are good biological reasons for choices to become habitual, including the choices involved with such creative/spiritual acts such as singing, dancing and praying. As an activity is repeated over and over, the neural circuitry of the brain responsible for these activities becomes "burned" in, which means that it can operate more efficiently. In some cases, an activity can become so "hardwired" that even the location of the circuitry in the brain changes, sinking down below the brain proper and into the spinal cord.[36] This turns out to have huge evolutionary benefits. Routinized behaviors require much less energy than those that require conscious thought.[37] Once routinized, these behaviors not only tend to operate more efficiently, they also tend to operate more effectively. Ironically, people are capable of being more creative, and spiritual, if they are operating in an unconscious, "automatic" mode. Virtually everything a person does over the course of a day, from engaging in conversation to playing music, from walking to playing basketball, is better when conscious thought is absent from the process.[38] One of the reasons professional athletes preform at such high levels of effectiveness is because they play "in the zone," in other words without having to be conscious of their playing. Years of practice and repetition enable them to make the right choices at the right time. In other words, not only are the behaviors routinized but so are the decision trees for choices, both of which are likely to be unavailable to self-reflection and description. This turns out to be true not only for Creativity & Spirituality-related choice making, but of all choice-making across all modalities of need.[39]

Pulling together the insights from these last two sections—the high degree of neural integration between Creativity & Spirituality-related Well-Being Systems and other Well-Being Systems and the critical role that repetition plays in the establishment of Creativity & Spirituality-related Well-Being Systems—provides some insights into how and why the needs of these systems could have evolved to be so salient for people. Although considerable time and even training might be required to develop the cognitive associations between creative or spiritual acts and positive well-being, once established, individuals would be highly pre-disposed to re-enact them again and again. Thus, whether responding to a need such as sickness or in anticipation of beginning an uncertain but important undertaking like setting out on a hunt, individuals would purposefully engage their Creativity & Spirituality-related Choice-Well-Being Systems in the expec-tation that past associations between these acts and positive well-being would result in future well-being. Importantly, the neurological connections so forged would have not only changed the ways well-being was perceived but opened the door to entirely new ways for achieving well-being; organized religion is one such example.

## Religion

It was long believed that big-S types of spirituality, namely religiosity, were com-mon to all humans. Although most present-day anthropologists do agree that spir-itual beliefs, often including belief in magical or miraculous events, are a cultural product created by all human communities, many now question whether these tendencies always become formalized into religious practices and thus whether religion itself can accurately be considered as something universally human.[40] Back in the mid-twentieth century when most did think that religious practice was a universal human trait, the influential anthropologist Clifford Geertz put forth the following explanation for religion. Religion is: "(1) a system of symbols which acts to (2) establish powerful, pervasive, and long-lasting moods and moti-vations in men by (3) formulating conceptions of a general order of existence and (4) clothing these conceptions with such an aura of factuality that (5) the moods and motivations seem uniquely realistic."[41]

Today Geertz's definition is controversial. Although some anthropologists believe that much of this definition still has validity, many others outright reject it because of what is assumed to be a Euro-centric bias in Geertz's categories.[42] Although there may or may not be a universally valid way to define and categorize religious-like beliefs, it does seem clear that all humans have both the capacity and propensity to consciously think about themselves in relation to a broader uni-verse of realities, frequently involving the placement of human existence within some larger system that transcends the immediate here and now. However, much like what distinguishes little-c creativity from big-C creativity, what distinguishes the type of little-s spirituality referred to above from the big-S spirituality associ-ated with religion is clearly formality and scale. Religion, as suggested by Geertz, has many dimensions, but arguably the most important of these is the highly social nature of religion. Religion is a group phenomenon, typically one that involves nearly every member of a person's immediate social network.

Religion is certainly a powerful meme. Worldwide, nearly 85% of the world's people identify with some religious group.[43] Religion is also a very complex meme.

The Well-Being Systems associated with religious practices and beliefs are by their nature typically quite abstract and complex, and so too the perceived needs associated with these Systems.

Like little-s spirituality, the benefits that derive from big-S spirituality, religion, involve learned associations. However, since the practices and beliefs associated with most religious Well-Being Systems are typically highly complex and often highly abstract, developing these Systems takes even more training and repeated exposure than do those associated with little-s spirituality. This is why most people find the practices and beliefs of unfamiliar religions strange or difficult to fathom. In fact, most people find the rules and practices of unfamiliar religions to be totally disconnected from their own needs and Well-Being Systems.[44] Instant conversions, celebrated as a miracle by many religions, are indeed miraculous because it is theoretically almost impossible for a single exposure to effect the kind of neural connectivity required to make religious beliefs effectively meet people's immediate well-being-related needs.

Without making a value judgment as to the veracity of any particular religious belief system, considerable time and repetitive teachings/training are required to build up sufficient connections between religious-related Choice-Well-Being Systems and a person's other Well-Being Systems. And such teaching/training is best started at an early an age; the earlier in life and the stronger the training is, the stronger and more permanent are the connections.[45] However, if and when such Systems do become intertwined, then the Well-Being Systems associated with religious practices can become immensely seductive and powerful.[46] This is a major goal and arguably at least much of the benefit that religion offers.[47]

Successful religions seek to connect every facet of a person's life to religious beliefs; with rules and practices associated with the foods one eats, the clothes one wears, methods for insuring one's health and safety, how and when to have sex, whom one should associate with and why. Religion specifically is focused on connecting to feelings of love and belonging, and religious communities shower esteem upon those individuals deemed to possess the strongest beliefs. Religions also forge connections to the Well-Being Systems of Reflectivity by providing guidance for how to make satisfying life-choices. And in all cases, religions teach their disciples that the positive emotions that flow from successful satisfaction of these other Well-Being Systems are directly associated with the Well-Being Systems of religious practice and beliefs.[48]

Of course even with deep and early training, a person can "lapse," their various Well-Being Systems becoming disconnected from their religious Well-Being Systems. However, under the right conditions, earlier developed connections can be rekindled. The trigger for such reconnections are often some kind of trauma such as depression, sickness or despair; in such cases the once learned relationship between religion and now compromised Well-Being Systems can be seen as a potential solution.[49] And if those connections are successfully reestablished, then the religious beliefs can once again win the neural Darwinian struggle for time and attention of a person's Well-Being Systems, even after the crisis subsides.

## The Satisfactions of Creativity and Spirituality-Related Well-Being Systems

The ultimate goal of all choice-making is the creation of feelings of well-being; this is true of the oldest and most biologically concrete Well-Being Systems and it is true of the most recently evolved and intellectually abstract Well-Being Systems. As evidenced by religion, but equally the case for other dimensions of Creativity and Spirituality such as the sciences, arts or sports, years of training and experience can result in the neural rewards of multiple Choice-Well-Being Systems becoming inextricably connected with a person's Creativity & Spirituality-related Choice-Well-Being Systems. The satisfactions a person derives through pursuits in the latter area can feel almost identical to the perceptions of well-being that a person typically associates with satisfactions in the former areas.[50] Ample examples of this occurring exist.

One scientist recently enumerated a long list of activities that he perceived made science fun.[51] Below are some of the activities he mentioned:

- Making discoveries via conducting experiments.
- Being the very first to discover something.
- Working closely with students, postdocs, research technicians and collaborators.
- Seeing a former graduate student or postdoctoral fellow you have trained go on to become a very successful independent investigator.
- Receiving public recognition such as being put in charge of a research group or facility, or being elected to a leadership position in a science society.
- Publishing a long and detailed research report in a science journal, or being invited to write a review article or to contribute a chapter for a new edited book.
- Presenting one's work at an annual science society meeting or an international science congress.

Most of these activities relate to the social modalities of Well-Being and involve feelings of connectedness and esteem, but one can project that other modalities are involved as well, including and particularly the modality of Reflectivity. However what should be clear from this listing of what is satisfying about being a scientist is that the sense of well-being afforded by these experiences can only accrue to someone deeply ensconced in the culture of science. In fact these activities would only be enjoyable to someone who was enculturated into these types of practices through years of learning and experience. Most non-scientists would find very few of these activities particularly "fun." Every person, though, through their own learning and experience, develops connections and associations between their Creativity and Spirituality-related Choice-Well-Being Systems and their other Well-Being Systems, connections and associations that they find personally satisfying and fun; only some of which others, including the average scientist, might share.

Not everyone is a scientist, an artist or a devout spiritualist, but there are many other ways to find Creativity or Spirituality-related well-being. Large percentages of Americans, for example, spend time on pursuits such as gardening, working on cars, square dancing, exploring their genealogy or collecting every imaginable type of memorabilia, all of which yield a significant measure of well-being.[52] Leisure pursuits such as these provide a useful window through which to view how the seven modalities of Well-Being Systems, winnowed through the lens of lived experiences, generate self-related needs and drive choice-making. This is why I utilize leisure-related choice-making as the backdrop for much of the final section of the book, the section where I strive to show how the Well-Being Systems model actually works in practice.

## Notes

1. Cosgrove, T. (2014). LIFE at Lascaux: First color photographs from another world. *Time*. Retrieved July 26, 2016. http://time.com/3879943/lascaux-early-color-photos-of-the-famous-cave-paintings-france-1947/#
2. Boesch, C. (2009). *The real chimpanzees: Sex strategies in the forest*. Cambridge: Cambridge University Press.
3. Pringle, H. (2013). The origin of human creativity was surprisingly complex. *Scientific American*. Retrieved July 26, 2016. www.scientificamerican.com/article/the-origin-human-creativity-suprisingly-complex/
4. Semendeferi, K., Armstrong, E., Schleicher, A., Zilles, K. & Van Hoesen, G.W. (2001). Prefrontal cortex in humans and apes: A comparative study of area 10. *American Journal of Physical Anthropology*, 114(3), 224–241.
5. Gabora, L. & Kaufman, S. (2010). Evolutionary perspectives on creativity. In J. Kaufman & R. Sternberg (Eds.), *The Cambridge handbook of creativity* (pp. 279–300). Cambridge, UK: Cambridge University Press.
6. Amabile, T. (1996). *Creativity in context: Update to the social psychology of creativity*. Boulder, CO: Westview Press.
7. Pringle, H. (2013). The origin of human creativity was surprisingly complex. *Scientific American*. Retrieved July 26, 2016. www.scientificamerican.com/article/the-origin-human-creativity-suprisingly-complex/
8. Tomasello, M., Kruger, A. & Ratner, H. (1993). Cultural learning. *Behavioral and Brain Sciences*, 16, 495–552; Tennie, C., Call, J. & Tomasello, M. (2009). Ratcheting up the ratchet: On the evolution of cumulative culture. *Philosophical Transactions of the Royal Society of London, B Biological Sciences*, 364(1528), 2405–2415.
9. Beppu, A. & Griffiths, T.L. (2009). Iterated learning and the cultural ratchet. In N. Taatgen, H. van Rijn, L. Schomaker & J. Nerbonne (Eds.). *Proceedings of the 31st annual conference of the cognitive science society* (pp. 2089–2094). Austin, TX: Cognitive Science Society.
10. Griffiths, T.L., Christian, B.R. & Kalish, M.L. (2008). Using category structures to test iterated learning as a method for identifying inductive biases. *Cognitive Science*, 32(1), 68–107.
    Stephan Lewandowsky, S., Griffiths, T.L. & Kalish, M.L. (2009). The wisdom of individuals: Exploring people's knowledge about everyday events using iterated learning. *Cognitive Science*, 33(6), 969–998.
11. Wikipedia. (2016). *Paleolithic religion*. Retrieved July 26, 2016. https://en.wikipedia.org/wiki/Paleolithic_religion
12. Clark, R. (2015). Mystery man. *National Geographic*, 228(4), 30–57.
13. Narr, K. (2008). Prehistoric religion. *Britannica online encyclopedia*. Retrieved July 26, 2016. www.britannica.com/topic/prehistoric-religion

14. Crawford, B. (2016). Earliest evidence of religious beliefs. *People of: Our everyday life*. Retrieved July 26, 2016. http://peopleof.oureverydaylife.com/earliest-evidence-religious-beliefs-4240.html

15. Based on the biggest and most detailed analysis of African DNA, the San people of southern Africa, who have lived as hunter-gatherers for thousands of years, are considered to be the oldest population of humans on Earth. According to these findings the San, also known as bushmen, are directly descended from the original population of early human ancestors who gave rise to all other groups of humans (Tishkoff, S., Reed, F., Friedlaender, F., Ehret, C., Ranciaro, A., Froment, A., Hirbo, J., Awomoyi, A., Bodo, J.-M., Doumbo, O., Ibrahim, M., Juma, A., Kotze, M., Lema, G., Moore, J., Mortensen, H., Nyambo, T., Omar, S., Powell, T., Pretorius, G., Smith, M., Thera, M., Wambebe, C., Weber, J. & Williams, S. (2009). The genetic structure of Africans and African Americans. *Science*, 324(5930), 1035–1044.).

16. Jaynes, J. (1976). *The origin of consciousness in the break-down of the bicameral mind*. Boston: Houghton Mifflin.

17. cf., Henrich, J., Heine, S. J. & Norenzayan, A. (2010). The weirdest people in the world? *Behavioral and Brain Sciences*, 33(2–3), 61–83.

18. Wiggins, G.A., Tyack, P., Scharff, C. & Rohrmeier, M. (2015). The evolutionary roots of creativity: Mechanisms and motivations. *Philosophical Transactions of the Royal Society B*, 370, 99–108.

19. For example, theories on the evolution of creativity typically begin with animal models of natural selection as the need to explore new territories or sexual selection, such as the creative use of song by birds and whales in mate selection (cf., Wiggins, G.A., Tyack, P., Scharff, C. & Rohrmeier, M. (2015). The evolutionary roots of creativity: Mechanisms and motivations. *Philosophical Transactions of the Royal Society B*, 370, 20140099), while theories on spirituality typically evoke social relationship building (e.g., Graziano, M. (2011). Is spirituality a byproduct of evolution? *Huffington Post*. Retrieved January 15, 2017. www.huffingtonpost.com/michael-graziano/spirituality-as-byproduct-of-evolution_b_918801.html) or even a genetic mutation that created a "God gene" or "God Spot" in the parietal lobes of the brain (cf., Cookson, J. (2013). The neurological origins of religious belief. *Big Think.com*. Retrieved January 13, 2017. http://bigthink.com/going-mental/the-neurological-origins-of-religious-belief).

20. Sternberg, R. J. (2011). *Creativity: Cognitive psychology* (6th ed.). Boston: Cengage Learning.

21. Simonton, D.K. (2001). *The psychology of creativity: An historical perspective*. Paper presented at the Green College Lecture Series on The Nature of Creativity: History Biology, and Socio-Cultural Dimensions, University of British Columbia, 2001. Retrieved July 26, 2016. http://simonton.faculty.ucdavis.edu/wp-content/uploads/sites/243/2015/08/HistoryCreativity.pdf

22. Pringle, H. (2013). The origin of human creativity was surprisingly complex. *Scientific American*. Retrieved July 26, 2016. www.scientificamerican.com/article/the-origin-human-creativity-suprisingly-complex/

23. cf., Fasko, D., Jr. (2006). Creative thinking and reasoning. In J.C. Kaufman & J. Baer (Eds.), *Creativity and reason in cognitive development* (pp. 159–176). New York: Cambridge University Press.

24. For example, a range of research has established a correlation between creativity, particularly artistic creativity, and mental illness (e.g., Batey, M. & Furnham, A. (2009). The relationship between creativity, schizotypy and intelligence. *Individual Differences Research*, 7, 272–284; Furnham, A., Batey, M., Anand, K. & Manfield, J. (2008). Personality, hypomania, intelligence and creativity. *Personality and Individual Differences*, 44, 1060–1069; Kyaga, S., Lichtenstein, P., Boman, M., Hultman, C., Långström, N. & Landén, M. (2011). Creativity and mental disorder: Family study of 300 000 people with severe mental disorder. *The British Journal of Psychiatry*, 199(5), 373–379).

25. Barber, N. (2012). *Why atheism will replace religion: The triumph of earthly pleasures over pie in the sky*. E-book, www.amazon.com/Atheism-Will-Replace-Religion-ebook/dp/B00886ZSJ6/

26. e.g., Stuckey, H.L. & Nobel, J. (2010). The connection between art, healing, and public health: A review of current literature. *American Journal of Public Health*, 100(2), 254–263.

Kaimal, G., Ray K. & Muniz, J. (2016). Reduction of cortisol levels and participants' responses following art making. *Art Therapy*, 33(2), 74–80.

Fukui, H. & Toyoshima, K. (2008). Music facilitates the neurogenesis, regeneration and repair of neurons. *Medical Hypotheses*, 71(5), 765–769.

Yamamoto, M., Naga, S. & Jun Shimizu, J. (2007). Positive musical effects on two types of negative stressful conditions. *Psychology of Music*, 35(2), 249–275.

27. Barber, N. (2012). Why did religion evolve? *Psychology Today*. Retrieved January 15, 2017. www.psychologytoday.com/blog/the-human-beast/201206/why-did-religion-evolve

28. Barber, N. (2012). *Why atheism will replace religion: The triumph of earthly pleasures over pie in the sky*. E-book. www.amazon.com/Atheism-Will-Replace-Religion-ebook/dp/B00886ZSJ6/

29. Paul-Labrador, M.D., Polk, J.H., Dwyer, I., Velasquez, S., Nidich, S., Rainforth, M., Schneider, R. & Merz, C.N. (2006). Effects of a randomized controlled trial of transcendental meditation on components of the metabolic syndrome in subjects with coronary heart disease. *Archives of Internal Medicine*, 166, 1218–1224.

30. Edison, T.A. (c. 1903). Spoken statement, published in *Harper's Monthly* (September 1932).

31. Gladwell, M. (2008). *Outliers*. New York: Little, Brown and Company.

32. Ferro, S. (2014). Scientists debunk the myth that 10,000 hours of practice will make you an expert. *FastCompany*. Outliers. Retrieved February 12, 2017. www.fastcodesign.com/3027564/asides/scientists-debunk-the-myth-that-10000-hours-of-practice-makes-you-an-expert

33. cf., Bransford, J.D., Brown, A.L. & Cocking, R.R. (Eds.). (2000). *How people learn: Brain, mind, experience, and school*. Washington, DC: National Academy Press.

34. de Groot, A. (1965). *Thought and choice in chess*. The Hague, Netherlands: Mouton.

35. Bransford, J.D., Brown, A.L. & Cocking, R.R. (Eds.). (2000). *How people learn: Brain, mind, experience, and school*. Washington, DC: National Academy Press, p. 44.

36. Eagleman, D. (2015). *The brain: The story of you*. New York: Pantheon.

37. Eagleman, D. (2015). *The brain: The story of you*. New York: Pantheon.

38. Eagleman, D. (2015). *The brain: The story of you*. New York: Pantheon.

39. Duhigg, C. (2012). *The power of habit*. New York: Random House.

40. Guthrie, S.E. (2000). Projection. In W. Braun & R.T. McCutcheon (Eds.), *Guide to the study of religion* (pp. 225–226). London: Cassell.

41. Geertz, C. (1966). Religion as a cultural system. In M. Banton (Ed.), *Anthropological Approaches to the study of religion* (pp. 1–46). London: Tavistock.

42. i.e., a WEIRD bias.

43. Pew (2012). The global religious landscape. *Pew Research Center for Religion & Public Life*. Retrieved January 15, 2017. www.pewforum.org/2012/12/18/global-religious-landscape-exec/

44. This reality is the bane of all proselyting religions. Seemingly there are good biological reasons why it's hard to convert the heathens (cf., Barber, N. (2012). *Why atheism will replace religion: The triumph of earthly pleasures over pie in the sky*. E-book. www.amazon.com/Atheism-Will-Replace-Religion-ebook/dp/B00886ZSJ6/).

45. Piedmont, R. & Village, A. (Eds.). (2009). *Research in the social scientific study of religion* (Vol. 20). Leiden, The Netherlands: Brill.

46. Many neuroscientists have taken too reductionist an approach to thinking about the neurobiology of religion; seeking to find the brain's religious center/"God spot" rather than appreciating that the Well-Being Systems associated with religion, like most neural processes, are highly distributed.

47. I personally do not believe it is necessary for there to be metaphysical/super-natural reasons for why religion helps people live more satisfying lives, but I will not here dispute the possibility that such additional reasons could be at play.

48. Borg, J., Andree, B., Doderstrom, H. & Farde, L. (2003). The serotonin system and spiritual experiences. *American Journal of Psychiatry*, 160(11), 1965–1969.
    Tiger, L. & McGuire, M. (2010). *God's brain*. Amherst, NY: Prometheus.
49. Alister, H. (1979). *The spiritual nature of man*. Oxford, UK: Clarendon Press.
50. Borg, J., Andree, B., Doderstrom, H. & Farde, L. (2003). The serotonin system and spiritual experiences. *American Journal of Psychiatry*, 160(11), 1965–1969.
    Tiger, L. & McGuire, M. (2010). *God's brain*. Amherst, NY: Prometheus.
51. Dr. M. (2015). What is fun about being a scientist. Dr. M. on Science, Research & Scientists. Retrieved January 15, 2017. http://dr-monsrs.net/tag/scientist-career-satisfaction/
52. Gelber, S.M. (1999). *Hobbies: Leisure and the culture of work in America*. New York: Columbia University Press.

# PART III

# Applying the Well-Being Systems Model

# 14

# UNDERSTANDING THE INDIVIDUAL IN THE MOMENT

This is the point in the book where I move from the theoretical to the practical, where I attempt to directly show how the Well-Being Systems model provides insights into why people make the choices they do. As discussed at the end of the first section of the book, human Well-Being Systems are influenced by events happening along a vast continuum, from the subatomic to the galactic, and on timescales of nanoseconds to eons; humans generally only perceive events within a fairly narrow subset of these experiences. I have labeled this area of perceptual focus the "language sphere" because everyday language evolved specifically to describe the self-related needs and choices, events and feelings occurring within this grain size of human experience. Although I point out that exclusively focusing on this narrow perspective has down sides, it clearly is an important human domain. The first two chapters in this section focus on understanding a single individual within this language sphere using leisure as the broad contextual vehicle. These chapters use as a case study a single leisure event in the life of a retired American male; an outing with friends occupying the better part of a single day.

## Leisure Time

There are a couple of reasons why leisure is a particularly useful context in which to examine Well-Being Systems and choice-making. The first reason is that leisure, more than any other human endeavor, affords people an opportunity to proactively choose to act in ways that comport with their conceptions of well-being; to more or less act in ways consistent with one's perceptions of how one would live one's life if one had total control.[1] Although all seven modalities of Well-Being Systems play a role in leisure choices and behaviors, the modality of Reflectivity plays a particularly important role since many leisure activities involve some measure of conscious deliberation and choice. As a consequence, once again using the paint-mixing metaphor introduced in Chapter 5, all leisure choices have at least a little bit of Reflectivity "pigment" within them. This represents the second big advantage to using leisure experiences as a case study on understanding choice-making. Despite the inherent limitations of language as a device for explaining choice-making in general, language-based explanations remain one of the most powerful tools currently available to social science for "peering inside" a person's mind. Given the direct relationship between conscious reflection and language, people find it easier to describe the needs that motivate their Reflectivity-related choices than they do describing those underlying many other types of choices. To set the context for using leisure time as a case study for choice-making, the following overview of leisure is useful.

Leisure is not, as some might presume, a modern invention. It has been suggested, based on studies of modern-day hunter-gatherer peoples, that humans historically had considerable leisure time.[2] That reality changed for millennia after the shift to an agrarian lifestyle. Although many agrarian peoples in the world today continue to eke out a living without measurable leisure time, an ever increasing percentage of the world's population has begun to once again reclaim the joys of having "idle" time. Although the concept of leisure time, time when someone is free from the immediate responsibilities of daily life, is common to all humans, the exact expression of leisure, what someone might actually choose to do during that leisure time, is always highly influenced by culture and context.

Over the past 100+ years in the industrialized world, the vast majority of people used leisure as a mechanism for escaping from the physical and mental drudgery and exhaustion of factory work. Classic 20th century responses were the escapism fostered by Disney and other theme parks or a week spent on vacation at the beach or some other resort doing "nothing."[3] Although these leisure diversions are still popular, their market share is declining.[4] As the world of work has become increasingly centered around mental rather than physical labor, more and more of the public's leisure time is being filled with experiences designed to support a range of essentially mental entertainments rather than just physical relaxation. Rather than vegetating under a palm tree at the beach, people increasingly see their leisure time as an opportunity to be enervated by immersing themselves in new ideas, spaces and experiences.[5] In the early years of the 21st century, more passive forms of leisure pursuit are being supplanted by activities designed to understand and push the limits of the body such as hiking, rafting or sports or to expand one's understanding of one's self and world such as visits to historic and natural settings, genealogical research and visits to museums.[6] According to leisure researcher Geof Godbey, "leisure should resemble the best aspects of work: challenges, skills and important relationships."[7] Regardless of whether an individual's free-time is designed to restore the body, build relationships, invigorate the mind or increasingly some combination of these, the key is that people are increasingly attempting to mindfully and pro-actively spend their time doing things they perceive maximize personal well-being.

All leisure decision-making increasingly comes down to a series of value-related cost-benefit choices in which time plays a crucial role. Whether it's a short trip to the downtown to visit the shopping mall, a day-long trip to a museum or natural site, or a multi-day journey to a domestic or foreign destination that might include a multitude of activities, including shopping, museum-going and hiking, people weigh the costs and values of the experience and roughly "calculate" how an investment of time in this activity or another will benefit them and their loved ones, actively selecting the option(s) they perceive will afford them maximal satisfaction, i.e., satisfy their most important self-related needs. What is it that would make a leisure good or service rise above the crowded field? Rather than selecting leisure experiences based merely on their utility, today's increasingly affluent leisure consumers make decisions based on an experience or product's ability to satisfy their perceived personal desires and lifestyles. So complete has been this transformation amongst the affluent that today a majority of the people living in Europe, Asia, the Americas and throughout the Pacific region have largely exhausted the things they *have* to purchase or do; instead they now focus on what they *want* to purchase or do.[8]

When asked, people provide a diversity of self-aspects to describe the well-being they seek in leisure. Some people say they engage in leisure pursuits because it makes them happy. Others say that they seek leisure activities that allow them to be better partners, parents or friends, while others emphasize that leisure helps them become more knowledgeable and competent individuals. Still others say they seek out specific leisure experiences in order to nourish and rejuvenate their spirit or give meaning to their life.[9] Whatever the self-aspects of well-being people use, all reveal a basic truth. People today engage in leisure for much the same reasons people have always engaged in leisure, in order to create a sense of well-being through satisfaction of one or some combination of the seven basic modalities of need.

## In Pursuit of Well-Being: A Case Study

It is with this context in mind that we now turn to the leisure experience of Daniel,[10] a recently retired, highly educated, middle-income white male. The transcript below was drawn from an interview I conducted just prior to Daniel's day-trip to Silver Falls State Park, one of Oregon's premier scenic areas.[11]

Q: So tell me, why did you want to go on this trip today?

A: Well, this is a good way to share quality time with my friends Jack and Linden. [Silver Falls] where we will be visiting is a rare, beautiful place. I've spoken of it before and want to share it with my friends. It's an ideal day—timing, weather. I'm looking forward to it stimulating creativity and pleasure, of it being an invigorating but not daunting hike. I spent a lot of time calculating and sharing its potential.

[I'm looking forward to] my friends and I having a learning experience together—not profound/academic learning, but enjoyable learning. Even though I have been there before, it's a new day, a new walk. I'll learn from my friend, things like birds and plants.

Q: Why is this important to you? Are these leisure goals you have frequently or is today and this site special?

A: I think of myself as a curious person, about everything. I prize learning. Also I've become increasingly attentive to the interests of other people in the social situations I or others construct. [Today] seems like a good opportunity. It's always an adventure, but it's a leap into the unknown; stretching [the capabilities of] my creaky limbs through a 3-mile hike. [I'm aware that] there's a finite number of times I might be able to do this kind of hike; I won't be able to do this forever.

Q: Why do you think Silver Falls will be a good place for accomplishing these goals?

A: One overall framing reason. I've been thinking about both the pleasure and the shadow of my limited time left. The ability to arrange things the way you want them in life. In addition to things said before, the light and shadow.

Both of us [Daniel and his partner Kate] have been to Silver Falls and had pleasant experiences. Kate had good experiences and has probably been 10 times or more. I've been four or five times; each one was positive, and several were quite special. . . . So I have a deep association between Silver Falls and a kind of renewal. So going there, for me, is associated with nature, pleasure and renewal; that's the feeling I have about that place. . . . I have been eager to share this experience with my friends Jack and Linden who have not been there before. . . .

Hiking is not an insignificant part of my and my wife's life, and my wife specifically likes that locale. These two facts made it even more appealing as a venue to visit. Both of us like to walk and be in nature; the novelty of the day. In fact, experiences in nature are always good for providing me with the novelty of presented phenomenon. I find this uniquely appealing. Also, I knew that this [particular walk] was not going to be [physically] challenging.

As for Jack and Linden, I've been hiking with them in the past, both on short and extended trips. They too like to attend to nature and find such pastimes pleasurable. Each of us brings our own interests and expertise to the event, the combination is mutually satisfying.

Q: Given your expectations and past experience what preparation or planning did you do for today?

A: In the context of wanting to have a really special time today with friends, of wanting this to be a really nice day, Kate and I gave a bit more attention to the rigor of the various walk options. We wanted to constrain the choices and advise our friends on options so we could maximize the quality of the experience. Other than that, just the normal stuff of getting gear and food together.

Daniel clearly perceived that he had considerable choice and control over how he spent his leisure time. Consistent with the brief review at the beginning of this chapter, Daniel proactively sought to craft a leisure experience that would support his and his friend's well-being based on a set of clearly perceived self-related needs and prior experiences, both his own and those of his partner and friends.

## Preparing for Leisure: How Needs Drive Choice-Making

As the interview above with Daniel reveals, he like so many others today is motivated to use his leisure time in ways that are designed to satisfy very specific leisure-related needs. In Daniel's case he cited several very specific desires that he hoped his day trip to Silver Falls State Park would satisfy; the desire to spend quality time with friends, a desire to learn and satisfy his personal curiosity, a desire to partake in invigorating but not exhausting physical exercise, a desire to take advantage of good weather and the park's amenities and the desire to experience a beautiful place. The choice of Silver Falls for this day's outing was not coincidental. Silver Falls was actively chosen as the destination because Daniel's prior experiences suggested that it would be a place that would support these multiple goals; it would be a good place to facilitate his friendship, satisfy his curiosity about and enjoyment of the natural world and a good place to hike, have a picnic lunch, and enjoy a beautiful spring day.

This framing of choice-making through the lens of need-satisfaction is totally consistent with my proposed Well-Being Systems model. It is also consistent with the findings of a host of leisure researchers,[12] who beginning in the late 1960s began to realize that leisure experiences should not be viewed merely as an activity such as hiking, fishing, camping or shopping but rather "should be conceptualized as a psychophysiological experience that is self-rewarding, occurs during non-obligated free time, and is the result of free-choice."[13] From this perspective, individuals do not randomly engage in leisure but rather pursue leisure for specific purposes, and if not totally mindfully, at least do so with the partial awareness that their leisure pursuit is intended to satisfy one or several specific need-related goal(s). Although the assumption that people should be able to describe, before the fact, why they are engaging in the particular leisure they have chosen to do seems unremarkable and totally and self-evident, it actually is non-trivial. The idea that leisure choices, in fact all choices, are directly connected to self-related needs is a critical insight and totally changed the way researchers thought about the hows and whys of leisure.

Hence, as evidenced by my interview with Daniel, when someone is asked prior to his actual leisure experience, why are you doing this today, they have no trouble responding:

> Well, this is a good way to share quality time with my friends Jack and Linden. [Silver Falls] where we will be visiting is a rare, beautiful place. I've spoken of it before and want to share it with my friends. It's an ideal

day—timing, weather. I'm looking forward to it stimulating creativity and pleasure, of it being an invigorating but not daunting hike. I spent a lot of time calculating and sharing its potential.

Starting in the 2000s I began trying to apply these ideas to better understanding why people visited museum-like settings;[14] asserting that museum-going was a purposeful act designed to satisfy specific self-related needs.[15] My research, along with that of others, not only confirms that people can readily explain their reasons for visiting museum-like settings during leisure, but more importantly it shows that although people offer up a diversity of explanations for why they are visiting such a setting, these diverse reasons all converge on a relatively small number of motivational categories.[16] People invariably offered up visit reasons that clustered around a finite set of museum-specific affordances that directly related to those individuals' desire to use their leisure experience as a vehicle for satisfying one or more self-related needs, needs that not only had a psychological but also a biological basis.

As outlined in earlier chapters, the actual machinery of the Well-Being Systems that determine perceived needs and choices largely operates below the level of awareness. However, people typically have some perception of these leisure-related internal goings-on and can verbally represent these events through socially and culturally constructed conventions called self-aspects—self-referential conceptualizations of perceived inner states, situations, attributes or relationships framed within the current linguistic vernacular of their society and culture. Because these self-aspects do not represent actual representations of underlying processes they cannot necessarily be taken literally or just accepted at face value. One needs to ask what is really going on here; how do a person's self-aspects map onto one or some combination of the seven basic modalities of well-being-related needs described in this book—Continuity, Individuality, Sexuality, Sociality, Relationality, Reflectivity and Creativity/Spirituality?

The self-aspects that emerge most prominently in Daniel's response relate to his perceived role as a friend. Daniel desires to do things he believes that friends do, things such as spending time together and doing things together that are mutually enjoyable. Daniel also reveals a desire to satisfy his own intellectual, physical and spiritual needs by selecting a setting for the outing that he perceives, based on prior experience, possesses these affordances.

From these self-aspects we can in turn infer that certainly some aspect of the self-related needs of Sociality appear to be important to Daniel, so too the self-related needs associated with Creativity/Spirituality and Continuity. But as with nearly all perceived needs, they represent not a single need but rather a complex blending of needs drawn from multiple modalities. Embedded in Daniel's description are clear references to friendship, learning and the physical benefits and joys of exercise but also allusions to aesthetics—"[Silver Falls] is a rare, beautiful place"—and the complex construct of "convenience." Daniel also gives as a reason that "It's an ideal day—timing, weather." Depending upon the situation and prior, lived experience, every human is continuously mixing and matching their various core self-related needs, often quite creatively, in an effort to maximize well-being by efficiently trying to satisfy multiple competing needs simultaneously. Thus, as described earlier from just seven core needs, a person is able to make an almost infinite variety of self-related choices.

## The Role of Prior Experience and Opportunity Costs

But what my research suggests is that Daniel's choices were not exclusively determined by his internally perceived needs. Equally important were what options he perceived were available for satisfying those needs. Daniel, like most people, could think of several alternatives, but not an infinite number. The usual leisure-time suspects might have included going to a movie, visiting a museum, sampling wine at a local winery or site-seeing and shopping at one of several nearby small towns. But none of these particularly appealed to him. Daniel chose to go hiking at a particular state park. In making this choice, Daniel was reflecting both his own personal preferences for how to satisfy his own perceived self-related needs as well as what he perceived his friends too might find satisfying. Since the primary goal of the day was to facilitate a positive social experience, to support Sociality-related needs, Daniel would not purposefully select an activity he felt his friends would find unenjoyable. But Daniel's leisure choices, like everyone's leisure choices, must be based on some prior experience or knowledge. Daniel could not select an activity for his leisure experience that he was totally unaware of, nor would he select something he, or in this case his friends, totally hated doing.

As described towards the end of the previous chapter, habit plays an important role in all human choices, including leisure. Most hikers are people who have hiked before and found it enjoyable. Most art museum-goers are people who have been to an art museum before and have found it satisfying. The same is true for movie goers, wine-tasters, shoppers and every other form of leisure. By and large, the people one finds engaged in any particular leisure pursuit are individuals with prior, positive experiences doing similar things.[17] Success breeds success, and the more a particular activity is found to be pleasurable, the more likely is a person to want to repeat that activity. The fact that Daniel and his partner had had extensive and particularly positive experiences with this particular venue was important. So too was the fact that Daniel knew that his friends enjoyed hiking and nature and that the two couples had enjoyed hiking together in the past. This knowledge, combined with the fact that Jack and Linden had never been to this particular site before all figured into Daniel's choice-making. So too was the fact that Silver Falls State Park was a relatively short drive from Daniel and his friends' home, was relatively inexpensive and afforded amenities beyond hiking such as nice places for a picnic lunch. Leisure, and arguably all other forms of choice-making as well, represent the confluence of three elements—self-related need, prior experience and opportunity costs and benefits. These three combine to form the why, where, when and how of (leisure) choice-making.

Different leisure settings afford different things. For example, natural areas clearly afford the ability to hike, bike or even run. They also afford the opportunity for social interactions as well as intellectual and aesthetic enrichment.

However, they are generally not the best places to go if one is seeking a gourmet meal, pre-packaged digital entertainment or a particular outfit to buy for next week's party. Over a number of years, colleagues and I have looked extensively at the reasons people visit a range of leisure settings, particularly museum-like settings such as art, natural history, history and children's museums, science centers, zoos and aquariums, botanical gardens and the like. As a consequence, data has now been collected from several thousand individuals visiting more than 50 institutions, across more than a dozen countries on four continents.

What this research reveals is that although the specific self-aspects used by these thousands of people to explain their motivations for visiting these sites varies widely, well over 90% of these self-aspects can be comfortably sorted into just a half dozen or so major self-related need categories.[18] Borrowing from people's self-aspect descriptions of the basic underlying self-related needs that I believed motivated people to visit these settings, more than a decade ago I chose to label the most common of these museum visit categories: *explorers*; *facilitators*; *experience seekers*; *professionals/hobbyists*; *amenity seekers*; and *rechargers*.[19] However these names and even the exact number of categories are arbitrary, reflecting my interpretation of how people's self-aspects aligned with my interpretation of underlying self-related needs.[20] What is important is that despite the amazing diversity of all these settings and the obvious diversity of the roughly one billion individuals worldwide who visit such settings every year, only a relatively small subset of reasons are required to explain why all of these people visit, and those reasons are directly related to the relationship between visitors' perceptions of their self-related needs and equally their perceptions of how these kinds of sites might satisfy those needs.[21]

Interestingly, despite the fact that individuals appreciate that any given leisure setting is capable of satisfying multiple needs and typically say that they are visiting because all, or at least many, of these affordances are important to them, if asked they typically have no difficulty specifying which of these many affordances is most important to them.[22] For example, Daniel gave multiple reasons for wanting to go hiking at Silver Falls, but on this particular day one motivation stood out above all others. The primary reason, according to Daniel, for going hiking this day at Silver Falls was social, falling within the category I have called a *facilitator* motivation (Figure 14.1). If Daniel did not perceive that Silver Falls was a place that could support his facilitator motivation, he would have selected another setting to visit that day.

The point is that these categories not only end up reflecting the reasons people have for visiting places like museums, but importantly they provide insights into the basic modalities of well-being an individual hopes to satisfy during their visit as well as reflecting the basic leisure attributes the public perceives that these kinds of best afford. In this case they provide a glimpse into this hybrid thing my colleague Lynn Dierking and I have called the museum-visitor experience.[23] They are not a complete description of museums, since all museums can be and arguably are more multifaceted and capable of supporting more than just these six categories of need-related behaviors and benefits. And they are certainly not fully descriptive of visitors and their unique well-beings, since each of the roughly one billion people who visit museums each year clearly are far more complex and

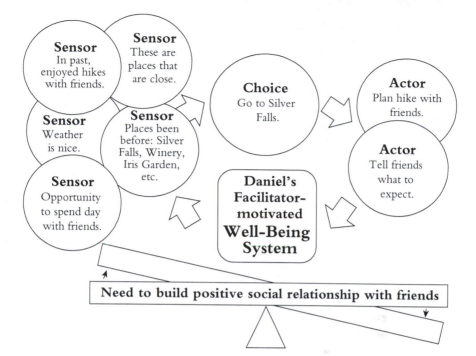

**FIGURE 14.1**  Daniel's Facilitator-Motivated Well-Being System at time 1

desirous of satisfying many more than just these six self-related needs. But what this simplified model of the world does seem to successfully describe is that unique confluence of biological, psychological and physical realities; where the ways most people who visit museums perceive their well-being and self-related needs intersect with their perceptions of the affordances of these particular types of physical settings.[24] Every single leisure experience and venue can be analyzed similarly.

Whether the leisure experience is a visit to a natural area or a shopping mall, attending a music festival or playing a game of bridge, going to a party or spending the evening in front of the television, all share this same relationship. Each potential experience represents a convergence between the participating individual's desire for well-being, as expressed through perceptions of her self-related needs and her perceptions of the affordances offered by the setting or activity that she believes will enable her to satisfy those needs. Then, and only then, each option is sifted through the opportunity-cost filters of time, price and convenience.

## Engaging in Leisure: How Expectations Drive Actions

The power of the Well-Being Systems model is that not only does it describe why a person would choose to engage in a particular leisure pursuit; it predicts that actions too are driven by those same Systems. As it turns out, not just immediate actions like Daniel actually following through and visiting Silver Falls, but longer-term actions as well. As discussed in detail in Chapter 12, the model predicts that if a person's self-related needs are sufficiently strong to motivate them to invest the significant energy required to initiate a complex leisure behavior they should also be sufficiently strong to influence how that leisure behavior is enacted. In other words, leisure motivations are also significant drivers of ALL behaviors associated with that leisure experience.

Again, let's turn to the example of Daniel's trip to Silver Falls. The following transcript comes from the interview I conducted with Daniel about two hours after he had completed his visit to Silver Falls State Park.

> Q: So, tell me about your experience at Silver Falls today. What were some of the highlights for you?

> A: Well first off, the day easily met my expectations. It was a lovely day—weather, agreeableness of climate and set-up. I enjoyed the company of my companions and the interactions I had with each of them. Globally, all of the arrangements were successful as they led to maximum opportunity for satisfaction. We had a really nice meal, in a good spot that was new to us. A fine and lively conversation, different from just the normal dinner time talk.

> We had a really nice walk out in nature. That part too went well. I learned something from my friend, as well as shared some learning experiences back. Overall, it was a good definition of quality time, well spent with friends in a beautiful setting.

> [I was] not exactly challenged [by the terrain], but it was a different sort of activity [than I'm used to]. It underscored that this is not as easy as it was 30 years ago and that I've a finite window for such things [like hiking].

> But, good weather and uncrowded; there were a constellation of dimensions that made it very conducive to a quality day. It is not often easy for me to spend such a nice day, sustained at such a high pitch, all day. The novelty was well set up to accomplish many of the objectives I had set for myself—high level of conversation about politics, etc. I can't think of a moment that wasn't agreeable.

> Q: What event or aspect of the trip did you find most satisfying?

> A: Without hesitation, I'd say that it was that [my friends] Jack and Linden enjoyed themselves. It was deeply satisfying to share an experience like this with them. At this point in my life, it is really important to me to share such things—good humor, not hilarity, but enjoyable times.

> Q: What event or aspect of the trip did you find most unsatisfying?

> A: There really was nothing that was unsatisfying. Clearly this kind of experience, to me, is a component of a life well-lived—of a different kind from the satisfaction I typically engage in which is more overtly intellectual. It was a kind of refreshment, a nice change but not compensatory. [I'm] not sure it was a sublime moment, but [it was a] time of novelty and wonderment. For example, my slow-motion pictures of the falls; not a deep experience, but

deeply satisfying. It was a walk in the woods with loved ones, not like playing a French horn, but very fine![25]

Q: Was there anything that arose today that you found particularly problematic or unpleasant?

A: Because of my desire to have other people be pleased, I had to make a deduction that everyone was enjoying themselves. Everyone seemed to be well.

There was a shared desire for civility—which is a quality of friendship. The shadow side, it was a little bit more taxing, are people really enjoying themselves or just pretending? One can never be absolutely sure what others are really feeling. But I've a high degree of confidence in my friend Jack, more than in most people in my life. I always believe he will be honest with me.

And then there was the slight mishap of Kate bumping her head [on an overhanging tree].

Q: If you happened to be talking to a friend about Silver Falls in the next few days or weeks, what based on today would you tell him or her?

A: Alone with Kate [wife], I might wonder if [other friends] have been here before. I'm thinking we should tell them about it. It's a highly manageable day. [Wife's niece] too, it would be good for her [as she'll be visiting soon]. The locale and organization of the day was confirmed as something possible and pleasing; which recommends it well as a good day trip. Perhaps when [wife's] brother comes to visit, it would be a good day trip for him too.

I can see this becoming part of our visitor repertoire; a reliable activity. [I] now have confidence [in this activity] that I can feel reasonably assured that it will feel like a good time for others.

As this follow-up interview reveals, Daniel's initial expectations and self-related motivations for the visit did indeed seem to act as a frame of reference for the trip. Daniel states that all his expectations for the visit were indeed met—it was a beautiful day, it did support his desire to use the experience to reinforce his friendship with Jack and Linden, he learned some things from his friends (and felt they learned from him as well), the weather and picnic lunch were indeed as hoped for and he found the hike to be within his level of expertise and abilities. All in all, as Daniel states, "Overall, it was a good definition of quality time, well spent with friends in a beautiful setting." Every self-related need Daniel had indicated he hoped his hike to Silver Falls would fulfill was, according to Daniel, satisfied.

As indicated above, Daniel's primary reason for going hiking this particular day at Silver Falls was social.[26] Ultimately, the criterion a facilitator such as Daniel would use to judge the success of a particular leisure experience would be whether or not he perceived that others in his group had a positive experience. As Daniel said, he perceived that the day was a success because he perceived that his friends enjoyed themselves, though he admits he could only infer that this was true.

My experiences as a social science researcher have taught me that one useful way to probe an individual's true feelings about an experience is to ask them how they would describe their experience to someone else, as I did in the final question above. Daniel's answer provides further evidence that this facilitator role dominated his valuing of the day. He says he would likely share with his partner Kate how nice this particular day visit to Silver Falls State Park would be for other friends and relatives they care about, that "I can see this becoming part of our visitor repertoire; a reliable activity. [I] now have confidence [in this activity] that I can feel reasonably assured that it will feel like a good time for others" (see Figure 14.2).

Daniel's description of his hike at Silver Falls provides a fascinating lens through which to better understand how the choices individuals make around their self-related needs help drive actual lived experiences; both the prospective choices and the actual, minute-by-minute choices and actions people engage in. Over the past 20 years I've now conducted hundreds of interviews with individuals like Daniel following one type of leisure experience or another, and time and time again in such interviews what leaps out is how profoundly personal such experiences are, how strongly tied each experience is to that individual's particular perception of self-related needs as well as how strongly each person's unique, prior lived experience influences what they do and recall. No two individuals experience the world in exactly the same way and so even individuals having just had what ostensibly is the exact same experience will provide very different narratives of the experience.

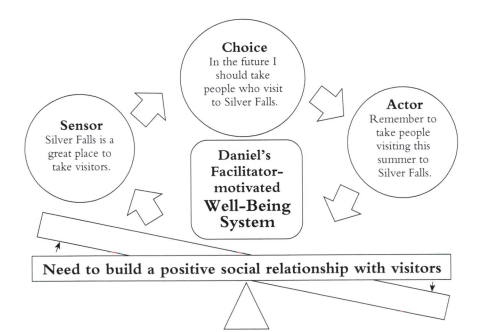

**FIGURE 14.2** Daniel's future-oriented Facilitator-Motivated Well-Being System

Yet, what is equally striking is how consistently an individual's post-experience narrative relates to their entering expectations. In other words, prior to spending the day hiking at Silver Falls Daniel talked about how this visit was all about his desire to spend time with his friends Jack and Linden, to enjoy the beauty and amenities of the setting, to have an exhilarating but not exhausting hike and potentially to satisfy his curiosity by learning new things. And after the experience, Daniel highlighted that what he remembered about the experience was that it was very satisfying to spend time with his friends Jack and Linden, that he enjoyed the beauty and amenities of the setting, that it was a healthy but not overly challenging hike and that he was able to satisfy his curiosity by learning new things. In other words, Daniel and others humans: 1) perceive needs based on their desire to achieve well-being; 2) plan their leisure experiences in ways that they hope will satisfy those needs; and then 3) use their leisure experience as a vehicle for fulfilling those needs and achieving well-being.

In others words, Daniel wanted to take a hike with his friends Jack and Linden first and foremost because he expected that it would result in an enhanced bond with these particular friends, which in turn would extend his Sociality-related needs, which would result in an enhanced perception of well-being. Likely, Daniel was only consciously mindful of the very first part of this outcome equation, but certainly unconsciously he was also at some level cognizant of the latter two parts as well. From past experience he understood that enhanced friendships increased feelings of well-being. Thus his expectations for the day helped to shape what he found salient and thus how he actually spent his time; and ultimately what he found satisfying.

## Satisfaction as an Indicator of Well-Being

Most people have a pretty good sense of what it means to be satisfied. Satisfaction is the neuro-physiological experience of feeling content and at ease with one's situation and is one of the ways people judge their well-being; high satisfaction equals high well-being. Considerable research has been conducted specifically on the topic of leisure satisfaction, particularly of late using what is called the *Dynamic Model* of leisure experience.[27] Basically leisure researchers have defined the dynamic leisure experience as a balance between a participant's entering expectations for a leisure experience and the set of interactions that the leisure participant has during a leisure experience, including all the social and physical context interactions she participates in—a model not unlike the one I've been laying out in this book. Since most leisure researchers are quantitatively-minded, they tend to couch their models accordingly. Thus, according to the leisure research literature, a leisure participant's overall experience can be conceived as the sum of the experiences that occur during the leisure event, with each episode having the potential to confirm or disconfirm the individual's entering expectations. What are these episodes? Well again according to leisure researchers, these episodes include both situational factors such as the presence of litter or crowds, as well as subjective factors such as the perception that things were easy to find, the extent to which goals were met or the perceived quality of what was seen. Although most leisure investigators, as well as most leisure purveyors, tend to be overly concerned with situational factors since these are presumed to be the things they think they can control, e.g., litter can be picked up and crowds managed, these turn out to not be the factors most people find most important, most of the time.

As leisure researchers Alan Graefe and Anthony Fedler and independently Steven Whisman and Steven Hollenhorst discovered, leisure satisfaction was most strongly influenced by people's subjective evaluations of the elements of the experience and only indirectly by the situational aspects.[28] In other words, perceptions of the experience were far more important than were actual conditions, and the emotional valence of those perceptions was paramount. These ideas were followed up in depth by leisure researchers Bongkoo Lee, Scott Shafer and Inho Kang, and they confirmed that indeed emotionally salient perceptions were more important than situations. Although the overall calculus of how visitors rated their satisfaction included many factors, overwhelmingly the most important consideration was whether or not individuals perceived that their entering self-related needs were satisfied.[29] These results have now been confirmed by a number of other studies.[30]

One other important and somewhat curious result emerges from this line of leisure and tourism research on expectations and satisfaction. People who perceived that a leisure situation did not quite fit their initial expectations will actually manipulate the recollection of their expectations so that they do fit. Research by Spanish tourism researchers Ignacio Rodrıguez del Bosque and Hector San Martin found that tourists consistently tended to adjust their perceptions to fit their realities in order to minimize cognitive dissonance.[31] The *Theory of Cognitive Dissonance* holds that inconsistency among beliefs or behaviors will cause an uncomfortable psychological tension. Frequently this perceived psychological tension leads people to change their beliefs to fit their actual behaviors, but the opposite can also happen.[32] The research of del Bosque and Martin seems to suggest that in the case of leisure and tourism, people routinely seem to place such high importance on achieving satisfaction that they will "modify" their expectations so that the two align. For example, Daniel's comment about how the hike, though not creating too much of a physical challenge for him, was still more difficult for him now than it had been on earlier visits, suggests that he found the hike more challenging than he expected or at least hoped it would be. In other words, when people like Daniel occasionally experience something that does not exactly match up with their expectations they will tend to excuse away these minor discrepancies as relatively insignificant in the grand scheme of things. Again as described earlier, e.g., Chapter 12, humans regularly act in ways that are designed to insure that their prior expectations are satisfied.[33]

And so it is for most of the leisure, and other, choices people make most of the time; but not always. Again using the example of museum visits, well over 95% of all visitors to museums claim to find the experience not just satisfying but *very satisfying*.[34] Even assuming that most museums are good places to visit, they cannot all be that good, all the time, for so many people, without something like this circular, self-reinforcing system being at work. However, the exceptions to this rule are very informative. It is those few percent of museum visitors who are dissatisfied that help elucidate how this self-reinforcement cycle actually works. They are the proverbial exceptions that prove the rule.

As part of a study to better understand the short and long-term experiences of visitors to museum-like settings, my colleague Martin Storksdieck and I randomly identified, interviewed, tracked and re-interviewed nearly 200 individuals who had visited a particular science center. All of these hundreds of individuals told us that they found their experience very satisfying; all that is except for one individual.[35] This one man claimed he was very dissatisfied with his visit. This individual had determined, based on a single very brief prior visit, that the science center was a good place for teaching children specific facts and concepts, that it was pretty much just like a school.

A few months later he came to the conclusion that his children needed to learn a specific science and health lesson. Based on this perceived Sociality-related need and his perceptions about the affordances of the science center, he decided that he would take his children to the science center with the expectation that the visit would result in his children learning these specific lessons he wanted them to learn. In his entry interview, he very explicitly articulated the specific content areas he expected his children to learn that day,

> Well my kids are a little chubby so [my visit is intended] as an encouragement for them to [more actively] exercise, [to learn] how important it is. And even P.E. [physical education], if they do it every day at school, to take it seriously during that hour because it's very important for their bodies to maintain the functioning and, you know, so we went [to the science center]. I wanted instead of, you know, sometimes we talk to the children but they don't listen. So instead of my talking to them, we [would] go and take them over there and have them sit down and have [the exhibit] do a little presentation [so they would] learn [this important idea].[36]

This was a message he felt was not being sufficiently taught in school, one that he felt was difficult for him to teach at home, and based on his earlier experience he had the expectation it could be successfully taught to his children at the science center.

However, once at the science center he discovered that his recollection of how the exhibits "taught" was not totally accurate; at least his children did not seem to respond to the exhibits in the way he hoped they would. His children became quite excited by their first visit to this free-choice, hands-on museum and were disinclined to focus on the specific exhibits their father wanted them to attend to. In short, the actual affordances of the science center the man and his children experienced that day significantly deviated from what the man had thought they were. During the visit, he even attempted to enact his pre-visit self-related expectations by forcing his children to sit and learn from the specific exhibits he had chosen for them but again the lived realities of the science center conspired to undermine his desires. The man discovered, much to his chagrin, that children in an interactive, hands-on science museum are not easily compelled to sit still and "learn" in a traditional sense.[37]

By the time the visit ended, this man was not only dissatisfied with his museum visit, he stated that he intended to share his dissatisfaction with his peers and swore that he, at least, would never again visit this particular institution. This example illuminates an important point. Although typically the choices people make involve expectations and often, but not always, represent self-fulfilling events where minor discrepancies can be papered-over, this does not happen 100% of the time. In fact, even when someone's expectations are well-matched to the typical affordances of a situation, unexpected things can happen. The reality of human lived experience is that life is inherently unpredictable and people can never be totally in control of their lives. Obviously affluence, knowledge and technology can tilt things towards increased control, but even the most affluent and knowledgeable person, surrounded by the best technologies is never in total control of their life circumstances. Efforts at affecting well-being always need to accommodate to the actual life-realities encountered.

## Responding to the Randomness of Actual Experience

Although Daniel, by virtue of past experience was able to predict much of what would happen during his visit to Silver Falls, he could not totally predict everything that actually happened. For example, Daniel remarked on the quality of the picnic lunch the two couples had collectively assembled, as well as the quality of the lunch-time conversation—both of which he had some but not total control over. Also remarked on were experiences that, though not totally planned for, emerged as salient and satisfying, e.g., "my slow-motion pictures of the falls." Most of the unanticipated events, fortunately for him, were positive and reinforcing, except that is for his partner hitting her head on an overhanging log. Fortunately, this was a minor accident, but life is not always so kind and cooperative.

After all, a hike along sometimes steep and slippery forest trails poses dangers one cannot always predict or avoid, even in a relatively benign setting like a state park. What if Daniel's partner had not just bumped her head but gashed her head on the overhanging tree or someone in the party had slipped while on the trail and taken a nasty fall? Or what would have happened if an unexpected argument flared up between one or some combination of the individuals on the hike? Should any of these or some other such negative event have transpired, Daniel's satisfaction with the day would surely have been diminished; as would his perception of his well-being. Unanticipated events can and regularly do occur; even in situations where an individual can reasonably assume that she understands and can predict most of what will transpire. It all comes back to the relative balance and management of competing self-related needs. Although people regularly make choices and deliberately attempt to follow their chosen scripts, events outside their control can loom large. As my model suggests, when self-perceived needs are subverted, when one's self is out of balance with the environment, perceived well-being is diminished. New needs will emerge and people will modify their choices and actions accordingly in an effort to reinstate well-being. My proposed model suggests a way to capture at least some of this complexity.

## Measuring Well-Being

In addition to the qualitative post-visit interview excerpted above, I also attempted to create a quantitative measure of Daniel's sense of well-being. The *Well-Being Expectation/Experience Index* I developed assumes that well-being is based on a multidimensional assessment of need satisfaction in which expectations are compared with actual experience.

Specifically, in any given situation an individual would need to balance the competing demands from each of the seven Well-Being System modalities, with the needs of each modality influencing the individual's overall perception of well-being. However, based on expectations, it is likely that one or several particular sets of need would predominate, in other words be weighted more heavily in importance. Given the importance of expectations, ultimate feelings of well-being would be based on how closely actual experiences and expectations align.

Following these ideas I developed a well-being satisfaction survey. The survey contained a list of twenty-one statements—three statements related to each of the seven core need-related Well-Being System modalities described in this book—Continuity, Individuality, Sexuality, Sociality, Relationality, Reflectivity and Creativity/Spirituality. Both the pre-event survey and post-experience survey contained identical questions.[38] The pre-event survey asks individuals to rate each of the 21 statements based on their expectations while the post-event survey asks individuals to rate each of the same 21 statements based on their sense of what actually transpired during the experience.

I created a customized version of this survey, i.e., questions appropriate to the context and reality of Silver Falls State Park, and administered it to Daniel twice, in the morning prior to Daniel's visit to Silver Falls and again later the same day, approximately two hours after the completion of Daniel's hike.

Basically each of the 21 statements were designed to measure Daniel's perceptions of the relative state of one aspect of need satisfaction, either prospectively as he hoped the event would play out or retrospectively as he perceived things actually transpired. In theory, Daniel's rating of each item was based on two perceptions: his perception of the relative importance of that particular need; and his perception, either prospectively or retrospectively, of the relationship between the leisure experience and the likelihood that this particular self-related need was satisfactorily satisfied. I assumed that this first criteria would create an implicit "weighting" of each item, since an item perceived to be of little importance would likely be rated low regardless of expectations, while items of high importance would receive higher ratings, at least during the expectation stage. I also assumed, as described above, that expectations should influence experiences. Therefore, the final experience ratings should roughly track expectation ratings; higher priority items should receive higher ratings than low priority items. In other words, any discrepancy, positive or negative, should be reflective of the actual quality of the event, i.e., feelings of satisfaction, and thus indicative of perceived well-being. If the event was perceived as supporting positive well-being, if the individual found their experience satisfying, then dividing total experience scores by total expectation scores should result in a number equal to or greater than 1.0. If, however, the ratio of experience to expectation fell below 1.0, it would be indicative that the person felt a sense of dissatisfaction with their experience; that their overall sense of well-being was diminished.

For example, in the realm of Continuity, Daniel expected the hike to be somewhat challenging, though he did not expect that it would present too many physical discomforts such as cold, rain, biting insects or hunger. He also was hoping for a nice picnic lunch. His experience generally tracked with his initial assumptions although he found the hike slightly more challenging than expected but with fewer physical discomforts than expected and a more enjoyable lunch experience than expected. By contrast, the Individuality-related questions asked Daniel to rate his perceptions of the safety and security of the setting. In this case his perceptions of the actual experience exceed his expectations. Sexuality was not high on Daniel's list of hoped for needs to be satisfied, and thus both his expectation and experience ratings for these items were low. Still, his ratings of this actual experience related to Sexuality exceeded his expectations. For example, he particularly enjoyed watching other people and found the people he saw more attractive than he anticipated. As expected, Daniel had high expectations for the social aspects of the trip and these were rewarded by comparably high ratings on all three social experience statements. Events on the trip proceeded more smoothly than he had envisaged as did the opportunities for intellectual growth; hence both Daniel's Reflectivity and Creativity/Spirituality experience scores exceeded his expectation scores as well.

Using a measure such as the *Well-Being Expectation/Experience Index* it was possible to derive a quantitative measure of Daniel's perceived satisfaction with his experience at Silver Falls, or more specifically, a measure of Daniel's perceived well-being during the time of his hike. The sum of Daniel's total experience scores divided by the sum of his total expectations scores equaled **1.43**; well within the positive range of this hypothetical well-being continuum. This score aligned well with Daniel's overall highly positive self-assessment of the day as revealed by his immediate post-hike interview (above). Again in theory, individuals should have feelings of well-being surrounding an event whenever their perceptions of their actual experiences equal or exceed their expectations for the event; this was the case for Daniel.

This is a very different way of measuring satisfaction/well-being than has typically been used. Given that, as I have proposed, perceptions of satisfaction, which in this instance are highly correlated with perceptions of well-being, are always both a biological and psychological construct that is continually in a process of construction and reconstruction, then it follows that satisfaction needs to be measured as such. What is not dissimilar in my approach so far, as compared with other social science investigators, is the timeframe/grain size of experience investigated. Investigations of specific events such as Daniel's are the norm.

People can and regularly do parse their lives into definable timeframes such as a day-trip hike to Silver Falls, each time period defined by the choices made in pursuit of well-being. These timeframes can overlap and they are not always contiguous in time, but because they are defined by choices, they are discriminable as discrete events. Thus, Daniel had no difficulty conceiving of his day-trip to Silver Falls as a distinct event in time, despite the fact that the actual event, if one includes planning for the trip and thoughts about the trip after the hike, occurred across multiple days and bled into other experiences. This was also the case for the other examples used in this book. For example, Teresa (Chapters 2–6) was able to think of her whole multi-month-long ordeal of emigrating to the U.S. as a single event despite the fact that other relevant events happened to her before and after the actual migration period. This is because the most consciously salient and memorable parts of any enacted Well-Being System are the choices and the sense of well-being that result; everything else, including much of the actual detail of life, including even the underlying needs and actions taken, tend to slowly disappear. The proposed Well-Being Systems model provides a mechanism for capturing and making sense of these events by compensating for partial and selective memory and enabling an investigator to fill-in the full complement of likely underlying processes involved.

## Notes

1. Kelly, J. (1996). *Leisure* (3rd ed.). Boston: Allyn and Bacon.
2. Diamond, J. (2012). *The world until yesterday.* New York: Viking.
3. Of course, doing "nothing" is not really nothing. These pursuits are focused on satisfying primarily Continuity and Individuality-related needs of physical and mental relaxation, recovery and safety.
4. McLean, D. (2015). *Kraus's recreation and leisure in modern society* (10th ed.). Burlington, MA: Jones & Bartlett Publishers.
5. Falk, J.H., Ballantyne, R., Packer, J. & Benckendorff, P. (2012). Travel and learning: A neglected tourism research area. *Annals of Tourism Research,* 39(2), 908–927.
   McLean, D. (2015). *Kraus's recreation and leisure in modern society* (10th ed.). Burlington, MA: Jones & Bartlett Publishers.
6. Kelly, J.R. & Freysinger, V.J. (2000). *21st century leisure: Current issues.* State College, PA: Venture Publishing.
   Freysinger, V.J. & Kelly, J.R. (2004). *21st century leisure: Current issues.* State College, PA: Venture Publishing.
7. Sandberg, J. (19 July 2006) It doesn't sound like a vacation to me. *Wall Street Journal Online.*
8. Sagon, C. (2004). Formerly known as Sutton Place. F1, *Washington Post,* April 7.
   Zuboff, S. & Maxmin, D. (2002). *The support economy: Why corporations are failing individuals and the next episode of capitalism.* New York: Viking Press.

9. Freysinger, V. J. & Kelly, J.R. (2004). *21st century leisure: Current issues.* State College, PA: Venture Publishing.

   Obviously, the rich "leisure classes" of former years engaged in this style of leisure long before the 21st century, but it represents a major shift that it now represents the norm for such a large percentage of the population.

10. Daniel and all of the rest of the names referred to in this interview are pseudonyms.

11. Full transcripts of all interviews and data used in this and the subsequent chapter are available from the author upon request.

12. e.g., Kelly, J.R. (1977). *Situational and social factors in leisure decisions.* Technical Report. ERIC #:ED153143.

    Driver, B.L. & Tocher, S.R. (1970). Toward a behavioral interpretation of recreational engagements, with implications for planning. In B.L. Driver (Ed.), *Elements of outdoor recreation planning: Proceedings of a national short course held in Ann Arbor, Michigan, May 6–16, 1968* (pp. 9–31). Ann Arbor, MI: University of Michigan.

    Beard, J.G. & Ragheb, M.G. (1980). Measuring leisure satisfaction. *Journal of Leisure Research,* 12, 20–33;

    Knopf, R.C., Driver, B. L. & Bassett, J. IL. (1973). Motivations for fishing. *Transactions of the 28th North American Wildlife and Natural Resources Conference* (pp. 191–204). Washington, DC: Wildlife Management Institute.

    Manfredo, M. J. & Driver, B.L. (1996). Measuring leisure motivation: A meta-analysis of the recreation experience preference scales. *Journal of Leisure Research,* 28(3), 188–213.

13. Manfredo, M. J. & Driver, B.L. (1996). Measuring leisure motivation: A meta-analysis of the recreation experience preference scales. *Journal of Leisure Research,* 28(3), 188–213.

14. Included in the category of "museum-like settings" are of course museums of all kinds—art, history, natural history and children's museums and science centers, as well as botanical gardens, arboretums, zoos and aquariums. Also falling into this category are places like national parks, monuments and historical sites.

15. Falk, J.H. (2006). The impact of visit motivation on learning: Using identity as a construct to understand the visitor experience. *Curator,* 49(2), 151–166.

    Falk, J.H. (2009). *Identity and the museum visitor experience.* Walnut Creek, CA: Left Coast Press.

16. e.g., Ashton, S.D. (2014). *Application of John Falk's visitor identities at Thanksgiving Point.* Poster. Visitor's Studies Association Annual Conference, Albuquerque; Christopher, A. (2013). *Practical applications of the Falk visitor identity model.* Colorado-Wyoming Association of Museums Annual Meeting, Golden, Colorado, April 25, 2013.

    Blokland, S. (2013). *Application of identity-related motivation instrument in Teylers Museum the Netherlands.* Unpublished Manuscript. Haarlem: The Netherlands.

    Covel, J. (2009). *Using Falk's identity-related motivations to support guest services at the Monterey Bay Aquarium.* Paper presented at the Annual Meeting of the American Association of Museums, May 1, 2010, Philadelphia, PA.

    Elizando, D. (2014). *Adicionalmente al SAV 2013, la antigua Dirección de Mediación y Evaluación realizó un estudio basado en el Modelo de la Experiencia de los Visitantes diseñado por John Falk.* Unpublished Manuscript. Mexico City: Papalote.

    Falk, J.H., Heimlich, J. & Bronnenkant, K. (2008). Using identity-related visit motivations as a tool for understanding adult zoo and aquarium visitor's meaning making. *Curator,* 51(1), 55–80.

    Falk, J.H. & Storksdieck, M. (2010). Science learning in a leisure setting. *Journal of Research in Science Teaching,* 47(2), 194–212.

    Hyunh, S. (2016). *Motivations of visitors to participate in fee-based aquarium programs.* Unpublished Masters Thesis. Oregon State University, Corvallis, OR.

    Koke, J. (2009). *The use of identity-related motivations to frame experiences and design at the Art Gallery Ontario.* Paper presented at the Annual Meeting of the American Association of Museums, May 1, 2010, Philadelphia, PA.

    Koke, J. (2010). *AGO visitor motivation study: Cumulative report.* Technical Report. Toronto: Art Gallery of Ontario.

Leason, T. & Filippini-Fantoni, S. (2013). *Adapting Falk's museum visitor experience model.* Paper presented at Visitor Studies Association Annual Conference, July 15–19, 2013, Milwaukee, Wisconsin.

Lundgaard, I.B., Jensen, J.T. & Foldgast, A.M. (2013). *User survey 2012.* Copenhagen: Danish Agency for Culture.

Meluch, W. (2011). *Profile of visitors to Iloni Palace.* Unpublished Technical Report. San Diego, CA: Meluch & Associates.

Smola, M. & Meluch, W. (2011). *Profile of visitors to Mission House Museum.* Unpublished Technical Report. San Diego, CA: Meluch & Associates.

Stein, J. (2007). *Adapting the visitor identity-related motivations scale for living history sites.* Paper presented at the Visitor Studies Association Annual Meeting, Toronto, Canada, July 19, 2007.

Storksdieck, M. & Stein, J. (2007). *Using the visitor identity-related motivations scale to improve visitor experiences at the US Botanic Garden.* Paper presented at the Visitor Studies Association Annual Meeting, Toronto, Canada, July 19, 2007.

Tinworth, K. (2010). *Denver—All city—Preliminary implementation of Falk's Visitor Identity-Related Motivation typology.* Technical Report. Denver: Denver-Area Cultural Evaluation Network.

Trainer, L., Steele-Inama, M. & Christopher, A. (2012). Uncovering visitor identity: A citywide utilization of the Falk Visitor-Identity Model. *Journal of Museum Education,* 37(1), 101–114.

17. Falk, J.H. (2009). *Identity and the museum visitor experience.* Walnut Creek, CA: Left Coast Press.

18. Ashton, S.D. (2014). *Application of John Falk's visitor identities at Thanksgiving Point.* Poster. Visitor's Studies Association Annual Conference, Albuquerque; Christopher, A. (2013). *Practical applications of the Falk visitor identity model.* Colorado-Wyoming Association of Museums Annual Meeting, Golden, Colorado, April 25, 2013.

Blokland, S. (2013). *Application of identity-related motivation instrument in Teylers Museum, The Netherlands.* Unpublished Manuscript. Haarlem: The Netherlands.

Covel, J. (2009). *Using Falk's identity-related motivations to support guest services at the Monterey Bay Aquarium.* Paper presented at the Annual Meeting of the American Association of Museums, May 1, 2010, Philadelphia, PA.

Elizando, D. (2014). *Adicionalmente al SAV 2013, la antigua Dirección de Mediación y Evaluación realizó un estudio basado en el Modelo de la Experiencia de los Visitantes diseñado por John Falk.* Unpublished Manuscript. Mexico City: Papalote.

Falk, J.H., Heimlich, J. & Bronnenkant, K. (2008). Using identity-related visit motivations as a tool for understanding adult zoo and aquarium visitor's meaning making. *Curator,* 51(1), 55–80.

Falk, J.H. & Storksdieck, M. (2010). Science learning in a leisure setting. *Journal of Research in Science Teaching,* 47(2), 194–212.

Hyunh, S. (2016). *Motivations of visitors to participate in fee-based aquarium programs.* Unpublished Masters Thesis. Oregon State University, Corvallis, OR.

Koke, J. (2009). *The use of identity-related motivations to frame experiences and design at the Art Gallery Ontario.* Paper presented at the Annual Meeting of the American Association of Museums, May 1, 2010, Philadelphia, PA.

Koke, J. (2010). *AGO visitor motivation study: Cumulative report.* Technical Report. Toronto: Art Gallery of Ontario.

Leason, T. & Filippini-Fantoni, S. (2013). *Adapting Falk's museum visitor experience model.* Paper presented at Visitor Studies Association Annual Conference, July 15–19, 2013, Milwaukee, Wisconsin.

Lundgaard, I.B., Jensen, J.T. & Foldgast, A.M. (2013). *User survey 2012.* Copenhagen: Danish Agency for Culture.

Meluch, W. (2011). *Profile of visitors to Iloni Palace.* Unpublished Technical Report. San Diego, CA: Meluch & Associates.

Smola, M. & Meluch, W. (2011). *Profile of visitors to Mission House Museum.* Unpublished Technical Report. San Diego, CA: Meluch & Associates.

Stein, J. (2007). *Adapting the visitor identity-related motivations scale for living history sites.* Paper presented at the Visitor Studies Association Annual Meeting, Toronto, Canada, July 19, 2007.

Storksdieck, M. & Stein, J. (2007). *Using the visitor identity-related motivations scale to improve visitor experiences at the US Botanic Garden.* Paper presented at the Visitor Studies Association Annual Meeting, Toronto, Canada, July 19, 2007.

Tinworth, K. (2010). *Denver—All city—Preliminary implementation of Falk's Visitor Identity-Related Motivation typology.* Technical Report. Denver: Denver-Area Cultural Evaluation Network.

Trainer, L., Steele-Inama, M. & Christopher, A. (2012). Uncovering visitor identity: A citywide utilization of the Falk Visitor-Identity Model. *Journal of Museum Education,* 37(1), 101–114.

19. Falk, J.H. (2009). *Identity and the museum visitor experience.* Walnut Creek, CA: Left Coast Press.

20. Some individuals have sub-divided some of these categories and not everyone totally agrees on the names and definitions.

21. There is not a one-to-one relationship between the self-aspect defined motivational categories I have found to correlate with "museum"-going and the seven Well-Being modules. Each represents a blending of modalities; some more "pure" than others. For example I would speculate that the six common self-related motivations I have listed are likely indicative of the following modalities of need, though as advertisers' lawyers insist they say, "results may vary." *Explorers = Reflectivity with a dash of Creativity & Spirituality; Facilitators = Sociality, Reflectivity and often Individuality as well (e.g., safety); Experience Seekers = Relationality, Reflectivity and perhaps Sociality, Continuity, Sexuality and Creativity & Spirituality as well; Professionals/Hobbyists = Creativity & Spirituality with a dash of Reflectivity; Amenity Seekers = Continuity, Reflectivity and perhaps Individuality and Rechargers = Reflectivity, Creativity & Spirituality and a bit of Continuity.*

22. Falk, J.H., Heimlich, J. & Bronnenkant, K. (2008). Using identity-related visit motivations as a tool for understanding adult zoo and aquarium visitor's meaning making. *Curator,* 51(1), 55–80.

    Falk, J.H. (2009). *Identity and the museum visitor experience.* Walnut Creek, CA: Left Coast Press.

23. cf., Falk, J.H. & Dierking, L.D. (2015). *The museum visitor experience revisited.* Walnut Creek, CA: Left Coast Press.

24. Of course such "confluences" are always socially and culturally specific, and always represent a moment in time. Twenty years from now the public could perceive the affordances of museums differently, and potentially their needs as well. At that point, my model should still predict who does and does not visit museums, but the specific self-related needs visitors might seek to satisfy and the perceptions of what museums afford would be different than today.

25. NOTE: At the time of this interview Daniel was writing a book on the "sublime and opera"—which no doubt influenced him to suggest this was not necessarily a sublime moment, comparable to the playing of the French horn.

26. A key aspect of this approach to understanding human behavior is that this way of categorizing people is not based on some permanent aspect of the individual such as demographic variables like gender, nationality or race/ethnicity, as has been the practice of much of social science research for nearly 100 years, but rather categorizing people based on their situated and ephemeral perceived self-related needs. The key to what constitutes well-being for a person during their leisure or other time, what emerges for that person as relevant self-related needs, are a person's lived experiences. Sometimes a person's perceived needs correlate with large-scale demographic variables like age, race/ethnicity, gender and religion but not always. On the day in question Daniel was motivated to go to Silver Falls for primarily social reasons; another day he may be primarily motivated to go there for creativity reasons, e.g., to take photographs. Not only his motivations but his

behaviors within the setting will be entirely different on those two days despite the fact that demographically he would remain the same person on both outings (cf., Falk, J.H. (2009). *Identity and the museum visitor experience*. Walnut Creek, CA: Left Coast Press).

27. Lee, B.K. & Shafer, C.S. (2002). The dynamic nature of leisure experience: An application of Affect Control Theory. *Journal of Leisure Research*, 34(2), 290–310.

Lee, B.K., Shafer, C.S. & Kang, I. (2005). Examining relationships among perceptions of self, episode-specific evaluations, and overall satisfaction with a leisure activity. *Leisure Sciences*, 27, 93–109.

Mannell, R. & Iso-Ahola, S.E. (1987). Psychological nature of leisure and tourism experience. *Annals of Tourism Research*, 14, 314–331.

Stewart, W.P. (1998). Leisure as multiphase experiences: Challenging traditions. *Journal of Leisure Research*, 30(4), 391–400.

Stewart, W.P. & Hull IV, B.R. (1992). Satisfaction of what? Post hoc versus real-time construct validity. *Leisure Sciences*, 14, 195–209.

28. Graefe, A.R. & Fedler, A.J. (1986). Situational and subjective determinants of satisfaction in marine recreational fishing. *Leisure Sciences*, 8, 275–295.

Whisman, S.A. & Hollenhorst, S.J. (1998). A path model of white-river boating satisfaction on the Cheat River of West Virginia. *Environmental Management*, 22(1), 109–117.

29. Lee, B.K., Shafer, C.S. & Kang, I. (2005). Examining relationships among perceptions of self, episode-specific evaluations, and overall satisfaction with a leisure activity. *Leisure Sciences*, 27, 93–109.

30. e.g., del Bosque, R., Martin, H.S. & Collado, J. (2006). The role of expectations in the consumer satisfaction formation process: Empirical evidence in the travel agency sector. *Tourism Management*, 27, 410–419.

del Bosque, I.R. & Martin, H.S. (2008). Tourist satisfaction: A cognitive-affective model. *Annals of Tourism Research*, 35(2), 551–573.

Falk, J.H. & Storksdieck, M. (2010). Science learning in a leisure setting. *Journal of Research in Science Teaching*, 47(2), 194–212.

Yoon, Y. & Uysal, M. (2005). An examination of the effects of motivation and satisfaction on destination loyalty: A structural model. *Tourism Management*, 26, 45–56.

31. del Bosque, I.R. & Martin, H.S. (2008). Tourist satisfaction: A cognitive-affective model. *Annals of Tourism Research*, 35(2), 551–573.

32. Harmon-Jones, E. & Mills, J. (1999). *Cognitive dissonance: Progress on a pivotal theory in social psychology*. Washington, DC: American Psychological Association.

33. Merton, R.K. (1957). *Social theory and social structure* (rev. ed.). New York: Free Press.

34. Falk, J.H. & Dierking, L.D. (2014). *The museum experience revisited*. Walnut Creek, CA: Left Coast Press.

35. Falk, J.H. & Storksdieck, M. (2010). Science learning in a leisure setting. *Journal of Research in Science Teaching*, 47(2), 194–212.

36. Falk, J.H. & Storksdieck, M. (2010). Science learning in a leisure setting. *Journal of Research in Science Teaching*, 47(2), 194–212.

37. There's plenty of evidence to suggest that this man's children likely learned during their visit, just not in the traditional school sense of learning their father had hoped for (cf., Falk, J.H. & Dierking, L.D. (2014). *The museum experience revisited*. Walnut Creek, CA: Left Coast Press; Falk, J.H. & Dierking, L.D. (in press). *Learning from museums* (2nd ed.). Lanham, MD: Rowman Littlefield).

38. Each question phrased in a situationally specific/appropriate manner.

# 15

# UNDERSTANDING THE INDIVIDUAL OVER TIME

In the previous chapter I presented a focused view of a one-day leisure time experience of a man named Daniel, a retired American professional male. In this chapter I continue an analysis of this particular leisure experience, fast-forwarding several weeks. I explore what happens to life experiences over time, how they become embedded into existing Well-Being Systems and influence perceptions of both past and future needs, choices and actions.

## Leisure Recalled: How Choice-Making Influences Memory

Q: So, do you remember the trip you took to Silver Falls about a month ago? Tell me about it.

A: I haven't really thought about it actively since the trip. I've been quite pre-occupied with other things.

[Pause]

Okay, I vividly recall having a good time with close friends. It met my incoming expectations for an enjoyable, nice day with close friends. Plus, it was an opportunity to introduce a lovely place to my friends and share this choice locale with them; a preferred place.

Beyond that, I remember that we planned so as to provide more than just the walk's opportunity for a pleasant day. We jointly prepared lunch and we planned to have dinner together afterwards; all of which I knew the foursome enjoys. But the highlight was sharing the place we knew. Plus, enjoying individual knowledge with each other—experiences if selected well, can provide [one with] feedback; the feedback is part of the pleasure.

Q: Any details you can remember?

A: Quality and interest, "conduct" of the conversation, ease, joy, rapport that comes as part of a friendship.

We lucked out with the weather, it was a nice day. We would have been really pissed-off if it had been raining. [I remember] the way our gang enjoys and promotes others in the group. Learning about things from each other; for example, what plants and birds are present, sharing photography. The key is, though, was my motivation to share; to make [the day] mutually enjoyable.

I don't recall any moments of tension or displeasure. . . . [I recall the] pleasure of being out in a natural environment, [an environment] if not unique, [that is] very special (as opposed to going to a bowling alley). It was a place that appealed to all of us because of our values. While there is no guarantee, the day was calculated to be an enjoyable time.

Q: Now that a little time has gone by, what event or aspect of the trip did you find most satisfying?

A: Working on the assumption that nothing in life is guaranteed, the apparent confirmation of [a reinforced] friendship and enjoyment of a well-planned day were the highlight for me.

Putting this in context, shit can happen. People can get sideways about things. That didn't happen. Particularly with close friendships, we typically assume they are durable, but they benefit from being renewed with new, diverse, unusual experiences. That is a good thing, the cultivation of friendship. On this day I felt my friendships were deepened and sustained. This event was all about friendship.

Q: What event or aspect of the trip did you find most unsatisfying?

A: I can't think of anything. I'm not one who suffers dissatisfaction easily. If I was unhappy, I'd let people know. I can't think of anything unpleasant about the day. All was good.

Q: Over the past few weeks did you have occasion to think about this trip or discuss it with anyone?

A: Yes, there were some conversations. I talked with Kate afterwards as we were considering locations to take visiting out-of-town guests; people we care about. Silver Falls was confirmed as a reliably pleasing place for such visits.

I also mentioned it to my close friends Bob and Joyce.[1] Although I was pretty sure they'd been there I asked them if they had been recently. I also promoted it to some other friends, Bill and Susan.[2] I was thinking of this as a spillover to Susan's interest in visiting the Iris Farm and I suggested that we might want to connect these two trips.

I also recently watched the Ken Burns National Parks program on PBS. National Parks are obviously monumental but important features of American life, and it's important to preserve these places. [The show] made me think of Silver Falls and what a wonderful place it was to refresh one's self and one's friendships.

This third interview with Daniel occurred approximately five weeks after his visit to Silver Falls State Park with his partner and friends. As the interview clearly reveals, over time Daniel's memories of the day had slightly morphed. Even though this experience had only happened about a month earlier, much of the detail of the day had fallen away, leaving only a generalized gestalt of the event in its place.[3] However, what remained was consistent with his previous interviews, in particular the centrality of social relationship building as a core focus. Not only did Daniel's visit expectations of satisfying a Sociality-related need influence how he actually experienced the day, it equally affected his long-term autobiographical memories of the day. His most salient long-term memories all revolved around this theme. He said that he was happy he was able to play a role in helping to solidify his relationship with his friends, and he was particularly pleased at how well this particular setting that he and his partner selected for the outing worked out in terms of this goal. After a month of intervening events and experiences, what he was able to recall was a generalized sense of a beautiful day and setting, good food, good conversation and good cheer. Absent were most of the details such as the slow-motion filming of the waterfall or the fact that his wife bumped her head. No doubt these memories could have been retrieved if prompted, but for the purposes of his still developing autobiographical memories of the day, these specifics had faded away; arguably because they were not essential to the basic narrative he had constructed about the event. The primary meaning Daniel attached to this day-trip concerned the fulfillment of the Sociality-related needs he sought to satisfy.

People always preferentially attend to the aspects of an action or experience which they perceive to be most meaningful; virtually everything else is ignored. Let me make this point crystal clear. As suggested in previous chapters, there were myriad realities that Daniel could have experienced that day, for example the physical terrain of Silver Falls State Park, the behavior of Daniel's friends Jack and Linden, the salience of the waterfalls Daniel encountered, the dozens of other people walking the Silver Falls trails that day, the plant and animal life present in the Park, the planes flying overhead, the snippets of conversation floating through the air or even the fluctuations in temperature and humidity as Daniel moved through the different microclimates present at Silver Falls. Exactly which of these realities Daniel would actually attend to could be only somewhat predicted. In other words, the fact that they existed and were available for perception was no guarantee that they would be attended to.

On any given day, two people might walk the same trails at Silver Falls, at more or less exactly the same time, and each would come away having seen and thought about entirely different things. One person might attend to the wild flowers and be oblivious to the other people passing by, while the second might never notice any wildflowers but be quite attentive to the other people on the trail. The perceived *reality* of each of these two individuals would be determined largely by the sum of their past experiences and interests, and of course what their expectations for the day were. These prior experiences and expectations would have not only influenced what they noticed and paid attention to but also what they ended up encoding in memory about the experience. The lived experience of a person is always a personally constructed reality and is not tied, one-to-one, with any fixed entity, space or event. Not only is it assured that two people would have entirely different experiences while visiting Silver Falls State Park, it is equally assured that even the same individual will have a different experience if she visits the same Park on two different days. In part this is because the people, plants, animals, weather and even the falls a person is likely to encounter on those two days would be different, but more importantly, the individual herself will also be different by virtue of likely having (even if only slightly) different expectations for her visit.[4]

As predicted by the Well-Being Systems model, Daniel's needs, in this particular case Sociality-related needs, framed his visit reality at Silver Falls State Park. He also remembered the shared meals and amiable conversations, and he recalled, and reveled, in the shared intellectual pursuits. It can be inferred that the reason Daniel found these particular events memorable was because these self-related needs all directly connected to what Daniel considered defining qualities of this particular friendship on this particular day.

The visit to Silver Falls enabled Daniel to enact his self-aspect role of the "good friend." In his recollection narrative, Daniel gives us some insights into what he perceives the role of being a "good friend" involves. He states, "Particularly with close friendships, we typically assume they are durable, but they benefit from being renewed with new, diverse, unusual experiences. That is a good thing, the cultivation of friendship." In other words, Daniel believes that being a good friend requires constant work. He perceived that this was the "work" he was attempting to do on this particular day, and he determined that he had indeed been successful at it. "On this day I felt my friendships were deepened and sustained. This event was all about friendship."

Everyone regularly chooses to engage in experiences that support their well-being goals, though not everyone is as self-aware and self-reflective of this process as Daniel. Many people make choices and pursue well-being without even being totally aware of why they are doing what they are doing. Not surprisingly then, in situations where a person lacks conscious self-awareness of their motivations and expectations, their autobiographical memories are likely to reflect this lack of self-awareness. In fact, it is totally possible in such cases for people to do things designed to support their expectations and needs without realizing they are doing such things; when this happens it is as if the events never happened. An example of this phenomenon emerged as part of a recent investigation of youth at a science museum.

The youth in question were engaged in a series of activities at an engineering exhibit. Researchers found that participants who had at least one encouraging check-in with one of the educators staffing the exhibition stayed significantly longer at the exhibit than did those who lacked an interaction with an educator. Individuals having an interaction with an educator, even a very brief one, also demonstrated a greater depth of engagement with the exhibit as measured by a statistically significant increase in the number of "designs" they tested.[5] However, the researchers also were struck by what they found to be an interesting, though to them somewhat peculiar, finding. They discovered that a surprisingly large percentage of the youth in the study who were observed being supported by educators, and hence facilitated in their inquiries, when asked after the experience whether or not they had received any support or encouragement from an educator, responded "NO."[6] Arguably many if not most of these youth were oblivious to adult intervention since these kinds of social interactions, representative of the underlying self-related need for Sociality or even Relationality, were not at all part of their conscious personal motivations/expectations for their visit.

As has been found to be the case for many youth who visit museums, these youth were likely predominantly focused on their Reflectivity and/or Creativity/Spirituality-related needs, in particular satisfying their own personal interests and curiosity needs or the desire to achieve a sense of intellectual mastery from the experience.[7] The result, as documented by this research, was that they were either unaware of the educator's interventions or, more likely, just did not find this aspect of their experience sufficiently salient to encode in memory. What is so interesting about this particular example is that unlike Daniel, it is reasonable to assume that many if not most of these youth did not spend hours and days planning for their visit and hence did not enter the museum with a strong conscious awareness of their self-related visit motivations. Nonetheless, just like Daniel (and the laboratory rats described in an earlier chapter with reference to placebo experiments), their perceptions of satisfaction were influenced by their pre-visit needs and expectations. These pre-defined expectations functioned as a strong filter for both how they behaved during the visit and what they remembered after the visit. Clearly they took advantage of the educator's facilitation to achieve their agenda of greater exploration and mastery, but interacting with educators was not part of their visit agenda and thus not sufficiently salient to them to become encoded as part of their memory of the experience. The events people find most memorable are those that directly relate to and support the satisfaction of expected need-related goals. Everything else is filtered out as noise. Fulfilling needs is very emotionally satisfying, and thus as described earlier, is both very salient and very memorable.

## The Building of Autobiographical Memories

Emotion played a significant and non-trivial role in Daniel's memories of his day at Silver Falls. What I'm referring to is not that Daniel was so moved by his visit to Silver Falls that he broke down and wept when I talked to him. Rather what I am referring to is the fact that it was clear that Daniel's experience and his subsequent memories of that experience involved not just cold, rational descriptions of what he saw and did but expressions of feelings, attitudes and beliefs.

As described in detail in Chapter 5, neural and cognitive scientists have only relatively recently come to fully appreciate the key role played by the emotional processing systems in the brain, in particular the role of emotions in the forming of autobiographical memories. The stronger the emotional "valence" and "arousal," the more likely it is for a perception to pass into memory;[8] and interestingly, pleasant experiences are strongly favored over unpleasant ones.[9] Evolution has insured that learning, memory and survival are interconnected and interdependent processes, and by virtue of their relationship to the limbic system, more often than not the former two processes are intrinsically pleasurable and rewarding.[10] If a contextually appropriate emotion is triggered, the brain marks the experience as meaningful, and stores memory of it in the networks activated by the emotion and similar experiences. Memory, at least longer term memory, requires an emotional "tag" to become permanent."[11]

For Daniel, and other individuals I have interviewed, the interconnection between perceived achievement of self-related needs and a sense of satisfaction always emerges, and this achievement in turn always elicits positive emotions which figure prominently in the person's memories.[12] Although I currently do not have a definitive way to empirically prove it, it seems clear from the interviews I conducted with Daniel that most of the specific experiences that he found memorable were ones that had high emotional value for him.[13] And by and large, the experiences with the highest emotional value were those connected to achievement of his Sociality-related needs.

Daniel was seeking to be a supportive friend in a beautiful natural setting, so particularly emotionally satisfying times for him were times when he felt that the confluence of setting and social interaction met that goal. Particularly salient were the times he perceived that both he and his friends were enjoying themselves, such as the effortless and stimulating conversation, the jointly shared aesthetic moments and the mutually appreciated meals. These were emotionally rich moments for Daniel because these were times when his self-related goals and his direct experience converged (in his mind) and reinforced his overarching "good friend" self-aspect. These emotional highpoints became marker events for the day at Silver Falls and were encoded in memory as such. The glue that held all these markers together for Daniel, as I would argue happens for all people in all circumstances, was Daniel's perceptions that this experience enhanced his sense of well-being. As pointed out by anthropologist Jay Rounds, a large part of how a person judges her experiences, in fact judges and understand her sense of self, comes through such *post hoc* processes of interpretation; a looking-backward process supported by autobiographical memory. "We understand backwards by looking at what we did, and considering how we felt about doing it, and asking what sort of person it is who acts and feels that way. We explain ourselves to ourselves, using our actions as evidence. You can't know who you are until you see what you do."[14] This process of backwards looking self-appraisal, of continuous construction and then reconstruction of one's sense of self relative to well-being is an on-going, never-ending process.[15]

As I have now observed across countless interviews similar to Daniel's, people utilize their self-related needs as motivations/expectations for choosing an experience and precipitating actions. These choices and actions and the perceptions of need-satisfaction that result from these choices and actions are all framed through the lens of self-aspects. It is these self-aspects rather than necessarily the specifics of need and choices that ultimately form the linguistic scaffolding of autobiographical memory. Although invariably a few specifics and perceived realities of the actual experience hang on the scaffolding, it is the overall self-aspect-defined feelings of well-being that are most vividly highlighted during recall.[16] "I haven't really thought about it actively since the trip. . . . [Pause] Okay, I vividly recall having a good time with close friends. It met my incoming expectations for an enjoyable, nice day with close friends."

With these insights as a "Rosetta Stone," it is now possible to "decode" people's self-reports of their experiences, and in the process understand why people behave in the ways they do, as well as how and why they construct meaning from those behaviors. Autobiographical memories typically feature self-referentially defined explanations of choices made and actions taken. Instances of perceived satisfaction are typically called-out. Using the Well-Being Systems model as a guide, it is now possible to read between the lines and appreciate what exactly these self-aspect-framed assessments represent. All autobiographical memories are well-being tales designed to create a consistent and ideally compelling tale about the satisfaction of one's self-related needs. Highlighted in memory are the events that most compellingly reinforce the well-being narrative; ultimately, experiences that best exemplify the satisfaction of self-related needs are most likely to endure.

## Well-Being Systems Over Time

Although it is possible to document that Daniel's day at Silver Falls was very satisfying, the well-being it generated will be fleeting. Although it is possible to "stop the film" and analyze this one day in Daniel's life, the actual film that is Daniel's life continues to run. Daniel will need to continually find additional ways on future days to support his well-being. He will also need to continually work on his self-aspect of being a good friend to Jack and Linden. Despite all this ephemera, there was at least one aspect of this experience that I can be reasonably certain resulted in long-lasting and tangible changes. Daniel's brain is almost certainly different than it was before this event. He has strengthened and potentially added to his synaptic connections between the ideas "building good friendships" and "visiting Silver Falls State Park." Obviously these ideas had to already have been connected in Daniel's mind, or at least existed in the distributed mind of Daniel and Kate in order for this particular outing with Jack and Linden to have occurred in the first place. But it is reasonable to assume that, after this particular "successful" day, those connections are now a considerably stronger and more elaborated part of the neural architecture of Daniel's brain.

An intriguing and important part of Daniel's final interview was evidence of this strengthened neural connection. As he predicted in his initial post-experience interview and then confirmed in his second post-experience interview, Daniel and his wife discussed the upcoming visit of several relatives and agreed that Silver Falls State Park would serve as an excellent place to take these visiting relatives. Thus it is possible to speculate that the neuronal networks, the Well-Being Systems in Daniel's brain associated with a particular physical place—Silver Falls State Park—and the Well-Being Systems associated with the Sociality-related need to build strong social connections with family and friends, became more firmly interconnected and strengthened each time he thought about this relationship. And if, as planned, Daniel and his wife follow through on their plans and actually take additional trips to Silver Falls with family and friends, these connections will become even more deeply etched, eventually even becoming habitual.

Amazingly and equally importantly though, the new Well-Being Systems being formed through the interconnections between these two ideas—Silver Falls and social relationships—were not merely happening within Daniel's mind but also simultaneously within Well-Being Systems of other people's minds. This surprising statement arises because Daniel did not merely think about this interconnection between a place and social relationship building; he also shared it with others. He discussed this idea with his wife as well as with several of his other close friends. In so doing, Daniel unwittingly contributed in some small way to the larger society's perceptions about the use and nature of leisure time in general and the value of outdoor places like Silver Falls State Park in particular.

## The Distributed Nature of Well-Being Systems

The sharing of experiences is a universal human activity[17] and has been argued by some to be the reason autobiographical narrative evolved in the first place.[18] Virtually every person, to a greater or lesser extent, freely shares with friends and relatives details of their leisure experiences, and they do this whether their perceptions of the experience were positive, as was the case for Daniel, or negative, as was the case of the unhappy museum visitor described in the previous chapter. After all, every person who has a leisure experience, great or small, comes away from that experience with a little more understanding of what that kind of experience was like and what the particular situation or setting that supported that experience affords. As suggested above, typically the perceptions a person has about their experience is framed by their entering choices, which are determined by their self-related needs. For Daniel, choosing to visit Silver Falls was based on a desire to build a better relationship with people he cared about, his friends Jack and Linden. And this is exactly the context he shared with others—talking to his spouse about Silver Falls as an ideal venue for taking soon-to-visit relatives as well as promoting to other friends the idea of visiting this site as part of a future social outing. Other individuals could visit the same site and perceive other affordances there, for example as a great place to jog or as an ideal place for viewing spring wildflowers. Still others could have the same general self-related goal of building social relationships as Daniel but choose to satisfy that goal by going shopping with a friend or organizing an evening of board games.

Individually, each of these conversations between friends and family has only a local impact, but collectively their impact is huge, affecting whole communities and even cultures. These shared autobiographical memories of experience become part of the larger societal understanding of the nature of the world people live in. Just as Daniel ended up sharing his Silver Falls experience with his friends Bob and Joyce and Bill and Susan, so too do others use their autobiographical memories of their lives as vehicles for sharing their experiences with others.[19] And it is through this process that ultimately every person, including individuals such as Daniel, comes to "know" about the opportunities that exist within the world, and which experiences are most suitable for supporting the satisfaction of specific self-related needs.

Arguably one of the key functions of culture is to foster these word-of-mouth connections between needs and solutions. The result is that people living in all healthy societies across time perceive that by and large there is a setting, context, situation or individual somewhere in their sphere capable of fulfilling whatever self-related need they might have. And typically, as was the case for Daniel, people rarely have to dig too deeply into their experiential repertoire to find these matches. The person's past experiences with this or some similar situation are drawn upon to support their self-related choices. And if personal experiences prove insufficient, then friends and associates, or as is the case in current society, online "friends and associates" are tapped to supplement personal experience. As Daniel's interviews revealed, he based his choice of Silver Falls as an excellent place for this outing on extensive prior experience—both his own and that of his wife. And nothing occurred on this particular day to change his perceptions of the affordances of this particular site.

Collectively, this all represents an enormous social-cultural feedback loop, a form of distributed Well-Being Systems that supports large numbers of individuals' choices of where and how to engage in specific leisure (and other) pursuits in order to support shared perceptions of need. Countless "Daniels" end up pursuing their need satisfaction in similar ways, for example hiking at Silver Falls with friends in order to support social relationships, and then valorize the satisfaction of those pursuits in autobiographical memory because the experience fulfilled their needs. These same people then share those autobiographical memories with others, in large part because such sharing builds and reinforces the storyteller's own identity.[20] Collectively, all of the pieces fitting together provide *post-hoc* coherence and meaning to the experience.[21]

Like all feedback loops, this process becomes self-reinforcing, both for the individual and for the society collectively. Ultimately, if these kinds of autobiographical memories cum word-of-mouth recommendations are repeated enough times, they become shared community knowledge; shared Well-Being Systems.

If these shared community Well-Being Systems become sufficiently well known, then eventually, over time they can even become accepted cultural norms; Well-Being Systems culturally passed on from one generation to the next.[22] Much as individual drops of rain collect to form rivulets, rivulets collect to form streams, streams become rivers and rivers ultimately combine to form oceans, the shared autobiographical memories of individuals combine to create the shared cultural knowledge of networks of individuals, some ultimately connecting to whole societies. Also totally analogous to waterways, repetition creates ever deeper, more indelible pathways. Although every rivulet, stream, river and ocean can and does take a slightly different shape and possesses unique features, all share many readily recognizable characteristics in common. So also is the case with human settings and contexts and the ways the public uses them to create cultural norms and expectations.

People make a constant string of choices, each overlapping in time and space with a vast array of other choices. Some choices are discrete and "knowable" and others not. Although the realities that underlie each of the millions of choices a person makes over a lifetime makes each particular choice unique, the basic outlines of why and how choices are made follows a fairly similar pattern. That pattern operates on the 11 premises laid out in Chapter 6, following a process similar to that outlined above for leisure. In Table 15.1, I take these same basic ideas and summarize them in a more concrete and elaborated way:[23]

Although few of life's choices and actions are as consciously scripted and discrete as the leisure experiences described in this and preceding chapter, all choices and resulting actions follow this basic pattern. All choices are designed to satisfy self-related needs. These choices in turn all have the goal of satisfying personal well-being. Feelings of well-being are perceived as emotionally positive, while negative emotions accompany perceptions of diminished well-being. Emotionally rich experiences, positive or negative, are memorable. Those associated with positive emotions are logged in memory (consciously or unconsciously) as worth repeating again, while negative emotions are logged as choices to be avoided in the future. These memories form the basis of all future perceptions of self-related need. Since feelings of well-being are always ephemeral, this process needs to be repeated endlessly across a lifetime.

Although the general outlines of the model described above provides a basic description of how and why human choices are made, it actually only describes the simplified functioning of Well-Being Systems within a specific realm of the human condition. The true nature of human choice and behavior is much more complex and, as mentioned several times, extends beyond the limits of current language and the traditional social science methods and tools employed. In the next and final chapter, I speculate on what Well-Being Systems in other realms might look like and how the model I have proposed might be applied to better describing and to a degree predicting human functioning beyond the language sphere.

**TABLE 15.1** The Well-Being System

| Time | Well-Being System Processes |
|------|------------------------------|
| 1a. | A person perceives a range of self-related needs emanating from one or some combination of the seven Well-Being System modalities (if consciously perceived, it is typically framed in terms of a self-aspect). |
| 1b. | Competing needs are triaged based on their relative perceived costs and benefits—which need(s), if satisfied, will most likely result in the greatest well-being. This is typically not an either-or choice, but a series of both-and-choices (typically the benefits of short-term outcomes carry more weight in this calculus than the benefits of longer-term outcomes). |
| 1c. | The person considers (consciously, unconsciously or some combination of the two) possible ways to resolve their self-related needs, all of which are based on perceived possibilities/affordances of different actions (perceived possibilities/affordances can have one or some combination of sources—biologically inherited experience, culturally constructed experience, personal lived experience or socially shared experience). |
| 1d. | Practicality considerations are also applied, such as ease, cost, convenience, etc. |
| 1e. | Since humans live within a social-cultural context, some choices are further vetted with others and others' perceived needs and perceptions of possible actions, i.e., Steps 1a—1d, are evaluated socially prior to making a choice. |
| 1f. | A choice is made and expectations formed for how to act. These expectations match perceived self-related need(s) with perceived affordance(s) of particular actions, taking into account the relative costs and benefits of those actions based on prior experience and the perceived likelihood that the action(s) will satisfy the individual's self-related need(s) in ways that are assumed will result in maximization of perceived well-being. |
| 2a. | The person proceeds to act upon her choice with the (conscious, unconscious or some combination of the two) expectation that her actions will satisfy her perceived self-related need(s). |
| 2b. | The person's expectations provide a lens through which the ensuing action(s) tends to get filtered—a lens that both directs behavior as well as directs interpretation of events as they unfold. |
| 2c. | As the experiences unfold, the individual continually appraises the situation, and as long as actions appear to support the satisfaction and extension of perceptions of self-related needs at or above predefined threshold expectation levels, she continues to act in a consistent way. |
| 2d. | In addition to a person's expectations, her other inherited, socially and culturally acquired and lived experiences (i.e., prior knowledge, interests, beliefs, values, etc.) shape how she navigates the realities she encounters and perceives the relative balance of her self-related needs. |
| 2e. | Environmental realities, both anticipated and unanticipated, continually impinge on actions. Typically, these "realities" merely create the landscape in which behaviors are enacted and only moderately deflect a person's trajectory of action. Occasionally though, "realities" demand a total reset of a person's action trajectory, new self-related needs require the individual to return to Step 1a. |

| Time | Well-Being System Processes |
|------|------------------------------|
| 2f. | Aspects of the experience most likely to be salient are those that emotionally connect with the person's initial expectations and serve to maintain a positive sense of well-being; although unexpected or serendipitous events can also become emotionally salient due to their positive or negative valence and arousal for the individual and their impact on perceptions of well-being. |
| 2g. | Throughout, perceptions of well-being are continuously appraised based on the relationship between the expectation of satisfying self-related needs and the actual satisfaction of needs experienced. |
| 2h. | When this set of choices and actions are perceived to be complete, the individual reassesses her well-being and situational needs and decides what to do next (i.e., Step 1a). |
| 3a. | Afterwards, in parallel to other choices and actions, the individual selectively valorizes in memory the parts of the experience that were most (emotionally) salient; typically these memorable bits directly relate to the initial needs she hoped to satisfy, the choices she made in an effort to satisfy those needs and her self-perceptions of well-being derived. |
| 3b. | Over time, most of the details of the experience fade. Left behind as autobiographical memory is a generalized set of self-aspects that reflect the overall emotional state created by the satisfaction (or not) of the needs the experience was intended to support. Also recalled are a few specific examples that illustrate the satisfaction of needs. |
| 3c. | These memories are rehearsed and shared internally and with others as a way to provide coherence and meaning to the experience. |
| 4a. | Through this sharing process the individual adds to her own, as well as her social network's and the larger society's, store of understanding of how specific choices and actions directly map to specific self-aspects and indirectly how choices and actions connect with self-related needs and the creation of well-being. This process serves to inform both the individual's and others in her social network's future choices and actions. |

## Notes

1. Pseudonyms.
2. Pseudonyms.
3. This is a typical pattern, cf., Falk, J.H., Scott, C., Dierking, L.D., Rennie, L.J. & Cohen Jones, M. (2004). Interactives and visitor learning. *Curator*, 47(2), 171–198.
4. This is why demographic variables like age, gender, race/ethnicity and nationality only sometimes provide useful insights into why different people experience the world differently. As mentioned earlier, demographic variables are fixed; they do not take into account the variability and "situatedness" of people and experience. They are aspects of lived experience, but only sometimes are they the aspects of lived experience most critical to the situation.
5. Lussenhop, A., Auster, R. & Lindgren-Streicher, A. (2015). *Facilitation Research for Engineering Design Education (FREDE)*. Unpublished Research Report. Boston: Museum of Science. Retrieved April 28, 2016. www.informalscience.org/sites/default/files/2016-01-04_2015-3%20Facilitation%20Research%20for%20Engineering%20Design%20Education%20Research%20Report.pdf

6. Lussenhop, A., Auster, R. & Lindgren-Streicher, A. (2015). *Facilitation Research for Engineering Design Education (FREDE)*. Unpublished Research Report. Boston: Museum of Science. Retrieved April 28, 2016. www.informalscience.org/sites/default/files/2016-01-04_2015-3%20Facilitation%20Research%20for%20Engineering%20Design%20Education%20Research%20Report.pdf

7. Needs I have previously categorized as falling under the term "Explorers" (Falk, J.H. (2009). *Identity and the museum visitor experience*. Walnut Creek, CA: Left Coast Press).

8. Staus, N. & Falk, J.H. (in press). The role of emotion in science learning: Testing a preliminary model. *Mind, Brain & Education*.

9. Ben-Ze'ev, A. (2000). *The subtlety of emotions*. Cambridge, MA: MIT Press.

   Aggleton, J.P. (Ed.). (1992). *The Amygdala: Neurological aspects of emotion, memory, and mental dysfunction*. New York: Wiley-Liss.

   Damasio, A.R. (1994). *Descartes' error: Emotion, reasons, and the human brain*. New York: Avon Books.

10. Csikzentmihalyi, M. & Hermanson, K. (1995). Intrinsic motivation in museums: Why does one want to learn? In J. Falk & L. Dierking (Eds.), *Public institutions for personal learning*. Washington, DC: American Association of Museums.

11. Turner, J.H. (2000). *On the origins of human emotions: A sociological inquiry into the evolution of human affect*. Stanford, CA: Stanford University Press, p. 59.

12. Falk, J.H. (2009). *Identity and the museum visitor experience*. Walnut Creek, CA: Left Coast Press.

13. Although I could not prove this assertion relative to Daniel, it is supported by physiological research (cf., Staus, N. & Falk, J.H. (in press). The role of emotion in science learning: Testing a preliminary model. *Mind, Brain & Education*).

14. Rounds, J. (2006). Doing identity work in museums. *Curator*, 49(2), 138.

15. One that some individuals are capable of doing consciously but all people do at some level unconsciously.

16. Falk, J.H. (2009). *Identity and the museum visitor experience*. Walnut Creek, CA: Left Coast Press.

17. Gottschall, J. (2012). *The storytelling animal: How stories make us human*. New York: Houghton Mifflin Harcourt.

18. McAdams, D.P. (2008). Personal narratives and the life story. In O. John, R. Robins & L.A. Pervin (Eds.), *Handbook of personality: Theory and research* (3rd ed., pp. 242–262). New York: Guilford Press.

19. McAdams, D.P. (2008). Personal narratives and the life story. In O. John, R. Robins & L.A. Pervin (Eds.), *Handbook of personality: Theory and research* (3rd ed., pp. 242–262). New York: Guilford Press.

   Gottschall, J. (2012). *The storytelling animal: How stories make us human*. New York: Houghton Mifflin Harcourt.

20. Gottschall, J. (2012). *The storytelling animal: How stories make us human*. New York: Houghton Mifflin Harcourt.

21. cf., Hood, B. (2012). *The self illusion*. Oxford: Oxford University Press.

   Laird, J.D. (2007). *Feelings: The perception of self*. Oxford: Oxford University Press.

22. Gladwell, M. (2000). *The tipping point: How little things can make a big difference*. New York: Little, Brown and Company.

23. NOTE: Although the sequence is constant, the time periods required for each of the three sets of events can vary in length—from microseconds to days or weeks—and may be directly connected temporally or separated by intervening choices, actions and memories.

# 16

## UNDERSTANDINGS BEYOND THE INDIVIDUAL

The Well-Being Systems model provides a robust and parsimonious framework for understanding the nature of individual human choice-making, particularly the types of "language sphere" choices most people are used to thinking about. In this final chapter I explore the opportunities suggested and questions posed by extending the Well-Being Systems model to the human realms that lie below the level of the individual as well as those involving multiple individuals. I begin by discussing how the current Well-Being Systems model raises many, currently unresolved questions at the smaller grain-sizes of neural and cellular functioning. Next I explore the implications for extending the Well-Being Systems model to very large grain sizes, for example at the level of organizations or ecological communities. I follow this with a discussion of how the Well-Being Systems model lends itself to thinking across grain sizes, as for example suggested in the previous chapter where an individual's leisure choice-making is both influenced by and in turn influences the larger society. I have chosen to focus on just a few examples within each of these grain-size categories, and much of what I discuss remains highly speculative. However, *IF* Well-Being Systems are truly as pervasive and fundamental as I assert, the number of possible examples and applications are limitless. My caveat *IF* is intentional. In the final section I offer up some final thoughts on both the remaining opportunities and significant challenges posed by the model.

### Well-Being Systems Smaller Than the Language Sphere

At the end of the first section of the book I argued that much of the focus of human discourse, as well as social science research, has been restricted to a subset of human-influencing events and experience (see Figure 16.1). A lot happens within the "language sphere"—events happening primarily within time frames of minutes to days or weeks or maybe a few years and experiences primarily perceived

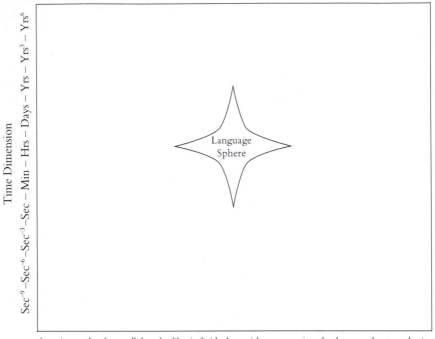

FIGURE 16.1  The scope and scale of human experience

to be happening at the margins of the whole body and community levels—and inarguably what happens within this perceptual sphere is important to the human experience. Though largely imperceptible to most humans, events and experiences happening at other scales are also important, including events involving the very small or the very big, the very quick or the very slow. Well-Being Systems exist at all of these levels as well; many but likely not all of which directly and regularly interconnect with Well-Being Systems operating at the level of the language sphere.

Investigations of the very small and very short duration have been a major focus of much of the natural sciences for the past century; with physics, chemistry, physiology and microbiology dominating the first half of the past century and biochemistry, genomics and neuroscience dominating the second half. In this section I will discuss possible ways that the Well-Being Systems model might inform or be informed by further work in several of these areas, starting with the neurosciences.

Throughout this book I've attempted to reconcile my model with current understandings of the mind, as well as support my claims with the most current neuroscience research.[1] However there are also some examples of where my model suggests things about how the mind should work that are currently poorly supported by at least my understanding of the research. For example, I speculated that the competing needs of the various Well-Being Systems are "negotiated" through a process comparable to Edelman's ideas of Neural Darwinism.[2] The logic of Edelman's ideas are compelling but the exact mechanism by which this triage actually occurs remains unclear, or at least unclear to me. How are individual neurons recruited into neural nets/Well-Being Systems? How are specific threshold activation states within neuronal networks/Well-Being Systems established, and how does this vary as a function of the type of neural net/Well-Being System in play?

For example, even within the same behavioral condition, considerable variability in neural response has been found.[3] However most of this variability has been studied at the level of individual cell responses rather than at the level of whole networks.[4] One of the important conclusions of the Neural Darwinism theory is that neuronal groups/Well-Being Systems should be capable of self-learning. Recent evidence from both laboratory studies and computer-based simulations based on Edelman's model suggested that this is indeed what happens across a diversity of neuronal functions.[5] Although what remains unclear is exactly what the drivers of these learning processes are, specifically how neuronal systems come to choose between competing signals and learn how to appropriately and situationally respond to the complexities and ambiguities of the world.

Edelman's model appears to suggest that selection is generally winner-take-all, with the "loudest" and/or most "relevant" signals attended to. This assumption makes sense in general and lends itself well to laboratory and/or computer simulation experimentation, which as suggested above have been done. However, in such experiments, the number of competing signals/variables are by necessity artificially restricted. Although there clearly are cases, e.g., emergencies or habitual activities where such simple, all-or-none choice-making no doubt occurs, it is open to question whether such situations are really the norm. The survival of complex vertebrates like humans has always been predicated on situational flexibility and the ability to locate and exploit scarce resources within a spatially and temporally complex world.[6]

As predicted by my model and observed in humans, it would make more sense to hypothesize that more nuanced neuronal group selective processes are at work. At least based on observable human choices and actions, it appears that neuronal groups are regularly using some kind of more complex algorithm of activation since behaviors invariably appear to reflect an integrative response to competing well-being-related needs/signals rather than an all-or-none response. In other words, people like Daniel decide to go hiking at Silver Falls State Park not SOLELY because such an activity has the potential to satisfy Sociality needs, but because this choice represents a good compromise between the competing needs of multiple modalities of well-being-related needs. The complexities of how this happens at the neuronal group level, particularly given the important role of neural chemistry, continues to remain elusive. It would seem that useful ideas for how this might work within the complex world of neuronal groups might be found in the only slightly less complex world of inter-cellular physiology.

A key underlying premise of my model is that Well-Being Systems, including those involved in neural processing, connect in an unbroken line to evolutionary events arising at the onset of the evolution of life some 3.7+ billion years ago, in particular biochemical processes that biologists typically refer to as homeostasis. Through exaptations, living systems have progressively evolved ever more sophisticated Well-Being Systems, each adapted for supporting and maintaining one particular aspect of well-being. As a consequence of the selective pressures resulting from the evolution of increasingly complex, highly mobile, multicellular organisms, an increasing percentage of these Well-Being Systems became centralized within neural ganglia, and ultimately brains, with the human brain representing an extreme example of this evolutionary process. However, despite the centralization of many of humanity's Well-Being processes within the brain, many Well-Being Systems remain tied to historic, non-neural, cell-to-cell communication pathways. Thus the model I propose predicts that understandings derived from the first principles of physiology might yield important understandings in neural processing.[7]

According to medical evolutionary biologist John Torday, a physiological explanation of Well-Being Systems might go something like the following:

> [Well-Being Systems/Homeostatic] processes have memory and allow for change. When stress is sensed by the organism, i.e. the [Well-Being System/ homeostatic] set-points are disturbed, the internal mechanisms that mediate [Well-Being System/homeostasis] will adjust to alleviate the stresses, but only within limits. If the stresses are too great the cells/tissues produce inflammatory mediators like Radical Oxygen Species (ROS). ROS cause gene mutations and duplications. Such genetic mutations occur within the constraints of the evolutionary "history" of the organism by trial and error until the stress (i.e. ROS) is alleviated by a new physiologic configuration mediated by soluble growth factors and their ligands on the cell-types that formed the physiologic trait remodeling their niche during embryogenesis. In this way "ontogeny recapitulates phylogeny." Epigenetic inheritance directly from the environment also participates in this process, allowing for transgenerational inheritance via the epigenetic marks in the germ cells. This process is consistent with the "metabolism first" theory of the origins of life, facilitated by cell-environment and cell-cell interactions that foster cooperativity.[8]

It is quite possible, perhaps even likely, that similar Well-Being System mechanisms are at work within the brain and could be tested as explanations for how neural networks achieve adaptability and "learning."

The presumed homologous relationship between homeostatic/Well-Being Systems at all physiological levels has particular relevance as well for thinking about the role that the microbiome might play in influencing overall human well-being. The trillions of microbial cells that comprise the human microbiome have lived within and upon humans and their ancestors for tens if not hundreds of millions of years, even though it is only within the past couple decades that research is revealing just how integral these creatures are to many, if not most, human physiology-level Well-Being Systems.[9] It only makes sense that these microorganisms would have co-evolved complicated communication and interaction pathways with and between humanity's psychology-level Well-Being pathways. Preliminary evidence suggesting that the microbiome influences perceptions of anxiety and depression are likely just the first of many such instances. My model would suggest that the human microbiome should almost certainly influence, even if only moderately, all seven modalities of human Well-Being Systems, including those associated with the needs of Reflectivity and Spirituality/Creativity, through a co-evolutionary process depending as much, if not more, on real-time adaptations and immunologic responses as on random mutation and genetically-based natural selection.[10]

Like many if not all Well-Being Systems, an individual's relationship to his microbiome is diachronic, meaning it develops over time. People acquire an initial inoculation of symbiotic microbes from their mother as they pass through the birth canal, but the vast majority of an individual's microbiome are acquired through eating, living in the world and interacting with others.[11] In this way the impact of Well-Being Systems occurring at the level of the very small extend into the realm of Well-Being Systems that operate on time scales of the very long.

## Well-Being Systems Larger Than the Language Sphere

Humans possess strong connections to particular physical settings, often referred to as their sense of place.[12] Like other Well-Being Systems, the human relationship to place is also diachronic. Preferences for specific landscapes, for example, develop over time. Findings from my own research on human landscape preferences support the idea that the Well-Being Systems associated with human relationship to place, including specifically Systems that result in feelings of emotional attachment to specific types of landscape, arise through a mix of genetic and learned factors.[13] All people seem to start out life with an innate "habitat preference" for savanna-like settings—short grass and scattered trees.[14] As discussed at length in Chapter 12, modern humans are the product of millions of years of evolution, 99+% of which was spent living in and adapting to African savanna-like landscapes. And even when these early ancestral humans migrated out of Africa, they clung to similar savanna-like habitats as they followed game animals across Eurasia. Although modern humans now live in every imaginable habitat on earth, they retain a genetic predisposition towards savanna-like landscapes. But this genetic legacy is not fixed; all humans come to equally prefer the landscapes they actually live in. Early to late adolescence appears to be a particularly critical time period in this learning process.[15]

Although it makes perfect sense that humans should be acutely aware of and sensitive to their physical context, until quite recently relatively few social scientists took this idea seriously. Research on the effects of physical settings on human well-being have long been conspicuously absent in mainstream social science literature, except in the writings of archaeologists, anthropologists and a handful of psychologists. The result has been a century or more of social science research possessing a glaring "blind spot" with regards to the critical role that sense of place and the environment played in human perceptions of need and well-being. That reality is slowly changing. Recent neuroscience research has shown that individuals do indeed build a self-related cognitive identity with the physical world in which they live,[16] and a new generation of psychologists have begun exploring these relationships. However, much of this research has suffered from a lack of theoretical grounding. Potentially this new model of Well-Being Systems, building on understandings of how such Systems work across a variety of contexts, could provide some useful future structure to this line of investigation.

Another example of how the Well-Being Systems model could be extended to new investigative domains would be to apply the model to entities larger than the individual, for example to collections of individuals such as family groups, organizations or even whole communities. What the proposed Well-Being Systems model predicts is that at every level, systems have evolved to support well-being through the perception of needs, the collection and analysis of relevant information, the making of choices and initiation of actions. Such Well-Being Systems should exist within family groupings, organizations, whole communities and even potentially at the level of ecosystems.[17] And much like the Well-Being Systems at the cellular or individual levels, each of these higher order Systems should be adaptive, designed to support and regulate well-being in relation and response to the System's social, economic and ecological history and current reality. Depending upon these histories and realities, a family, organization or community's well-being should be easier or harder to attain and maintain. The model also predicts that all smaller systems within that larger social entity, e.g., individuals within a corporation or corporations within a community, should most of the time, but not all of the time, work to maintain the collective well-being of the larger entity using the same basic, self-related processes, forming a nested system of Well-Being Systems. It also explains why higher level systems are so dependent on the well-being of lower levels. The needs of Systems at lower levels always take precedence. Only if those lower level needs are satisfied will Systems at lower levels expend any effort on satisfying the needs of higher levels.[18]

From this perspective then, it should be possible to analyze the choice-making of a complex social construct like a corporation or non-profit organization using very similar logic and tools as I used to analyze Daniel's day trip to Silver Falls. Like individuals, corporations and organizations make an endless stream of choices, some of which reflect conscious decision making but many of which are "culturally" determined, read unconscious, and seemingly develop over-time through custom or out of habit.[19] Specifically then, what do the choices a corporation or organization make say about that entity's perceptions of well-being? Does one find the same modalities of Well-Being System within corporations and organizations as in individual humans, i.e., the modalities of Continuity, Individuality, Sexuality, Sociality, Relationality, Reflectivity and Creativity/Spirituality? If so, what are the analogs at these higher levels of organization? What different or additional modalities of well-being exist at these higher levels of organization? What insights about an organization could be gleaned by better understanding how an organization triages the needs of the many, many selves it comprises when making choices? What mechanisms exist within organizations to sense these various needs and are there needs that seem to consistently be unheard or disproportionately ignored? Which modalities of need, and under what conditions, seem to dominate organizational choice-making? Such an analysis would arguably go a long way towards improving both the understanding and functioning of not only organizations but social systems of all kinds.

Arguably the most exciting insight that the Well-Being Systems model affords is the idea that given the common origins of all Well-Being Systems, similar processes are likely working at all levels, from the smallest intracellular homeostatic system all the way up to the largest, ecosystem-level system. Implicit in this idea is that understandings generated about the functioning of Well-Being Systems at any level are potentially directly applicable to understandings at other levels. In other words, insights related to homeostatic processing of calcium might actually yield insights about how humans interact within organizations or communities, while insights about ecosystem functioning might advance understanding of how individual humans make choices.

## Well-Being Systems Across Different Levels

In all of the examples used in this chapter, a consistent observation is the importance of interactions of Well-Being Systems across multiple levels of organization. This idea was introduced in the last chapter in relation to Daniel's leisure choice-making. In this and many other ways, the Well-Being Systems model I have described fits the description of what has come to be called *complex-adaptive systems theory*.[20] This idea of interactions across multiple levels is just one of the many qualities that define complex adaptive systems. Other important characteristics are that in complex systems the number of interacting elements are sufficiently large and interdependent that conventional descriptions are impractical and cease to assist in understanding the system; the interaction of elements are dynamic and non-linear; the overall behavior of the system is not dictated by the actions of any individual part of the system; and the system operates far from equilibrium conditions.[21] The Well-Being Systems I have described meet all these criteria. Whether at the cellular or organizational level they, like all complex adaptive systems, are dynamic and ever changing; constantly evolving in response to both past and current events.

A key benefit of conceptualizing Well-Being Systems as complex adaptive systems is that it is possible to build on existing theoretical frameworks such as complexity theory which enable examination of entities existing within a hierarchy of interrelated but different organizational levels.[22] These frameworks have now been used to study a variety of other types of complex systems such as ecosystems, economies, transportation networks, epidemics and neural systems.[23] The key insight of complex system analysis is that the combination of local interactions and feedback loops between different hierarchical levels gives rise to self-organized structural, spatial and temporal patterns that are neither completely ordered (equivalent to a uniform spatial pattern or temporal equilibrium) nor disordered (random or chaotic).

Adapting a model developed by Parrott,[24] the example from the previous chapter on leisure choice-making could be schematically represented as shown in Figure 16.2 (Note: Daniel would be represented by one of the shapes located in the bottom part of the diagram). As the diagram suggests, events at each level interact with and effect events at other levels. As a consequence, it is not possible to fully understand what is happening at any given level without also understanding what is happening at superordinate and subordinate levels. As illustrated by Daniel's leisure experiences, the experiences of other people occurring prior to the day of Daniel's trip to Silver Falls subtly influenced Daniel's experience, just as Daniel's experience ultimately influenced future visitors to Silver Falls. All of this happened independently of whether or not any of these actors were consciously aware of each other.

An interesting example of how such interacting Well-Being Systems might function comes from a preliminary cross-sector analysis of the U.S. science, technology, engineering and mathematics—STEM—learning ecosystem.[25] It is typically assumed that schooling is the main driver of learning not only in the classroom but over the lifetime of the individual, and that it is first and foremost schooling that establishes learning Well-Being Systems, particularly for academic subject areas such as STEM.[26] Certainly schools have long employed the kind of socialization processes designed to train children to associate learning with well-being, not dissimilar from the training and habituation processes alluded to in Chapter 13 when discussing Creativity & Spirituality systems. And for some children this type of continually reinforced, extrinsic reward system—doing well results in praise and good grades—seems to work; however, for many children not so much. Over the last decades consistent data has been emerging that provides a more complex picture about where, when and why children learn things like science, math, engineering and technology; data that disputes the assumption that schooling is the primary source of STEM learning.[27]

STEM learning appears to be the result of multiple sources, and as is the case with all Well-Being Systems, is a consequence of protracted and adaptive forces occurring over time. For example, all U.S. national and international standardized tests of STEM understanding show that the single most significant factor affecting test scores is not school quality or the nature of instruction utilized but home environment.[28] Data from a recent U.S. 2014 National Assessment of Educational Progress assessment of digitally-based Technology and Engineering Literacy of 8th graders found that while 52% of youth reported taking a course on technology or engineering in school, 63% reported that their family members taught them most of what they know about building things, fixing things or how things work. In

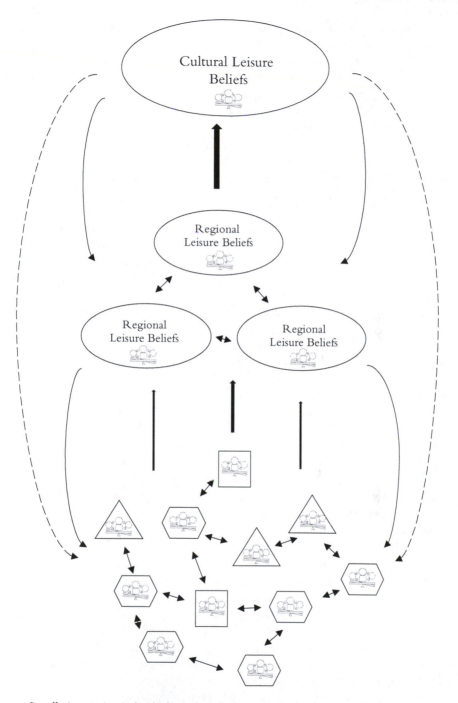

Locally interacting individuals, each with their own leisure experiences and beliefs

**FIGURE 16.2** Conceptual model of interconnected leisure Well-Being Systems

fact, nearly 90% reported that learning about figuring out why something was not working in order to fix it happened exclusively outside of school.

The influence of home-life on schooling begins early and is long-lasting. And although these parental influences correlate with demographic factors like parental educational attainment and socio-economic status, they occur independently of these factors. Three-year-olds whose low income mothers nurtured their math skills through play performed significantly better on preschool and first-grade math skills tests than did children from comparable backgrounds whose mothers did not engage in these activities with them.[29] Parental influences, across all demographic categories, have been shown to persist year after year, with the children receiving the most parent support consistently out-achieving less supported children both in school and later in life.[30]

What is less well understood is exactly how parental support directly leads to improved school performance, since there is not always a one-to-one relationship between parental attitudes towards schooling and student success.[31] Again I would argue that the Well-Being Systems model provides a better answer than the usual assumptions that what determines school success is parental attitudes towards the importance of schooling. Over many years, acquired both explicitly through parental instruction and arguably even more importantly acquired implicitly through modeling of parents,[32] children develop a range of Well-Being Systems related to learning. The more these learning-related Systems are positively associated with perceptions of positive well-being, the more likely children will strive to invest in future learning—in or out-of-school.

All young children have strong Sociality-related needs, the need to feel loved and appreciated by their parents. If parents spend quality time with their children doing activities like reading, building things and asking and answering questions, then children grow up believing that activities like reading, making things and being curious result in feelings of well-being. As children's reflective needs develop, for example the needs associated with planning and creativity, they model their parents' well-being strategies. For example, when a child has a toy that does not work, through their actions parents teach their children, again either by instruction or more likely through modeling, how one responds to unforeseen circumstances. If the parent helps the child discover that rather than throwing the toy away the toy can be fixed, the child learns to develop the self-reliance necessary to fix toys, and other aspects of life that become broken, by themselves. Presumably, this kind of parent also praises their child when she tries to fix things herself. For these children learning to fix things themselves becomes strongly associated with positive rewards and pleasurable experiences; engaging in these kinds of experiences become highly salient and memorable and something the child seeks to repeat as frequently as possible, potentially all the way through employment. The association between positive emotion and learning, between learning and well-being, initially developed at home, becomes transferred to other situations as well, including school, the workplace and the larger world.[33]

## Towards Better Choice-Making

The need for improved choice-making has arguably been a major driver of both biological and cultural evolution; throughout history better choices equated with greater survivability. This reality is as true today as ever. Although everyone believes the world they live in is complex and challenging, there is no questions that this aptly describes present reality. The climate is dramatically changing, world populations are bumping up against limits in critical resources like water and food, and people worldwide are being forced to choose between increasingly divergent political and social ideologies. Finding a tool that could help to better navigate these issues and choices would be wonderful. Unfortunately, this new model of choice-making, despite providing considerable explanatory powers, does not explicitly address how to make better choices.[34] Generally, the Well-Being Systems model is designed to explain *why* and *how* choices are made, not *what* choices should be made. That said, there are a few insights about improved choice-making that can be gleaned from this model.

One important insight the Well-Being Systems model suggests is the importance of bodily needs. For too long, it was assumed that personal well-being was primarily achieved through maximization of financial and/or intellectual needs. The model suggests that the needs of Continuity, Individuality and Sexuality are important pathways to well-being, both in the moment and over time. Thus at the individual level, choices should be made that focus on nurturing the body, doing things that lead to improved health, and yes, having a healthy and satisfying sex life.

Another important insight is the importance of social relationships. The model suggests that Sociality-related needs are critical to overall well-being, arguably disproportionately important because of their durability. These Systems tend to be more stable, and though not exactly easy to maintain at a high state of equilibrium, they are easier to maintain than many other Well-Being Systems. The consistent feelings of well-being provided by strong friendships and positive family relationships can help individuals weather the vicissitudes of diminished well-being caused by sickness, depression and a host of other life crises.

Insights the model affords about the workings of groups also can lead to better choice-making. Since the model predicts that the needs of Systems at lower levels always take precedence, individuals charged with maintaining group welfare would be well advised to always place the well-being of the individuals within the group ahead of the well-being of the collective. If lower level needs are not satisfied, individuals will be loath to expend any effort helping to satisfy the needs of the larger group.

Individuals familiar with this model have reported that it has helped them make better choices merely by making them stop and think about why they feel the need to make a particular choice. Why do they feel they need to eat that extra helping, is this just a message from some part of the microbiome seeking to serve its own best interests? Is the impulse to not exercise satisfying a short-term well-being need at the expense of a long-term well-being need? Applications of the model in this way facilitate increased self-control, what psychologists call executive functioning.[35] Connecting the parts of the brain involved in executive functioning to Well-Being Systems typically disconnected from these "higher" cognitive functions has been shown to result in improvements in the quality of choice-making.[36]

Finally, if nothing else, the model makes clear the central role that well-being plays in life; that pursuit of well-being is not a nicety but a necessity. It also makes clear that well-being is not a destination but an on-going set of stops along the way. In other words, people should live their life in ways that allow them to enjoy their triumphs when they happen and accept and move on from their tragedies when these too inevitably happen. Life is a roller coaster ride of good moments and bad moments, good and bad choices. Unlike a real roller coaster which is on a fixed path, people through their choices and actions have some modicum of control. This perhaps is the ultimate take away of the Well-Being Systems model. Life courses are not pre-defined. Despite societal constraints, every individual has considerable control over their own life trajectory. Every individual, each in his own way, has the ability to define what constitutes needs, and then choose to seek, or not, actions that he perceives will result in happiness. If there is one thing the Well-Being Systems model reveals, nothing is totally pre-ordained. Perceptions of need and the choices that emanate from those perceived needs are all capable of change; life courses are malleable.

## Next Steps & Further Questions

I offer this Well-Being Systems model at this time not because I believe the model is complete or perfect the way it is; quite the contrary. I know that the current model is a work in progress and without question will be found to have flaws and require modifications or elaborations. I am presenting this model now because I think it is far enough along in its development to offer some important new insights.

Obviously how one defines and measures an individual's self-related needs, and thus utilizes these as indicators of choice and well-being, is a critical issue. In creating the current model, I erred on the side of trying to simplify what is clearly an exceedingly complex reality. My goal was to create a model that was simultaneously comprehensible and more or less realistic while at the same time both useable and generalizable; a feat inherently challenging for any model.[37]

Greater detail and precision would undoubtedly insure a closer fit to particular contexts and life situations, but it would also result in a poorer fit in other circumstances. That might be a worthwhile tradeoff in trying to describe the specific choices and behaviors of a particular group of individuals within some specific constrained context, but it seems like a bad tradeoff when trying to create a generalizable model for something as diverse and heterogeneous as human choice-making. Thus the way I have parsed the universe of Well-Being Systems represents an overly reduced and simplified view of the world, erring on the side of being a "lumper" rather than a "splitter." To begin with, it should be clear to any thoughtful reader that there are not in fact just seven critical modalities of Well-Being Systems, there are more likely dozens if not thousands. However, I know through my initial work with museum-like settings that creating a larger number of categories, rather than seven I have proposed here, would of course enable a better mapping between theory and reality but would also inevitably diminish the model's practicality and acceptance. Perhaps because of the way the human mind is constructed,[38] keeping the number at seven (plus or minus two) is more cognitively manageable, particularly for those people who might actually want to apply these ideas to real people in the real world. At the moment, the current Well-Being Systems model based on seven evolutionarily defensible modalities seems to make sense and can be supported by initial data. However, more data and more testing of how the model actually works in practice are clearly required, and when collected, it may turn out to be important to expand the number of modalities considered and otherwise complexify the processes described.

Additionally, I know that the strategies my colleagues and I have used to date for measuring an individual's self-related needs and motivations remain quite crude and overly dependent upon autobiographical memory and self-report, in short consciously constructed language. As discussed in the previous chapters, missing are accurate tools for delving into all of the various factors and myriad processes driving self-related perceptions of need and choice-making, most of which lie below the level of human conscious awareness. As suggested by the model, only some aspects of some choices are likely available to conscious, language-driven explanations. Clearly additional tools are needed that can circumvent these limitations.

Some may raise concerns about the lack of coherence between my model and a range of widely tested and currently accepted psychological models of choice, including many of the models summarized in these pages. Actually I would begin by suggesting that my model actually does appear to be consistent with much of the data used to create these various models; it merely deviates from the theoretical frameworks used to explain the data. I would suggest as well that almost without exception all of the cited models were generated through the conscious, language-driven self-reports of primarily WEIRD people—Western, Educated, Industrialized, Rich and Democratic.[39] As earlier discussed, this is a problematic population on which to base a generalized model for humanity.[40] These models make sense as long as the same subject pool and context in which they were generated are maintained, however they often do not hold up as well when these conditions are not met.

Awareness of the inherent biases created by culture is not new. Mindful of these challenges, there has been a tendency for many in the social sciences to assert that all human behavior is relative and lacking in generalizability. That too I believe is a bias; one that stems from an undue dependence on conscious, language-driven self-reports. As physiologists discovered a long time ago, although humans superficially appear quite diverse, at their core they are quite similar. So too I would argue are social processes. Although explanations for choices are strongly influenced by social, cultural and lived experiential factors, at their core they too are likely quite similar. All human choice-making is driven by the same fundamental modalities of self-perceived needs that all humans share as a consequence of their common evolutionary heritage.[41] Nonetheless, there is no getting around the fact that my model too is disproportionately based on data from WEIRD populations. This is a flaw that although totally mindful of, I currently am unable to remedy. However, without question, there is a need for additional research to determine if the model I have proposed holds for humans across a range of cultures and contexts.

A key aspect of the model I have proposed is that it seeks to describe the ongoing, continuous biological process of choice-making. The model asserts that this dynamic choice-making process can best be understood as a series of never-ending snap-shot assessments of well-being. Of course the actual biology of this process is only hinted at. But much as the term homeostasis has come to generically describe a host of self-regulating physiological processes, so too do the Well-Being Systems operating within the Language Sphere generically describe a host of self-regulating psychobiological processes. The parallels as I have hypothesized are not just analogous but homologous. This assertion, like every one of the proposed implications listed above, represents a testable hypothesis. It should be possible to devise experiments that examine both the validity and reliability of each assertion. To date, only a few of these ideas have been tested, and these primarily in leisure contexts. Although they are promising I am hopeful that I and others will examine the accuracy of this model across a wider range of situations and of course, as suggested above, with a greater diversity of humankind.

Although the goal of this book was to explain human choice-making, it should be clear given the deep evolutionary roots of Well-Being Systems that much of what has been discussed here has implications for non-human organisms as well. Every living organism regularly exercises choices, each in its own way attempting to maximize perceived well-being. Each of these species-specific perceptions of well-being are indicative of how that species attempts to maximize its fitness. Hence it should be possible to use the Well-Being Systems model presented here as a vehicle for making useful predictions about the lives of other organisms, either by starting with needs and predicting choices, or starting with choices and predicting needs. Obviously the more closely related a species is to humans, the greater will be the commonality between the self-related needs and choices of the target organism and human self-related needs and choices, but even distantly related species are likely to share considerable overlap. There has been a longstanding tradition of applying insights from "lower" life forms to humans, but the reverse has historically been taboo due to long-standing concerns about anthropomorphism. However, given the amazingly conservative nature of life, it would make good sense for there to be a surprising number of insights about other life forms that could be realized by applying insights gained from the study of human Well-Being Systems.

Of course the model I have posed here raises as many questions as it seeks to answer. One could ask questions such as: Are all actions really the product of choice or even justified as a choice? Is having choice always a good thing? There is evidence that too many choices can be as problematic as too few choices; what are evolutionary constraints on choice-making imposed by the structure and function of Well-Being Systems? Is there a rule of thumb about what constitutes optimal conditions for choice-making or is every situation unique? And if there is a rule of thumb, what is the biological basis for that rule? What are the advantages and disadvantages of consciousness with regard to choice? Finally, is it possible that choice as well as the perceptions of choice have no real biological basis? That choice, like virtually all human activity, is merely a socially and culturally constructed epiphenomenon. I will not attempt to answer these questions now, nor presume that this list raises all of the important issues needing answering. I have no doubt that others will raise many additional, perhaps even more important, questions. All are fair game and will need to be addressed down the road.

No matter what the outcome of the questions posed and the tests of my model conducted, I am hopeful that the ideas presented in this book will stimulate discussions and possibly even debates within and ideally between the social and natural science communities. Such conversations will certainly be interesting, and hopefully even result in better understandings of humans and other life forms. I would assert that the only ways one can make sense of a person, as well as arguably the social systems in which they function, be that social system a family, corporation or a whole society, is by understanding the whys and hows of the needs perceived and the choices made. I would further assert that regardless of whether the choices an individual makes are unique or similar in form and substance to those made by other humans, whether the choices are specific to humans or congruent with the choices of other types of life, all choices are made in order to facilitate and maintain well-being. If true, this insight alone will result in an enhanced understanding of the ways people operate within the world, make meaning and ultimately seek to control their individual fitness.

## Notes

1. A caveat to this statement is in order. In actual fact, aligning my model with the best and most current neuroscience has been extremely challenging. The neurosciences are an extremely dynamic field, with new and often contradictory results emerging almost daily. I do not regularly read neuroscience journals, and even if I did, there are currently 70 or more such journals.
2. Edelman, G. (1989). *Neural Darwinism—The theory of neuronal group selection.* New York: Basic Books.
3. Dinstein, I., Heeger, D.J. & Behrmann, M. (2015). Neural variability: Friend or foe? *Trends in Cognitive Science*, 19, 322–328.
4. Chervyakov, A.V., Sinitsyn, D.O. & Piradov, M.A. (2016). Variability of neuronal responses: Types and functional significance of neuroplasticity and Neural Darwinism. *Frontiers of Human Neuroscience.* Retrieved February 1, 2017. https://doi.org/10.3389/fnhum.2016.00603

5. Chervyakov, A.V., Sinitsyn, D.O. & Piradov, M.A. (2016). Variability of neuronal responses: Types and functional significance of neuroplasticity and Neural Darwinism. *Frontiers of Human Neuroscience.* Retrieved February 1, 2017. https://doi.org/10.3389/fnhum.2016.00603

6. Falk, J.H. & Lynch, J.F. (1981). *The evolution and ecology of information.* Unpublished Manuscript.

7. A case in point would be the insights Gerald Edelman had about neural processing represented a direct extension of insights he developed about the functioning of the immune system.

8. Torday, J.S. (2015). Homeostasis as the mechanism of evolution. *Biology,* 4, 573–590.

9. Miller, W.B., Jr. (2013). *The microcosm within: Evolution and extinction within the hologenome.* Boco Ratan, FL: Universal-Publishers.

10. Miller, W.B., Jr. (2013). *The microcosm within: Evolution and extinction within the hologenome.* Boco Ratan, FL: Universal-Publishers.

11. Ursell, L.K., Metcalf, J., Parfrey, L.W. & Knight, R. (2012). Defining the human microbiome. *Nutritional Review,* 70(Suppl. 1), S38–S44.

12. Tuan, Y.F. (1990). *Topophilia: A study of environmental perception, attitudes and values.* New York: Columbia University Press.
    Cresswell, T. (2005). *Place: A short introduction.* Hoboken, NJ: Blackwell Publishing.

13. cf., Falk, J.H. (in press). Human landscape preference. In T. Shackelford & V. Weekes-Shackelford (Eds.), *Encyclopedia of evolutionary psychological science.* New York: Springer.

14. Falk, J.H. & Balling, J.D. (2010). Evolutionary influence on human visual preference. *Environment and Behavior,* 42, 479–493.

15. Falk, J.H. & Balling, J.D. (2010). Evolutionary influence on human visual preference. *Environment and Behavior,* 42, 479–493.

16. Lengen, C. & Kistemann, T. (2012). Sense of place and place identity: Review of neuroscientific evidence. *Health & Place,* 18, 1162–1171.

17. cf., Lovelock, J.E. (1972. Gaia as seen through the atmosphere. *Atmospheric Environment,* 6, 579–580.

18. It is this phenomenon that likely contributed to Maslow observing a hierarchy of needs. The demands of the trillions of selves within humans, both those genetically related as well as those unrelated, "demand" that their well-being be satisfied. When these needs are not met, they make it difficult for other levels of self-related need to break through the cacophony of demands, but not impossible.

19. e.g., Denison, D. (1990). *Corporate culture and organizational effectiveness: Wiley series on organizational assessment and change.* Oxford, UK: John Wiley & Sons.

20. Gell-Mann, M. (2003). Regularities and randomness: Evolving schemata in science and the arts. In J. Casti & A. Karlqvist (Eds.), *Art and complexity* (pp. 47–58). New York: Elsevier.
    Ahmed, A., Elgazzar, A.E. & Hegazi, A.S. (2005). An overview of complex adaptive systems. *Mansoura Journal of Mathematics,* 32, 6059. Retrieved January 31, 2017. https://arxiv.org/pdf/nlin/0506059.pdf

21. Cilliers, P. (1998). *Complexity and postmodernism: Understanding complex adaptive systems.* Retrieved January 31, 2017. http://14.139.206.50:8080/jspui/bitstream/1/1690/1/Cilliers,%20Paul%20-%20Complexity%20and%20Postmodernism.pdf

22. e.g., Parrott, L. (2002). Complexity and the limits of ecological engineering. *Transactions of the ASAE,* 45(5), 1697–1702.
    Hammond, R.A. (2009). Complex systems modeling for obesity research. *Preventing Chronic Disease,* 6(3). Retrieved March 17, 2012. www.cdc.gov/pcd/issues/2009/Jul/09_0017.htm

23. cf., Boccara, N. (2004). *Modeling complex systems.* New York: Springer.

24. Parrott, L. (2002). Complexity and the limits of ecological engineering. *Transactions of the ASAE,* 45(5), 1697–1702.

25. Falk, J.H., Storksdieck, M., Dierking, L.D., Babendure, J., Canzoneri, N., Pattison, S., Meyer, D., Verbeke, M., Coe, M. & Palmquist, S. (2017). The learning SySTEM. In

R. Ottinger, (Ed.), *STEM ready America*. Flint, MI: Charles Stewart Mott Foundation. http://stemreadyamerica.org/read-the-compendium/ Retrieved June 5, 2017.

26. Falk, J.H. & Dierking, L.D. (2010). The 95% solution: School is not where most Americans learn most of their science. *American Scientist*, 98, 486–493.

27. Azevedo, F.S. (2011). Lines of practice: A practice-centered theory of interest relationships. *Cognition and Instruction*, 29, 147–184.

Department for Children, Schools, and Families. (2008). *The impact of parental involvement on children's education*. Nottingham, UK: DCSF Publications.

Dudo, A., Brossard, D., Shanahan, J., Scheufele, D.A., Morgan, M. & Signorielli, N. (2011). Science on television in the 21st Century: Recent trends in portrayals and their contributions to public attitudes toward science. *Communication Research*, 38(6), 754–777.

Falk, J.H., Dierking, L.D., Staus, N., Penuel, W., Wyld, J. & Bailey, D. (2016). Understanding youth STEM interest pathways within a single community: The Synergies Project. *International Journal of Science Education, Part B*, 6(4), 369-384.

Falk, J.H. & Needham, M. (2011). Measuring the impact of a science center on its community. *Journal of Research in Science Teaching*, 48, 1–12.

Fehrmann, P.G., Keith, T.Z. & Reimers, T.M. (1987). Home influence on school learning: Direct and indirect effects of parental involvement on high school grades. *Journal of Educational Research*, 80, 330–337.

Happer, C. & Philo, G. (2013). The role of the media in the construction of public belief and social change. *Journal of Social and Political Psychology*, 1(1). Retrieved June 21, 2016. http://jspp.psychopen.eu/article/view/96/37

Horrigan, J. (2006). *The internet as a resource for news and information about science*. Washington, DC: Pew Internet & American Life Project.

Ito, M., Baumer, S., Bittanti, M., Boyd, D., Cody, R., Herr-Stephenson, B., Horst, H.A., Lange, P.G., Mahendran, D., Martinez, K.Z., Pascoe, C., Perkel, D., Robinson, L., Sims, C. & Tripp, L. (2010). *Hanging out, messing around, and geeking out: Kids living and learning with new media*. Cambridge, MA: MIT Press.

Lewenstein, B.V. (2009). Science books since World War II. In D.P. Nord, M. Schudson & J. Rubin (Eds.), *The Enduring book: Publishing in Post-War America*. Chapel Hill: University of North Carolina Press.

Maltese, A.V. & Tai, R.H. (2010). Eyeballs in the fridge: Sources of early interest in science. *International Journal of Science Education*, 32(5), 669–685.

McCreedy, D. & Dierking, L.D. (2013). *Cascading influences: Long-term impacts of informal STEM experiences for girls*. Philadelphia: The Franklin Institute.

National Research Council. (2009). *Learning science in informal environments: People, places, and pursuits*. Washington, DC: The National Academies Press. doi:10.17226/12190

National Science Board. (2015). *Science and Engineering Indicators: 2014*. Washington, DC: Government Printing Office.

Takahashi, B. & Tandoc, E.C., Jr. (2015). Media sources, credibility, and perceptions of science: Learning about how people learn about science. *Public Understanding of Science*. Retrieved June 21, 2016. http://pus.sagepub.com/content/early/2015/03/18/0963662515574986

TASC. (2014). *After school and beyond*. New York: The After School Corporation. http://expandedschools.org/sites/default/files/TASC_LegacyReport_for_web.pdf

28. El Nokali, N., Bachman, H. & Votruba-Drzal, E. (2010). Parent involvement and children's academic and social development in elementary school. *Child Development*, 81(3), 988–1005.

29. Casey, B., Lombardi, C., Thomson, D., Nguyen, H.N., Paz, M., Teriault, C. & Dearing, E. (2016). Maternal support of children's early numerical concept learning predicts preschool and first-grade math achievement, *Child Development*. Retrieved January 23, 2017. http://onlinelibrary.wiley.com/doi/10.1111/cdev.12676/

30. Bonci, A., Mottram, E., McCoy, E. & Cole, J. (2011). A research review: The importance of families and the home environment. *National Literacy Trust*. Retrieved January 24,

2017. www.literacytrust.org.uk/assets/0000/7901/Research_review-importance_of_families_and_home.pdf

Dubos, E., Boxer, P. & Huesmann, L.R. (2009). Long-term effects of parental involvement on children's educational and occupational success: Mediation by family interactions, child aggression, and teenage aspirations. *Merrill Palmer Quarterly*, 55(3), 224–249.

31. The entire "unschooling" movement is predicated on this assumption (cf., Illich, I. (1971). *Deschooling society*. New York: Harper & Row; Holt, J. (1977–2001). *Growing Without Schooling Newsletter*.

32. Presumably very similar in process and product to the enculturation of religious beliefs described in Chapter 12.

33. Support for this assertion comes from the research of Carol Dweck (Dweck, C. (2000). *Self-Theories: Their role in motivation, personality and development*. New York: Psychology Press).

34. The model does predict that the most likely choice a person will make in any given moment is one that is exactly the same as the one that immediately preceded it. But in those relatively rare moments when a new choice needs to be made, the model cannot exactly predict what direction that new choice will take.

    The model also predicts that all choices are perceived by the individual making the choice as likely to satisfy a need and yield (short-term) well-being, but such choices may or may not pan out as "good" choices. And although all choices involve logic (the logic of satisfying critical needs), relatively few choices involve logical deliberation and even when they do, a person's choices might appear irrational to a third-party.

35. cf., Diamond, A. (2013). Executive functions. *Annual Review of Psychology*, 64, 135–168.

36. Mischel, W. (2014). *The marshmallow test: Conquering self-control*. New York: Little, Brown. Theoretically, one of the ways a variety of anti-depressive and attention deficit disorder medications might function is by slowing down the Well-Being System processes sufficiently to allow this kind of executive functioning to kick-in.

37. cf., discussion on models in: Levins, R. (1968). *Evolution in changing environments: Monographs in population biology, Number 2*. Princeton: Princeton University Press.

38. e.g., Miller, G.A. (1956). The magical number seven, plus or minus two: Some limits on our capacity for processing information. *Psychological Review*, 63(2), 81–97.

39. And as is typical in the social sciences, the self-reports of many people are elicited in response to a common set of treatments, often highly artificial treatments at that, and results are collected and statistically analyzed for patterns. Based on these patterns, WEIRD scientists assign names to the resulting categories, such as Deci and Ryan's autonomy, competence and relatedness categories (Deci, E.L. & Ryan, R.M. (1985). *Intrinsic motivation and self-determination in human behavior*. New York: Plenum). It is not that these categories are inherently wrong, in fact they are quite robust within the context in which they are used, it is just that they are descriptive, psychological abstractions. Describing a phenomenon is not the same as characterizing the underlying causative mechanisms.

40. An error that I too am of course making.

41. Social science has long lacked sufficient tools for measuring need-based choice-making across time; the analog of the time and energy studies of vertebrates. Also lacking are true cross-cultural measures of perceived need and choice-making. If such studies were conducted through the lens of Well-Being Systems I would predict that human choice-making will be found to be far more homogeneous than existing language- and behavior-based explanations have led us to believe.

# AFTERWORD

I can still remember the moment as if it was yesterday. It was early spring 1980 and I was in a hotel room in Chicago, having recently returned from a research trip to Africa. I was just awakening from a nap. Still half asleep, I suddenly realized that the key to understanding people and the choices they make lay in knowing how each individual perceived and acted upon their self-related needs. As I reflected further on this insight I had an *ah-ha* moment. In a flash I appreciated that the ability to respond to self-related needs is inherent in what it means to be alive—all living things make such choices, while non-living things do not. So too, the ability to perceive well-being. That from the beginning of life on earth, life's ability to maintaining well-being, and hence influence its survivability, depended upon its ability to have a sense of self, initially defined as the difference between "inside" and "outside." My insight was that all living things make choices, and the goal of these choices, whether accomplished or not, is to maximize perceptions of well-being, and in so doing increase the probabilities of survival.

If true, the implication of this insight was that choice-making in humans, as well as the dependence of choice on the perception of self-related needs, was highly unlikely to be a totally unique human phenomenon as it was typically treated within all of the social science models of which I was aware. Perhaps I thought, by better understanding the evolutionary roots of self-perceived needs, I could figure out how people perceive and attempt to advance their well-being, and in so doing, how and why people make the choices they do. If so, I reasoned, perhaps I could gain significant insights into the complexities of human behavior. At the time this seemed simple and straightforward, and even potentially groundbreaking. Many decades later I still think it is potentially a groundbreaking set of ideas, but it has turned out to be anything but simple and straightforward.

Nearly four decades have gone by and I am still thinking long and hard about these ideas. There were many reasons why this topic was so challenging. To begin with, every day, each human makes countless, seemingly unrelated choices. And that's just one person. Given that each person is different and each of the billions of people on the globe is engaged in an endless process of choice-making, what is the probability that all of these choices share anything in common? Further complicating matters, and arguably the most important challenge given the central role I imagined self-perceptions playing in this process, was the highly personal and infinitely complex ways that humans perceive and enact their sense of self.

Where and how to begin? Understanding the complexity of how humans make self-related choices requires insights from many fields, including in particular all of the social sciences—psychology, sociology, anthropology and even economics. In fact, the concept of the "self" plays a central role in all of these disciplines. However, issues of choice, self-perceptions of need and well-being play a central role in the humanities as well, including disciplines such as philosophy and religion. But implicit in my insight was that the roots of human choice, self-related needs and well-being go very, very deep; arguably reaching all the way back to the beginnings of life itself. Thus, my ability to understand these processes required transcending the social sciences and humanities and needed to include the biological sciences, and potentially the physical sciences as well. Particularly critical would be areas like evolutionary biology, microbiology, immunology, physiology, embryology, genetics and the wealth of new findings in the neural sciences.

Hence, the aptness of a quote by Edwin Schrodinger:

> We have inherited from our forefathers the keen longing for unified, all embracing knowledge . . . But the spread, both in width and depth, of the multifarious branches of knowledge during the last hundred odd years has confronted us with a queer dilemma. We feel clearly that we are only now beginning to acquire reliable material for welding together the sum total of all that is known into a whole; but, on the other hand, it has become next to impossible for a single mind fully to command more than a small specialized portion of it. I see no other escape from this dilemma (lest our true aim be lost forever) than that some of us should venture to embark on a synthesis of facts and theories, albeit with second hand and incomplete knowledge of some of them—and at the risk of making fools of ourselves.[1]

Specifically, it has become next to impossible for a single mind fully to command more than a small specialized portion of the vast knowledge represented by each of the many disciplines having important things to say about the topic of this book. Each of these numerous disciplines possesses a vast literature, each with its own unique jargon and each requiring at least some minimal knowledge in order to know where and how to even begin a meaningful inquiry. Although the task is now easier than ever before in human history due to the ubiquity of research literature on the Internet, it has been and remains a daunting journey. Nonetheless, it has been a journey I have enthusiastically embraced. To understand why requires knowing just a little bit about me, in other words, something about the choices I have made in my life.

I began my academic training pursuing dual interests in biology and education, in particular community ecology on the biology side, and a focus on how people learn on the education side. Unwilling to choose one of these two areas to focus on, I ended up conducting two studies and wrote two dissertations simultaneously, one in ecology and one in science learning. My first professional job after completing my joint doctorate was at the Smithsonian Institution's Chesapeake Bay Center for Environmental Studies,[2] a place where I could and did pursue both of my dual research agendas in ecology and educational psychology. For years, beginning in graduate school, I had been advised to pick one area or the other, but not both. Having already decided that working in two areas simultaneously was an okay idea, I blithely ignored this good advice. It was only around the early 1980s, nearly a decade after completing my doctoral work, and shortly after the epiphany referred to above, that I finally came to appreciate the wisdom of my elders. I realized I needed to focus my energies in just one research area lest I be doomed to a life of professional mediocrity, in not just one, but in both of my chosen areas. There just was not enough time to become excellent in each. Although I chose to pursue my social science interests, I never totally abandoned my deep and abiding interest in the biological sciences.

My work has always followed the path less trodden. For example, my biological research focused on the ecology of that quirky human invention the lawn, while my social science inquiries focused on how people learn, but not where most people studied learning, namely in either schools or laboratories, but in the places where people learn as part of their everyday lives. I studied lawns in order to better understand how humans impact the biological world and out-of-school, free-choice learning in order to understand how settings and situations affect what and why people choose to learn. I believe it is because of this personal quirk in my background and interests that I found myself willing and able to take on the challenges inherent in synthesizing the historically disparate realms of the social and biological sciences required for this book. It is my contention that the absence of this kind of synthesis in the past has contributed to the current general confusion and lack of unifying theory surrounding the nature of human choice, self, needs and well-being. Any useful insights that I might now offer in this regard are at least in part due to my unique perch in each of these broad arenas.

A thread running through all of my work through the years has been an effort to make sense of how organisms, be they flies or humans, perceive the world and choose to act upon those perceptions. For example, when I was 16 I wondered why people choose to walk down hallways in the ways they did—why did some people walk down the middle and others cling to the walls? Was there a preference for staying to the left or to the right? A decade later at 26 I was asking questions about why some kinds of insects choose to live in lawns and others not—why are spiders so common in prairie grasslands but rare in lawns? Simultaneously I was asking questions about why children learn differently in familiar and unfamiliar settings—what makes the learning that happens in places like museums so much more salient and memorable than the learning that typically happens in school? Another decade later I was now asking why some people choose to visit museums and others not—why would some people opt to visit a museum ten times a year while others never deign to set foot in such places? No matter what question I was pursuing though, I always enjoyed trying to see the world in a different way. And whether true or not, I always assumed that this openness to new perspectives afforded me insights others missed.

I know some will dismiss what I have written as nothing terribly new or profound; just a recasting of existing ways of thinking. For example, some have already suggested my Well-Being Systems model is nothing more than an updating of Maslow's Hierarchy of Needs. This would be a gross misunderstanding of both what my model represents as well as how I arrived at this new unified model of life processes. As suggested above I began with an insight that current explanations of human choice-making, as well as perceptions of self, need and well-being have been unduly constrained by the highly anthropocentric nature of most models. My starting point was trying to understand the evolutionary roots of these key processes; processes I believed went back to the beginnings of life. My ultimate goal was to develop a coherent theory that could accommodate not just observations of how people behaved under different circumstances but equally capable of accommodating current understandings derived from the neurosciences, physiology and biochemistry. I have always been data-driven. Though I did not begin my efforts with Maslow in mind, I came to appreciate, as many others have also, that Maslow was an astute observer of human behavior. This is why there is a high level of convergence between Maslow's efforts to explain human choice-making and mine.

Fortunately, over the three and a half decades that I have been pondering issues of choice, self-perception, self-related needs and well-being, the scientific enterprise has generated unprecedented insights into the biochemical machinery of life, the workings of the human brain and the evolutionary history of life in general, and humans, in particular. Although the basic outlines of the model I have presented in this book were formulated years ago, I have done my best to take advantage of as many of these new understandings as possible. Fortunately, as with Maslow, most of these new facts and findings seem to fit into the story I was trying to tell, but not always. Over the years, this model has undergone numerous revisions and refinements as I have attempted to insure that it is consistent with each new breakthrough. A truly unified theory needs to be consistent with all the data, not just some of it.

This is a daunting task. Every week someone tells me about a new book or article they think I should read and consider including in these pages. Writing a book like this is a little like painting a large bridge; in the time it takes to complete the task it is already clear that the process needs to begin anew. And so it has been. This book has had not only multiple drafts but multiple versions as I continually arrive at new understandings and think of new and better ways to communicate my ideas. By my count, this particular version represents the eleventh unique effort I made over the years to encapsulate these ideas within book form, each version involving multiple drafts. Each rewriting resulted in improvements, but ultimately I needed to declare, the bridge is painted!

I have no regrets though about investing the time and effort in bringing this book to fruition. If, as I believe, Well-Being Systems are inextricably linked to all life processes, then it follows that virtually everything now discovered about life in general and humans in particular must in some way connect to these processes. This is the gist of the grand tale I have spent more nearly 40 years pondering and a disproportionate amount of my days over the past six years attempting to capture in book form. In presenting this new model of Well-Being Systems I aspired to make my case authoritatively with ample references while eschewing the use of jargon and unnecessarily technical detail. From the beginning, my goal was to write a short, readable, academic book—three descriptors not often used in the same sentence. I wanted to do this so that this book would be accessible to as wide a range of readers from across both the social and biological sciences as possible, as well as the informed general public. Hopefully I got the balance right.

## In Appreciation

Whether I did get the balance right or not, I owe a sincere debt to a long list of individuals whose ideas both helped to frame my thinking and whose writings provided significant undergirding for the model I've created. All books, but certainly a book of this nature, arises from the collective ideas of many people. In particular I have been influenced by the thinking and writings of Antonio Damasio, Jerrold Siegel, Joseph LeDoux, John Torday, Paul Dolan, Bernd Simon, Mihayli Csikszentmihalyi, Eva Jablonka and Marion Lamb, Edward Deci and Richard Ryan, Francisco Varela, Lynn Margulis, Bruce Hood, Richard Dawkins, Michael Graziano and Sabine Kastner, Ed Diener, William James, Abraham Maslow, John Maynard Smith and Eors Szathmary, Daniel Kahneman, Erving Goffman, Jared Diamond, Albert Bandura, Merlin Donald and Dan McAdams.

I am also indebted to Lauren Leotti, Sheena Iyengar and Kevin Ochsner for not only their important scholarship but for coming up with such a compelling article title, which I shamelessly stole as the main title for this book.

Finally, I would particularly like to thank the following people who have encouraged and supported me during the writing of this book. Thank you to Nalini Nadkarni, Nicole Ardoin, Scott Pattison, Bill Penuel, Suzanne Hidi, Jeremy Babendure, Pat Shein, Martin Storksdieck, Dennis Schatz, Richard Toon, Doug Coulson, Ann Renninger, Areti Damala, Martha Fleming, Jack FitzSimmonds, Krissi Hewitt and Chris Bayne for reviewing and commenting on early drafts.

Particular thanks to Mitch Allen for believing in me and this book project and to John Torday for your inspired thinking, writings and intellectual guidance.

I also want to thank my Routledge editors Louisa Vahtrick and Marc Stratton, production manager Christine Cottone and copyeditor Charlotte Kading. Special thanks to my publicist John Madera for all his efforts on my behalf.

Also thank you to Nelda Reyes for identifying, interviewing and translating "Teresa's" amazing story. And to Nicolette Canzoneri for assisting with all of the End Notes and Bibliography.

Last, but definitely not least I am grateful to both my dear friend Joe Cone and my partner and colleague Lynn Dierking for sticking with me through these many years: Lynn for nearly all of the 37 and counting years of this journey. I have benefited from both your reviews and thoughtful comments on my way too many versions. More importantly, without your constant encouragement and tolerance of my seemingly never-ending fixation on this project I would never have been able to persist long enough to bring this project to completion. Thank you!

## Notes

1. Schrödinger, E. (1992/1944). *What is life?* Cambridge: Cambridge University Press, p. 1.
2. Currently called the Smithsonian Environmental Research Center.

From one, many.
From many, one.

# BIBLIOGRAPHY

Abramson, P.R. & Pinkerton, S.D. (1995). *With pleasure: Thoughts on the nature of human sexuality.* New York: Oxford University Press.

Achenbach, J. (2016). 3.7-billion-year-old fossils may be the oldest signs of life on Earth. *Washington Post.* Retrieved August 31, 2016. www.washingtonpost.com/news/speaking-of-science/wp/2016/08/31/3-7-billion-year-old-fossils-may-be-the-oldest-signs-of-life-on-earth/?utm_term=.a2c769c27e3f

Adami, C., Ofria, C. & Collier, T.C. (2000). Evolution of biological complexity. *Proceedings of the National Academy of Sciences* (USA), 97, 4463–4468.

Aggleton, J.P. (Ed.). (1992). *The Amygdala: Neurological aspects of emotion, memory, and mental dysfunction.* New York: Wiley-Liss.

Ahmed, A., Elgazzar, A.E. & Hegazi, A.S. (2005). An overview of complex adaptive systems. *Mansoura Journal of Mathematics,* 32, 6059. Retrieved January 31, 2017. https://arxiv.org/pdf/nlin/0506059.pdf

Ajzen, I. (1991). The theory of planned behavior. *Organizational Behavior and Human Decision Processes,* 50(2), 179–211.

Alister, H. (1979). *The spiritual nature of man.* Oxford, UK: Clarendon Press.

Amabile, T. (1996). *Creativity in context: Update to the social psychology of creativity.* Boulder, CO: Westview Press.

Andersson, M. (1994). *Sexual selection.* Princeton: Princeton University Press.

Ariely, D. (2016). *Payoff: The hidden logic that shapes our motivations.* New York: Simon & Schuster.

Aristotle, *Metaphysics,* Book I, chapter II. Retrieved January 17, 2016. http://classics.mit.edu/Aristotle/metaphysics.1.i.html

Armony, J. & Vuilleumier, P. (Eds.). (2013). *Cambridge handbook of human affective neuroscience.* Cambridge: Cambridge University Press.

Ashton, S.D. (2014). *Application of John Falk's visitor identities at Thanksgiving Point.* Poster presented at the Visitor's Studies Association Annual Conference, Albuquerque, NM.

Awramik, S.M. (1983). Filamentous fossil bacteria from the Archean of Western Australia. *Precambrian Research,* 20(2–4), 357–374.

Azevedo, F.S. (2011). Lines of practice: A practice-centered theory of interest relationships. *Cognition and Instruction,* 29, 147–184.

Bailenson, J., Yengar, S., Yee, N. & Collins, N. (2008). Facial similarity between voters and candidates causes influence. *Public Opinion Quarterly*, 72(5), 935–961.

Baker, D. & Keramidas, N. (2013). The psychology of hunger. *Monitor on Psychology*, 44(9), 66–67.

Bandura, A. (1977). Self-efficacy: Toward a unifying theory of behavioral change. *Psychological Review*, 84(2), 191–215.

Bandura, A. (1986). *Social foundations of thought and action: A social cognitive theory*. New York: Prentice-Hall.

Barber, N. (2012). *Why atheism will replace religion: The triumph of earthly pleasures over pie in the sky*. www.amazon.com/Atheism-Will-Replace-Religion-ebook/dp/B00886ZSJ6/

Barber, N. (2012). Why did religion evolve? *Psychology Today*. Retrieved January 15, 2017. www.psychologytoday.com/blog/the-human-beast/201206/why-did-religion-evolve

Bardack, N. & McAndrew, F. (1985). The influence of physical attractiveness and manner of dress on success in a simulated personnel decision. *Journal of Social Psychology*, 125, 777–778.

Bargh, J.A. (1997). The automaticity of everyday life. In R.S. Wyer, Jr. (Ed.), *Advances in social cognition* (Vol. 10, pp. 1–62). Hillsdale, NJ: Erlbaum.

Bargh, J.A. & Ferguson, M.J. (2000). Beyond behaviorism: On the automaticity of higher mental process. *Psychological Bulletin*, 126, 925–945.

Barnard, C.I. (1938). *The functions of the executive*. Cambridge, MA: Harvard University Press.

Baron-Cohen, S. (1995). *Mindblindness: An essay on autism and theory of mind*. Cambridge, MA: MIT Press.

Barrett, L., Henzi, P. & Dunbar, R. (2003). Primate cognition: From 'what now?' to 'what if?'. *Trends in Cognitive Science*, 7(11), 494–497.

Bartlett, F. (1932). *Remembering*. Cambridge: Cambridge University Press.

Batey, M. & Furnham, A. (2009). The relationship between creativity, schizotypy and intelligence. *Individual Differences Research*, 7, 272–284.

Baumeister, R. & Leary, M. (1995). The need to belong: Desire for interpersonal attachment as a fundamental human motivation. *Psychological Bulletin*, 117, 497–529.

BBC (2014). How parasites manipulate us. *BBC News Magazine*. Retrieved July 13, 2016. www.bbc.com/news/magazine-26240297

Bea, K. (2007). *Federal emergency management policy changes after Hurricane Katrina: A summary of statutory provisions*. Washington, DC: Congressional Research Service. Retrieved February 10, 2014. www.fas.org/sgp/crs/homesec/RL33729.pdf

Beard, J.G. & Ragheb, M.G. (1980). Measuring leisure satisfaction. *Journal of Leisure Research*, 12, 20–33.

Bekoff, M. (2001). Observations of scent-marking and discriminating self from others by a domestic dog (Canis familiaris): Tales of displaced yellow snow. *Behavioural Processes*, 55(2), 75–79.

Bell, D.E. (1982). Regret in decision making under uncertainty. *Opinions Research*, 30(5), 961–981.

Bem, D.J. (1972). Self-perception theory. In L. Berkowitz (Ed.), *Advances in experimental social psychology* (Vol. 6, pp. 1–62). New York: Academic Press.

Ben-Ze'ev, A. (2000). *The subtlety of emotions*. Cambridge, MA: MIT Press.

Beppu, A. & Griffiths, T.L. (2009). Iterated learning and the cultural ratchet. In N. Taatgen, H. van Rijn, L. Schomaker & J. Nerbonne (Eds.). *Proceedings of the 31st annual conference of the cognitive science society* (pp. 2089–2094). Austin, TX: Cognitive Science Society.

Berger, S.L., Kouzarides, T., Shiekhattar, R. & Shilatifard, A. (2009). An operational definition of epigenetics. *Genes Development*, 23(7), 781–783.

Berke, J.D. & Hyman, S.E. (2000). Addiction, dopamine, and the molecular mechanisms of memory. *Neuron*, 25(3), 515–532.

Berntson, G.G. & Caciaoppo, J.T. (1990). From homeostasis to allodynamic regulation. In J.T. Cacioppo, L.G. Tassinary & G.G. Berntson (Eds.), *Handbook of psychophysiology* (2nd ed., pp. 459–481). Cambridge: Cambridge University Press.

Biello, D. (2007). Evolving a mechanism to avoid sex with siblings. *Scientific American*. Retrieved February 7, 2014. www.scientificamerican.com/article/evolving-mechanism-avoid-sibling-sex/

Blokland, S. (2013). *Application of identity-related motivation instrument in Teylers Museum the Netherlands*. Unpublished Manuscript. Haarlem, The Netherlands.

Blouin-Hudon, E.-M. & Pchyl, T. (2015). Experiencing the temporally extended self: Initial support for the role of affective states, vivid mental imagery, and future self-continuity in the prediction of academic procrastination. *Personality and Individual Differences*, 86, 50–56.

Blower, T.D., Short, F.L., Rao, F., Mizuguchi, K., Pei, X.I., Finneran, P.C. & Luisi, B.F. (2012). Salmond GP identification and classification of bacterial Type III toxin-antitoxin systems encoded in chromosomal and plasmid genomes. *Nucleic Acids Research*, 40, 6158–6173.

Bluck, S. & Gluck, J. (2004). Making things better and learning a lesson: Experiencing wisdom across the lifespan. *Journal of Personality*, 72, 543–572.

Blume, L.E. & Easley, D. (2008). Rationality. In S. N. Durflauf & L. E. Blume (Eds.). *The New Palgrave Dictionary of Economics* (2nd ed.) (pp. 884–893). London: Macmillan.

BobB. (2010). Same name, two different things. *Chowhound*. Retrieved November 13, 2016. www.chowhound.com/post/725469

Boccarra, N. (2004). *Modeling complex systems*. New York: Springer.

Boesch, C. (2009). *The real chimpanzees: Sex strategies in the forest*. Cambridge: Cambridge University Press.

Bonci, A., Mottram, E., McCoy, E. & Cole, J. (2011). A research review: The importance of families and the home environment. *National Literacy Trust*. Retrieved January 24, 2017. www.literacytrust.org.uk/assets/0000/7901/Research_review-importance_of_families_and_home.pdf

Bonnellan, M.B., Trzesniewski, K.H., Robins, R.W., Moffitt, T.E. & Caspi, A. (2005). Low self-esteem is related to aggression, antisocial behavior, and delinquency. *Psychological Sciences*, 16(4), 328–335.

Bonner, J.T. (1980). *The evolution of culture in animals*. Princeton, NJ: Princeton University Press.

Bonner, J.T. (2006). *Why size matters*. Princeton: Princeton University Press.

Borg, J., Andree, B., Doderstrom, H. & Farde, L. (2003). The serotonin system and spiritual experiences. *American Journal of Psychiatry*, 160(11), 1965–1969.

Botvinick, M. & Cohen, J. (1998). Rubber hands 'feel' touch that eyes see. *Nature*, 391, 756.

Bradberry, T. (2015). Do you have emotional intelligence? Here's how to know for sure. *Inc.* Retrieved March 15, 2016. www.inc.com/travis-bradberry/are-you-emotionally-intelligent-here-s-how-to-know-for-sure.html

Brand, R.J., Markey, C.M., Mills, A. & Hodges, S. (2007). Sex differences in self-reported infidelity and its correlates. *Sex Roles*, 57, 101–109.

Bransford, J.D., Brown, A.L. & Cocking, R.R. (1999). *How people learn: Brain, mind, experience, and school*. Washington, DC: National Academy Press.

Breed, M. & Sanchez, L. (2012). Both environment and genetic makeup influence behavior. *Nature Education Knowledge*, 3(10), 68.

Brini, M., Call, T., Ottolini, D. & Carafoli, E. (2013). Chapter 5 Intracellular calcium homeostasis and signaling. In L. Banci (Ed.), *Metallomics and the cell: Metal ions in life sciences* (Vol. 12, pp. 119–168). Dordrecht: Springer.

Bronfenbrenner, U. (1979). *The ecology of human development.* Cambridge, MA: Harvard University Press.

Brooker, L. & Woodhead, M. (2008). *Developing positive identities.* London: The Open University.

Brown, G., Fairfax, S., Sarao, N. & Anonymous, S. (2013). *Human evolution.* Retrieved August 11, 2013. http://tolweb.org/treehouses/?treehouse_id=3710

Bruner, J. (1986). *Actual minds, possible worlds.* Cambridge, MA: Harvard University Press.

Burgess, H. (2003). Stereotypes/characterization frames. In G. Burgess & H. Burgess (Eds.), *Beyond intractability.* Boulder, CO: Conflict Information Consortium, University of Colorado. Retrieved July 24, 2014. www.beyondintractability.org/essay/stereotypes

Burt, A. (2000). Perspective: Sex, recombination, and the efficacy of selection—Was Weismann right? *Evolution,* 54(2), 337–351.

Buss, D.M. (2003). *The evolution of desire: Strategies of human mating* (rev. ed.). New York: Basic Books.

Caldarado, N. (2007). Caching, money, magic, derivatives, mana and modern finance. *Journal of World Anthropology: Occasional Papers,* 3(2), 1–47.

Calvin, W.H. (1997). *How brains think.* New York: Basic Books.

Cantor, N., Mischel, W. & Schwarz, J. (1982). A prototype analysis of psychological situations. *Cognitive Psychology,* 14, 45–77.

Casey, B., Lombardi, C., Thomson, D., Nguyen, H.N., Paz, M., Teriault, C. & Dearing, E. (2017). Maternal support of children's early numerical concept learning predicts preschool and first-grade math achievement. *Child Development,* 88(1), 263–281.

Cavalier-Smith, T. (2004). The membranome and membrane heredity in development and evolution. In R.P. Hirt & D.S. Horner (Eds.), *Organelles, genomes and eukaryote phylogeny: An evolutionary synthesis in the age of genomics* (pp. 335–351). Boca Raton, FL: CRC Press.

Cha, A.J. (2016). People on the autism spectrum live an average of 18 years less than everyone else study finds. *Washington Post.* Retrieved March 18, 2016. www.washingtonpost.com/news/to-your-health/wp/2016/03/18/people-on-the-autism-spectrum-live-an-average-of-18-years-less-than-everyone-else-study-finds/?hpid=hp_hp-cards_hp-card-national%3Ahomepage%2Fcard

Chai, S.K. (2001). *Choosing an identity.* Ann Arbor, MI: University of Michigan Press.

Chervyakov, A.V., Sinitsyn, D.O. & Piradov, M.A. (2016). Variability of neuronal responses: Types and functional significance of neuroplasticity and Neural Darwinism. *Frontiers of Human Neuroscience.* https://doi.org/10.3389/fnhum.2016.00603

Chimpanzee Protection. (n.d.). Retrieved March 20, 2016 from Jane Goodall Institute of Canada: www.janegoodall.ca/about-chimp-behaviour-diet.php

Chomsky, N. (2002). *On language and nature.* Cambridge: Cambridge University Press.

Christiansen, M. & Kirby, H. (2003). Consensus and controversies. *TRENDS in Cognitive Sciences,* 7(7), 300–307.

Christopher, A. (April 2013). *Practical applications of the Falk visitor identity model.* Colorado-Wyoming Association of Museums Annual Meeting, Golden, CO.

Cilliers, P. (1998). *Complexity and Postmodernism: Understanding complex adaptive systems.* http://14.139.206.50:8080/jspui/bitstream/1/1690/1/Cilliers,%20Paul%20-%20Complexity%20and%20Postmodernism.pdf

Clark, A. (1997). *Being there: Putting brain, body and world together again.* Cambridge: MIT Press.

Clark, R. (2015). Mystery man. *National Geographic,* 228(4), 30–57.

Clasadonte, J., McIver, S.R., Schmitt, L.I., Halassa, M.M. & Haydon, P.G. (2014). Chronic sleep restriction disrupts sleep homeostasis and behavioral sensitivity to alcohol by reducing the extracellular accumulation of adenosine. *Journal of Neuroscience*, 34, 1879–1891.

Cloninger, C.R. (2004). *Feeling good: The science of well-being.* Oxford: Oxford University Press.

Cofer, C.N. & Appley, M.H. (1964). Homeostatic concepts and motivation. In C.N. Cofer & M.H. Appley (Eds.), *Motivation: Theory and research* (pp. 302–365). New York: Wiley.

Constable, T. (2001). *Chimpanzees: Social climbers of the forest.* New York: Dorling Kindersley.

Contie, V. (2012). Organ transplants without lifelong drugs. *NIH Research Matters.* Retrieved March 14, 2014. www.nih.gov/researchmatters/march2012/03192012transplants.htm

Conway, M.A. & Loveday, C. (2015). Remembering, imagining, false memories & personal meanings. *Consciousness and Cognition*, 33, 574–581.

Cookson, J. (2013). The neurological origins of religious belief. *Big Think.com.* Retrieved January 13, 2017. http://bigthink.com/going-mental/the-neurological-origins-of-religious-belief

Cooper, C.R. (1999). Multiple selves, multiple worlds: Cultural perspectives on individuality and connectedness in adolescence development. In A. Masten, (Ed.), *Minnesota symposium on child psychology: Cultural processes in development* (pp. 25–57). Mahwah, NJ: Lawrence Erlbaum Associates.

Cooper, M.D. & Herrin, B.R. (2010). How did our complex immune system evolve? *Nature Reviews Immunology*, 10, 2–3.

Cosgrove, T. (2014). LIFE at Lascaux: First color photographs from another world. *Time.* Retrieved July 26, 2016. http://time.com/3879943/lascaux-early-color-photos-of-the-famous-cave-paintings-france-1947/#

Costello, J. (1985). *Love sex and war: Changing values, 1939–45.* London: William Collins.

Cottrell, L. (1968). *The warrior pharaohs.* London: Evan Brothers.

Crabbe, J.C. (2002). Genetic contributions to addiction. *Annual Review of Psychology*, 53, 435–462.

Covel, J. (2009). *Using Falk's identity-related motivations to support guest services at the Monterey Bay Aquarium.* Paper presented at the Annual Meeting of the American Association of Museums, May 1, 2010, Philadelphia, PA.

Crawford, B. (2016). Earliest evidence of religious beliefs. *People of: Our everyday life.* Retrieved July 26, 2016. http://peopleof.oureverydaylife.com/earliest-evidence-religious-beliefs-4240.html

Cresswell, T. (2005). *Place: A short introduction.* Hoboken, NJ: Blackwell Publishing.

Crucianelli, L., Metcalf, N.K., Fotopoulou, A. & Jenkinson, P.M. (2013). Bodily pleasure matters: Velocity of touch modulates body ownership during the rubber hand illusion. *Frontiers of Psychology*, 4, 1–7.

Cruwys, T., Bevelander, K.E. & Hermans, R. (2015). Social modeling of eating: A review of when and why social influence affects food intake and choice. *Appetite*, 86, 3–18.

Csikszentmihalyi, M. (1990). *Flow: The psychology of optimal experience.* New York: Harper Perennial.

Csikszentmihalyi, M. & Hermanson, K. (1995). Intrinsic motivation in museums: Why does one want to learn? In J. Falk & L. Dierking (Eds.), *Public institutions for personal learning.* Washington, DC: American Association of Museums.

Damasio, A.R. (1994). *Descartes' error: Emotion, reason, and the human brain.* New York: Avon Books.

Damasio, A.R. (1999). *The feeling of what happens: Body and emotion in the making of consciousness.* New York: Harcourt Brace & Company.

Damasio, A.R. (2010). *Self comes to mind.* New York: Vintage.

Damasio, A.R. (2011). Neural basis of emotions. *Scholarpedia*, 6(3), 1804. Retrieved December 8, 2016. www.scholarpedia.org/article/Neural_basis_of_emotions

Damasio, A.R. & Damasio, H. (2016). Exploring the concept of homeostasis and considering its implication for economics. *Journal of Economic Behavior & Organization*, 126, 125–129.

Darwin, C. (1871). *The Descent of man, and selection in relation to sex*. London: John Murray.

Dawkins, R. (1976). *The selfish gene*. Oxford: Oxford University Press.

Dawkins, R. (1986). *The blind watchmaker: Why the evidence of evolution reveals a universe without design*. New York: Norton.

Dawkins, R. & Krebs, R.J. (1979). Arms races between and within species. *Proceedings of the Royal Society Biological Sciences Series B*, 205, 489–511.

Deamer, D.W. (1986). Role of amphiphilic compounds in the evolution of membrane structure on the early earth. *Origins of Life and the Evolution of the Biosphere*, 17, 3–25.

Deamer, D., Dworkin, J.P., Sandford, S.A., Bernstein, M.P. & Allamandola, L.J. (2002). The first cell membranes. *Astrobiology*, 2, 371–381.

Decety, J. & Chaminade, T. (2003). Neural correlates of feeling sympathy. *Neuropsychologia*, 41, 127–138.

deCharms, R. (1968). *Personal causation: The internal affective determinants of behavior*. New York, NY: Academic Press.

Deci, E.L. & Ryan, R.M. (1985). *Intrinsic motivation and self-determination in human behavior*. New York: Plenum.

Deci, E.L. & Ryan, R.M. (2000). The 'what' and 'why' of goal pursuits: Human needs and the self-determination of behavior. *Psychological Inquiry*, 11, 227–268.

de Groot, A. (1965). *Thought and choice in chess*. The Hague, Netherlands: Mouton.

del Bosque, I.R. & Martin, H.S. (2008). Tourist satisfaction: A cognitive–affective model. *Annals of Tourism Research*, 35(2), 551–573.

del Bosque, I.R., Martın, H.S. & Collado, J. (2006). The role of expectations in the consumer satisfaction formation process: Empirical evidence in the travel agency sector. *Tourism Management*, 27, 410–419.

DeMoraes, C.M., Lewis, W.J., Pare, P.W., Alborn, H.T. & Tumlinson, J.H. (1998). Herbivore-infested plants selectively attract parasitoids. *Nature*, 393, 570–573.

Denison, D. (1990). *Corporate culture and organizational effectiveness: Wiley series on organizational assessment and change*. Oxford: John Wiley & Sons.

Dennett, D. (1978). *Brainstorms: Philosophical essays on mind and psychology*. Cambridge, MA: MIT Press.

Dennett, D. (2013). *Intuition pumps and other tools for thinking*. New York: W. W. Norton & Company.

Department for Children, Schools, and Families. (2008). *The impact of parental involvement on children's education*. Nottingham, UK: DCSF Publications.

Descartes, R. (1960). *Discourse on method and meditations*. L.J. Lafleur (trans). New York: The Liberal Arts Press.

Desrumaux, P., De Bosscher, S. & Leoni, V. (2009). Effects of facial attractiveness, gender, and competence of applications on job recruitment. *Swiss Journal of Psychology*, 68(1), 33–42.

Diamond, A. (2013). Executive functions. *Annual Review of Psychology*, 64, 135–168.

Diamond, J. (1997). *Why is sex fun? The evolution of human sexuality*. New York: Basic Books.

Diamond, J. (2012). *The world until yesterday*. New York: Viking.

Diener, E. (2015). *Subjective well-being scales*. Retrieved December 8, 2016. https://internal.psychology.illinois.edu/~ediener/scales.html

Diener, E. & Biswas-Diener, R. (2008). *Happiness: Unlocking the mysteries of psychological wealth.* Malden, MA: Blackwell Publishing.

Dinstein, I., Heeger, D.J. & Behrmann, M. (2015). Neural variability: Friend or foe? *Trends in Cognitive Science,* 19, 322–328.

Di Pellegrino, G., Fadiga, L., Fogassi, L., Gallese, V. & Rizzolatti, G. (1992). Understanding motor events: A neurophysiological study. *Experimental Brain Research,* 91, 176–180.

Dolan, P. (2014). *Happiness by design: Finding pleasure and purpose in everyday life.* London: Penguin.

Dolan, R.J. (2002). Emotion, cognition, and behavior. *Science,* 298(5596), 1191–1194.

Donald, M. (2012). Evolutionary origins of autobiographical memory systems: A retrieval hypothesis. In D. Berntsen & D.C. Rubin (Eds.), *Understanding autobiographical memory: Theories and approaches* (pp. 269–289). Cambridge: Cambridge University Press.

Driver, B.L. & Tocher, S.R. (1970). Toward a behavioral interpretation of recreational engagements, with implications for planning. In B.L. Driver (Ed.), *Elements of outdoor recreation planning: Proceedings of a national short course held in Ann Arbor, Michigan, May 6–16, 1968* (pp. 9–31). Ann Arbor, MI: University of Michigan.

Dr. M. (2015). What is fun about being a scientist. Dr. M. on Science, Research & Scientists. Retrieved January 15, 2017. http://dr-monsrs.net/tag/scientist-career-satisfaction/

Dubos, E., Boxer, P. & Huesmann, L.R. (2009). Long-term effects of parental involvement on children's educational and occupational success: Mediation by family interactions, child aggression, and teenage aspirations. *Merrill Palmer Quarterly,* 55(3), 224–249.

Dudo, A., Brossard, D., Shanahan, J., Scheufele, D.A., Morgan, M. & Signorielli, N. (2011). Science on television in the 21st century: Recent trends in portrayals and their contributions to public attitudes toward science. *Communication Research,* 38(6), 754–777.

Duhigg, C. (2012). *The power of habit.* New York: Random House.

Dunbar, R. (1992). Neocortex size as a constraint on group size in primates. *Journal of Human Evolution,* 22(6), 469–493.

Dunbar, R. (1998). The social brain hypothesis. *Evolutionary Anthropology,* 6, 178–190.

Dweck, C. (2000). *Self-theories: Their role in motivation, personality and development.* New York: Psychology Press.

Dwyer, G. (1985). *War.* New York: Crown.

Eagleman, D. (2011). *Incognito: The secret lives of the brain.* New York: Vintage.

Eagleman, D. (2015). *The brain: The story of you.* New York: Pantheon.

Early Human Culture. (n.d.). Retrieved August 11, 2013 from palomar.edu: http://anthro.palomar.edu/homo/homo_4.htm

Eccles, J.C. (1992). Evolution of consciousness. *Proceedings of the National Academies of Science USA,* 89, 7320–7324.

Edelman, G. (1978). *The mindful brain.* Cambridge, MA: MIT Press.

Edelman, G. (1989). *Neural Darwinism—The theory of neuronal group selection.* New York: Basic Books.

Edelman, G. & Tononi, G. (2000). *A universe of consciousness.* New York: Basic Books.

Edelman, G. & Tononi, G. (2000). Reentry and the dynamic core. In T. Metzinger (Ed.), *Neural correlates of consciousness: Empirical and conceptual questions* (pp. 121–138). Cambridge, MA: MIT Press.

Edison, T.A. (c. 1903). Spoken statement, published in *Harper's Monthly* (September 1932).

Edward, D.A. (2014). The description of mate choice. *Behavioral Ecology,* 26, 301–310.

Eid, M. & Larsen, R.J. (Eds.). (2008). *The science of subjective well-being.* New York: The Guildford Press.

Elder, G.H.J. (1969). Appearance and education in marriage mobility. *American Sociological Review,* 34(4), 519–533.

Elizando, D. (2014). *Adicionalmente al SAV 2013, la antigua Dirección de Mediación y Evaluación realizó un estudio basado en el Modelo de la Experiencia de los Visitantes diseñado por John Falk.* Unpublished Manuscript. Mexico City: Papalote.

El Nokali, N., Bachman, H. & Votruba-Drzal, E. (2010). Parent involvement and children's academic and social development in elementary school. *Child Development*, 81(3), 988–1005.

Erikson, E.H. (1963). *Childhood and society* (2nd ed.). New York: Norton.

Ersner-Hershfield, H., Elliott Wimmer, G. & Knutson, B. (2009). Saving for the future self: Neural measures of future self-continuity predict temporal discounting. *Social Cognitive and Affective Neuroscience*, 4(1), 85–92.

Falk, J.H. (1981). *The origin of self.* Unpublished Manuscript.

Falk, J.H. (2006). An identity-centered approach to understanding museum learning. *Curator*, 49(2), 151–166.

Falk, J.H. (2009). *Identity and the museum visitor experience.* Walnut Creek, CA: Left Coast Press.

Falk, J.H. (2016). Museum audiences: A visitor-centered perspective. *Loisir et Société/Leisure and Society*, 39(3), 357–370.

Falk, J.H. (in press). Human landscape preference. In T. Shackelford & V. Weekes-Shackelford (Eds.), *Encyclopedia of evolutionary psychological science.* New York: Springer.

Falk, J.H., Ballantyne, R., Packer, J. & Benckendorff, P. (2012). Travel and learning: A neglected tourism research area. *Annals of Tourism Research*, 39(2), 908–927.

Falk, J.H. & Balling, J.D. (2010). Evolutionary influence on human visual preference. *Environment and Behavior*, 42, 479–493.

Falk, J.H. & Dierking, L.D. (2000). *Learning from museums.* Lanham, MD: Altamira Press.

Falk, J.H. & Dierking, L.D. (2010). The 95% solution: School is not where most Americans learn most of their science. *American Scientist*, 98, 486–493.

Falk, J.H. & Dierking, L.D. (2015). *The museum visitor experience revisited.* Walnut Creek, CA: Left Coast Press.

Falk, J.H. & Dierking, L.D. (in press). *Learning from museums* (2nd ed.). Lanham, MD: Rowman Littlefield.

Falk, J.H., Dierking, L.D., Staus, N., Penuel, W., Wyld, J. & Bailey, D. (2016). Understanding youth STEM interest pathways within a single community: The Synergies Project. *International Journal of Science Education, Part B*, 6(4), 369–384.

Falk, J.H., Heimlich, J. & Bronnenkant, K. (2008). Using identity-related visit motivations as a tool for understanding adult zoo and aquarium visitor's meaning making. *Curator*, 51(1), 55–80.

Falk, J.H. & Lynch, J.F. (1981). *The evolution and ecology of information.* Unpublished Manuscript.

Falk, J.H. & Needham, M. (2011). Measuring the impact of a science center on its community. *Journal of Research in Science Teaching*, 48, 1–12.

Falk, J.H., Scott, C., Dierking, L.D., Rennie, L.J. & Cohen Jones, M. (2004). Interactives and visitor learning. *Curator*, 47(2), 171–198.

Falk, J.H. & Storksdieck, M. (2010). Science learning in a leisure setting. *Journal of Research in Science Teaching*, 47(2), 194–212.

Falk, J.H., Storksdieck, M., Dierking, L.D., Babendure, J., Canzoneri, N., Pattison, S., Meyer, D., Verbeke, M., Coe, M. & Palmquist, S. (2017). The learning SySTEM. In R. Ottinger, (Ed.), *STEM ready America.* Flint, MI: Charles Stewart Mott Foundation. Retrieved June 5, 2017. http://stemreadyamerica.org/read-the-compendium/

Faragher, E.B., Cass, M. & Cooper, C.L. (2005). The relationship between job satisfaction and health: A meta-analysis. *Occupational & Environmental Medicine*, 62, 105–112.

Fasko, D., Jr. (2006). Creative thinking and reasoning. In J.C. Kaufman & J. Baer (Eds.), *Creativity and reason in cognitive development* (pp. 159–176). New York: Cambridge University Press.

Fearon, J.D. (1999). *What is identity (as we now use the term)?* Unpublished Manuscript. Retrieved July 10, 2013. www.stanford.edu/~jfearon/papers/iden1v2.pdf

Fehr, E. & Fischbacher, U. (2003). The nature of human altruism. *Nature*, 425, 785–791.

Fehrmann, P.G., Keith, T.Z. & Reimers, T.M. (1987). Home influence on school learning: Direct and indirect effects of parental involvement on high school grades. *Journal of Educational Research*, 80, 330–337.

Fernández-Huerga, E. (2008). The economic behavior of human beings: The institutional/Post-Keynesian model. *Journal of Economic Issues*, 42(3), 709–726.

Ferrari, P.F. & Rizzolatti, G. (2014). Mirror neuron research: The past and the future. *Philosophical Transactions of the Royal Society B*, 269, 169–173.

Ferro, S. (2014). Scientists debunk the myth that 10,000 hours of practice will make you an expert. *FastCompany*. Outliers. Retrieved February 12, 2017. www.fastcodesign.com/3027564/asides/scientists-debunk-the-myth-that-10000-hours-of-practice-makes-you-an-expert

Finn, P. (2006). Bias and blinding: Self-fulfilling prophecies and intentional ignorance. *The ASHA Leader*, 11(8), 16–17, 22.

Fishbein, M. & Ajzen, I. (1975). *Belief, attitude, intention, and behavior: An introduction to theory and research*. Reading, MA: Addison-Wesley.

Fivush, R. & Nelson, K. (2004). Culture and language in the emergence of autobiographical memory. *Psychological Science*, 15, 573–577.

Flegr, J. (2007). Effects of *Toxoplasma* on human behavior. *Schizophrenia Bulletin*, 33(3), 757–760.

Foster, K.R., Wenseleers, T. & Ratnieks, F.L.W. (2006). Kin selection is the key to altruism. *TRENDS in Evolution and Ecology*, 21(2), 57–59.

Freeman, W. (2000). *How brains make up their mind*. New York: Columbia University Press.

Freysinger, V.J. & Kelly, J.R. (2004). *21st century leisure: Current issues*. State College, PA: Venture Publishing.

Friedman, M. (1953). *Essays in positive economics, Part I—The methodology of positive economics*. Chicago: University of Chicago Press.

Fukui, H. & Toyoshima, K. (2008). Music facilitates the neurogenesis, regeneration and repair of neurons. *Medical Hypotheses*, 71(5), 765–769.

Furnham, A., Batey, M., Anand, K. & Manfield, J. (2008). Personality, hypomania, intelligence and creativity. *Personality and Individual Differences*, 44, 1060–1069.

Gabora, L. & Kaufman, S. (2010). Evolutionary perspectives on creativity. In J. Kaufman & R. Sternberg (Eds.), *The Cambridge handbook of creativity* (pp. 279–300). Cambridge, UK: Cambridge University Press.

Galaburda, A.M. & Kosslyn, S.M. (2002). *Languages of the brain*. Cambridge, MA: Harvard University Press.

Gallup, G.G., Jr., Anderson, J.R. & Shillito, D.J. (2002). The mirror test. In M. Bekoff, C. Allen & G. M. Burghardt (Eds.) *The cognitive animal: Empirical and theoretical perspectives on animal cognition* (pp. 325–333). Cambridge, MA: MIT Press.

Gangestad, S.W., Haselton, M.G. & Buss, D.M. (2006). Evolutionary foundations of cultural variation: Evoked culture and mate preferences. *Psychological Inquiry*, 17(2), 75–95.

Gardner, H. (1983). *Frames of mind: The theory of multiple intelligences*. New York: Basic Books.

Garner, D.M. & Garfinkel, P.E. (Eds.). (1997). *Handbook of treatment for eating disorders* (2nd ed., Chapter 8, pp. 145–177). New York: Guilford Press.

Gauthier, D. (1986). *Morals by agreement.* Oxford: Oxford University Press.

Gazzaniga, M.S. (2008). *Human: The science behind what makes your brain unique.* New York: HarperCollins.

Gee, J.P. (2001). Identity as an analytic lens for research in education. *Review of Research in Education,* 25, 99–125.

Geertz, C. (1966). Religion as a cultural system. In M. Banton (Ed.), *Anthropological approaches to the study of religion* (pp. 1–46). London: Tavistock.

Geertz, C. (1973). *The interpretation of cultures.* New York: Basic Books.

Gelber, S.M. (1999). *Hobbies: Leisure and the culture of work in America.* New York: Columbia University Press.

Gell-Mann, M. (2003). Regularities and randomness: Evolving schemata in science and the arts. In J. Casti & A. Karlqvist (Eds.), *Art and complexity* (pp. 47–58). New York: Elsevier.

Gerald Edelman. (n.d.). Retrieved January 7, 2017 from Wikipedia: https://en.wikipedia.org/wiki/Gerald_Edelman

Gilbert, S.F. (2001). Ecological developmental biology: Developmental biology meets the real world. *Developmental Biology,* 233, 1–12.

Giordano, M. (2013). Homeostasis: An underestimated focal point of ecology and evolution. *Plant Sciences,* 211, 92–101.

Gladwell, M. (2000). *The tipping point: How little things can make a big difference.* New York: Little, Brown and Company.

Gladwell, M. (2006). *Blink: The power of thinking without thinking.* New York: Little, Brown.

Glassey, S. (2010). Owners willing to risk lives for pets—Survey. *News.com.au.* Retrieved February 7, 2014. www.news.com.au/breaking-news/owners-willing-to-risk-lives-for-pets-survey/story-e6frfku0-1225834438263

Gladwell, M. (2008). *Outliers.* New York: Little, Brown and Company.

Goffman, E. (1959). *The presentation of self in everyday life.* New York: Doubleday.

Goldman, D. (2012). *Our genes our choices: How genotype and gene actions affect behavior.* Amsterdam: Elsevier.

Goldstein, J.S. (2001). *War and gender: How gender shapes the war system and vice versa.* Cambridge: Cambridge University Press. Retrieved February 11, 2016. www.warandgender.com/wggensex.htm

Goleman, D. (2006). *Social intelligence: The new science of human relationships.* New York: Bantam Books.

Goleman, D. (2011). Are women more emotionally intelligent than men? *Psychology Today.* Retrieved January 11, 2017. www.psychologytoday.com/blog/the-brain-and-emotional-intelligence/201104/are-women-more-emotionally-intelligent-men

Gompers, S. (1890). *What does the working man want?* Retrieved March 10, 2016. www.historymuse.net/readings/GompersWhatdoestheworkingmanwant.htm

Gordon, C. & Heath, J. (1986). Integration and central processing in temperature regulation. *Annual Review of Physiology,* 48, 595–612.

Gottschall, J. (2012). *The storytelling animal: How stories make us human.* New York: Houghton Mifflin Harcourt.

Gould, S.J. (1990). *The Panda's Thumb: More reflections in natural history.* Harmondsworth: Penguin Books.

Gould, S.J. & Vrba, E.S. (1982). Exaptation—A missing term in the science of form. *Paleobiology,* 8(1), 4–15.

Graefe, A.R. & Fedler, A.J. (1986). Situational and subjective determinants of satisfaction in marine recreational fishing. *Leisure Sciences,* 8, 275–295.

Grafen, A. (1998). Green beard as death warrant. *Nature,* 394(6693), 521–522. http://users.ox.ac.uk/~grafen/cv/grbeard.pdf

Gramling, C. (2016). Hints of oldest life on earth. *Science.* Retrieved August 31, 2016. www.sciencemag.org/news/2016/08/hints-oldest-fossil-life-found-greenland-rocks

Gray, P. & Garcia, J. (2013). *Evolution and human sexual behavior.* Cambridge, MA: Harvard University Press.

Graziano, M. (2011). Is spirituality a byproduct of evolution? *Huffington Post.* Retrieved January 15, 2017. www.huffingtonpost.com/michael-graziano/spirituality-as-byproduct-of-evolution_b_918801.html

Graziano, M. (2013). *Consciousness and the social brain.* Oxford: Oxford University Press.

Graziano, M.S.A. & Kastner, S. (2011). Human consciousness and its relationship to social neuroscience: A novel hypothesis. *Cognitive Neuroscience,* 2, 98–113.

Green, M.J. & Phillips, M.L. (2004). Social threat perception and the evolution of paranoia. *Neuroscience and Biobehavioral Reviews,* 28, 333–342.

Griffin, D.R. & Speck, G.B. (2004). New evidence of animal consciousness. *Animal Cognition,* 7(1), 5–18.

Griffiths, T.L., Christian, B.R. & Kalish, M.L. (2008). Using category structures to test iterated learning as a method for identifying inductive biases. *Cognitive Science,* 32(1), 68–107.

Grupe, D.W. & Nitschke, J. (2013). Uncertainty and anticipation in anxiety. *National Review of Neuroscience,* 14(7), 488–501.

Guthrie, S.E. (2000). Projection. In W. Braun & R.T. McCutcheon (Eds.), *Guide to the study of religion* (pp. 225–226). London: Cassell.

Habermas, T. & Bluck, S. (2000). Getting a life: The emergence of the life story in adolescence. *Psychological Bulletin,* 126, 748–769.

Habermas, T. & Paha, C. (2001). The development of coherence in adolescents' life narratives. *Narrative Inquiry,* 11, 35–54.

Halassa, M.M., Florian, C., Fellin, T., Munoz, J.R., Lee, S.Y., Abel, T., Haydon, P.G. & Frank, M.G. (2009). Astrocytic modulation of sleep homeostasis and cognitive consequences of sleep loss. *Neuron,* 61, 216–219.

Hall, B.K., Hallgrímsson, B. & Strickberger, M.W. (2008). *Strickberger's evolution: The integration of genes, organisms and populations* (4th ed.). Sudbury, MA: Jones and Bartlett Publishers.

Hall, S. (1992). The question of cultural identity. In S. Hall & T. McGrew (Eds.), *Modernity and its futures* (pp. 273–326). Cambridge: Polity Press.

Hamilton, W.D. (1964). The genetical evolution of social behaviour. I. *Journal of Theoretical Biology,* 7, 1–16.

Hammond, R.A. (2009). Complex systems modeling for obesity research. *Preventing Chronic Disease,* 6(3). Retrieved March 17, 2012. www.cdc.gov/pcd/issues/2009/Jul/09_0017.htm

Hampton, R.R. (2001). Rhesus monkeys know when they remember. *Proceedings of the National Academy of Sciences,* 98(9), 5359–5362.

Happer, C. & Philo, G. (2013). The role of the media in the construction of public belief and social change. *Journal of Social and Political Psychology,* 1(1). Retrieved June 21, 2016. http://jspp.psychopen.eu/article/view/96/37

Harland, D.P. & Jackson, R.R. (2004). Portia perceptions: The Umwelt of an araneophagic jumping spider. In F.R. Prete (Ed.) *Complex worlds from simpler nervous systems* (pp. 5–40). Cambridge, MA: MIT Press.

Harmon-Jones, E. & Mills, J. (1999). *Cognitive dissonance: Progress on a pivotal theory in social psychology.* Washington, DC: American Psychological Association.

Harold Gillies. (n.d.). Retrieved March 14, 2014 from Wikipedia: https://en.wikipedia.org/wiki/Harold_Gillies

Harris, K.J. (2015). *Leaving ideological social groups behind: A grounded theory of psychological disengagement.* Retrieved March 13, 2016. http://ro.ecu.edu.au/theses/1587

Hart, B.L., Hart, L.A., McCoy, M. & Sarath, C.R. (2001). Cognitive behaviour in Asian elephants: Use and modification of branches for fly switching. *Animal Behaviour,* 62(5), 839–847.

Hastie, R. & Park, B. (1986). The relationship between memory and judgment depends on whether the judgment task is memory-based or on-line. *Psychological Review,* 93, 258–268.

Haught, H.M., Rose, J., Geers, A. & Brown, J.A.J. (2015). Subjective social status and well-being: The role of referent abstraction. *Social Psychology,* 155(4), 356–369.

Hawkley, L.C. & Cacioppo, J.T. (2007). Aging and loneliness: Downhill quickly? *Current Directions in Psychological Science,* 16, 187–191.

Hawkley, L.C., Thisted, R.A., Masi, C.M. & Cacioppo, J.T. (2010). Loneliness predicts increased blood pressure: Five-year cross-lagged analyses in middle-aged and older adults. *Psychology and Aging,* 25, 132–141.

Heikkila, R., Mantyselka, P. & Ahonens, R. (2011). Price, familiarity, and availability determine the choice of drug—A population-based survey five years after generic substitution was introduced in Finland. *BMC Clinical Pharmacology,* 11, 20–24.

Helliwell, J., Layard, R. & Sachs, J. (Eds.). (2016). *World happiness report 2015.* New York: Earth Institute. Retrieved December 8, 2016. http://worldhappiness.report/wp-content/uploads/sites/2/2015/04/WHR15.pdf

Henrich, J., Heine, S.J. & Norenzayan, A. (2010). The weirdest people in the world? *Behavioral and Brain Sciences,* 33(2–3), 61–83.

Hicks, S. (2012). Measuring subjective well-being: The UK Office for National Statistics experience. In J.F. Helliwell, R. Layard & J. Sachs (Eds.), *World happiness report.* New York: Earth Institute.

Hill, R. & Dunbar, R. (2003). Social network size in humans. *Human Nature,* 14, 53–72.

Ho, D.Y.F. (1995). Selfhood and identity in Confucianism, Taoism, Buddhism, and Hinduism: Contrasts with the West. *Journal for the Theory of Social Behaviour,* 25(2), 115–139.

Hodgins-Davis, A., Adomas, A.B., Warringer, J. & Townsend, J.P. (2012). Abundant gene-by-environment interactions in gene expression reaction norms to copper within Saccharomyces cerevisiae. *Genome Biology and Evolution,* 4(11), 1061–1079.

Hogan, R., Jones, W.H. & Cheek, J. (1985). Socioanalytic theory: An alternative to armadillo psychology. In B.R. Schlenker (Ed.), *The self and social life* (pp. 175–198). New York: McGraw-Hill.

Holland, D., Lachicotte, W., Jr., Skinner, D. & Cain, C. (1998). *Identity and agency in cultural worlds.* Cambridge: Harvard University Press.

Holland, M. (2004). *Social bonding and nurture kinship: Compatibility between cultural and biological approaches.* Unpublished Doctoral Dissertation. London: London School of Economics.

Holt, J. (2016). *Growing Without Schooling: The Complete Collection Volume 1 1977–1981.* Medford, MA: HoltGWS.

Hood, B. (2012). *The self illusion.* Oxford: Oxford University Press.

Horrigan, J. (2006). The internet as a resource for news and information about science. *Pew Research Center.* www.pewinternet.org/2006/11/20/the-internet-as-a-resource-for-news-and-information-about-science/

Hosoda, M., Stone-Romero, E. & Coats, G. (2003). The effects of physical attractiveness on job-related outcomes: A meta-analysis of experimental studies. *Personnel Psychology,* 56(2), 431–462.

Howe, M.L. & Courage, M.L. (1997). The emergence and early development of autobiographical memory. *Psychological Review*, 104, 499–523.

Human Brains. (n.d.). Retrieved August 9, 2013 from Smithsonian National Museum of History: http://humanorigins.si.edu/human-characteristics/brains

Humphrey, N.K. (1976). The social function of intellect. In P. Bateson & R. Hinde (Eds.), *Growing points in ethology*. Cambridge: Cambridge University Press.

Hunt, G.R. & Gray, R.D. (2003). Diversification and cumulative evolution in New Caledonian crow tool manufacture. *Proceedings of the Royal Society of London B: Biological Sciences*, 270(1517), 867–874.

Hyunh, S. (2016). *Motivations of visitors to participate in fee-based aquarium programs*. Unpublished Master's Thesis. Corvallis, OR: Oregon State University.

Icobani, M. (2008). *Mirroring people: The new science of how we connect with others*. New York: Farrar, Stuaus and Giroux.

Illich, I. (1971). *Deschooling society*. New York: Harper & Row.

Immordino-Yang, M.H. (2015). *Emotions, learning, and the brain: Exploring the educational implications of affective neuroscience*. New York: W. W. Norton & Co.

Invisible Hand. (n.d.) Retrieved March 10, 2016 from Investopedia: www.investopedia.com/terms/i/invisiblehand.asp#ixzz42WpCoL7O

Itkowitz, C. (2016). Harvard researchers discovered the one thing everyone needs for happier, healthier lives. *The Independent*. Retrieved March 2, 2016. www.independent.co.uk/life-style/harvard-researchers-discover-the-one-thing-everyone-needs-for-happier-and-healthier-lives-a6907901.html

Ito, M., Baumer, S., Bittanti, M., Boyd, D., Cody, R., Herr-Stephenson, B., Horst, H.A., Lange, P.G., Mahendran, D., Martinez, K.Z., Pascoe, C., Perkel, D., Robinson, L., Sims, C. & Tripp, L. (2010). *Hanging out, messing around, and geeking out: Kids living and learning with new media*. Cambridge: MIT Press.

Jablonka, E. & Lamb, M. (2014). *Evolution in four dimensions: Genetic, epigenetic, behavioral and symbolic variation in the history of life*. Cambridge: MIT Press.

James, W. (1884). What is an emotion? *Mind*, 9(34), 188–205.

James, W. (1890). *The principles of psychology*. New York: Henry Holt and Company.

Jaremka, L.M., Fagundes, C.P., Glaser, R., Bennett, J.M., Malarkey, W.B. & Kiecolt-Glaser, J.K. (2012). Loneliness predicts pain, depression, and fatigue: Understanding the role of immune dysregulation. *Psychoneuroendocrinology*, 38(8), 1310–1317. doi: 10.1016/j.psyneuen.2012.11.016.

Jaynes, J. (1976). *The origin of consciousness in the breakdown of the bicameral mind*. Boston: Houghton Mifflin.

Jeannerod, M. (2003). The mechanism of self-recognition in human. *Behavioral Brain Research*, 142, 1–15.

Jiddu Krishnamurti. (n.d.). Retrieved January 5, 2017 from BrainyQuote: www.brainyquote.com/quotes/keywords/sick.html

Johansson, P., Hall, L., Sikstrom, S. & Olsson, A. (2005). Failure to detect mismatches between intention and outcome in a simple decision task. *Science*, 310, 116–119.

Johnson, F. (1985). The Western concept of self. In A.J. Marsella, G. DeVos & F.L.K. Hsu (Eds.), *Culture and self: Asian and Western perspectives* (pp. 91–138). New York: Tavistock.

Jolly, A. (1966). Lemur social behavior and primate intelligence. *Science*, 153, 501–506.

Jones, S. (2003). *Y: The descent of men*. New York: Houghton Mifflin.

Jussim, L. & Harber, K.D. (2005). Teacher expectations and self-fulfilling prophecies: Knowns and unknowns, resolved and unresolved controversies. *Personality and Social Psychology Review*, 9, 131–155.

Kahan, D.M. (2017). The expressive rationality of inaccurate perceptions. *Behavioral and Brain Sciences*, 40. Retrieved June 11, 2017. https://www.cambridge.org/core/journals/behavioral-and-brain-sciences/article/expressive-rationality-of-inaccurate-perceptions/0B7D1B92F41B5408FBA7EFFFD78CD25E

Kahneman, D. (2000). Experienced utility and objective happiness: A moment-based approach. In D. Kahneman and A. Tversky (Eds.). *Choices, values and frames* (pp. 673–692). New York: Cambridge University Press.

Kahneman, D. (2011). *Thinking, fast and slow.* New York: Farrar, Straus and Giroux.

Kahneman, D. & Tversky, A. (1972). Subjective probability: A judgment of representativeness. *Cognitive Psychology*, 3, 430–454.

Kaimal, G., Ray, K. & Muniz, J. (2016). Reduction of cortisol levels and participants' responses following art making. *Art Therapy*, 33(2), 74–80.

Kamierczak, J. & Kempe, S. (2004). Calcium build-up in the Precambrian seas. In J. Seckbach (Ed.), *Origins* (pp. 329–345). Dordrecht, The Netherlands: Kluwer.

Karama, S., Armony, J. & Beauregard, M. (2011). Film excerpts shown to specifically elicit various affects lead to overlapping activation foci in a large set of symmetrical brain regions in males. *PLoS ONE*, 6(7), e22343. doi:10.1371/journal.pone.0022343

Kashdan, T.B. (2016). 13 reasons why people have sex. *Psychology Today.* Retrieved January 8, 2017. www.psychologytoday.com/blog/curious/201601/13-reasons-why-people-have-sex

Keeler, J., Roth, E., Neuser, B., Spitsbergen, J.M., Waters, D. & Vianney, J.-M. (2015). The neurochemistry and social flow of singing: Bonding and oxytocin. *Frontiers of Human Neuroscience*, 9, 518–525. Retrieved December 31, 2016. www.ncbi.nlm.nih.gov/pmc/articles/PMC4585277/

Keller, L. & Ross, K. (1998). Selfish genes: A green beard in the red fire ant. *Nature*, 394(6693): 573–575. doi:10.1038/29064

Kelly, J.R. (1977). *Situational and social factors in leisure decisions.* Technical Report. ERIC #: ED153143.

Kelly, J.R. (1996). *Leisure* (3rd ed.). Boston: Allyn and Bacon.

Kelly, J.R. & Freysinger, V.J. (2000). *21st century leisure: Current issues.* State College, PA: Venture Publishing.

Kenrick, D.T., Griskevicius, V., Neuberg, S.L. & Schaller, M. (2010). Renovating the pyramid of needs: Contemporary extensions built upon ancient foundations. *Perspectives on Psychological Science*, 5, 292–314.

Keys, A., Brožek, J., Henschel, A., Mickelsen, O. & Taylor, H.L. (1950). *The biology of human starvation* (2 Vols). St. Paul, MN: University of Minnesota Press.

Kirshenbaum, S. (2011). *The science of kissing.* New York: Grand Central Publishing.

Koke, J. (2009). *The use of identity-related motivations to frame experiences and design at the Art Gallery Ontario.* Paper presented at the Annual Meeting of the American Association of Museums, May 1, 2010, Philadelphia, PA.

Koke, J. (2010). *AGO visitor motivation study: Cumulative report.* Technical Report. Toronto: Art Gallery of Ontario.

Kokko, H., Brooks, R., Jennions, M. & Morley, J. (2003). The evolution of mate choice and mating biases. *Proceedings of the Royal Society B*, 270(1515), 653–664.

Koob, G.F., Ahmed, S.H., Boutrel, B., Chen, S., Kenny, P., Markou, A., O'Dell, L., Parsons, L. & Sanna, P. (2004). Neurobiological mechanisms in the transition from drug use to drug dependence. *Neuroscience and Biobehavioral Reviews*, 27(8), 739–749.

Koonin, E.V. (2007). The Biological Big Bang model for the major transitions in evolution. *Biology Direct*, 2, 21–30. Retrieved July 5, 2013. www.biology-direct.com/content/2/1/21

Koonin, E.V. & Makarova, K.S. (2013). CRISPR-Cas: Evolution of an RNA-based adaptive immunity system in prokaryotes. *RNA Biology*, 10(5), 679–686.

Knapp, M., Romeo, R. & Beecham, J. (2007). *The economic consequences of Autism on the U.K.* London: Foundation for People with Learning Disabilities.

Knopf, R.C., Driver, B.L. & Bassett, J. IL. (1973). Motivations for fishing. *Transactions of the 28th North American Wildlife and Natural Resources Conference* (pp. 191–204). Washington, DC: Wildlife Management Institute.

Krebs, J. & Carafoli, E. (2016). Why calcium? How calcium became the best communicator. *The Journal of Biological Chemistry*, 29(40), 20849–20857.

Kuhlmeier, V., Wynn, K. & Bloom, P. (2003). Attribution of dispositional states by 12-month olds. *Psychological Science*, 14, 402–408.

Kuo, R.C., Baxter, G.T., Thompson, S.H., Stricker, S.A., Patton, C., Bonaventura, J. & Epel, D. (2000). NO is necessary and sufficient for egg activation at fertilisation. *Nature*, 406, 633–636.

Kyaga, S., Lichtenstein, P., Boman, M., Hultman, C., Långström, N. & Landén, M. (2011). Creativity and mental disorder: Family study of 300 000 people with severe mental disorder. *The British Journal of Psychiatry*, 199(5), 373–379.

Laird, J.D. (2007). *Feelings: The perception of self.* Oxford: Oxford University Press.

Landau, E. (2013). Rare skull sparks human evolution controversy. *CNN*. Retrieved July 24, 2016. www.cnn.com/2013/10/17/world/europe/ancient-skull-human-evolution/#

Lapointe, M.-C. & Perreault, S. (2013). Motivation: Understanding leisure engagement and disengagement. *Society and Leisure*, 36(2), 136–144.

Lazarus, R.S. (1966). *Psychological stress and the coping process.* New York: McGraw-Hill.

Leary, M.R. & Tangney, J.P. (2003). The self as an organizing construct in the behavioral and social sciences. In M.R. Leary & J.P. Tangney (Eds.), *Handbook of self and identity* (pp. 3–14). New York: Guilford Press.

Leason, T. & Filippini-Fantoni, S. (2013). *Adapting Falk's museum visitor experience model.* Paper presented at Visitor Studies Association Annual Conference, July 15–19, 2013, Milwaukee, Wisconsin.

LeDoux, J. (2002). *Synaptic self: How our brains become who we are.* New York: Penguin.

Lee, B.K. & Shafer, C.S. (2002). The dynamic nature of leisure experience: An application of Affect Control Theory. *Journal of Leisure Research*, 34(2), 290–310.

Lee, B.K., Shafer, C.S. & Kang, I. (2005). Examining relationships among perceptions of self, episode-specific evaluations, and overall satisfaction with a leisure activity. *Leisure Sciences*, 27, 93–109.

Leeming, D.A. (2010). *Creation myths of the world* (2nd ed.). New York: ABC-CLIO.

Lehman, L. & Keller, L. (2006). The evolution of cooperation and altruism: A general framework and a classification of models. *Journal of Evolutionary Biology*, 19, 1364–1375.

Leliveld, L., Langbein, J. & Puppe, B. (2013). The emergence of emotional lateralization: Evidence in non-human vertebrates and implications for farm animals. *Applied Animal Behaviour Science*, 145(1–2), 1–14.

Lengen, C. & Kistemann, T. (2012). Sense of place and place identity: Review of neuroscientific evidence. *Health & Place*, 18, 1162–1171.

Leotti, L.A., Iyengar, S.S. & Ochsner, K.N. (2010). Born to choose: The origins and value of the need for control. *Trends in Cognitive Sciences*, 14(10), 457–463.

Lester, D. (1990). Maslow's hierarchy of needs and personality. *Personality and Individual Differences*, 11, 1187–1188.

Letters from a German Soldier in WWI to his mother. (n.d.) Retrieved March 3, 2014 from TeenInk.com: www.teenink.com/fiction/historical_fiction/article/517658/Letters-From-a-German-Soldier-in-WWI-to-his-mother/

Leuchter, A.F. (2002). Changes in brain function of depressed subjects during treatment with Placebo. *American Journal of Psychiatry*, 159, 122–129.

Levins, R. (1968). *Evolution in changing environments: Monographs in population biology, Number 2*. Princeton: Princeton University Press.

Lewenstein, B.V. (2009). Science books since World War II. In D.P. Nord, M. Schudson & J. Rubin (Eds.), *The Enduring book: Publishing in Post-War America*. Chapel Hill: University of North Carolina Press.

Lewis, M. (1990). Intention, consciousness, desires and development. *Psychological Inquiry*, 1, 278–283.

Lewis, M. (2011). *The big short*. New York: Norton.

Lieberman, D.E. (2013). *The story of the human body*. New York: Pantheon.

Lieberman, M. (2013). *Social: Why our brains are wired to connect*. New York: Crown.

Lieberman, P. (2000). *Human language and our reptilian brain: The subcortical bases of speech, syntax and thought*. Cambridge, MA: Harvard University Press.

Linville, P.W. (1985). Self-complexity and affective extremity: Don't put all your eggs in one cognitive basket. *Social Cognition*, 3, 94–120.

Linville, P.W. (1987). Self-complexity as a cognitive buffer against stress-related illness and depression. *Journal of Personality and Social Psychology*, 52, 663–676.

Litman, G.W., Cannon, J.P. & Dishaw, L.J. (2005). Reconstructing immune phylogeny: New perspectives. *Nature Reviews: Immunology*, 5(11), 866–879.

Little, A.C., Burriss, R.P., Jones, B.C. & Roberts, S.C. (2007). Facial appearance affects voting decisions. *Evolution and Human Behavior*, 28, 18–27.

Little, A.C., Jones, B.C. & DeBruine, L. (2011). Facial attractiveness: Evolutionary based research. *Philosophical Transactions of the Royal Society London B: Biological Sciences*, 366(1571), 1638–1659.

Long, C.H. (1963). *Alpha: The myths of creation*. New York: George Braziller.

Lovelock, J.E. (1972). Gaia as seen through the atmosphere. *Atmospheric Environment*, 6, 579–580.

Love, Sex and War—From Chapter 14: The Girls They Met 'Over There'. (n.d.) Retrieved February 10, 2016. www.heretical.com/costello/14govert.html

Lundgaard, I.B., Jensen, J.T. & Foldgast, A.M. (2013). *User survey 2012*. Copenhagen: Danish Agency for Culture.

Lundin, M. (2007). Explaining cooperation: How resource interdependence, goal congruence, and trust affect joint actions in policy implementation. *Journal of Public Administrative Research Theory*, 17(4), 651–672.

Lussenhop, A., Auster, R. & Lindgren-Streicher, A. (2015). *Facilitation Research for Engineering Design Education (FREDE)*. Unpublished Research Report. Boston: Museum of Science. Retrieved April 28, 2016. www.informalscience.org/sites/default/files/2016-01-04_2015-3%20Facilitation%20Research%20for%20Engineering%20Design%20Education%20Research%20Report.pdf

Lyons, W. (1995). *Approaches to intentionality*. Oxford: Oxford University Press.

Lynn Dierking in discussion with the author, November 12, 2016.

Madon, S., Guyll, M., Spoth, R.L., Cross, S.E. & Hilbert, S.J. (2003). The self-fulfilling influence of mother expectations on children's underage drinking. *Journal of Personality and Social Psychology*, 84, 1188–1205.

Makarova, K.S., Wolf, Y.I. & Koonin, E.V. (2013). Comparative genomics of defense systems in archaea and bacteria. *Nucleic Acids Research*. Retrieved July 30, 2013. http://nar.oxfordjournals.org/content/early/2013/03/06/nar.gkt157.full

Makarova, K.S., Wolf, Y.I., Snir, S. & Koonin, E.V. (2011). Defense islands in bacterial and archaeal genomes and prediction of novel defense systems. *Journal of Bacteriology*, 193, 6039–6056.

Makepeace, C. (2011). Sex and the Somme: The officially sanctioned brothels on the front line laid bare for the first time. *Daily Mail.* Retrieved February 10, 2016. www.daily-mail.co.uk/news/article-2054914/Sex-Somme-Officially-sanctioned-WWI-brothels-line.html#ixzz3znAdTiqM

Maltese, A.V. & Tai, R.H. (2010). Eyeballs in the fridge: Sources of early interest in science. *International Journal of Science Education*, 32(5), 669–685.

Manfredo, M.J. & Driver, B.L. (1996). Measuring leisure motivation: A meta-analysis of the recreation experience preference scales. *Journal of Leisure Research*, 28(3), 188–213.

Mannell, R. & Iso-Ahola, S.E. (1987). Psychological nature of leisure and tourism experience. *Annals of Tourism Research*, 14, 314–331.

Marieb, E.N. (2006). *Essentials of human anatomy and physiology* (8th ed.). Retrieved March 14, 2014. www.google.com/search?q=Cummings,+B.+%282006%29.+Pearson+Educational+Publishing.+homeostasis&biw=1368&bih=772&source=lnms&tbm=isch&sa=X&ved=0ahUKEwje8LDLnZ3SAhUJ6WMKHciLArgQ_AUIBigB&dpr=2#imgrc=ZND6LDnTwMlm5M

Margulis, L. (1998). *Symbiotic planet: A new look at evolution.* New York: Basic Books.

Margulis, L. & Sagan, D. (1986). *Microcosmos.* New York: Summit Books.

Markus, H.R. & Kitayama, S. (1991). Culture and the self: Implications for cognition, emotion, and motivation. *Psychological Review*, 98, 224–253.

Martin, W. & Russell, M.J. (2003). On the origin of cells: A hypothesis for the evolutionary transitions from abiotic geochemistry to chemoautotrophic prokaryotes, and from prokaryotes to nucleated cells. *Philosophical Transactions of the Royal Society of London, B-Biological Sciences*, 358(1429), 59–85.

Maslow, A.H. (1943). A theory of human motivation. *Psychological Review*, 50(4), 370–396.

Maslow, A.H. (1970). *Motivation and personality.* New York: Harper & Row.

Matthius, J. (2013). Why I teach programming to my co-workers. *SendGrid.* Retrieved July 21, 2016. https://sendgrid.com/blog/why-i-teach-programming-to-my-co-workers/

Mayberg, H., Silva, A., Brannan, S.K., Tekell, J.L., Mahurin, R.K., McGinis, S. & Jerbek, P. (2002). The functional neuroanatomy of the placebo effect. *American Journal of Psychiatry*, 159, 728–737.

Maynard Smith, J. (1978). *The evolution of sex.* Cambridge: Cambridge University Press.

McAdams, D.P. (1990). *The person: An introduction to personality psychology.* Orlando, FL: Harcourt Brace Jovanovich.

McAdams, D.P. (2008). Personal narratives and the life story. In O. John, R. Robins & L.A. Pervin (Eds.), *Handbook of personality: Theory and research* (3rd ed., pp. 242–262). New York: Guilford Press.

McAdams, D.P. (2013). The psychological self as actor, agent, and author. *Perspectives in Psychological Science*, 8(3), 272–295.

McAuliffe, K. (2012). How your cat is making you crazy. *The Atlantic.* Retrieved June 18, 2013. www.theatlantic.com/magazine/archive/2012/03/how-your-cat-is-making-you-crazy/308873/

McCreedy, D. & Dierking, L.D. (2013). *Cascading influences: Long-term impacts of informal STEM experiences for girls.* Philadelphia: The Franklin Institute.

McEwan, B.S. & Wingfield, J. (2010). What is in a name? Integrating homeostasis, allostasis and stress. *Hormones and Behavior*, 57, 105–111.

McGaugh, J.L. (2003). *Memory & emotion: The making of lasting memories.* New York: Columbia University Press.

McLean, D. (2015). *Kraus's recreation and leisure in modern society* (10th ed.). Burlington, MA: Jones & Bartlett Publishers.

Meany, M.J. (2010). Epigenetics and the biological definition of gene environment interactions. *Child Development*, 81(1), 41–79.

Meluch, W. (2011). *Profile of visitors to Iloni Palace*. Unpublished Technical Report. San Diego, CA: Meluch & Associates.

Mennecke, B.E., Townsend, A.M., Hayes, D.J. & Lonergan, S.M. (2007). A study of the factors that influence consumer attitudes toward beef products using the conjoint market analysis tool. *Journal of Animal Science*, 85, 2639–2659.

Merton, R.K. (1957). *Social theory and social structure* (rev. ed.). New York: Free Press.

Meston, C. & Buss, D. (2007). Why humans have sex. *Archives of Sexual Behavior*, 36(4), 477–507.

Military Leadership Diversity Commission (2010). *Reenlistment rates across the services by gender and race/ethnicity*. Issue paper #31, Retention. Retrieved February 12, 2017. http://diversity.defense.gov/Portals/51/Documents/Resources/Commission/docs/Issue%20Papers/Paper%2031%20-%20Reenlistment%20Rates%20Across%20the%20Services.pdf

Miller, G.A. (1956). The magical number seven, plus or minus two: Some limits on our capacity for processing information. *Psychological Review*, 63(2), 81–97.

Miller, G.A. (2000). *The mating mind: How sexual choice shaped the evolution of human nature*. London: Heineman.

Miller, W.B., Jr. (2013). *The microcosm within: Evolution and extinction within the hologenome*. Boco Ratan, FL: Universal-Publishers.

Milton, L.P. & Westphal, J.D. (2005). Identity confirmation networks and cooperation in work groups. *Academy of Management Journal*, 48(2), 191–212.

Minority Nurse. (2011). Retrieved March 10, 2016. minoritynurse.com: http://minoritynurse.com/nursing-volunteer-efforts/

Mintz, S.W. & du Bois, C.M. (2002). The anthropology of food and eating. *Annual Review of Anthropology*, 31, 99–119.

Mischel, W. (2014). *The marshmallow test: Conquering self-control*. New York: Little, Brown.

Moalem, S. (2009). *How sex works: Why we look, smell, taste, feel, and act the way we do*. New York: Harper Perennial.

Moerman, D.E. (2002). *Meaning, medicine and the 'placebo effect'*. Cambridge, UK: Cambridge University Press.

Moore, H., Dvoráková, K., Jenkins, N. & Breed, W. (2002). Exceptional sperm cooperation in the wood mouse. *Nature*, 418, 174–177.

Motion Picture Editors Guild. (2010). Retrieved March 10, 2016. www.editorsguild.com/labornews.cfm?LaborNewsid=2926

Mulkidjanian, A.Y., Galperin, M.Y. & Koonin, E.V. (2009). Co-evolution of primordial membranes and membrane proteins. *Trends in the Biochemical Sciences*, 34(4), 206–215.

Mulkidjanian, A.Y., Galperin, M.Y., Makarova, K.S., Wolf, Y.I. & Koonin, E.V. (2008). Evolutionary primacy of sodium bioenergetics. *Biology Direct*, 3, 13-32.

Murray, P. (2013). How emotions influence what we buy: The emotional core of consumer decision-making. *Psychology Today*. Retrieved February 11, 2016. www.psychologytoday.com/blog/inside-the-consumer-mind/201302/how-emotions-influence-what-we-buy

Nakamura, J. & Csikszentmihalyi, M. (2009). Flow theory and research. In C.R. Snyder & S.J. Lopez (Eds.), *Handbook of positive psychology* (pp. 195–206). Oxford: Oxford University Press.

Narr, K. (2008). Prehistoric religion. *Britannica online encyclopedia*. Retrieved July 26, 2016. www.britannica.com/topic/prehistoric-religion

National Research Council. (2009). *Learning science in informal environments: People, places, and pursuits*. Washington, DC: The National Academies Press. doi:10.17226/12190

National Science Board. (2015). *Science and Engineering Indicators: 2014.* Washington, DC: Government Printing Office.

Neiworth, J. (2009). Thinking about me: How social awareness evolved. *Current Directions in Psychological Science,* 18(3), 143–147.

Nestler, E.J. (2001). Total recall—The memory of addiction. *Science,* 292(5525), 2266–2267.

Nichols, J. (1998). The origin and dispersal of languages: Linguistic evidence. In N. Jablonski & L.C. Aiello (Eds.), *The origin and diversification of language* (pp. 127–170). Memoirs of the California Academy of Sciences, 24. San Francisco: California Academy of Sciences.

Nisbet, E.G. & Sleep, N.H. (2001). The habitat and nature of early life. *Nature,* 409(6823), 1083–1091.

Nozick, R. (1990). *A normative model of individual choice.* New York: Garland Press.

Oliver, R.L. (1980). A cognitive model of the antecedents and consequences of satisfaction decisions. *Journal of Marketing Research,* 17, 460–469.

Olivio, C. & Todorov, A. (2009). The look of a winner: The emerging—And disturbing— Science of how candidates' physical appearances influence our choice in leaders. *Scientific American.* Retrieved February 11, 2016. www.scientificamerican.com/article/the-look-of-a-winner/#

Omarzu, J., Miller, A.N., Schultz, C. & Timmerman, A. (2012). Motivations and emotional consequences related to engaging in extramarital relationships. *International Journal of Sexual Health,* 24(2), 154–162.

Organ transplantation. (n.d.). Retrieved March 14, 2014. http://en.wikipedia.org/wiki/Organ_transplantation

Ortner, S.B. (1984). Theory in anthropology since the sixties. *Comparative Studies in Society and History,* 151. Retrieved July 14, 2016. http://mysite.du.edu/~lavita/anth-3135-feasting-13f/_docs/ortner_theory_in_anthropology.pdf

Paleolithic religion. (2016). Retrieved July 26, 2016. https://en.wikipedia.org/wiki/Paleolithic_religion

Parrott, L. (2002). Complexity and the limits of ecological engineering. *Transactions of the ASAE,* 45(5), 1697–1702.

Passi, V., Bryson, S. & Lock, J. (2003). Assessment of eating disorders in adolescents with anorexia nervosa: Self-report questionnaire versus interview. *Eating Disorders,* 33(1), 45–54.

Pasupathi, M. & Mansour, E. (2006). Adult age differences in autobiographical reasoning in narratives. *Developmental Psychology,* 42, 798–808.

Paul-Labrador, M.D., Polk, J.H., Dwyer, I., Velasquez, S., Nidich, S., Rainforth, M., Schneider, R. & Merz, C.N. (2006). Effects of a randomized controlled trial of transcendental meditation on components of the metabolic syndrome in subjects with coronary heart disease. *Archives of Internal Medicine,* 166, 1218–1224.

Peoples, H., Duda, P. & Marlowe, F. (2016). Hunter-gatherers and the origins of religion. *Human Nature,* 1, 1–22. doi:10.1007/s12110-016-9260-0

Perdue, S.S. (2015). Immune system. In *Encyclopedia Britannica.* Retrieved February 7, 2016. www.britannica.com/science/immune-system/Evolution-of-the-immune-system

Perreault, C. & Mathew, S. (2012). Dating the origin of language using phonemic diversity. *PLoS ONE,* 7(4), e35289.

Personal diary of William J. 'Bill' Schira in World War I. (n.d.) Retrieved March 4, 2014. http://net.lib.byu.edu/estu/wwi/memoir/Schira/Schira.htm

Pew (2012). The global religious landscape. *Pew research center for religion & public life.* Retrieved January 15, 2017. www.pewforum.org/2012/12/18/global-religious-landscape-exec/

Piaget, J. (1957). *Construction of reality in the child.* London: Routledge & Kegan Paul.

Piedmont, R. & Village, A. (Eds.). (2009). *Research in the social scientific study of religion* (Vol. 20). Leiden, The Netherlands: Brill.

Pinder, C.C. (1984). *Work motivation: Theory, issues, and applications*. Glenview, IL: Scott, Foresman and Company.

Pinker, S. (1994). *The language instinct*. New York: HarperCollins.

Plotnik, J.M., de Waal, F. & Reiss, J. (2006). Self recognition in an Asian elephant. *Proceedings of the National Academy of Sciences of the USA*, 103(45), 17053–17057.

Plutchik, R. (2003). *Emotions and life: Perspectives from psychology, biology and evolution*. Washington, DC: American Psychological Association.

Porter, L.W. & Lawler, E.E. (1968). *Managerial attitude and performance*. Homewood, IL: Irwin-Dorsey.

Pradeu, T. & Carosella, E.D. (2006). The self model and the conception of biological identity in immunology. *Biology and Philosophy*, 21, 235–252.

Prakash, S. (December 2008). Yeast gone wild. *Seed*. Retrieved November 29, 2009. http://seedmagazine.com/content/article/yeast_gone_wild/

Price, D.D., Chung, S.K. & Robinson, M.E. (2005). Conditioning, expectation, and desire for relief in placebo analgesia. *Seminars in Pain Medicine*, 3(1), 15–21.

Pringle, H. (2013). The origin of human creativity was surprisingly complex. *Scientific American*. Retrieved July 26, 2016. www.scientificamerican.com/article/the-origin-human-creativity-suprisingly-complex/

Prior, H., Schwarz, A. & Güntürkün, O. (2008). Mirror-induced behavior in the magpie (Pica pica): Evidence of self-recognition. *PLoS biology*, 6(8), e202.

Privette, G. (1983). Peak experience, peak performance, and flow: A comparative analysis of positive human experiences. *Journal of Personality and Social Psychology*, 45(6), 1361–1368.

Puts, D.A., Dawood, K. & Welling, L.L. (2012). Why women have orgasms: An evolutionary analysis. *Archives of Sexual Behavior*, 41(5), 1127–1143.

Queller, D.C., Ponte, E., Bozzaro, S. & Strassmann, J. (2003). Single-gene greenbeard effects in the social amoeba Dictyostelium discoideum. *Science*, 299(5603), 105–106. doi:10.1126/science.1077742

Raafat, R. M., Chater, N. & Frith, C. (2009). Herding in humans. *Trends in Cognitive Sciences*. 13(10), 420–428.

Raven, D., van Vucht Tijssen, L. & de Wolf, J. (Eds.). (1992). *Cognitive relativism and social science*. Piscataway, NJ: Transaction Publishers.

Rawls, J. (1971). *A theory of justice*. Cambridge: Belknap Press of Harvard University.

Rennell, T. (2014). Horror Beyond Imagination: The most haunting account of the trenches you'll ever read—From a brilliant anthology by Birdsong author Sebastian Faulks. *Daily Mail*. Retrieved July 7, 2015. www.dailymail.co.uk/news/article-2715098/The-haunting-account-trenches-ll-read-brilliant-anthology-Birdsong-author-Sebastian-Faulks.html

Reynolds, G. (October 25, 2015). A sexually aware immune system? *Well: New York Times Magazine*. New York: New York Times.

Reynolds, V., Falger, V.S.E. & Vine, I. (Eds.). (1987). *The sociobiology of ethnocentrism: Evolutionary dimensions of xenophobia, discrimination, racism and nationalism*. London: Croom Helm.

Ridaura, V.K., Faith, J.J., Rey, F.E., Cheng, J., Duncan, A.E., Kau, A.L., Griffin, N.W., Lombard, V., Henrissat, B., Bain, J., Muehlbauer, M.J., Ilkayeva, O., Semekovich, C.F., Funai, K., Hayashi, D.K., Lyle, B.J., Martini, M.C., Ursell, L.K., Clemete, J.C., Van Treuren, W., Walters, W.A., Knight, R., Newgard, C.B., Heath, A.C. & Gordon, J.I.

(2013). Gut microbiota from twins discordant for obesity modulate metabolism in mice. *Science*, 341(6150), 1214.

Rizzolatti, G., Camarda, R., Fogassi, L., Gentilucci, M., Luppino, G. & Matelli, M. (1998). Functional organization of inferior area 6 in the macaque moneky. II. Area F5 and the control of distal movements. *Experimental Brain Research*, 71, 491–507.

Rizzolatti, G. & Sinigaglia, C. (2010). The functional role of the parieto-frontal mirror circuit: Interpretations and misinterpretations. *Nature Reviews Neuroscience*, 11, 264–274.

Roach, N.T., Venkadesan, M., Rainbow, M.J. & Lieberman, D.E. (2013). Elastic energy storage in the shoulder and the evolution of high-speed throwing in Homo. *Nature*, 498(7455), 483–486.

Rounds, J. (2006). Doing identity work in museums. *Curator*, 49(2), 133-150.

Rozin, E. (1973). *The flavor-principle cookbook*. New York: Penguin.

Ryan, B. & Gross, N. (1950). *Acceptance and diffusion of hybrid corn seeds in two Iowa communities*. Research Bulletin 372. Agricultural Experiment Station, Iowa State College of Agriculture and Mechanic Arts, Ames, IA.

Ryff, C.D. (1989). Happiness is everything, or is it? Explorations on the meaning of psychological well-being. *Journal of Personality and Social Psychology*, 57(6), 1069–1081.

Ryff, C.D. (2014). Psychological well-being revisited: Advances in the science and practice of Eudaimonia. *Psychotherapy & Psychosomatics*, 83(1), 10–28.

Sagon, C. (April 2004). Formerly known as Sutton Place. *Washington Post*. www.washington post.com/archive/lifestyle/food/2004/04/07/formerly-known-as-sutton-place/5ab 70392-4adb-464a-b804-e0c9ca5851d3/?utm_term=.f34c23fbfa3b

Sampson, E.E. (1988). The debate on individualism. *American Psychologist*, 43, 15–22.

Sandberg, J. (July 2006). It doesn't sound like a vacation to me. *Wall Street Journal Online*. www.wsj.com/articles/SB115317337878109062

Sapolski, R.M. (2004). Social status and health in humans and other animals. *Annual Review of Anthropology*, 33, 393–418.

Scaruffi, A. (2006). *The nature of consciousness*. Retrieved June 27, 2013. www.scaruffi.com/ nature/

Schacter, D.L. (1996). *Searching for memory*. New York: Basic Books.

Schacter, D.L., Wegner, D. & Gilbert, D. (2007). *Psychology*. New York: Worth Publisher.

Schmidt-Rhaesa, A. (2007). *The evolution of organ systems*. Oxford: Oxford University Press.

Schmitt, D.P. (2005). Sociosexuality from Argentina to Zimbabwe: A 48-nation study of sex, culture, and strategies of human mating. *Behavioral and Brain Sciences*, 28(2), 247–274.

Schrödinger, E. (1992/1944). *What is life?* Cambridge: Cambridge University Press.

Schutte, N.S., Kenrick, D.T. & Sadalla, E.K. (1985). The search for predictable settings: Situational prototypes, constraint, and behavioral variation. *Journal of Personality and Social Psychology*, 51, 459–462.

Scott, C. (2000). Rational choice theory. In G. Browning, A. Halcli & F. Webster (Eds.), *Understanding contemporary society: Theories of the present*. Beverly Hills, CA: Sage Publications. Retrieved July 14, 2016. www.soc.iastate.edu/sapp/soc401rationalchoice.pdf

Sears, W. (2016). *Month-to-month guide to baby's milestones*. Retrieved January 7, 2017. www. parenting.com/article/month-by-month-guide-to-babys-milestones

Seigel, J. (2005). *The idea of the self: Thought and experience in Western Europe since the eighteenth century*. Cambridge: Cambridge University Press.

Seligman, M. (2002). *Authentic happiness: Using the new positive psychology to realize your potential for lasting fulfillment*. New York: Free Press.

Semendeferi, K., Armstrong, E., Schleicher, A., Zilles, K. & Van Hoesen, G.W. (2001). Prefrontal cortex in humans and apes: A comparative study of area 10. *American Journal of Physical Anthropology*, 114(3), 224–241.

Sen, A. (2008). Rational behavior. In S. N. Durflauf & L. E. Blume (Eds.). *The New Palgrave Dictionary of Economics* (2nd ed.) (pp. 68–76). London: Macmillan.

Shiffrin, R. & Schneider, W. (1977). Controlled and automatic human information processing: II: Perceptual learning, automatic attending, and a general theory. *Psychological Review*, 84(2), 127–190.

Shreeve, J. (2015). This face changes the human story: But how? *National Geographic*. Retrieved July 24, 2016. http://news.nationalgeographic.com/2015/09/150910-human-evolution-change/

Seigel, J. (2005). *The idea of the self: Thought and experience in Western Europe since the seventeenth century*. Cambridge: Cambridge University Press.

Simandan, D. (2014). Omitted variables in the geographical treatment of well-being and happiness. *Geography Journal*. Retrieved May 18, 2017. http://dx.doi.org/10.1155/2014/150491

Simon, B. (2004). *Identity in modern society: A social psychological perspective*. Oxford: Blackwell.

Simon, H.A. (1956). Rational choice and the structure of the environment. *Psychological Review*, 63, 129–138.

Simonton, D.K. (2001). *The psychology of creativity: An historical perspective*. Paper presented at the Green College Lecture Series on The Nature of Creativity: History Biology, and Socio-Cultural Dimensions, University of British Columbia. http://simonton.faculty.ucdavis.edu/wp-content/uploads/sites/243/2015/08/HistoryCreativity.pdf

Sinervo, B., Chaine, A., Clobert, J., Calsbeek, R., Hazard, L., Lancaster, L., McAdam, A.G., Alonzo, S., Corrigan, G. & Hochberg, M.E. (2006). Self-recognition, color signals, and cycles of greenbeard mutualism and altruism. *Proceedings of the National Academy of Sciences of the USA*, 103(19), 7372–7377.

Smith, A.P. (1776). *An inquiry into the nature and causes of the wealth of nations* (1st ed.). London: W. Strahan.

Smith, A.P. (2012). Effects of the common cold on mood, psychomotor performance, the encoding of new information, speed of working memory and semantic processing. *Brain, Behavior, and Immunity*, 26(7), 1072–1076.

Smith, A.P. (2013). Twenty-five years of research on the behavioural malaise associated with influenza and the common cold. *Psychoneuroendocrinology*, 38(6), 744–751.

Smith, J.M. & Szathmary, E. (1995). *The major transitions in evolution*. Oxford: Oxford University Press.

Smith, P.A. (June 2015). Can the bacteria in your gut explain your mood? *New York Times*. Retrieved June 27, 2015. www.nytimes.com/2015/06/28/magazine/can-the-bacteria-in-your-gut-explain-your-mood

Smithsonian Institution. (2016). *What does it mean to be human?* Retrieved July 24, 2016. http://humanorigins.si.edu/human-characteristics/brains

Smola, M. & Meluch, W. (2011). *Profile of visitors to Mission House Museum*. Unpublished Technical Report. San Diego, CA: Meluch & Associates.

Smukalla, S., Caldara, M., Pochet, N., Beauvais, A., Guadagnini, S., Yan, C., Vinces, M.D., Jansen, A. & Prevost, M.C. (2008). FLO1 is a variable green beard gene that drives biofilm-like cooperation in budding yeast. *Cell*, 135(4), 726–737.

Social Science. (n.d.). Retrieved January 17, 2016. www.encyclopedia.com/topic/social_science.aspx#

Soyer, O.S. (2010). The promise of evolutionary systems biology: Lessons from bacterial chemotaxis. *Science Signals*, 3(128), 23–48.

Stam, J.H. (1976). *Inquiries into the origins of language*. New York: Harper and Row.

Staus, N. & Falk, J.H. (in press). The role of emotion in science learning: Testing a preliminary model. *Mind, Brain & Education*.

Stein, E. (1996). *Without good reason: The rationality debate in philosophy and cognitive science.* Oxford: Oxford University Press.

Stein, J. (2007). *Adapting the visitor identity-related motivations scale for living history sites.* Paper presented at the Visitor Studies Association Annual Meeting, Toronto, Canada, July 19.

Stephan Lewandowsky, S., Griffiths, T.L. & Kalish, M.L. (2009). The wisdom of individuals: Exploring people's knowledge about everyday events using iterated learning. *Cognitive Science*, 33(6), 969–998.

Steptoe, A., Pollard, T.M. & Wardle, J. (1995). Development of a measure of the motives underlying the selection of food: The food choice questionnaire. *Appetite*, 25, 267–284.

Sterelny, K. (2007). *Dawkins vs. Gould: Survival of the fittest.* Cambridge: Icon Books.

Sternberg, R.J. (2011). *Creativity: Cognitive psychology* (6th ed.). Boston: Cengage Learning.

Stewart, W.P. (1998). Leisure as multiphase experiences: Challenging traditions. *Journal of Leisure Research*, 30(4), 391–400.

Stewart, W.P. & Hull IV, B.R. (1992). Satisfaction of what? Post hoc versus real-time construct validity. *Leisure Sciences*, 14, 195–209.

Storksdieck, M. & Stein, J. (2007). *Using the visitor identity-related motivations scale to improve visitor experiences at the US Botanic Garden.* Paper presented at the Visitor Studies Association Annual Meeting, Toronto, Canada, July 19.

Stringer, C. (2011). *The origin of our species.* London: Allen Lane.

Stuckey, H.L. & Nobel, J. (2010). The connection between art, healing, and public health: A review of current literature. *American Journal of Public Health*, 100(2), 254–263.

Sukel, K. (2012). *This is your brain on sex.* New York: Simon & Schuster.

Swanson, A. (2016). The real reasons you procrastinate—And how to stop. *Washington Post*. Retrieved April 28, 2016. www.washingtonpost.com/news/wonk/wp/2016/04/27/why-you-cant-help-read-this-article-about-procrastination-instead-of-doing-your-job/?hpid=hp_hp-more-top-stories_wonk-procrastinate-652pm%3Ahomepage%2Fstory

Takahashi, B. & Tandoc, E.C., Jr. (2015). Media sources, credibility, and perceptions of science: Learning about how people learn about science. *Public Understanding of Science*. Retrieved June 21, 2016. http://pus.sagepub.com/content/early/2015/03/18/0963662515574986

Tallerman, M. & Gibson, K.R. (2012). *The Oxford handbook of language evolution.* New York: Oxford University Press.

Tanner, J. & Raymond, M.A. (2012). *Marketing Principles, Chapter 3 Consumer behavior: How people make buying decisions.* Retrieved February 11, 2016. http://2012books.lardbucket.org/books/marketing-principles-v1.0/s06-consumer-behavior-how-people-m.html

TASC. (2014). *After school and beyond.* The After School Corporation, New York. http://expandedschools.org/sites/default/files/TASC_LegacyReport_for_web.pdf

Tauber, A.I. (1994). *The immune self: Theory or metaphor?* New York and Cambridge: Cambridge University Press.

Taylor, C. (1989). *Sources of the self: The making of the modern identity.* Cambridge, MA: Harvard University Press.

Tedeschi, J.T. & Felson, R.B. (1994). *Violence, aggression & coercive actions.* Washington, DC: American Psychological Association.

Teitelbaum, S. (2016). An Introduction to Compulsive Gambling. *Psych Central*. Retrieved July 17, 2017. https://psychcentral.com/lib/an-introduction-to-compulsive-gambling/

Tennesen, M. (2003). *Do dolphins have a sense of self?* Reston, VA: National Wildlife. Federation.

Tennie, C., Call, J. & Tomasello, M. (2009). Ratcheting up the ratchet: On the evolution of cumulative culture. *Philosophical Transactions of the Royal Society of London, B Biological Sciences*, 364(1528), 2405–2415.

Tenter, A.M., Heckeroth, A.R. & Weiss, L.M. (2000). Toxoplasma gondii: From animals to humans. *International Journal of Parasitology*, 30, 1217–1258.

The Human Condition. (n.d.). Retrieved June 26, 2013. https://en.wikipedia.org/wiki/Human_condition

Thompson, W.G. (2005). *The placebo effect and health—Combining science and compassionate care*. New York: Prometheus.

Thorndike, E.L. (1920). Intelligence and its use. *Harper's Magazine*, 140, 227–235.

Tiger, L. & McGuire, M. (2010). *God's brain*. Amherst, NY: Prometheus.

Tinworth, K. (2010). *Denver—All city—Preliminary implementation of Falk's Visitor Identity-Related Motivation typology*. Technical Report. Denver: Denver-Area Cultural Evaluation Network.

Tishkoff, S., Reed, F., Friedlaender, F., Ehret, C., Ranciaro, A., Froment, A., Hirbo, J., Awomoyi, A., Bodo, J.-M., Doumbo, O., Ibrahim, M., Juma, A., Kotze, M., Lema, G., Moore, J., Mortensen, H., Nyambo, T., Omar, S., Powell, T., Pretorius, G., Smith, M., Thera, M., Wambebe, C., Weber, J. & Williams, S. (2009). The genetic structure of Africans and African Americans. *Science*, 324(5930), 1035–1044.

Tobin, C. (2012). What are some examples of the same dish being prepared or served differently across different countries and/or cultures? *Quora*. Retrieved November 13, 2016. www.quora.com/What-are-some-examples-of-the-same-dish-being-prepared-or-served-differently-across-different-countries-and-or-cultures

Tolman, D.L. & Diamond, L. (Eds.). (2014). *APA handbook of sexuality and psychology*. Washington, DC: American Psychological Association.

Tomasello, M. & Call, J. (1997). *Primate cognition*. New York: Oxford University Press.

Tomasello, M., Kruger, A. & Ratner, H. (1993). Cultural learning. *Behavioral and Brain Sciences*, 16, 495–552.

Tononi, G. (2008). Consciousness as integrated information: A preliminary manifesto. *Biological Bulletin*, 215(3), 216–242.

Torday, J.S. (2015). A central theory of biology. *Medical Hypotheses*, 85, 49–57.

Torday, J.S. (2015). Homeostasis as the mechanism of evolution. *Biology*, 4, 573–590.

Torday, J.S. (2016). The cell as the first niche construction. *Biology*, 5, 19–26.

Torday, J.S. & Miller, W.B., Jr. (2016). Phenotype as agent for epigenetic inheritance. *Biology*, 5, 30–36.

Torday J.S. & Miller, W.B., Jr. (2017). A systems approach to physiologic evolution: From micelles to consciousness. *Journal of Cellular Physiology*. Retrieved June 7, 2017. https://www.unboundmedicine.com/medline/citation/28112403/A_systems_approach_to_physiologic_evolution:_From_micelles_to_consciousness.

Torday, J.S. & Rehan, V.K. (2012). *Evolutionary biology, cell-cell communication, and complex disease*. New York: John Wiley & Sons.

Trainer, L., Steele-Inama, M. & Christopher, A. (2012). Uncovering visitor identity: A citywide utilization of the Falk Visitor-Identity Model. *Journal of Museum Education*, 37(1), 101–114.

Trivers, R.L. (1971). The evolution of reciprocal altruism. *The Quarterly Review of Biology*, 46(1), 35–57.

Tuan, Y.F. (1990). *Topophilia: A study of environmental perception, attitudes and values*. New York: Columbia University Press.

Turner, J.H. (2000). *On the origins of human emotions: A sociological inquiry into the evolution of human affect*. Stanford, CA: Stanford University Press.

Tzu, S (circa 5th C BCE). *The art of war*. Retrieved July 16, 2016. www.goodreads.com/author/quotes/1771.Sun_Tzu

Ursell, L.K., Metcalf, J., Parfrey, L.W. & Knight, R. (2012). Defining the human microbiome. *Nutritional Review*, 70(1), S38–S44.

U.S. Bureau of Labor Statistics. (2014). Table A-1 Time spent in detailed primary activities: 2014 annual averages. Retrieved February 11, 2016. www.bls.gov/tus/tables/a1_2014. pdf

Varela, F. (1999). Steps to a science of Interbeing: Unfolding the Dharma implicit in modern cognitive science. In S. Bachelor, G. Claxton & G. Watson (Eds.), *The psychology of awakening.* New York: Rider/Random House.

Varela, F. (2000). Four batons for the future of cognitive science. In B. Wiens (Ed.), *Envisioning Knowledge.* Cologne: Dumont.

von Neumann, J. & Morgenstern, O. (1972). *Theory of games and economic behavior.* Princeton: Princeton University Press.

Vroom, V. (1964). *Work and motivation.* New York: Jon Wiley & Sons.

Vygotsky, L.S. (1978). *Mind in society: The development of higher psychological processes.* Cambridge, MA: Harvard University Press.

Waldinger, R. (2015). *What makes a good life? Lessons from the longest study on happiness.* Retrieved March 2, 2016. www.ted.com/talks/robert_waldinger_what_makes_a_good_life_lessons_from_the_longest_study_on_happiness?language=en

Wegner, D.M. (2002). *The illusion of conscious will.* Cambridge, MA: MIT Press.

Wells, C., Morrison, C.M. & Conway, M.A. (2014). Adult recollections of childhood memories: What details can be recalled? *Quarterly Journal of Experimental Psychology,* 67(7), 1249–1261.

Wenger, E. (1998). *Communities of practice: Learning, meaning, and identity.* Cambridge: Cambridge University Press.

West-Eberhard, M.J. (2004). *Developmental plasticity and evolution.* New York: Oxford University Press.

Whisman, S.A. & Hollenhorst, S.J. (1998). A path model of white-river boating satisfaction on the Cheat River of West Virginia. *Environmental Management,* 22(1), 109–117.

Whitbourne, S. (2012). It's a fine line between narcissism and egocentrism. *Psychology Today.* Retrieved December 28, 2016. www.psychologytoday.com/blog/fulfillment-any-age/201204/it-s-fine-line-between-narcissism-and-egocentrism

Why people work. (n.d.). Retrieved March 10, 2016. http://davetgc.com/Why_People_Work.html

Wiggins, D. (2001). *Sameness and substance renewed* (2nd ed.). Cambridge: Cambridge University Press.

Wiggins, G.A., Tyack, P., Scharff, C. & Rohrmeier, M. (2015). The evolutionary roots of creativity: Mechanisms and motivations. *Philosophical Transactions of the Royal Society B,* 370, 99–108.

Williams, G.C. (1975). *Sex and evolution.* Princeton: Princeton University Press.

Wilson, E.O. (1975). *Sociobiology: The new synthesis.* Cambridge, MA: The Belknap Press.

Wilson, T.D. (2002). *Strangers to ourselves: Discovering the adaptive unconscious.* Cambridge, MA: Belknap Press.

Wilson, T.D., Dunn, D.S., Kraft, D. & Lisle, D.J. (1989). Introspection, attitude change, and attitude-behavior consistency: The disruptive effects of explaining why we feel the way we do. In L. Berkowitz (Ed.), *Advances in experimental social psychology* (Vol. 23). New York: Academic Press.

Woese, C. (1998). The universal ancestor. *Proceedings of the National Academy of Sciences, USA,* 95(12), 6854–6859.

Wolf, F.W. & Heberlein, U. (2003). Invertebrate models of addiction. *Journal of Neurobiology,* 54, 161–178. Retrieved May 16, 2014. http://psychcentral.com/lib/an-introduction-to-compulsive-gambling/000360

Wolfe, N. (2013). Small, small world. *National Geographic,* 223(1), 136–147.

Wolpert, L. & Szathmáry, E. (2002). Multi-cellularity: Evolution and the egg. *Nature*, 420(6917), 745–751.

Wong, J.T. & Hui, E.C.M. (2006). Power of expectations. *Property Management*, 24, 496–506.

Woodward, K. (2002). *Understanding identity*. London: Arnold.

Yamamoto, M., Naga, S. & Jun Shimizu, J. (2007). Positive musical effects on two types of negative stressful conditions. *Psychology of Music*, 35(2), 249–275.

Yoon, Y. & Uysal, M. (2005). An examination of the effects of motivation and satisfaction on destination loyalty: A structural model. *Tourism Management*, 26, 45–56.

Zahn, R., Moll, J., Paiva, M., Garrido, G., Krueger, F., Huey, E. & Grafman, J. (2009). The neural basis of human social values: Evidence from functional MRI. *Cerebral Cortex*, 19, 276–283.

Zare, B. (2011). Reviews of studies on infidelity. *3rd International Conference on Advanced Management Science*, 19, 182–186. www.ipedr.com/vol19/34-ICAMS2011-A10054.pdf

Zimmer, C. (2010). Sizing up consciousness by its bits. *New York Times*. Retrieved August 11, 2013. www.nytimes.com/2010/09/21/science/21consciousness.html?pagewanted=all&_r=1&

Zimmer, C. (2014). Secrets of the brain. *National Geographic*, 225(2), 28–57.

Zuboff, S. & Maxmin, D. (2002). *The support economy: Why corporations are failing individuals and the next episode of capitalism*. New York: Viking Press.

Zürcher, E.J. (1999). The Ottoman conscription system in theory and practice, 1844–1918. In Erik Jan Zürcher (Ed.), *Arming the state: Military conscription in the Middle East and Central Asia*. London: I.B. Tauris.

# INDEX